Farm Boys

FARM BOYS

*Lives of Gay Men from
the Rural Midwest*

Collected and edited by
Will Fellows

THE UNIVERSITY OF WISCONSIN PRESS

The University of Wisconsin Press
1930 Monroe Street
Madison, Wisconsin 53711

3 Henrietta Street
London WC2E 8LU, England

9   8   7   6   5

Printed in the United States of America

Library of Congress Cataloging-in-Publication Data
Fellows, Will.
Farm boys: lives of gay men from the rural Midwest /
Will Fellows.
352 pp.   cm.
Includes bibliographical references.
ISBN 0-299-15080-1 (cloth: alk. paper)
ISBN 0-299-15084-4 (paper: alk. paper)
1. Gay men—Middle West—Case studies. 2. Farmers—
Middle West—Case studies. I. Title.
HQ76.2.U52M534   1996
305.38'9664—dc20   96-6058

Whatever actually happens to a man
is wonderfully trivial and insignificant,
—even to death itself, I imagine.
                    —*Henry David Thoreau*

CONTENTS

PART 3: *Coming of Age Between the Mid-1970s and Mid-1980s*

PREFACE

This work is about the lives of gay men who grew up on farms in the midwestern United States during the twentieth century. I have done this work in the interest of promoting a fuller appreciation of the varied origins of, and perspectives within, the population of gay men in the U.S. I hope that the reader will find these plain-spoken narratives to be engaging and illuminating in their candor, insight, and sense of humor. It is also my hope that this work will be of value to individuals who are exploring issues related to sexual and gender identity.

These men describe how they perceived and responded to a variety of conditions that existed in many of the farm communities and families of their boyhoods: rigid gender roles, social isolation, ethnic homogeneity, suspicion of the unfamiliar, racism, religious conservatism, sexual prudishness, and limited access to information. While none of these conditions is unique to farm culture, they operate in a distinctive synergy in that setting.

They also have a lasting impact. More than just boyhood memories, these stories describe the long-term influences that many of these men believe their upbringings have had on the course and character of their lives. How has their farming heritage influenced their choices and identities as gay men? How do they see themselves in relation to gay men from urban or suburban backgrounds? How do they fit into their local gay communities? Inherent in these stories are the very different experiences and perspectives of men who came of age in earlier decades of this century and those who came of age in more recent decades—especially in the 1970s and 1980s.

In preparing these narratives from interviews, I have seen myself as something of a midwife, listening to men who had something to say and delivering their experiences and perspectives to the reader in their own distinct voices. If I had believed that soliciting contributions from professional writers would have yielded as diverse a cross-section of gay "farm boys," I might have chosen to edit their writings and organize them in a collection. In the interest of presenting a greater range of largely unheard voices, I have collaborated with my own group of subjects to shape auto-biographical narratives from their interview transcripts. Because very few of these men were writers, it is unlikely that most of these stories would have been told unless someone had come along with a litany of questions and a tape recorder.

Despite my efforts to let these men's words speak for them, my own background has no doubt influenced the ways in which I have gone about asking them to talk about their lives, as well as the ways in which I have understood and edited their words. I was born in 1957 and grew up on a Wisconsin dairy farm that had been in the family for more than a century. Apart from the inevitable jolts and angst of growing up, my childhood was one of naivety, safety, stability, and freedom. My parents expected me to do a certain amount of housework and farmwork, but my childhood was not consumed by endless toil or rigid expectations.

Living five miles from town, with few neighbor kids my age, I played mostly with my two younger sisters and weathered typical fraternal ha-rassment from my older brother. I pleased my teachers at public school and Baptist church in town, played with my toy printing press, collected coins, and completed 4-H projects in drama, woodworking, and nature conservation. My feelings of rootedness and belonging were strengthened as I researched my father's family history, tracing our tenure on the farm back to its beginnings in the 1850s.

I chose to spend a lot of time with my paternal grandmother who lived in the old farmhouse next door, surrounded by her beloved antiques and books and other fine things. For several years in my teens, I operated a small antique shop in an old poultry shed that my father helped me re-furbish. Through high school I was essentially a sexually naive loner, feel-ing no great inclination to date girls or to fool around with boys. I edited the school newspaper, wrote for a local weekly paper, and spent a summer as a foreign exchange student (feeling homesick much of the time). Com-ing out to myself and my family between eighteen and twenty-one years of age was relatively free of pain.

My life since leaving the farm for college has been largely urban, mid-western, and variously fulfilling. There is much I have come to like about city life, but I have tended to feel like an outsider in the gay communities of the cities in which I have lived. And I have had similar feelings in rela-tion to the larger gay "community" in the United States, as represented in popular gay-themed books, periodicals, and movies. In an effort to gain a better understanding of what I bring to the experience of being gay as a result, perhaps, of my farm upbringing, I have looked for books telling about my kind of childhood. The body of literature that examines the lives of gay men has expanded greatly in recent years and has enriched my life in many ways, but it neglects the experiences and perspectives of gay men who grew up in farm families. Urban or suburban experiences are central to the lives of most gay men, but they constitute only part of the story.

It is not uncommon for gay men who grew up on farms to regard their rural roots as irrelevant or embarrassing. Those attitudes tend to be reinforced by the popular gay press, in which the most common representations of the rural childhood experience include a variety of farm-boy stereotypes, fantasies, and romanticized, back-to-nature images. Charles Silverstein described some of these popular perceptions in his 1981 book, *Man to Man: Gay Couples in America.*[1]

> City gays imagine the boys on the farm as somehow more wholesome than themselves. Soaking up the sun while pitching a bale of hay, their bodies taking on a bronze glow, these promising young men develop tight muscles from manual labor and hardiness; the lines in their faces and the callouses on their hands are the results of wind, rain, and the warming sun. In short, they are pictured as country bumpkins with rosy cheeks, ready to be plucked if they venture into the big city (p. 241).

In our interview, Clark Williams described his own experience with these stereotypical perceptions.

> A lot of men idealize the naive, good-looking, tanned farm boy. "Wouldn't you love to go to bed with him? Wouldn't you love to have him, to take him down?" I've had some guys take that kind of approach with me. I'm supposed to be wide-eyed, naive, less intelligent, and in denial about who I am. They'll ask me, "Are you married? Do you have a girlfriend?"

The life stories presented here are not primarily those of gay men who stayed in the rural farming communities where they grew up. A large majority of these men have left farming and rural communities, choosing to live in or near relatively large midwestern cities. Richard Kilmer was succinct in assessing his own choice to leave.

> If I had stayed on the farm, I would have never dealt with being gay. I would have probably gotten married and had sex with men on the side. I think a lot of gays don't leave the farm, so there's probably a lot of people out there who are doing that. So many people there are alcoholics, and I think that's what a lot of gays gravitate towards, to kind of deaden their feelings.

Barney Dews grew up on a farm in East Texas in the 1960s and 1970s, and was living in Minneapolis at the time of our interview. Although he is not a midwesterner, his description of "a centrifugal force that slings gay people as far away as possible, to escape," is relevant to many of these men's experiences. It seems likely that by having uprooted and distanced themselves from the families and communities of their childhoods, these men were able to look at their lives with more insight and clarity than would have been possible had they stayed. As these stories reveal, their views of growing up range widely, from bitter to beatific.

NOTE

1. Silverstein, Charles. 1981. *Man to Man: Gay Couples in America*. New York: Quill.

ACKNOWLEDGMENTS

The idea for this project was conceived as the result of conversation over dinner with my friend Karl Wolter. Clarification and refinement of this original idea were enhanced by conversations with many others, especially Doug Bauder, John Berg, Françoise Crélerot, Joanne Csete, Carlos Dews, Kim Karcher, Ming Liang Kwok, Lon Mickelsen, Sarah Newport, Brian Powers, Larry Reed, Julia Salomón, Martin Scherz, Jack Siebert, and Jane Vanderbosch. I thank all of my friends and family members for their contributions to making things happen as well as they did.

Early interest in the Gay Farm Boys Project was shown by The New Harvest Foundation of Madison, Wisconsin, the Cream City Foundation of Milwaukee, Wisconsin, and The Madison Community United. I am indebted to them, as I am to my friend Joanne Csete, for generous and encouraging financial support.

Bonnie Denmark Friedman was a superb transcriber and Jeff Kopseng has been a dream of an illustrator. This work has been greatly improved by the efforts of Rosalie M. Robertson and Raphael Kadushin at the University of Wisconsin Press, and by the encouraging editorial advice of David Bergman, David Román, and Reed Woodhouse. I thank Robert Peters for permission to use excerpts from his book, *Crunching Gravel: A Wisconsin Boyhood in the Thirties* (University of Wisconsin Press, 1993). I am grateful to all of the men who agreed to be interviewed, including those whose stories I have not been able to include in this volume.

As a 1975 graduate of Evansville (Wisconsin) High School, I was honored to receive the Helen Smith Literary Award, named for a local writer. Dr. Smith's early encouragement has been important to me.

I dedicate this work to my abundantly loving mate, Bronze Quinton, and to my splendid parents, David and Catharine Fellows.

HOW THESE STORIES
WERE DISCOVERED

Interview subjects were recruited by publicizing the Gay Farm Boys Project through press releases sent during the summer of 1992 to twenty-six gay and lesbian community publications in the midwestern United States. These included: Chicago, Illinois—*Gay Chicago, Outlines, Windy City Times;* Rockford, Illinois—*Rock River News;* Indianapolis, Indiana—*Fever, Indiana Word;* Ann Arbor, Michigan—*Michigan Tribune, Out and About;* Detroit, Michigan—*Cruise, Metra;* Minneapolis, Minnesota—*Equal Time, GAZE;* Kansas City, Missouri—*Alternative News;* St. Louis, Missouri—*News-Telegraph;* Omaha, Nebraska—*New Voice;* Cincinnati, Ohio—*Nouveau Midwest;* Cleveland, Ohio—*Gay People's Chronicle, Valentine News;* Columbus, Ohio—*Free Press, Gaybeat;* La Crosse, Wisconsin—*Leaping La Crosse News;* Madison, Wisconsin—*Frontiersman;* Milwaukee, Wisconsin—*In Step, Wisconsin Light;* Wausau, Wisconsin—*Lifeline;* Westby, Wisconsin—*New Beginnings.*

To give the editors of these publications flexibility in publicizing the project, the appeal for interview subjects was provided in two forms—as a standard press release and a letter to the editor. The text of the standard release follows:

Farm Boys Sought for Interviews

Are you a gay man who grew up on a farm? If so, your experience as a farm boy is an important and largely neglected part of gay culture. Urban experiences are central to the lives of most gay men, but they're far from being the whole story.

The Gay Farm Boys Project is intended to give gay men who grew up on farms—whether or not they are still involved in farming—a chance to talk about their experiences and the ways in which their farm upbringings have influenced their lives.

If you are a gay man who grew up in a farming household and you think you might be interested in contributing to this cultural research project by talking about your experiences, please contact Will Fellows at

[phone number] for more information or to arrange for an interview.
You can write to Fellows at [P.O. box address].

   A gay farm boy himself, Fellows is an experienced researcher and
writer who would like to consider your story for inclusion in a book
based on the "gay farm boys" theme. Whatever your age and whatever
your life is about now, your story is a unique and valuable part of gay culture. If anonymity is desired, names and other key details can be changed.

Approximately 120 men responded by telephone and mail to this publicity. A few emphasized the importance of discretion and anonymity in
this initial contact, but most seemed trusting and uninhibited in their responses. Some of those who wrote sent brief notes requesting that more
information be sent, sometimes to a post office box address. Others wrote
longer, more engaging letters describing their interest in the project and
their qualifications for being interviewed. For example, one man wrote:

> I grew up in the sixties on a small farm in a Mennonite community in a
> rural area south of Cleveland, Ohio. The whole family took an active part
> in the daily chores of milking cows, plowing, working the gardens, clean-
> ing the pens, killing chickens on Saturdays, and acting like saints in
> church on Sundays. The horrors on the farm for this guy were too many,
> and now in my forties I live in a suburban area outside of Cleveland.
> After those days in the country, I don't have and won't have even a pet,
> at least not four-legged.

Apparent in some letters and phone conversations was an assumption,
suspicion, or hope that the Gay Farm Boys Project would prove to be a
networking service for men in rural areas, men with fantasies about "farm
boys," men with fantasies about sex with animals, or some combination
thereof. One man wrote from rural Minnesota:

> I am interested in your research and how you plan to process the infor-
> mation. Is this for your edification? A chance to compare notes with
> other respondents and form some sort of support group? An opportunity
> to meet others in the same boat and socialize? Or what? You may have
> tapped a good market for this kind of research. As I expect you know, the
> chance to make rural contacts is very limited.

The allure of the farm-boy fantasy was brought home to me in an im-
ploring letter from a man in suburban Chicago. Would I help him make
pen-pal connections with midwestern farm boys who might be interested
in hosting a city boy for a couple of days? "I love the country, and I've always wanted to have an adventure with a real cute farm boy way out there
in the loft of the barn—wake up to fresh ground coffee, scrambled eggs
with sausage, toast, and a good horse ride. I'm crazy for blond, blue-eyed
hunks." Although I could appreciate the difficulties of making satisfying
connections, I did not intend the project to serve matchmaking purposes.

Thus, I avoided interviewing men whose interest in the project appeared to hinge greatly on the prospect of social or sexual networking possibilities.

A man in Chicago wrote to say that his years on a dairy farm in Ohio had given him "many tales to tell of sex with animals. Is this what you are interested in? Do you want all the naughty but nice details?" He would tell me all about it if I promised I was not with the cops. Two men in Canada sent along cartoons relating to bestiality. I had no desire to avoid the exploration of this subject, which seems to be quite strongly linked with farm life in the popular imagination. However, I had no interest in interviewing individuals whose responses to the project appeared to be entirely salacious in nature. My preference was to involve those who evinced broader imagination and greater thoughtfulness related to the stated themes of the project. Overall, I was very pleased with the magnitude and caliber of the response to my press release.

In addition to those recruited for interviews through publicity, I enlisted a relatively small number of subjects personally. These men were generally friends or acquaintances, or strangers referred to me by people I knew. All prospective interview subjects were sent the following letter describing the project and the interview process:

> Thanks for your interest in the Gay Farm Boys Project. This cultural research project is intended to give you—a gay man who grew up in a farming household—a chance to talk about your experiences and the ways in which your farm upbringing has influenced your life. I am gay, grew up on a dairy farm, and am an experienced interviewer and writer. Your words will be used as part of a book based on the "gay farm boys" theme.
>
> Life stories rooted in farm childhoods have been largely neglected in the growing literature that documents the lives of gay men in the U.S. If you grew up on a farm—whether or not you are still farming—I welcome your participation in changing this situation. Whatever your age and whatever your life is about now, your story is a unique and valuable part of gay culture.
>
> Here are some basic details about being interviewed:
>
> • The interview is informal, in-depth, and is meant to be a relaxed and enjoyable experience. Please try to set aside two to three hours for it.
> • We can hold the interview at your home or at some other mutually agreeable location.
> • The format and content of the interview are flexible and specific to the individual. General areas that we are likely to cover include: childhood experiences; family relationships; parental values, beliefs and attitudes; development of your sexual awareness, understanding and self-acceptance; your present life situation, values, beliefs, attitudes, etc.

- The interview will be recorded (audio, not video) and portions of the transcript will be used as part of a book based on the "gay farm boys" theme.
- There is no payment for being interviewed or for any use that may be made of the content of the interview, but your participation will be duly acknowledged.
- If you desire anonymity, names and other key details of your story can be changed. At the interview, we will come to an agreement about these matters—on which you are free to change your mind later.
- If you would like further information, please contact me at the address or phone number listed above.

Between the spring of 1992 and the autumn of 1993, I conducted interviews with seventy-five men from rural farming backgrounds. Ages of subjects ranged from twenty-five to eighty-four years, with men in their twenties, thirties, and forties representing more than three-quarters of those interviewed. All subjects were European-American, reflecting the vastly dominant ethnic profile of the rural farming population in the midwestern U.S.

Most of the men I interviewed lived in, or near, relatively large midwestern cities and were no longer engaged in farming. This prevailing profile may result from a number of factors. First, this research project was publicized in gay and lesbian community publications centered primarily in larger cities. In addition, a greater proportion of gay-identified men from rural farming backgrounds may live in larger cities rather than small cities and towns or rural areas. Further, several men living in small towns and rural areas declined to be interviewed for reasons that appeared to center around concern about their identities being revealed.

The men I interviewed seemed to possess a wide range of sometimes mixed motives for agreeing to participate: they hoped that by telling their stories they could contribute to illuminating people's minds and hearts, thus making a positive difference for future generations; they were simply responding enthusiastically to a project that struck them as "a great idea," and wanted to help out so that the project would be successful; they wanted to tell what they considered to be interesting stories about their lives. A self-therapeutic motive was evident in some interviews; these subjects seemed to be influenced by a confessional or cathartic impulse to tell all, perhaps in an effort to pull together life's loose ends and enhance their self-understanding. It was evident, as well, that some subjects hoped that their participation would assist them in meeting other men with similar backgrounds, interests, and values.

Most interviews were conducted in the midwestern United States, including the states of Ohio, Indiana, Illinois, Wisconsin, Minnesota, Iowa, Missouri, Kansas, and Nebraska. One interview was held in California. Subjects participated with the understanding that they would not be paid for any use that might be made of interview material. Most interviews were two to three hours in length, exploring many facets of the individual's life. I was often surprised and moved by the extent to which the men I interviewed seemed to make open books of their lives. I took a casual, conversational, free-form approach to interviewing, letting the subject have primary influence on the structure of the interview. While the scope of my questioning was consistent from one interview to another, the sequencing of, and relative emphasis given to, the various lines of inquiry were influenced greatly by the ways in which each subject was inclined to talk about his own life. A summary of the major areas of inquiry follows.

CHILDHOOD BACKGROUND

- Where did you live as a child? What kind of farm was it?
- How would you describe your involvement in farm work? In house work?
- How would you describe your childhood relationships with your parents? With your siblings?
- Besides your parents, did any other adult play a significant role in your childhood on a day-to-day basis?
- Where did you go to school as a child?
- Describe your playmates/friends in elementary, junior high, and senior high school.
- Were you involved in any school-related activities in junior or senior high school?
- Were you involved in any non-school-related activities during junior or senior high school?
- Was there any particular place on or near the farm where you would go to be by yourself?

FAMILY ATTITUDES, BELIEFS, VALUES

- How would you describe the beliefs/attitudes within your family when you were a child about people who were different from yourselves because of race, ethnicity, or religion? What were your family's prevailing attitudes regarding gender roles, sexuality, and homosexuality?

- How would you describe the influence of church/religion on your childhood?

Coming Out to Self and Others

- When did you first become aware of your same-sex orientation? How would you describe your reaction? Did you talk with anyone or do anything else about it?
- Do you recall any books, magazines, movies, TV shows, or other forms of popular information or entertainment that were important to you in coming to understand your sexual identity?
- At any time during your childhood, did you know (or know of) someone who was gay—and you were aware of it *then?*
- Did you have any intimate physical or sexual experiences while growing up?
- How would you describe the influence of the farm culture of your childhood on your ability to recognize and come to terms with your sexual orientation?
- Is there any particular theory explaining the causes of homosexuality that you are especially inclined to believe?
- To what extent have you come out to your parents and other family members?
- Were you ever married?
- When did your parents and other family members learn that you were gay? What were their reactions?
- How would you describe your current relationships with your parents and other family members?

Beyond Coming Out

- *If subject did not stay in farming:* Did you ever seriously consider farming for a living? Was being gay a factor in deciding not to farm?
- *If subject stayed in farming:* How does being gay fit into your life as a farmer?
- *If subject has lover/partner/mate:* How, when, and where did you meet? Did he grow up on a farm? Has he gotten to know your parents and other family members? How would you describe his relationship with them?

- How would you describe your attitudes about intimate relationships with men?
- How would you describe your involvement in the gay community?
- How would you describe your political perspectives, especially with regard to issues of concern to gay people?

GENERAL REFLECTIONS

- What are your best memories of growing up on a farm? What are your worst?
- How would you describe the influence that your farm upbringing has had on the character and quality of your life?
- How would you describe your current feelings about being a gay man?
- How do you feel about the life choices you have made in light of being gay?

The fact that all interviews were based on the same range of questions contributes to a similarity in the topical range of these narratives. However, interview subjects differed greatly in how they responded to the interview process. Some subjects seemed to be most comfortable with a very clearly delineated question-and-answer format, and tended not to go off on their own. Others were more self-directed in what they had to say; I would ask a question to get things going, ask questions for follow-up or refocusing as I was inclined, move things along occasionally with a new line of questioning, and the subject would take it from there. These were generally the best interviews, driven less by my questions than by the force of the subject's narrative spontaneity.

Earnestness abounds in these stories. While the reader will find moments of humor and light-heartedness throughout this collection, many of these stories are largely serious in tone. I believe this results from several conditions. First, it seems likely that the more serious-minded would choose to participate in an in-depth autobiographical interview as part of a cultural research project, especially when they know that portions of what they say may be published. In addition, many of those who chose to tell their stories had some distinctly serious things to talk about. There is also the editorial reality that humorous exchanges in conversation do not always translate effectively in print. More fundamentally, though, I believe that many of these men were less interested in entertaining me and my potential readers than in telling about their lives and being heard.

It was fascinating to experience the various ways in which these men approached telling me—a stranger in most cases—about themselves. Some men seemed to be quite comfortable talking frankly about intimate matters; others seemed nervous or embarrassed. Some were inclined to take an orderly, linear, chronological approach in recounting the events of their lives. (One man in his early seventies reported the exact dates of several events of his personal development during the 1930s, including that of his pubescence.) Other men seemed to prefer a looser, more thematic approach to talking about their lives, which was more compatible with my style of questioning.

Some men were quite inclined to reflect on and analyze their experiences, and to talk about the emotional and psychological aspects of things. Others were more disposed to talk about specific people, places, and events. Most gratifying to me were those occasions when rich surface details came accompanied by insightful analysis and reflection. The questions that seemed to be most challenging for many subjects were two that I asked in tandem toward the end of the interview: How would you describe your current feelings about being a gay man? How do you feel about the life choices you have made in light of being gay?

Somewhat less than half of the men represented in this collection used pseudonyms, including Henry Bauer, Dennis Lindholm, James Heckman, Norm Reed, Ronald Schoen, David Foster, Doug Edwards, Bill Troxell, Martin Scherz, Heinz Koenig, Dale Hesterman, Everett Cooper, David Campbell, Richard Hopkins, Lon Mickelsen, Steven Preston, and Connie Sanders. All prospective interview subjects were informed that their names and other identifying details would be changed if they so desired. At the time of the interview, each subject was asked to specify the extent to which he wished to have these things changed. Some subjects stated that a simple change of their own names would be sufficient, while others desired a more thorough masking of identities by giving pseudonyms to other individuals mentioned by name in their interviews. If the subject desired geographical anonymity as well, the locale of his childhood was obscured by describing it in terms of a county or general region of a state, with no specific place name. Thus, the only names that have been replaced by pseudonyms are those of persons, not places.

I generally did not ask any interview subject to explain either his desire to have his identity concealed or his willingness to have it revealed. We simply came to an understanding on the matter and left it at that. I took this approach because I did not want the issue to get in the way of their talking comfortably with me about their lives. It was apparent from the interviews that the desire to conceal was generally rooted in considerations of personal and family privacy, as well as privacy for other individuals whose lives were touched on during the interviews. Also of concern to some subjects were their employment security, personal safety, and the sensitive nature of some of the things they talked about.

While I liked the idea of using real names, obtaining a candid, uncensored account of these men's lives was much more important to me. In some cases it seemed that a desire or willingness to be identified by real name, however daring or courageous, was accompanied by a disinclination to be fully candid. Moreover, the desire or willingness to be identified by a real name did not seem to be consistent with an overall openness about being gay in day-to-day life. Some of the men who elected to have their stories presented pseudonymously seemed to be quite open about being gay. Conversely, some of the men who chose to be identified by their real names did not seem to be especially open about being gay in their daily lives; in these cases, electing to be identified by a real name may have been motivated by a desire to take advantage of the opportunity to come out, in print, once and for all.

Of the seventy-five audio-taped interviews, I selected the fifty most substantive and representative to be professionally transcribed. I then selected approximately half of these fifty to shape into full-length narrative chapters. Each of these interview subjects was then invited to review a draft of his chapter, with the following instructions.

Thanks for your willingness to review the enclosed draft of your life story as adapted from your interview. I would like you to check it for accuracy and for speaking style. Does it reflect your way of saying things? You may find that reading it out loud is helpful. In shaping your spoken words into text, I have adhered to your own word choices as much as possible. Because I try to avoid over-editing and imposing my own words on you, this spoken-to-written transformation sometimes results in awkward wording. I hope that *you* will do what you wish to fix any grammatical awkwardness that you perceive.

I would also like you to consider whether the piece seems to be a fairly well-rounded, balanced presentation of your life story. If there are changes you could make that would clarify or enrich it, please do so. Keep in mind, however, that I am not looking for you to update your story. I want it to reflect your life as you saw it at the time of your interview. With that in mind, you are welcome to expand on anything, to add new material, or to delete material. Simply cross out any text to be changed or deleted and write in the new text, if any. You may write anywhere on these pages or on separate sheets of paper. Using a pencil is probably a good idea. It's likely that in most cases I will agree on the re-

visions that you specify, but I reserve the right to leave anything unchanged if that seems most appropriate to me.

All twenty-six subjects of these full-length chapters agreed to participate in the review process, which improved the narratives in important
ways. Most helpful was the addition of text that clarified or elaborated on
various topics that had not been covered adequately in the interview. Also
helpful were suggestions for rearranging portions of the text to enhance
flow and coherence. Some subjects made changes in wording that were
intended to soften their expressions of anger or other strong emotions or
opinions. In one narrative, for example, "It was a big, hot bitch of a day,"
got whittled down to, "It was a hot day." I believe this impulse was largely
the result of these subjects being struck by the sometimes startling force
of spoken words put down on paper. Some expressed misgivings about including text that they decided was too intimately revealing. Since all of
the men who made these problematic revisions had elected to use pseudonyms, I felt comfortable disregarding any of their requested revisions
that appeared to diminish the character and substance of their narratives.

I excerpted material from many of the transcribed interviews that were
not used as the basis of full-length chapters. The most substantive of these
excerpts were also made available for review by the interview subjects, with
instructions similar to those detailed above. These excerpt narratives are
shorter than the full-length autobiographical chapters, and they typically
address a single topic or theme. While they lack the larger context of the
longer chapters, they provide concise and engaging illustrations of important themes that emerge in the longer chapters.

Selected quotes for use in the introductory text were excerpted from
several of the interviews that were not fully transcribed. In addition, I invited all interview subjects to share with me any materials they had written that were relevant to the focus of the project. In the cases of five individuals, portions of these autobiographical writings were woven into their
transcript-based narratives.

I have chosen to arrange these life stories according to the subject's
year of birth. This arrangement appeals to me because it acknowledges the
primacy of time and fate. Moreover, it takes advantage of the historical
perspective on American culture which many readers will bring to their
understanding of these stories. It also allows the reader to perceive more
readily the ways in which the experience of growing up gay in the rural
Midwest has and has not changed through the century.

I have divided the narratives of these men, born from 1909 to 1967,
into three groups based on the calendar years during which they came of
age (by my judgement, the period between their fifteenth and twentieth

birthdays). The oldest of these three groups includes those who came of age anywhere between the mid-1920s and the mid-1960s. The middle period comprises those who came of age from the mid-1960s to the mid-1970s. The youngest group includes those who had their fifteenth and twentieth birthdays anywhere between the mid-1970s and mid-1980s. This chronological framework delineates three quite distinct eras in American mass culture with regard to the kind and amount of information about homosexuality and gay identity accessible to midwestern farm boys. Each of these three groups of life stories is preceded by a description of the era.

FARMING GLOSSARY

Farming has its own terminology, some of which may be unfamiliar. This glossary explains the meanings of potentially unfamiliar words used in these life stories.

Farming involves raising crops and/or livestock, and relying largely on the use of harvested crops to feed such livestock as dairy cattle, hogs, or poultry. By contrast, *ranching* involves raising livestock—such as beef cattle, sheep, or horses—by grazing them on large acreages of herbage, with little or no use of harvested crops. Thus, crop production is the major activity that distinguishes farming from ranching. Except for picking rock and walking beans, all of the crop-growing processes described here are done with tractor-pulled implements on most midwestern farms.

CROPS

Farmers prepare fields for planting by *plowing* to turn over the soil and then *harrowing* to pulverize and smooth the soil for planting. If the harrowing implement uses disk-shaped metal blades it is called *disk harrowing*, or simply *disking*. If it uses metal spikes, it is called *spike harrowing*, or *dragging*. Once the soil in a field has been prepared, the crop is planted using a *drill* or *planter*. This implement makes holes or furrows, deposits the seed and sometimes fertilizer and other chemicals, and covers them with soil. To minimize damage to equipment used in plowing, harrowing, and planting, farmers with rocky fields sometimes have to do *rock-picking* beforehand. This manual removal of rocks needs to be done from season to season, as plowing and frost-heave bring more rocks to the surface.

Corn and soybeans have become the predominant crops in midwestern farming. Many farmers rotate their planting of these two crops, growing soybeans in a particular field one year, corn the next year, and so on. An advantage of this rotation is that soybeans improve growing conditions for the following year's corn crop by adding nitrogen to the soil. A disadvantage of this rotation is that soybean fields are often infested with *vol-*

unteer corn, those plants that grow from the residue of the previous year's corn crop. Many farmers deal with this by *walking beans*—enlisting all available hands to walk through soybean fields to pull volunteer corn and weeds. In a corn field, this weeding process can be done mechanically. Once a corn crop has begun to grow, but is still young enough for a tractor to drive over it, the field is *cultivated* to loosen the soil and uproot weeds between the corn rows.

Summertime, while corn and soybean crops are growing, is time for *making hay.* This dry fodder for cattle, sheep, and horses is usually a mix of alfalfa, clover, and grasses such as timothy, orchard, or brome. First, the hay field is cut, often with an implement called a *haybine* or *windrower,* which leaves the cut hay in *windrows.* These are rows of herbage which can be easily picked up by a baling machine after they have dried in the sun. Use of a *hay rake* helps to turn the windrows over for better drying and easier pick-up by the baling machine. Once baled, hay is often stored in a *haymow* or *hayloft* above the level of the barn where livestock are housed and fed.

Also during the summer, an implement called a *corn chopper* is used to harvest immature corn plants, with which the *silo* is filled. A tall, cylindrical structure made of metal or concrete, the silo is sealed to exclude air once it has been filled with chopped corn. In the absence of oxygen, the corn is converted to *silage,* a succulent, fermented fodder.

Oats are usually harvested with a *combine* (emphasis on first syllable, rhymes with "tom"), a large piece of machinery that is so named because it combines in one machine two processes that had to be done separately in earlier years—cutting and threshing the grain. *Threshing* means separating the grain kernels from the stalk residue, or *straw.* Some farmers leave the straw on the field, to add organic matter to the soil. Others bale it for use as livestock bedding.

A *corn picker* is an implement that strips ears of mature corn from the corn stalk, but leaves the kernels of corn on the cob. This ear corn may then be stored in a *corn crib,* a ventilated storage building. The dry corn stalk residue is often harvested in chopped form for use as livestock bedding. Mature corn and soybeans are also harvested with the use of a combine, which strips the corn kernels from the cob or the beans from the pod. These harvests may be stored on-farm for use as livestock feed, or may be hauled to a commercial *grain elevator* for storage or sale.

LIVESTOCK

Common breeds of cattle in midwestern dairy farming are *Holstein* (large, black and white), *Guernsey* (grayish brown and white), and *Jersey* (small, yellowish brown). *Angus* is a common breed of beef cattle. Among cattle, a *bull* is an adult, uncastrated male; a *steer* is a male that has been castrated before sexual maturity, for beef production. A *cow* is an adult female; a *heifer* is a young cow that has not yet had her first calf. Many farmers use *artificial insemination* for breeding cattle. Semen is collected by a breeding service and frozen for later use, allowing farmers to do selective breeding without direct use of bulls. Breeding over many generations within a single breed produces *purebred* cattle, which may be *registered* with a breed association. Registered purebred dairy cattle have value as breeding stock in addition to their milk production value.

Milk from dairy herds is either *grade A,* for use as fluid milk, or *grade B,* for making cheese, butter, ice cream, and other dairy products. Health and sanitation standards are higher for grade A herds. On grade A farms, bacterial growth is inhibited in various ways, including spreading pulverized limestone *(barn lime)* on the floor of the dairy barn, and by periodically *whitewashing* the barn's walls and ceiling with an application of lime solution.

On some dairy farms, cows are milked while stanchioned in rows. The *stanchion* is a device that fits loosely around a cow's neck, restricting her movement in the stall. Behind the row of cows is a *gutter* to collect their excrement. Milking is more automated on some farms; cows walk through a *dairy parlor* for milking, and their milk is piped from the milking machine to a refrigerated *bulk tank* in the milk house. A *milkman* who works for a dairy cooperative or milk processing plant collects milk from bulk tanks on a number of farms. Earlier in this century, cow's milk was often put through a *cream separator* on the farm—a machine that instantly separated the cream or butterfat portion of whole milk from the nonfat portion. The cream was then put in jars and sold.

Among hogs, a *boar* is an adult, uncastrated male; a *barrow* is a male that has been castrated before sexual maturity, for pork production. A *sow* is an adult female; a *gilt* is a young sow that has not yet had her first litter of pigs. It is common for the hog farmer to have a *farrowing barn* in which sows give birth to and nurse their litters in individual pens. *Feeder pigs* are weaned pigs that eat corn and other feed until they reach market size.

Among draft animals, a *stallion* is an adult, uncastrated male horse. A *mare* is an adult female horse. A *mule* is a hybrid between a female horse (mare) and a male ass (jackass).

Farm Boys

Iowa Farm, by Jeff Kopseng, based on a photo courtesy of Jim Cross

Introduction

I HAVE VIEWED this work of inquiry as "research" only in the broadest sense of the word. I have not sought to quantify anything, nor to prove or disprove anything. My aim has been simply to collaborate with gay men in telling about their lives, and to assist the reader in understanding what these men have to say. This chapter describes midwestern farming and farm culture, and offers some generalizations about the experiences and perspectives represented in this collection of life stories. It is not intended as a summary of definitive conclusions, but simply as a background against which to regard the individual narratives.

FARMING

Midwestern farming has changed greatly during the twentieth century. In the early 1900s, farms were smaller, more numerous, and more diversified in their production. The typical midwestern farm of that era had a variety of livestock and crops, including work horses or mules, dairy and beef cattle, hogs, chickens, corn, hay, wheat, fruits, and garden vegetables. These farms provided most of their own subsistence needs in addition to producing goods for commercial markets.

Technology brought many changes to farming. From the 1920s to the 1950s, work horses and mules were replaced by gasoline-powered tractors. Electrical power became available to the majority of farmers from the mid-1930s through the 1950s. The use of hybrid seed and synthetic fertilizers proliferated during this century, as did the use of chemicals to control weeds and insect pests. These technological changes made greater mechanization possible, meaning that fewer farmers could farm more land more efficiently. Consequently, the number of farms declined and farm size increased as smaller farms were consolidated into fewer, larger operations using larger machinery.

To meet the market demands of an increasingly urbanized population, midwestern farms became more specialized as they became larger. Today, many farms produce only one kind of crop or livestock and even the farms that remain small and diversified have become more specialized. Hogs and beef cattle are of primary importance in midwestern livestock farming, followed by dairy cattle, poultry, and lamb. Crop farming in the Midwest has come to be dominated by corn and soybeans, thanks to lots of level land, fertile soil, and a warm, moist growing season. Secondary crops are hay, oats, grain sorghum (milo), barley, flaxseed, rapeseed, rye, sugar beets, and wheat. As climate, soil conditions, topography, and market access vary throughout the Midwest, so does the variety of crops grown in any particular area.

The men whose stories are presented here grew up on farms that were extremely varied, reflecting not only regional differences within the Midwest, but also changes in farming during this century. Some of the farms on which they lived were relatively small operations that represented only a portion of the family's livelihood; one or both parents worked at off-farm jobs as well. Other farms were larger operations that were the family's sole livelihood. Some farms were family-owned, others were rented. Some farms were specialized, but most had some mixture of animals and crops. On farms that specialized in grains, with little or no livestock, spring and fall tended to be exceptionally busy times, as the crops were planted and harvested. Summer and winter were much less busy. On farms that raised animals as well as the crops to feed them, work demands were more consistent from one time of year to the next. Farm animals, especially dairy cattle, guaranteed the daily grind of chores—feeding, milking, and cleaning.

COMMUNITY

In the early decades of the twentieth century, midwestern farming was an enterprise that relied heavily on relationships with neighbors and kin. Since then, it has become a highly individualized and mechanized enterprise. Technological changes beyond those related to farming methods have contributed greatly to this change. Automobiles, all-weather roads and high-speed highways, telephone, radio, and television have reduced the cultural insularity of farm communities. In doing so, they have eroded the differences between rural and urban life, contributing to a "suburbanization" of farm life.

A technology-induced decline in the rural population has been a major force in the disintegration of rural communities. The closing of rural and village churches and businesses, the demise of one-room country schools, the consolidation of school districts and the bussing of children to towns and cities all represent the loss of institutions central to community life. And as farming operations have become larger, farmers have spread out over the countryside, impeding neighborly relations.

These kinds of changes were lamented by Martin Scherz, who grew up on a small, diversified livestock and crop farm in southeastern Nebraska.

> In the area where I was raised, the old patterns of farming are disappear-
> ing year by year. You don't see nearly as much pasture and livestock. All
> you see is corn and soybeans, anymore. I don't like the direction that
> farming has taken, the increased industrialization and reliance on corpo-
> rate power and corporate structure. Bigger farms might mean more pro-
> duction, but the cost in human lives is far too great to be a good thing.
>   We've lost a lot of the independence of small communities such as the
> one I come from. For the most part, they continue on a blind descent
> into some kind of modern hell. The patterns of rural life have disinte-
> grated into a cheap imitation of suburban life. The kids are involved in
> the same shit that the urban and suburban kids are. They don't have
> much of a sense of community anymore. They lose their grocery store,
> they become just a collection of old people living off what years they have
> left and wondering what their kids are up to a thousand miles away.
> There's a center of life that has disappeared, and I'm not sure what any-
> body can do about it anymore. Bring in some Amish? I tend to be a ro-
> mantic, I guess. The Amish have a good way of life in many ways, and a
> lot of people could learn a lot of things from societies like that. I admire
> them, although I recognize that Amish culture can be oppressive to non-
> conformists.

Though Martin Scherz's sentiments about the disintegration of rural communities echo my own, I am struck by the irony of this perspective. As Martin observes with regard to the Amish, an openly gay identity—of the sort that I have embraced in one fashion or another all of my adult life—is essentially incompatible with traditional farm culture, where gen-der roles tend to be tightly defined and enforced. Thus, it seems that the possibilities of coming out relatively easily and even of living quite openly as a gay man in a farming community have been enhanced as the integrity of rural communities has been diminished.

In "suburbanized" farm communities you are not likely to know your neighbors very well, so you are less likely to be concerned with what they think about you. You probably consider your hand-picked social network of like-minded people to be your community, so the influence of the con-formist impulse in your rural neighborhood is lessened. You are probably exposed to, and identify substantially with, the urban culture by way of the mass media, so that the potential insularity and homogeneity of rural life are diminished. You are more likely to see farming as a business than as a way of life, so the social conventions of farming culture lose some of their authority.

The influence of rural community is illustrated by comparing and con-

trasting the experiences of Steve Gay and Todd Ruhter. Steve was born in
1959 and grew up on a Wisconsin dairy farm. Todd, born in 1967, grew
up on a Nebraska ranch. Both were raised in German families and in predominantly German communities, both came of age between the mid-
1970s and mid-1980s, and both went to college. But the ways in which
they had accommodated being gay in their daily lives differed greatly. Steve
Gay and his lover, Jim, lived just up the road from his parents' place, on
their own farm. Steve talked about his decision to be openly gay in a conservative farming community, despite estrangement from his parents and
siblings.

> I guess it's just the strong-willed part of me that some people have and
> some don't. You've got to say, hey, my life is going to be what *I* want, it's
> going to make *me* happy. If other people don't want to contribute to that,
> well, then they won't. If they can't handle it, that's too bad. It takes a lot
> of will and self-determination to go against your family and friends—to
> make people see you differently than they used to.

At the time of our interview, Todd Ruhter was getting ready to move
from Omaha back to his home ranch, to take care of the cattle for several
months while his father recuperated from surgery. Because he had made
large financial investments in the ranch and expected to have the chance
to take it over when his father retired, Todd expressed great ambivalence
about telling his parents that he is gay.

> I'm not out with my family. . . . Whenever they're ready to hear, which
> may never happen, they can hear. I don't have any problem with telling
> them. . . . But even if I thought they might be ready, I'm not sure I trust
> my judgment enough, considering what they have of mine financially,
> and how they could really hurt me. They are the keystone of my physical
> safety and my ability to interact in the community where I grew up. . . .
> [And] to make sure I never told anybody at home would be the ultimate
> damage control for them, because for anybody there to find out would
> theoretically destroy the business for them and destroy the way they're
> treated in town. I understand and respect that.

Both Steve and Todd had maintained close ties with the rural communities of their childhood in ways that suited the idiosyncrasies and ex-
igencies of their own lives. Todd's approach hinged on his attraction to
farming as a way of life, and his stated belief that "Where I came from is
as important as what I am." Steve's credo seemed to be a transposition of
that, the sense that what I am is as important as where I came from. Above
all, Steve said, "My life is going to be what I want." In contrast, Todd had
decided it was important that he go along with appearing to be what his
family and home community wanted him to be—for the sake of family

and community relations, investments, inheritance, and his future in ranching. For Todd, at age twenty-five, fitting into the rural community that he still thought of as home was more important than living openly as a gay man according to the model defined by urban gay culture.

ETHNICITY

As their surnames reveal, more than half of the men whose stories are presented here are of at least partial German heritage. This is consistent with the ethnic composition of the rural Midwest, which was settled during the nineteenth and early twentieth centuries by two main groups, Yankees and Germans. For well over a century now, the ethnic mosaic of this region has been dominated by these two groups.

The Yankees were native-born Americans who had British Protestant ancestry. Following the frontier, they migrated to the Midwest from their homelands in the Northeastern and Middle Atlantic states. Close on their heels were the Germans, new immigrants to the U.S. from Catholic and Protestant areas in Germany. Scandinavian immigrants from Denmark, Finland, Norway, and Sweden also established themselves as midwestern farmers during this era, with cultures that tended to be more Germanic than Yankee in character.

The distinct differences between Yankee and German farming cultures have been described by Sonya Salamon in her book, *Prairie Patrimony*. I have drawn on Salamon's work in the characterizations presented here, and illustrate her generalities with quotes from the life stories presented in this volume.

Compared to the Yankees, German farmers were strongly communalistic. They maintained a strong ethnic identity and very tight, kin-oriented social networks that were closed to outsiders. "We were very insular," Martin Scherz said of his German farm community in Nebraska. "A lot of the people were from the same villages in Germany and were all related for the most part. . . . Most of the community was Lutheran." Church and community were synonymous in German culture; the social and religious functions of the church were equally important. Children were raised to be obedient. Everyone tended to know everyone else's business and a steady stream of gossip and criticism helped to maintain conformity. There was little tolerance for diversity or nonconformity.

"There was prejudice and bigotry all over the place," said James Heckman of his German farm community in Indiana.

My grandmother thought the black stuff on black people would rub off, so she wouldn't shake hands with one. And you had to beware of the Jews and the Japs. There was a young girl in the area who went off to school in Chicago, and when she married a black guy her family disowned her. A good friend of our family said, "I could bury a child before I could accept that," and my parents agreed how terrible it was.

German farmers tended to be industrious, earnest, frugal, conservative, and slow to change their traditional farming practices. It was common for all family members, male and female, to be intensively involved in the farming operation. In Dennis Lindholm's view, "We very rarely did anything other than work. . . . [Dad] never slept beyond 4:00, and was up and gone by the time we got up, so we had to go out and help." Because family identity was very closely tied to the land, German parents did what they could to ensure that their farm would grow and prosper in succeeding generations. To this end, they reared their children—sons in particular—for commitment to farming.

Many a successful German patriarch "colonized" his rural neighborhood by acquiring adjacent farms for his sons to operate once they were married and raising families. Salamon tells of an eighty-five-year-old farmer who recalled, "I went into the service for four years and when I came back, I really wasn't so sure I wanted to be a farmer. But my dad told me that he'd raised me to be a farmer and that's what he wanted me to do. German fathers have a real influence on their sons. What else could I do?" (Salamon, p. 101).

Unlike the Germans, for whom the perpetuation of their farms and farming methods represented cultural continuity, the Yankees tended to take a more entrepreneurial and capitalistic approach. They saw farming as a business and land as a commodity; they farmed in order to make a profit and to increase the value of the farm. In comparison to the more traditional Germans, Yankees valued innovation in farming methods and equipment.

Yankee farmers were strongly individualistic and their communities more loosely organized. Their ethnicity was not so central to their identity. Households belonged to individualized social networks that were not necessarily kinship-based, and one's kin were often divided among different churches. The religious function of church was far more important than the social. Yankee children were raised to be more individualistic and autonomous, and the loose-knit community enhanced tolerance of diversity and unconventional behavior. Gossip and criticism were less important than among Germans as agents of conformity. Upon reaching adulthood, Yankee children were expected to distance themselves from their parents' authority, leave their childhood homes, and find their own way in the world. Consequently, the Yankee farmer was less likely than the German to pressure a son to take over the family farm.

The sharpness of this Yankee/German contrast has been eroded during this century, as various factors have led to a blending of these cultures. Nonetheless, it seems likely that these differences in farming culture would lead to different experiences for gay farm boys growing up in families dominated by Yankee or German values. Considering the German culture's greater emphasis on shaping oneself to conform to the expectations of others, it seems reasonable to assume that growing up in a German family would have been particularly problematic for a gay male. First, being gay would not satisfy rigorous family and community standards. In addition, since sons generally succeed fathers in taking over farms, fitting into the rural community and assuring the continuity of the family farm depends on marrying and having children. This could only intensify marital and reproductive imperatives in the coming-of-age experience of farm boys, especially those who have no brothers.

James Heckman became an only son as the result of his older brother's death as a child. With the collaboration of his parents and extended family, James did his best to fill his dead brother's shoes throughout childhood and well into adulthood. He sought to pattern his own identity after that of his idealized brother. At age twenty-seven, assured by a Catholic priest that he would grow into it, James married a woman because "she seemed to be the type of woman [my brother] might have married. And because my brother would have had children, I had children. There was a time when I thought of my own children as my brother's children." James's attempted suicide, psychiatric hospitalization, and coming out in his mid-thirties helped to end that role-playing era of his life.

In a less traumatic way, Joe Shulka's experience also exemplifies the pressure exerted by traditional farming parents on their sons. As an only son, Joe's decision not to go into farming created much disappointment and strife with his parents.

> [Dad] bought the farm from his father, and as soon as he had a son he
> figured it was going to continue on for generations. . . . [Now,] with
> Dad planning to sell the farm, there's a lot of people who are looking on
> it as a real loss, because he's been at it for fifty years in the same place,
> and the farm has really changed under him. I feel some guilt, but I think
> Dad and Mom have come to terms with the fact that I've chosen a life of
> my own.

Yankee parents were less likely to pressure a son to take over the family farm, even if they would have liked to see him do so. My own experience illustrates this dynamic, though, unlike James Heckman and Joe Shulka, I am not an only son. As a child I was very involved in the work of the farm, but much less than my brother, who has since taken over the homestead. Although my brother and I knew that we had the option of farming for a living, we were not raised to be farmers in the characteristic German fashion. It was always evident to us that our parents encouraged us to find our own paths in life. Finding out that being gay was part of my path has not been easy for my parents, but their disappointment over my not marrying and fathering children has not been accompanied by distress about the family farm's continuity.

My own upbringing was consistent with the Yankee profile in other ways as well. My extended family was large, but kinship connections were not tight; each nuclear family functioned as a discrete entity, with their own church affiliations and social networks. This is in marked contrast to the experience of Todd Ruhter, who grew up with a younger brother in a German Lutheran family in Nebraska. "My uncles and grandparents could discipline us just like my mother and father could. Everybody and everything was community property." Also, although I grew up in a community that included families of varied European heritage, I was essentially oblivious to ethnicity throughout childhood. Only as an adult did I come to realize that many of the surnames of my home community were of English, Irish, German, and Norwegian origin. Until then, they had been simply American.

Gender Roles

In most cases, growing up on a farm presented these boys with two quite distinct, gender-based spheres of work activity—farmwork and housework. Farmwork was largely the male's domain. It extended from the livestock in the barns and pastures to the crops in the fields, and to the maintenance and repair of farm machinery and vehicles. Housework was largely the female's domain, typically extending from the house to the garden. On some farms, caring for the chickens and milk cows was also seen as women's work, most often when these were relatively small operations. Until the 1950s, the sale of cream, eggs, and poultry by farm women was often an important supplement to farm income. As boys, several of the men I interviewed had been involved in raising and caring for chickens, with a particular interest in exotic breeds.

Any overlap or flexibility of male and female duties tended to occur most often in the gardens and barns, and least often in the houses, fields, and machine shops. But what was considered appropriate work for males and females varied by region, community, and family. In Todd Ruhter's experience, "There was the wife's role and the husband's role, and the only time they mixed was when the wife was helping the husband."

With few exceptions, the boys whose stories are presented here fit a common profile with regard to their involvement in farmwork. They generally sought to avoid fieldwork and the repair and maintenance of farm machinery and vehicles. This was typically attributed to an inherent "mechanical disability" and to the dusty, dirty, boring nature of driving machinery back and forth in the fields. Martin Scherz fit this profile, and felt deficient as a result.

> I felt like a damn fumbling idiot around farm machinery. My brother was good at that kind of stuff, and that made me worse by comparison. When I would screw up, my dad would say, "Oh, go up to the kitchen with your mother." I think it was his way of saying that I had to decide whether I was going to be a sissy or whether I could really help on the farm.

Dean Gray, born in 1962, grew up on a small dairy farm in central Wisconsin. Even in his preschool years, his attraction to animal husbandry was strong.

> There were lots of mechanical things on the farm that I was no help with, but I could handle the record-keeping and I loved taking care of the animals, which included delivering lots of calves. When I was four years old, we had a calf I named Todd. No one else knew he had a name. One morning I was in the barn and found out Todd was to be sold. I refused to go in the house for breakfast. Overwrought and crying, I stood in front of each cow in the barn and sang a song to each one—thirty-some songs I made up, looking for comfort.

To the extent that these boys were attracted to any aspect of farmwork, it was generally the care, feeding, and breeding of livestock and the cleaning and maintenance of these animals' shelters that they found most appealing and satisfying. This sort of work is essentially the "housework" of the farm. After a housekeeping apprenticeship with his mother in his early years, David Foster was expected to join his father and older brothers in doing some of the farm chores. "What I did, I did very well. I've always been a very thorough person, very organized and clean. I did farmwork that way too, cleaning the barn and sweeping the feed into the cribs. . . . My mother would say, 'David's the only one that sweeps it that clean.'"

The degree of rigidity with which the boundaries of gender-based work roles were enforced varied greatly among the families represented here. In most cases, enforcement tended to be especially strong for males. For females, things were more ambiguous and fluid. It was far more common for wives and daughters to do work related to livestock and crops, when their help was needed, than for husbands and sons to do housework, no matter how badly their help was needed. But it was common for everyone in the family, regardless of gender, to be involved in certain seasonal tasks requiring a large number of hands, such as "walking beans"—walking between rows of soybeans and pulling out weeds and unwanted "volunteer" corn sprouting from the residue of the previous year's crop.

A large majority of my subjects identified more closely with, and generally had richer and more satisfying relationships with, their mothers and other females than with their fathers and other males. With few exceptions, these boys tended to have a stronger inclination to work in the house and garden than to do farmwork. The extent to which they were allowed to indulge this domestic preference varied widely. In some cases it was welcomed, or at least it provoked no criticism or disapproval. Other boys, while not forbidden or discouraged from engaging in such activities as housecleaning, cooking, baking, sewing, gardening, canning, and freezing, had little time for these preferred domestic tasks because of the extent to which they were required to help with farmwork. In other cases, the boys were admonished or ridiculed as "sissies," most often by fathers, brothers, and other male relatives. From a young age, James Heckman learned to shun "girl stuff."

> Often I wished I could be at my mother's side to cook and bake and sew, but in German Catholic farm families only girls did those things. When we would go visiting, I was very interested in how the house was decorated, what type of food was on the table, how well-dressed they were. Needlework, knitting and crocheting fascinated me, and I really wanted to do them. But had I done them, I would have been ridiculed for being such a sissy. My uncle would have started it and it would have spread out from there. Even my grandfather would say, "Oh, you don't want to do that. That's girl stuff."

The degree to which rigid gender roles extended beyond the realms of work varied widely among families. Some boys were free to pursue their own interests, however unconventional, as long as they did the farmwork that was expected of them. Other boys found themselves bound by gender-based expectations in all arenas, even the make-believe play of early childhood. Terry Bloch, born in 1948 and raised on a crop and livestock farm in southwestern Minnesota, described an early message that had an enduring impact.

> When I was real little, playing with my sister and cousins, I would dress up like Annie Oakley. I'd put on a skirt over my jeans and cowboy boots,

and even had socks for boobs. My mom said, "Your dad doesn't like it when you dress up like that." The message was that I was not to be feminine and I was not to play the feminine role. I was to be masculine, butch. On the other hand, there was nothing wrong with a girl being a tomboy and holding her own. There was nothing wrong with my sisters driving a tractor, milking cows; my dad made us all work equally hard. But my sisters were expected to be girls and I was expected to be a boy. I tried to excel at sports, dated girls, and stayed in the closet, playing the butch role.

By marrying and fathering children, Terry continued to play the role that was expected of him. David Nordstrom, born in 1942 and raised on a small farm in southwestern Wisconsin, reflected on the role that his upbringing led him to assume.

Where I grew up, men were men and women were women and there really wasn't anything in between. Geared toward being strong, silent and tough, I accumulated lots of layers as I went along. I didn't *feel* tough at all, but I certainly created a veneer for myself, and that's been a wall, for me and for other people who have tried to communicate with me. I've been through some real tough times—an insane drinking career and insane relationships—and at forty-nine years of age I'm finally growing up and feeling some pride in myself.

Like Terry Bloch and David Nordstrom, many of these men grew up in families where gender-role enforcement was especially rigid and contrary to their inherent natures. In most cases, this gender-rigidity seemed to lead them to make more drastic efforts to deny or avoid their homosexuality. Common manifestations of this kind of response included getting married, having suicidal tendencies, and becoming immersed in religious pursuits. In contrast, the boy who was able to create and maintain a reasonably comfortable gender-identity niche that suited his own nature tended to have less difficulty in acknowledging and accepting the essential difference of his sexual identity.

Todd Moe, born in 1962, grew up on a small farm in east-central Minnesota. He found something of an alternative role model in the person of an elderly neighbor woman.

Minnie was an old maid, very manly in her dress, who lived her entire life on the farm where she was born. Whenever we went to her place to buy eggs, her house was as neat as a pin and her kitchen always had the smell of something freshly baked. She was very warm and had a distinctive, contagious laugh. She enjoyed chatting with my dad as much as with my mom. We sort of adopted Minnie as an aunt or grandmother. In one sense people probably thought, "How strange, living all by herself," but she was well-liked and respected by the neighboring farmers. She knew a lot about farm life and about the area. I really admired the respect that she commanded, and I sometimes thought that I would like to live like she did.

Many of these boys sought to strengthen their feelings of fitting in and being worthwhile, even though they didn't fit the conventional gender-role picture very well, by striving to be "the best little boy in the world." This common pattern of response to feelings of being a misfit was illustrated by author John Reid, who used the phrase as the title of his account of growing up gay, published in 1973. Typical elements of this "best little boy" response included exceptionally obedient and mature relations with parents and other elders, an earnest commitment to farm and household work responsibilities, above-average performance in school and other off-farm activities, and a devotion to religious belief and church involvement that often exceeded that of the parents. Richard Kilmer's experience was characteristic of this response.

> From my earliest memory, I knew I was gay, so I always had this part of me that I had to hide. I thought if people knew, they would never think I was this wonderful person, so I overcompensated by being a dutiful son—getting good grades, being polite, not drinking, doing the things I was supposed to, going to church and being the altar boy. I felt it wasn't fair that my mother would be out working on the farm and then she would have to come in and cook the meal while everybody else sat around. So I became her helpmate, setting the table and doing those kinds of things, even as I got older.

ISOLATION AND FREEDOM

The freedom to get away on their own in the large, open spaces of the farm had great positive significance for many of these boys. For many of them as well, this freedom was accompanied by isolation from social contact with people outside their own families. The degree of isolation varied greatly, determined not only by the farm's location in relation to neighbors and the nearest village or town, but also by the modes of transportation available and by the parents' attitudes toward the value of activities that would afford their children social contact.

Some boys were tied relentlessly to work responsibilities throughout their growing-up years; others had relatively few work responsibilities and were able to participate in outside activities quite freely. Some parents made an effort to overcome the geographical isolation of farm life for their children. Other parents, it seemed, were attracted to farming *because* it afforded a large degree of social isolation, which may have been consistent with their own natures and what they considered appropriate for their children. For the boys who were most isolated, the influence of home life was inevitably intensified.

Most of these boys lived in rural communities that were very homogeneous with regard to racial, ethnic, and religious heritage. Racism, religious intolerance, and a general suspicion of strangers were quite prevalent. Nonetheless, Tom Lewis said, "It was broadening to have grown up on a farm, which is ironic because I wasn't exposed to great diversity there." Tom, who grew up in northern Illinois and now lives in Chicago, attributed this broadening influence to having established a strong connection with the natural world, and having developed an appreciation for "the balance between humans, animals, and plants."

One of the fundamental characteristics of farming is that it deals with living, growing things and with the cycles of nature. The lack of human diversity in the social experiences of many of these boys appears to have been offset to some extent by their rich experience of the diversity of the nonhuman world. Essentially, the often subconscious message that many of them seemed to get from observing the inherent variability in animals and plants, both on the farm and in the wild, was that being different was unusual, sometimes strange, but very much a part of life nonetheless. This impression helped some of these boys accept the different sort of male they sensed themselves to be.

Wayne Belden, who grew up on a dairy farm in northwestern Illinois and now lives in Chicago, described what he considered to be an effect of the social isolation of farm life.

> In the city, your main reference point is people. You tend to think that everything that's holding you back or moving you forward has something to do with other people. When you make your living dealing with the cycles of nature, you know that there are other reference points outside human society and that you can't control everything.

A number of these men suggested that the isolation they experienced both hindered and helped them in coming to recognize and understand their differentness. While they missed out on the kind of information, perspective, and social experience that they may have had access to in a town or city, the potentially devastating expectations and ridicule of their peers were also avoided or diminished. Like many of these men, Everett Cooper experienced a lot of pressure to conform to standards of masculinity that prevailed in junior high and high school.

> If I'd had an inordinate amount of teasing on any given day, I would get real melancholy, and would sometimes go out in the woods to cry or to

fight things out inside myself. And I enjoyed riding my horse in the
openness and expanse of the fields. It was almost a gift to be able to get
away and think my own thoughts—to ride free and unrestrained. I often
wondered if my school friends in town were ever able to get away from
everything and get in touch with themselves.

In the relative isolation of the farm, some of these boys were better able
to avoid peer pressure and invent themselves according to their own in-
clinations and standards. Jim Cross believed that because his childhood
was so uncluttered, he was able to focus on the blossoming of his own in-
dividuality. The isolation of his growing-up years made it possible for him
to create his own frame of reference, his own gender identity.

These stories do not suggest that there was necessarily less pressure to
conform to expected gender roles on the farm than in town. They do suggest, however, that if these boys were going to have any success in creating and maintaining their own unconventional gender-identity niches, they
were more likely to do so in the arena of the immediate family than in the
larger community. As Barney Dews observed, "An eccentric is a person in
your own family; a freak is in someone else's." With a few exceptions, families tended to be more accommodating of these boys' differentness than
were peers in the larger community, most often encountered at school.
Donald Freed grew up on a farm near the small town of Loomis, in south-
central Nebraska. "In school, I was branded both a sissy and a smarty, and
that persisted all the way through high school. Thank god I grew up outside of town and not in it!"

"Growing up on the farm, if you don't want to deal with anybody outside of your own family, you don't have to," said Allen Victor. He was born
in 1955, the oldest of six children on a 160-acre crop farm near Sleepy
Eye, in south-central Minnesota. "It was a pretty blissfully ignorant existence, and I was free to be who I was. We were raised to be independent,
to think for ourselves—'Who cares what the neighbors think? They don't
have to live your life. You have to do what you feel is right for yourself.'
That came through real strong from my mom."

SEXUALITY

In her book, *Letters from the Country,* Carol Bly mused on "Scandinavian-
American sexual chill" in the prairie country of western Minnesota.

As your eye sweeps this landscape you can see five or six farmers'
"groves" (windbreaks around the farmhouses). At dawn and dusk the
groves look like the silent, major ships of someone else's navy, standing

well spaced, well out to sea. When I came out here . . . on my first visit,
we drove in the evening. The bare bulbs were lighted in the passing
farmyards. The barn lights were on for chores. I remember saying, "How
marvelous to think of night on this gigantic prairie—all the men and
women making love in their safe houses guarded by the gloomy groves!
Who wants to think of anyone making love in Los Angeles—but how
great to think of it in these cozy farmhouses!" The reply was: "That's
what *you* think!" (pp. 1–2)

It is a fairly common and sensible thing for people from urban backgrounds to assume that farm folks regard sex with a fairly comfortable mat-
ter-of-factness. After all, sex is central to raising livestock, and the livestock
usually do it in broad daylight. Nonetheless, in the experience of most of
these boys—Scandinavian-American or not—the blunt reality of sex among
the farm animals did not translate into open, comfortable attitudes about
human sexuality. In some cases, it appeared that even sex among farm animals was seen as a bad influence. Several of these boys were forbidden to
watch the breeding of horses or cattle, and John Berg was reprimanded
harshly when, at age seven or eight, his father found him engrossed in observing a boar mounting a sow.

On the other hand, John Beutel's mother was probably like many parents in her belief that sufficient sex education was afforded by observing
breeding among farm animals and pets. A large majority of these boys received no sex education from their parents and very little at school. Access
to other sources of information about sex varied greatly among these boys,
with generally greater access for those who came of age in more recent
decades. From Lon Mickelsen's perspective, sexuality was held in an undercurrent. Tom Lewis suggested that "sexuality was kind of like God—
you believed in it, but you didn't talk about it." In fact, God and sex were
closely connected, as religious influences appeared to be a major factor in
fostering sexual prudishness among conservative farm families. Silverstein
commented on the role of the church in his 1981 book, *Man to Man: Gay
Couples in America.*

Sex is not yet an idea whose time has come in the heartland. . . . The
churches teach generalized guilt concerning all feelings of sexuality. . . .
The force of religion and the lack of alternatives in the heartland have
unquestionably prevented many gay men from experiencing their homosexuality and in some cases prevented them from awareness of it until
later years (pp. 324–25).

Many of these men believed that growing up on a farm hindered the
development of their understanding of human sexuality in general. And
no matter when they began to sense something different about their own

sexuality, many of them believed that their farm upbringing hindered their ability to recognize, understand, and come to terms with their homosexual orientation. "In that farm environment, it's like I was in hibernation as to who I really was sexually," Robert Peters observed. Lon Mickelsen elaborated on that idea.

> It took longer to come to grips with being gay growing up on a farm, not so much because of the homophobia but because of the absence of homosexuality in that culture. It's not that homosexuality was frowned upon. It simply didn't exist. There were never any strong overtones about it being wrong, because it was never discussed.

This invisibility of homosexuality is not unique to farm communities, but it was probably enhanced by isolation, religious conservatism, and sexual prudishness. Further, the mixture of antipathy and fascination with which many farm people regard urban life seems to foster the belief that homosexuality is an unnatural phenomenon of the city that has no relevance to rural life. The silence surrounding homosexuality was compounded for a large majority of these boys by the fact that they were not aware of knowing any homosexual person throughout their growing-up years. Silverstein stated his impressions of a rural-urban difference.

> Repression of the homosexual identity appears more successful in the boondocks of America and in many of the small- to medium-sized cities of the South, the Southwest, and Midwest. Especially in the heartland of America, it's possible for men to reach age twenty or more before becoming aware of their homosexual needs; this is quite different from the case in larger cities in which some men make a *decision* to suppress and refuse their homosexuality. Men who have married without knowing they were gay live everywhere, but are probably less prevalent in the largest cities than elsewhere (pp. 322–23).

As with information about sex in general, access to information about homosexuality varied greatly, with generally greater access for those who came of age in more recent decades. For example, the June 26, 1964, issue of *Life* magazine carried a ground-breaking feature story, "Homosexuality in America," that was an important source of information for two of these individuals, one as a teenager and the other as a married man. Magazines, newspapers, and books appeared to have been most significant, with television having great importance for those who came of age between the mid-1970s and mid-1980s. Nonetheless, many of these boys made no particular effort to obtain information about homosexuality, and many who did make an effort tended to come up short. Dale Hesterman perused a health book that his parents had in the house. "The section on homosexuality talked about studies that had been done, and one had found that men whose right testicle hung lower than the left were more prone to homosexuality. I looked at mine and, doggone it, the right one *was* lower than the left."

For some, their ignorance was likely to have increased the chances that they would believe, as David Nordstrom did, that "to wind up being a queer was the worst thing I could think of." However, it's unlikely that much of the information that was available before the 1970s would have led any of them to a more favorable conclusion.

Some of these men, as boys, did not seem to need information about homosexuality in order to feel okay about themselves. Although Harry Beckner did not think of himself as homosexual during his adolescent years, he accepted his attraction to other males as a natural thing because he felt it to be so central a part of who he was. Nearly all of these men believed that they were essentially born with a homosexual orientation. The few who diverged from this perspective believed that their attraction to other males was fostered, at least in part, by receiving too little affectionate attention from their fathers and other males. Several men speculated that their fathers may have had strong but conflicted homosexual tendencies. More than one man wondered if his father's distance and lack of affection was the result of discomfort at seeing "gay" characteristics in his son.

The assumption that farm people are more comfortable and freewheeling about sex had become apparent to some of these men in their connections within the gay community. Clark Williams said, "Sometimes when I tell someone that I grew up on a farm, he'll ask if I had sex with the animals—or if there was a network of country boys who got together for circle jerks. God, I wish!"

In 1948, Kinsey, Pomeroy, and Martin wrote: "The city boy's failure to understand what life can mean to a boy who is raised on a farm, and the farm boy's idea that there is something glamorous about the way in which the city boy lives, apply to every avenue of human activity, including the sexual (p. 449)."

Among males, Kinsey's group reported, "sexual relations with animals of other species are, of necessity, most often found in rural areas" (p. 459). Several of the men whose stories are presented here engaged in sexual relations with farm animals and pet dogs. That several other men chose not to reveal having had sexual contact with animals became evident in conversations subsequent to their interviews. In most cases, these incidents of bestiality appeared to be isolated, experimental events of adolescence. However, animal contacts were a major sexual outlet for David Foster until he reached his early twenties.

Kinsey's group reported slightly lower frequencies of both total sexual activity and homosexual activity among rural males compared to urban (p. 464). In contrast, Silverstein stated that the greater freedom and privacy of the farm lead to a degree of sexual activity among rural boys that equals or exceeds that of urban boys (p. 262). In regard to the boys whose stories are presented here, it appears that the combined effects of social isolation and sexual ignorance and prudishness could have only served to restrict sexual activity.

A number of these boys had no sexual outlet throughout their teen years, with the exception of wet dreams. For others, masturbation was the sole sexual outlet. Nonetheless, many of these boys did have sexual relations with other males during their preadult years, most often with peers from neighboring farms or from school. In some cases these relations were naively exploratory and experimental, while in other cases they consisted of complete sexual acts engaged in repeatedly. Several boys had sexual relations with brothers; several others had sexual contacts with adult males, related and unrelated. None reported having sexual relations with his father.

Approximately one-quarter of these men married. One of these men, still married, arranged to be interviewed at a public library in Indiana. He talked about his intention to come out to his wife and adolescent children in the next several years. Several of these men, as adults, engaged in extensive psychiatric therapy or psychological counseling related to sexual identity issues. Cornelius Utz, born in 1909, stated that his Victorian upbringing led him to repress expression of feeling in general, and this repression was reinforced by several years of sex-focused psychiatric therapy in the late 1930s. He was married for nearly forty years, and came out shortly after his wife's death. Several of these men had seriously contemplated suicide, and one had attempted to kill himself in the midst of his marriage. The older men in my group were more likely than the younger men to have been married, to have engaged in extensive sex-related therapy or counseling, and to have contemplated or attempted suicide.

PRESENT LIFE

The men whose stories are presented varied greatly in the degree to which they were open about being gay, and in the extent of their involvement with their local gay communities. While some assumed an activist orientation, most tended to be more conservative in their attitudes toward gay politics. Tactics that were seen as rocking the boat were generally disdained. Some disapproved of gay pride parades or other highly visible events, and of gay men who are drag queens or who behave in flamboyantly effeminate ways. Tom Lewis stated that he has had difficulty accepting men who don't act like men did on the farm—"where men were men." Richard Hopkins described his view of being gay as a very private thing.

> I don't want to wear it on my sleeve. It's not open for discussion, and I don't ever intend it to be—with people I work with, the next-door neighbors, the family even. If you know me, you're either going to like me or you're not going to like me, but not because I'm wearing a banner up and down the street so everybody knows, or saying in your face, "I'm gay, like it or leave it."

In their approaches to socializing, these men tended to favor get-togethers among relatively small groups of friends rather than the more public and densely populated socializing that prevails in bars and clubs. Similarly, many of these men believed that they needed more solitary time than gay men from urban backgrounds required. Considering that many men seem to have a "loner" tendency—regardless of their sexual orientation and whether their upbringing was rural or urban—it is not surprising that a number of these men felt they lived on the fringes of their gay communities. It is likely, however, that the origin of these feelings goes beyond the typical male loner impulse. Most gay communities are urban phenomena, and although many of these men lived in or near relatively large cities, they were not *of* the city, as many of their gay peers were. Wayne Belden, who has lived in Chicago for about twenty years, said, "Here in the city I'm kind of out of my element. I just have to get on as best I can, gaining some things and losing some." Larry Ebmeier had a similar reaction to getting acquainted with the gay community in Lincoln, Nebraska, once he started to come out in his late twenties.

> It seemed like I was the peg that didn't fit—I wasn't a queen, I didn't like to dish. I always tended to feel more at home with some of my nongay friends. I still feel that way, but less so. It was somewhat of a dilemma, because I knew I was gay but I didn't enjoy the banter, I wasn't into the style, I wasn't into the things they did. People that I've come into contact with in the gay community tend to be more outgoing, more talkative, less introverted than I am. I wonder if there aren't other people out there who are like me, more quiet and more private, not like the gay mafia that you see so much of—the outgoing, outspoken, socialistic, activist, flamboyant and fast-paced, dishing, camping-it-up type of people who seem to dominate when gays come together in urban areas.

Allen Victor, who has been with his partner Jeff since 1979, ruminated on their efforts to create and sustain gay as well as mainstream community connections in a small city in southern Minnesota.

Jeff and I live in his hometown, so we're very involved with his family.
The house we bought was a block away from his grandmother's, an old
Norwegian lady who lived to be eighty-five. She and I got along very
well, always teasing each other. Once, when she thought I was putting
Jeff up to doing something she didn't quite approve of, she told him, "I
don't know if you should hang around with Allen—I think he's a homosexual. But he *is* a good cook."

When she passed away, we inherited her best friend from across the
street, and her next-door-neighbor friend. It's an old, established neighborhood, but through living here and doing things for his grandmother
and her friends, we've gotten to know our neighbors. We feel a little bit
more support from some of them than from the other gay people in
town—just because our values are more in tune with those of our neighbors, I guess. It seems like people here can handle gay and lesbian couples
who've been here a long time and live openly but quietly. There's one
couple that's been together here for close to forty years.

It's hard to be closeted in this town, because word gets around. When
we first moved here, a lesbian came to us and said, "All right, we're
here—we have to organize a little bit." So we got a post office box and
got a group of eight or ten people together. It started out to be a real
positive experience, but we ended up burning out on personality conflicts and bad feelings because of different outlooks on how to live in this
small town. Jeff and I felt like we were being pushed to the foreground.
Since we lived together, we could be the visible ones and take the flak.
We really resented that, because we had just bought a house and we were
trying to do business in the community.

Jeff and I try to keep informed through the gay press, give some
money to AIDS organizations, and get together with other local gay men
when we can. I've had a hard time socializing with other gay men, and
I've had a hard time getting the difference between "gay is good" and
"all gay people are good and everything they do is good." I know some
gay men who are real assholes. If they were straight I wouldn't give them
the time of day. And some of the things that gay people have done "for
the cause" I now see differently; it's easy to be more radical if someone
else pays the price. I don't know if this perspective is coming with age,
from owning more things, or from the small-town attitude rubbing off.

Approximately one-third of these men were in relationships with other
men at the time of their interviews. Being in a stable, long-lasting, committed relationship had great significance for a large majority of these men,
whether or not they were currently in one. Some of them attributed this
trait to the stability of their farm backgrounds where, as Tom Lewis described it, "friends remained friends and people stayed together." Quite a
number of the men who were interviewed expressed an interest in meet-

ing other men from farming backgrounds, and this interest was apparent in others who seemed reluctant to express it.

Some of these men expressed considerable enthusiasm about being gay. For others, feelings were more mixed. Although none indicated a desire to become heterosexual if that were possible, some men were clearly distressed by the ways in which being gay had affected the course of their lives. Nonetheless, many of these men reflected Harry Beckner's opinion that "farm people tend to be down to earth, to accept things for what they are." For some of these individuals, however, achieving that acceptance had been a very long and rough process.

These men varied greatly in the extent to which they were open with their parents or other family members about being gay. Some were actively open about it; some were passively open, making no particular effort to reveal or to conceal being gay. Others made a considerable effort to conceal their orientation—in some cases because they were not yet ready to take on the task of coming out, or because they believed that such self-disclosure would serve no useful purpose, or would give too much satisfaction to troublemaking family members.

Gary Christiansen's direct approach to telling his family about his sexual identity is most characteristic of the men who came of age since the mid-1970s. Born in 1967, Gary grew up with an older sister and brother on a mixed livestock and crop farm in western Iowa, between Missouri Valley and Logan. The coming-out letter that Gary sent to his parents and siblings when he was twenty-five included this statement: "From the very beginning, I have accepted that I am 'different' and I have never struggled with my identity or wished to change it. There is nothing to change, because I am the way God made me."

In our interview, Gary explained how his upbringing had influenced his response to being gay, including his decision to reveal that part of himself to his family.

> We were raised to face things, to do what you've got to do to take care of each problem as it comes up. Life is unfair, but you've got to bounce right back. You don't run away from your problems, because you aren't going to get anywhere. When a problem would come up, my dad would say, "Well, that's just the way it is—you'll just have to deal with it." When I realized I was gay, I didn't try to run and hide from it. Even though I knew my parents weren't going to like it, I knew that was just the way it was.
>
> I sent the letter to my mom and dad, my sister, and my brother and sister-in-law. My mom called and was in hysterics. "We don't understand this. It's abnormal. It's not right. We can't tell anybody about this." She said it was a good thing I lived in Omaha, because if I lived up there

they'd have to move. When she said she didn't know how she was going
to tell my dad, I said she didn't have to tell him. "That's why I sent the
letter—he can read it just like you did and fall off his chair if that's the
case." When my dad had a really hard time with it, I told him that "my
being gay is no different than your goddamned tractor having two flat
tires. That's just the way it is, and you'll just have to deal with it."

My mom was a lot calmer when she called two days later, but she said
she just didn't understand. I said, "Think back and put things together.
You must have at least suspected." But she said she'd had no idea. My dad
said that he had suspected, and then he said, "With modern medicine,
why can't you just take a pill to take care of it?" When my mom asked,
"What did we do wrong?," I told her that it was nothing she did that
made me this way. "It's kind of like a field of clover," I said. "Most of it
is three-leaf clover, but there's one that has four leaves. That's a gay
clover—it's different, but it serves its purpose. It's there with the rest of
them, just trying to survive and do its job." She didn't buy that analogy.

Since a few weeks after that letter, the subject hasn't been brought up.
I'd like to sit down with my parents and talk about it, but I know my dad
would just leave the room. I think, in time, my mom and I will discuss it
once in a while, as we feel a little more comfortable. It's a long process. I
don't know how to answer some of her questions, and it's hard for me to
talk to her about sex. Of course, she's worried about AIDS. I'm trying to
get into her mind that I don't sit around in bars and have sex all the
time. I get up, put my pants on, go to work, and pay my bills just like
anybody else.

In one of his radio monologues on "A Prairie Home Companion," Garri-
son Keillor stated that "every family needs at least one good sinner who
does it right out there where you can see it." By being open about being
gay, some of these men have played that role in their families. As a result,
they have experienced varying degrees of familial disdain and rejection. In
some cases these negative reactions have been rooted primarily in biblical
injunctions. In other cases, concern about the family's image in the community appeared to be the main consideration. The potential for disapproval, gossip, and ridicule tends to be an especially potent enforcer of conformity—or the appearance of conformity—in farm communities, where
families are often deeply rooted and thus less able to sever social ties or
move away in the face of disapproval.

Terry Bloch's description of the area where he grew up provides a vivid
snapshot of the force of conformity in a rural community, and how it affected his life as a gay man.

Southwestern Minnesota is white, conservative, Republican country
where, in those days, you didn't admit there was such a thing as child

abuse, you didn't admit that your husband was a wife-beating alcoholic, you didn't let yourself get a divorce. You'd go to church on Sunday, smiling and waving, and keep your skeletons in the closet. The husband was the strong, dominant one in a marriage, and he didn't talk about things. I brought those values into my relationship with Jahred, only to discover it wasn't right. We have to be equal, we have to be more open with our feelings and thoughts. Sometimes I do a real shitty job of that.

Despite the list of apparently negative influences that one could compile from these life stories, many of these men saw much that was positive in their childhoods. Lon Mickelsen's assessment is characteristic.

Looking back, the farm and my hometown seem like distant, impossible places—places where my life doesn't fit, and where "keeping it to yourself" is considered an admirable trait. But growing up on the farm didn't seem that limiting to me until I was no longer there. And though there were times when it was rough around the edges, my life on the farm gave me many of the things that I value most today: my appreciation of the importance of relying on others and allowing them to rely on me, of balancing work and play, of keeping a wide-eyed fascination in the world; my love of animals and nature, my work ethic, my desire to grow things.

Although it was common for these men to believe that their farm upbringings delayed their sexual self-understanding, they did not necessarily see that as a drawback. Barney Dews speculated that if he had grown up in a city he would have come out earlier and would likely be dead by now as the result of less-healthy living—drinking, smoking, and engaging in risky sex. "If I had come out when I was younger, I probably would have died of AIDS," Terry Bloch commented. "Growing up where I did made me conservative, traditional, straight-laced, slower to jump on the bandwagon."

Many of these men believed that their farm upbringings instilled in them a strong and persistent work ethic. "Be responsible, work hard, and win acceptance" appeared to be a central motivating principle in many of their lives. Mark Vanderbeek described the role of work in his life.

I tend to be an over-achiever. At times it's a blessing and at times it's a curse, but I don't want anyone at work to ever have reason to say, "Not only is he gay, but he doesn't do above and beyond the call of duty." You can call me a faggot, you can call me any slur you want to, but don't ever call me a sluff-off or someone who doesn't put out 110 percent. It's definitely a trait I picked up from my father. He would say, "Count your blessings for every day you can work."

Karl Gussow elaborated more broadly on the work-ethic theme.

> Farm life has a certain amount of genuineness to it—honesty and an in-
> ability to shirk responsibility. The cow's udder is going to burst if you
> don't milk it, the weeds are going to continue to grow if you don't hoe
> them, the hay is going to rot if you don't put it in the mow, the silage is
> going to reach its peak and go the other way if you don't get it put up. I
> think being reared where I was has caused me to be a little more appre-
> ciative of the urgencies and the responsibilities with which we have to ad-
> dress life.

It was common for these men to see the reality of their homosexual
orientation from a perspective very similar to Karl's view of udders, weeds,
hay, and silage. James Heckman compared his own homosexuality to a bull
that doesn't take to cows and concluded that, however inexplicable, it's
all a part of nature and must be accepted for what it is. Some of the men
for whom religious belief continued to be significant had a similar "that's
the way it is" way of looking at things. Their belief that God made them
the way they are and loves them the way they are seems to be a theologi-
cal extension of the belief that whatever nature creates is the way it's meant
to be.

In thinking about the farming country of his childhood, Barney Dews
acknowledged "something very organic that draws me back there because
it's familiar, it's home." Many of these men continued to feel strong connections to their rural midwestern homelands, but their feelings for these
places did not tend to be wistfully romantic or sentimental. Martin Scherz
described his feelings of a continuing connection to his Nebraska home.

> When I go back home, I feel a real connection with the land—a tremen-
> dous feeling, spiritual in a way. It makes me want to go out into a field
> and take my shoes off and put my feet right on the dirt, establish a real
> physical connection with that place. I get homesick a lot, but I don't
> know if I could ever go back there and live. . . . I feel alienated in a lot of
> ways, and it's not the kind of place that would welcome me if I lived
> openly, the way that I would like to live. I would be shunned.

For many years, Dean Gray concealed his rural heritage. After finishing college in the mid-1980s, he moved from the Midwest to New York
City, where he works in theater and lives in the West Village.

> Now I cherish having grown up on a farm. It's one of the first things I
> tell people about myself. People in New York say to me, "You're a farm
> boy. What are you doing here? Don't you miss the country, the open
> space, the animals?" I do. When I go back home to Wisconsin, I'm out in
> the barn first thing in the morning, feeding the animals and cleaning the
> barn. I feel something there I can't feel in New York.

However, apart from fantasizing about living on a few acres in the country, most of the men who were living in cities and towns were not looking to move back to farming communities. They tended to believe that, despite the appeal of certain aspects of farm life, urban life offered them as much or more promise of fulfillment. It appeared that what they valued most about their farming backgrounds they carried with them, wherever they lived.

REFERENCES

Adams, Jane. 1994. *The Transformation of Rural Life: Southern Illinois, 1890–1990.* Chapel Hill: University of North Carolina Press.

Alyson Publications. 1990. *The Alyson Almanac.* Boston: Alyson Publications.

Blumenfeld, Warren J., and Diane Raymond. 1989. *Looking at Gay and Lesbian Life.* Boston: Beacon Press.

Bly, Carol. 1982. *Letters from the Country.* New York: Penguin.

Katz, Jonathan. 1976. *Gay American History: Lesbians and Gay Men in the U.S.A.* New York: Crowell.

Katz, Jonathan. 1983. *Gay/Lesbian Almanac: A New Documentary.* New York: Harper & Row.

Kinsey, Alfred C., Wardell B. Pomeroy, and Clyde E. Martin. 1948. *Sexual Behavior in the Human Male.* Philadelphia: W. B. Saunders.

Nardi, Peter M., David Sanders, and Judd Marmor. 1994. *Growing Up before Stonewall: Life Stories of Some Gay Men.* New York: Routledge.

Reid, John. 1973. *The Best Little Boy in the World.* New York: Ballantine.

Salamon, Sonya. 1992. *Prairie Patrimony: Family, Farming, and Community in the Midwest.* Chapel Hill: University of North Carolina Press.

Silverstein, Charles. 1981. *Man to Man: Gay Couples in America.* New York: Quill.

Welch, Paul, and Ernest Havemann. "Homosexuality in America." *Life:* June 26, 1964, pp. 66–74, 76–80.

PART 1

*Coming of Age Before
the Mid-1960s*

Our Favorite Team, by Jeff Kopseng, based on a 1920 photo of an Indiana farm boy, courtesy of Larry Reed

Introduction

DESPITE PROFOUND changes in the character of U.S. life from the early 1900s to the mid-1960s, there was little change throughout this era in the kind or quantity of information about homosexuality accessible to a farm boy coming of age in the Midwest. The invisibility of homosexuality through the 1930s was described by Robert C. Reinhart in *A History of Shadows*.[1]

> Gays lived without a literature, a means of communication to serve their interests and needs, or any sense of community. . . . When gay people were even heard about, it was in the pages of psychiatric journals, annals of jurisprudence, or the news columns that chronicled sexual transgressions, but usually in such veiled terms that readers were hard put to know why the person had been sentenced to five years in jail (pp. 53–54).

The veil was drawn back from homosexuality in two novels published in 1948—Truman Capote's *Other Voices, Other Rooms*[2] and Gore Vidal's *The City and the Pillar*.[3] To the extent that mainstream publications gave these works any notice, their reviews ranged from disagreeable to hostile. The Kinsey report on American male sexual behavior, also published in 1948, was not so easily ignored.[4] The report stated that homosexual activity was much more common than generally believed, that very few individuals were exclusively homo- or hetero- in their sexual nature, and that many individuals had a mix of both homo- and heterosexual experience. Kinsey's findings challenged America's ability to sustain the denial, silence, and ignorance surrounding homosexuality, but even in the face of scientific evidence the facade of America's Victorian/Puritan sexual code did not crumble. The Kinsey report astonished, appalled, and fascinated millions without seeming to enlighten very many.

Throughout the 1950s, the efforts of Senator Joseph McCarthy and the Eisenhower administration to expel Communists, sex perverts, and other undesirables from influential positions captured headlines and spawned localized witch-hunts around the country. In the face of these oppressive attitudes, today's organized gay rights movement got started in the 1950s and early 1960s, but it was an exclusively urban phenomenon with very limited reach.

The tenor of prevailing notions about homosexuality was both reflected in, and reinforced by, the mass media. National mass-market peri-

odicals gave minimal coverage to the topic. In 1959, *Time* presented a psychiatrist's view that the homosexual is a "psychic masochist," a glutton for
punishment whose "distorted pleasures feed on the allure of danger."[5] The
gist of a 1960 article in *Newsweek*, "To Punish or Pity?," is conveyed effectively by the title.[6] *Newsweek* reported in 1961 that the number of homosexuals in the military was increasing. "These people are sick, they need
treatment. They can be cured if they want to be," a psychotherapist stated.
From a preventive perspective, he advocated school-based psychiatric treatment on the premise that homosexuals could be spotted as early as seven
years of age.[7]

For many of the men whose stories are presented here, coming of age
between the mid-1920s and the mid-1960s meant bearing a burden of un-
equivocally negative feelings toward their emerging selves. Some carried
this burden for decades, others for only a short time. For more than half
of them, this negativity was shouldered in tandem with the expectations
and responsibilities of marriage and parenting. Those who managed to
avoid marriage were faced with the task of creating a meaningful life focus
and identity apart from mainstream conventions and often without the
example of role models that were acceptable to them.

Henry Bauer's tale of psychoanalytic misadventure is emblematic of
coming of age during this era. So is Cornelius Utz's account of coming
out to himself in his seventies, after thirty-five years of marriage. Robert
Peters' reminiscences are snapshots from the life of a naive adolescent male
on a poor backwoods farm in the late 1930s. In light of the oppressiveness
of this period, the diversity of experience in this group of stories is no-
table. For example, Jim Cross and Dennis Lindholm were born within two
years of each other and both grew up in Iowa farm families, but that is
about the extent of their similarity. Jim came to grips with being gay in
his early twenties and with relatively little pain; Dennis came out in his
mid-forties and with much trauma.

In the face of a debilitating lack of self-confidence, John Beutel struggled to achieve a sense of self-worth through his work as a teacher. For
Ronald Schoen, being able to help a gay student through the uncertainties, fears, and isolation of his rural teenage years has been greatly reward-
ing. Myron Turk winces at seeing a nephew in the midst of a painful adolescence similar to his own. Norm Reed, who hoped that marriage and
religion would banish his homosexual feelings, continues to adhere to the
fundamentalist beliefs of the church that ostracized him. In contrast to
Harry Beckner's light-hearted account of growing up gay, James Heckman's suicide attempt is a reminder that many gay farm boys who were
fated to come of age in this era did not make it to the next.

Notes

1. Robert C. Reinhart. 1982. *A History of Shadows.* New York: Avon.
2. Truman Capote. 1948. *Other Voices, Other Rooms.* New York: Random House.
3. Gore Vidal. 1948. *The City and the Pillar.* New York: Dutton.
4. Alfred C. Kinsey, Wardell B. Pomeroy, and Clyde E. Martin. 1948. *Sexual Behavior in the Human Male.* Philadelphia: W. B. Saunders.
5. "The Strange World." *Time:* November 9, 1959, p. 66.
6. "To Punish or Pity?" *Newsweek:* July 11, 1960, p. 78.
7. "One Soldier in 25?" *Newsweek:* May 15, 1961, pp. 92, 94.

Cornelius Utz

Cornelius was born in 1909 in Buchanan county, northwestern Missouri, on a small farm about five miles south of the city of South St. Joseph, where his father was a horse and mule trader. Cornelius was the youngest of eleven children—eight boys and three girls. He was married for thirty-five years, is the father of two children, and had a career in social work. He lives in a retirement community in Cleveland, Ohio.

I AM DEEPLY saddened by the sociocultural pressure that's put on homosexual people. We're human beings and it just happens that the genes worked this way for us. I didn't learn this until I was practically eighty years old. Internalized homophobia affected my whole life in a sadly deleterious way. I couldn't happily be myself because I thought if people knew me they wouldn't accept me. I was afraid I would reveal my homosexuality, so I put the damper on all kinds of self-expression. I wanted to be liked, so I went out of my way to please people. I wanted to like myself, but I couldn't quite allow myself to do it. This damned internalized homophobia is just godawful, it's tragic, and it took me a long time to overcome it. I really feel good about myself and I think I'm a very lovable person, but I still struggle with it every once in a while.

When I decided to come out, I did it with a bang, and the heaviest weight descended from my shoulders. I never felt so free—released from a burden that had been with me all my life. With this release of creative energy, I have gotten tremendous satisfaction out of everything I've done, from writing to teaching to playing bridge and creating artwork. I get great accolades for the fiber artworks I produce, and I'm very proud of them. Hell of a long time I had to wait to get those kinds of satisfactions, but thank god they came. I've had a productive life and a good life, basically, but I weep sometimes at how much better it could have been had I not been so inhibited, had I had the freedom to put all of myself into learning my profession and creating my early artwork. I feel incredibly grateful that I finally learned to love myself enough so that here in my twilight years I can get tremendous satisfaction out of my artwork and my wonderful relationships.

The house I was born in was built of logs and we lived in that house until I was four years old—thirteen people in four rooms. My father then built a much larger house that would accommodate our family. We had a long dining table with benches on either side, six kids on one side and five on the other, father at one end and mother at the other. On Sunday mornings when I was a small child, my father would put an extra dollop of cream in his coffee, pour it in a saucer, and blow on it to cool it down, and then, with me in his lap, let me take a sip of it from the saucer. That sweet, creamy coffee tasted so good it made me tingle with pleasure. It was like sucking at my father's breast.

We had a lovely big fireplace in the living room of the new house, with a circle of chairs around it. One day, I had injured myself while playing and felt I deserved special treatment during my recovery, so I sat in my father's chair, the most comfortable one in the room. When he came home he was enraged that his youngest pipsqueak son would have the effrontery to be sitting in his chair, so he lifted me out of it by my ear, ignoring my injury. Crying, I started running upstairs and said, "Ain't you got no sense?" Like a flash, he caught me at the bottom of the stairs and gave me an awful licking—the only one I ever got from him.

My mother liked to have me learn poems or speeches, and she trained me to declaim. She would listen to me go over and over a piece, and instruct me in how to make it more powerful. There were contests in the county, and I won the first prize more than once with my declamations. My father would then insist that I perform at social gatherings. It scared me to pieces to be asked by my father, out of the blue, to get up in front of all those people, but I did it. I was afraid if I didn't deliver I'd get a whipping when I got home.

I loved it when we had company, because they related to me with great warmth. Once I cried because I couldn't ride along when somebody in the family was taking the company back home. My mother said, "So you cry when we say you can't go? I'll give you something to cry about!" and she whipped me with a switch, very hard, on my behind and legs. Experiences like these deeply affected my ability to be very spontaneous about any expression of feeling. You didn't have to get those kinds of whippings very often to begin to close up.

Surreptitiously I learned to crochet and embroider from my sisters. I was really quite good at handwork, but I wouldn't allow my brothers to see me doing it. When I was seven or eight, my mother got a new sewing machine—an old foot-pedal type—and taught me how to work it. I loved to work that machine and would sit at it for hours, hemming sheets and pillow cases. That was a great help to my mother, because we bought sheeting and pillow tubing by the bolt for that size family.

I learned to ride horseback when I was five or six years old, and from about age eight until twelve I was highly involved in the farm. We had a chunky little Shetland pony—just the dearest thing you could ever know—and I became so proficient that I could ride him at a gallop standing up on his rump. One of my chores was to ride the pony to the pasture and bring the cows in to be milked, then milk them and drive them down the long lane back to the pasture. I would also round up the sheep and bring them to the farmyard for protection from wolves and coyotes by night.

When we harvested wheat and oats, my oldest brother Millard drove the team that pulled the binder, a very heavy machine that cut the grain and bound it in bundles. Because the binder was so heavy, five horses or mules or some combination of the two were required to pull it, with two in front of three. Someone had to ride one of the lead horses to guide them. By the time I was eight years old, I was the chosen one since I weighed less than anyone else. It was a very exacting job. The binder cut a five- or six-foot swath of grain, and I had to guide the team so that it didn't leave little spaces that weren't cut. It was a pleasant enough chore for a short time, but a full day of it was hard work. I was always glad when those long, tiresome days on the horse came to an end.

With my little pony and cart, I was the water boy, wearing bib overalls, a large straw hat, and a bandanna tied about my neck to absorb perspiration. I would fill one-gallon stoneware jugs with water, put them in a burlap-lined fruit crate, and cover them with water-soaked burlap to keep them cool. I took this fresh, cold water to the men in the fields as they were loading the wagons to bring the sheaves of grain to the steam-driven threshing machine. Then I would go to the threshing machine and give the men there their water. That cold water was a godsend for those men, working in ninety-degree heat or even hotter, as it was some of those days in late July and early August. They greeted me with joy and pleasure.

My family were fairly strict Methodists, especially my father. He frowned on playing cards, dancing, smoking, and the use of alcohol. And in spite of the fact that we were eleven children, my parents had a good many inhibitions about sexuality. Anything sexual was to be controlled and denied. Once I was in the barn when a cow had a calf. It was incredibly exciting to me, but I was scared to death to let my family know that I had witnessed it, for fear I would be punished.

When I was about four years old, Rindy, our black laundress, came to our house and brought her grandson, Lester, who was about my age. He

"The house I was born in was built of logs and we lived in that house until I was four years old—thirteen people in four rooms." Cornelius Utz's mother and nine of his ten siblings in front of their four-room log house, about 1905. Courtesy of Cornelius Utz.

was a lively little boy and had an endless imagination of things to do. One day we ended up in the scale house, which was used as a garage for one of our buggies. He asked me to lie down, and he lay down on top of me. We had our clothes on and he was dry-fucking me. It was not unpleasant. He was quite aggressive and in control, and I was very docile in order not to displease him. I liked having kids my own age to play with and there weren't any in the neighborhood. Suddenly Rindy appeared and saw what was happening. She picked up a bridle with long leather reins and gave Lester a whipping within an inch of his life. She didn't say or do a thing to me, but she made it impossible for us to play together the rest of the day. After that, when Rindy and Lester came there were a lot of other kids with him, or Rindy would say, "Cornelius, why don't you ask your mother if you can go over and visit your friend." This younger neighbor kid had nice toys and we would play together, but there was nothing sexual at all. I think Rindy thought it would be all right if I had sex-play with other little white boys, but not with her grandson.

One summer afternoon when I was five years old I was in the cow barn and George, our new hired man, approached me. He patted me on the head and placed his hand on my shoulder, then squatted and hugged me

"I would also round up the sheep and bring them to the farmyard for protection from wolves and coyotes by night." Courtesy of Cornelius Utz.

gently. It felt good, so I let myself fall against him. We snuggled a bit, then he gently unbuttoned my pants and brought my penis out as if to help me pee, but I didn't need to pee. Instead, my skinny little penis became erect and he fondled me a bit, producing a feeling I had never had before. I liked it, but I felt a little fear as well. George stood up and took his penis out, asking me to hold it, and I did. It was not as hard as mine, but it felt okay in my hand. I began to feel afraid, so I stopped holding his penis, returned mine to my trousers, buttoned up, and went back to the house. Not long after this, my mother told my sister and me that we should never go to the cow barn alone if George were there. Shortly thereafter, George was gone for good.

In one way or another, I had sex-play with six of my seven brothers— fondling and masturbating each other to orgasm, dry-fucking by pressing against each other. It usually occurred at night when we would be sleeping together, like it was happening in our dreams, and we never spoke about it. I slept in my parents' bed until I was four years old, but when we moved into the new house my oldest brother Millard and I shared a bed. He was seventeen years older than I. Some mornings, he would feel my penis and stimulate me until it got hard, but he would never let me touch his. It was very titillating in a way, but he said, "You really shouldn't do this." When I was older, Millard and I had some sex-play together, but I don't think we ever came to orgasm together because "you shouldn't do that."

When I was five or six, I was out in a cornfield with my brother Lawrence, of whom I was quite fond. We both had to urinate, and he said, "Let me see your penis." As he looked, it got hard and he pulled the foreskin back and cut it a little bit with his thumbnail, saying it looked like it was growing over the head of my penis. He was very tender and gentle with me, but I think that was a bit of sadism on his part. Later, when I was adolescent, Lawrence and I had a number of episodes of sex-play whenever we slept together. He sucked me, but I couldn't suck him for any length of time—I guess because I wanted it so much that it gagged me. When I was probably thirteen, we had a black hired man. He and I had sex together a time or two, and shortly after that occurred my mother cautioned me that I should not do anything with him. I don't know how she knew I had done anything, if she did, or whether it came to her attention that he had made out with one of my brothers.

I had suspicions, but I really denied like hell that I was "that way." I grew up feeling that same-sex relations were immoral, and even to masturbate would cause you to have problems later. I masturbated an awful lot between twelve and sixteen or eighteen, sometimes two or three times a day. I would determine that I wasn't going to do it again—"I'll just do this now and I won't do it again today or tomorrow"—but I was highly sexually stimulated and felt bad about my tremendous sex drive. There were times when I would get extraordinarily hard and almost painful erections as I was riding my horse, and there was nothing I could do to subdue them.

My father had jackasses that were bred to grade mares to produce work mules. He also had a large white stallion for breeding mares to produce grade work horses. I was never permitted to be out there when breeding was going on, and there was a high board fence around the barnyard so that you couldn't see the breeding from the ground level, but from the window of my bedroom I could see what was going on and I would masturbate. I was highly excited by the animals. When cows are in heat they dribble something, and it would just drive me over the wall when our cows did that. It made me want to get up there and fuck them. We had an old mare who had been neutered and often when I was alone I would stick my arm down her vagina. She didn't seem to mind it at all. I tried to fuck her by standing on her hocks, but I wasn't very successful.

In 1921, my father's business failed and we lost the farm and everything. Two of my brothers who were renting a farm together let the remaining family move in with them, and we lived there for about two years. During those years, I slept a lot with my brother Lawrence and we had sex-play together. I was twelve or thirteen, and very interested in people slightly older. I was also highly stimulated by a very attractive hired hand they had. It was all I could do to keep my hands off of him. I wanted to play with his penis, and I thought it was just terrible that I had those kinds of feelings. That helped me restrain myself from acting on them.

I left the farm when I was fourteen. A sister and brother had established housekeeping in St. Joe, so we younger children lived with them and completed high school in the city. We had a coach in high school who really turned me on sexually. I loved being with him. He would shower with the rest of us and I would get a chance to see his equipment and fantasize about it. After football practice, those hunky football players would say, "How about a rubdown?" I loved doing it, and I'm sure it was sexually stimulating to them as it was to me. I became very adept at giving rubdowns.

I was highly attracted to a number of guys in high school, but I didn't dare let it be known. To be a good, sturdy, non-sissy guy, you had to be interested in sports like football and basketball. I really tried to be an athlete because I wanted to emulate my brother Sam. He was the first and only other man in our family who went through college, and he was greatly admired by my parents for doing that. Sam called everybody and his dog a sissy that wasn't a high-level football player. I really hated football, but I tried to play because it would make me more of a man.

The first time I had sex-play with Sam, I was on the track team in our high school. We had a track meet in Cameron, Missouri, where Sam was the coach. After the meet, he asked if I would like to stay overnight. We shared the bed where he roomed, and he initiated sex-play with me, which I welcomed. When I was in college in Columbia, he came down there on coaching business several times and spent the night with me and we would have sex-play. This was after he was married and had children. He told me that his wife was kind of nervous, like a Jersey cow.

In college, I heard about a biology professor who was homosexual. When I finally connected with him, he took me to a very lovely place in the country, a secluded and protected woodland area. We were enjoying the birds and the view when he put his arms around me, turned towards me and kissed me. That was the first time I'd ever been kissed by a man. He gave me a deep French kiss, which was highly exciting. We hugged each other a bit and then went to his house. He lived with his mother, who was closeted in the back of the house and told never to interfere when he had guests. We went to his bedroom and disrobed and made love some more. I took his tongue in my mouth and put my tongue in his mouth. I played with his cock some, but I could never suck him without gagging. He always sucked me, and never seemed to expect me to relieve him through masturbation or anything.

He really introduced me to what it can mean to have gay sex. It was an idyllic experience. I would feel ashamed of myself, but whenever I felt horny I would call him and ask if he would be home a little later. He always said yes. To a great extent, this took care of my sexual needs throughout the rest of college. I really think he fell deeply in love with me, but I couldn't allow myself to feel love for him, because that would make me a really full-blown "that way" person. (I didn't become familiar with the word homosexual until I was in graduate school in social work.) I denied that I was completely male-sex-oriented.

I enjoyed being with girls, had relationships with a number of girl-friends, and did a hell of a lot of necking. I'm sure they all wanted me to fuck them, but I never could bring myself to go that far. Consciously, I was scared to death I would impregnate them and then I'd be hooked because it would only be honorable for me to marry. I wasn't in a position to get married; I had no job, no capacity to support a family.

During my college years I carried on a correspondence with Karl, a friend from high school. It was a purely platonic relationship but I cared very much for him and he seemed to care very much for me. I asked if I could stop and visit him on my way to graduate school in New York. He was in graduate school in Philadelphia and lived in a neat little house out in the country with his roommate Ted, a biology professor. When it came time to go to bed, I was assigned a bed in the bedroom with Ted, upstairs, and Karl slept in the bedroom downstairs. Ted made a pass at me before we went to sleep and we had sex both nights I was there. The interchange was kind of electric between us, so that Ted and I developed a really wonderful relationship, and I continued to be a good friend of Karl's.

During my years in school in New York, I would go down to Philadelphia when I could scrape up enough money to spend a weekend with them. They did wonderful things to entertain me, and Ted and I always had our reunions in the bedroom. After Karl developed a brain tumor and died, Ted would come to New York to spend weekends with me. He fell in love with me and really wanted me to make my home with him. I liked him, and I'm sure he would have supported me if need be, but I just could not allow a feeling of love.

In college, I had learned enough psychology to become more and more concerned that I was homosexual, and I had to restrain myself from telling this to my close friends. In graduate school, we deep-dished into Freudian psychology and my being queer descended on me more and more. About 1936, I decided I couldn't live with it. I went to a female analyst—I was afraid to go to a male—and had a very comfortable interview with her. I didn't hold back anything. She said she thought I should have analysis, and she did not think I should go to a woman. She put me in touch with a Dr. Wiggers.

When I told Dr. Wiggers about Ted, he said, "It's up to you. I think if you continue seeing Ted you're not going to be able to give this up. I don't know whether you'll be able to give it up if you *don't* see him, but I don't think there's any chance of your coming through with a good heterosexual relationship if you continue seeing him."[1] The next time Ted came to visit, I told him that it would be our last weekend together—that I really wanted to see if I couldn't work this out. He understood and said we could still be friends, and I said I'd love to be friends with him.

Analyses are never completed, but after five years Dr. Wiggers and I decided we were as far as we could go. I had gone six days a week for the first two years and five days a week for the rest of the time. I continued to see him from time to time to talk about things that were troubling me. He gave me a great deal of confidence in myself, and my skill as a social worker grew by leaps and bounds as a result of my analysis. I feel incredibly grateful for my treatment because it enabled me to function as well as I did throughout the rest of my life. It enabled me to have sex with a woman and enjoy it, and as a result of that I have two lovely children and four beautiful grandchildren. I feel that having children contributed inordinately to my growth and development as a person.

I met and courted my wife while I was in analysis. I no longer had the need to tell anybody I was gay, and I never discussed it with my wife. For a few years we had very good and satisfying sex, but I simply could not control the drive to have sex with men. If ever I was out of town I would pick up somebody and have a one-night stand. None of them were very pleasant experiences because I would be half-drunk. I almost became an alcoholic during my marriage, and I smoked very heavily.

I couldn't keep up my correspondence with Ted because I felt I would have to explain it to my wife, so I just quit writing and didn't give him any explanation. He continued exchanging Christmas cards with one of my sisters, and every so often she would report to me what he was doing— that he was in the army in World War II, that he had moved from Philadelphia to Boulder. After my wife died in 1978, I got Ted's address from my sister and wrote him the kind of a letter you write to somebody thirty-five years later. I said I would love to hear from him if he felt like it. He wrote an incredibly nice letter back, inviting me to come and see him.

When I went to Boulder for a weekend to visit with Ted, I said I wanted to apologize for how I had terminated our relationship. He said, "Don't think a thing about it. I knew you were trying to get over it, but I knew you were queer and would always be queer." He said that it was in the genes and I couldn't get it out. We had better sex on that visit than we'd had thirty-five years before. I visited him twice after that long interval of nothing, and we had a wonderful visit each time, highly meaningful and exhilarating. I fantasied going out there and living with him the rest of our lives, but I don't think he wanted that, and I probably wouldn't have done it. He died a couple of years ago, so that's wiped out and washed up.

After my wife died, I decided to see what I could find out about the gay community, so I went to the baths on the west side in Cleveland. This was before the AIDS scare. While I was there I found out about Integrity and went to their next meeting.[2] One member of the group told me about somebody he had met who he thought really needed to talk to me—a fellow named Dave who was married and had a couple of kids. He gave me Dave's phone number at work, and eventually we met for lunch and talked. He was not happy and he and his wife hadn't had sex for years. I appreciated the struggle he was going through. He was still living with his wife, who was extraordinarily homophobic, and he didn't have enough sense to keep quiet about his gayness with her.

To seal our beginning friendship, Dave and I hugged and had a nice deep French kiss. I got a letter from him saying he wanted to see me again, that he had been so excited as a result of our kiss that he had to go to a public restroom and jack it off. So we met again and had incredibly beautiful sex with each other—the best sex with any man I had ever had. He began writing me love letters, and he was the first man I ever allowed myself to really feel love for. We had a sustained relationship for several weeks and then suddenly he got anxious and tried to break it off. I was disappointed and saddened.

Dave and I came together a number of times after that and they were pleasant encounters, but his restraint affected my ability to put myself quite as freely into the sexual relationship. We were incredibly compatible otherwise. He appreciated my artwork, he was a cultured person, we liked a lot of the same things. He played with the idea of getting a divorce and setting up housekeeping with me, and I said if he did I'd come out of the closet. But I finally wrote Dave a letter, saying that I felt he was treating me like a prostitute the last few times, and that I didn't want to continue that kind of relationship. He wrote back and said, "I loved you very much, and I still do, but I can't give up my relationship with my family. I've decided that's the way it has to be. I was afraid that if I kept seeing you I would lose control of myself, and lose my job and my family." As sad as it was, it was a beautiful experience, because it left me free to love other men. I don't hold back feelings of love as I always did before, when I was trying to avoid being a homosexual. I feel a lot of love for other men, whether I have sex with them or not.

In 1979 I joined the Unitarian Universalists for Lesbian and Gay Concerns. Two years later I was one of the organizing members of our local chapter, but I was snug in the closet and insisted on confidentiality outside our meetings. In 1985 I attended a continental UULGC meeting in San Diego. Both the gay and straight members of the First Unitarian Church there were incredibly loving, accepting, and supportive. In that atmosphere I began to love myself enough to decide I would be who I was, and I determined to come out of the closet, come hell or high water. I had not yet gotten a foothold in the gay community and had been fearful that in coming out I might lose my straight friends and then would be bereft. With my newfound confidence as a result of learning to love myself, I felt that if my straight friends weren't still my friends after I came out, they hadn't been my friends before.

With that resolution, I came out to a friend of fifty years living in San Diego, a guy who had been in the short course in social work. It didn't matter to him, and he said, "You're speaking more freely now than I've ever seen. You don't seem to be holding anything back now, as apparently you were before." My niece, also there in San Diego, could tell that I was a little bit nervous as I was coming out to her at dinner. She reached across the table and grasped my hands and said, "Uncle Cornelius, you've always been very dear to me, and you always will be." I thought, boy, this is not bad!

I wrote a letter to my two children and sent each of them a copy. My daughter and her husband were very accepting, and she's very interested in my continuing reports about UULGC meetings and other things. When I have initiated the conversation with my son a couple of times, he has said, "It's all right, but why do you have to say anything about it?" He said he couldn't understand why I chose this, and when I said there is no choice, it's in the genes, he said, "Well, you had a choice to give in to it." I said, "I'm sorry, Dave, that I haven't been able to handle this very well with you. I don't think you've really understood what I've been trying to tell you. Maybe sometime I'll find a way to make it clearer—I hope I can— but I may not be able to." He's been incredibly loving and caring and concerned about me, but this is a struggle for him. He may be worried that he's carrying that gene himself and that maybe his sons are too.

I don't have a lover and probably won't have, but I do have some people I occasionally play in the hay with. I have a lot of pen pals and some of them come to see me, so I have a love-in for two or three days. That's the best I can do, and hope springs eternal. It's reassuring to me at eighty-four that I can still get it off with joy. A man in Georgia has begged me to come and visit him. There's something about the foreskin of an uncut older man that turns him on incredibly. But I feel that there should be a real feeling of love along with the sex experience. There's an awful lot of emphasis on just getting it off. That may be pleasurable, but unless you can have a real feeling of love with your sexual partner, it doesn't mean very much.

I'm not in the gay community that much. I used to go to the bars, but I wouldn't put my foot inside one now because I can't stand the smoke. I smoked and drank to take care of stress for too long. That's why I have emphysema. And I got no fun out of being there. By the time I came out, I was so old that none of the young guys would look twice at me. They didn't know how attractive I would be if they'd get to know me. There's a group of older gay men that meets at somebody's home on the west side, but I haven't kept up with them because there was no one there who had any of the cultural or artistic interests that I do. For an ongoing relationship, those things are just as meaningful to me as sexual compatibility.

I've never felt comfortable in the gay community, but I have developed a pretty good tolerance for most gay people. We're all in this together, and if we can't love each other we'd better figure out where we're going to find people to love. The church is my community. It was through my experience with the UULGC that I found I loved myself enough to come out. When I don't show up at a meeting there are a lot of people who miss me, and they tell me so. I'm active on the Gay/Lesbian/Straight Task Force, which is working to combat homophobia in our church. I'm also in a men's group at the church, and I'm very open there. I feel an incredible love for all the members of my men's group and for people in the congregation of my church.

If I'm in a friendship that means anything to me and the person doesn't know that I have a same-sex preference, I will mention it at some point. I haven't really encountered any problems in being out with people that matter to me, and I'm not at a loss for friends. I've got my circle, both men and women. I came out to the social worker who interviewed me before I came to live here, but I haven't mentioned it to anyone else here. I haven't felt it would serve any special purpose. There's a group of men here who often eat in the dining room together. Every once in a while they'll make denigrating statements about homosexuals, and I'll say, "I don't know what's wrong with homosexuals. They're human beings like all the rest of us." That's as far as I've gone. In spite of their homophobia, I feel a lot of love for those old bastards.

NOTES

1. The psychiatric treatment of gay men in this era is described in Peter M. Nardi, David Sanders, and Judd Marmor. 1994. *Growing Up before Stonewall: Life Stories of Some Gay Men*. New York: Routledge.

2. Integrity, founded in 1974, is the gay and lesbian caucus of the Episcopal Church with chapters in many cities in the United States.

Robert Peters

Robert was born in 1924, the oldest of five children, and grew up on a poor scrub-sand farm of forty acres near Eagle River, in Vilas County, northern Wisconsin. He married and fathered four children. The author of more than thirty books of poetry, criticism, short stories, and plays, Robert retired in 1993 from teaching literature and writing at the University of California, Irvine. He lives in the Los Angeles area with his companion of many years, Paul Trachtenberg.

Robert Peters' autobiographical poetry may be found in his Poems: Selected and New, 1967–1991 *(Asylum Arts, 1992). The autobiographical prose pieces that follow are excerpted from his* Crunching Gravel: A Wisconsin Boyhood in the Thirties *(University of Wisconsin Press, 1993). In these excerpts, Old Crip is a rooster, Osmo Makinnen is the school bully, Lady is a cow, and Margie is Robert's sister.*

KILLING THE HEN

OLD CRIP DANCED on spurless legs, making deep-maw proprietary sounds. Once the hens were eating corn and chortling, he fed himself, keeping a wary eye on us.

We selected a large Rhode Island Red, one no longer laying. "Now," Dad said. "Point the barrel at her eye; then pull the trigger slow."

An olio of feelings: I did not want to shoot. I did not want to displease Dad. Oblivious, the hen pecked at her corn.

The trigger felt like ice. My index finger seemed jointless.

"Now, do it right," Dad warned.

The bird's yellowish ear was a minuscule sun. Stunned, she chortled, rattled, and fell, clawed the air, stiffened, and then stilled. Dad whipped out a pocketknife and slit her throat. "Wasn't too bad, was it?" He lifted the hen by its legs. "Nice fat one. Be good with dumplin's."

I plunged the bird into boiling water. The feathers loosened immediately and smelled like rancid rags. Then came the singeing and butcher-

47

ing. Mom planned an early supper, complete with blueberry pie, from berries picked the previous summer.

EASTER

As Easter neared, I read the Bible with increasing fervor. Whether I understood or not, each word was truth. Even the interminable "begat" verses were mines of spiritual ore. I meditated over the saccharine color prints of Jesus with lambs, of Jesus being scourged, of Jesus dying, and I began to talk to Jesus, shaping the air with my hands, imagining Him as my very own.

The circumstance resolving my struggle was my first ejaculation. I had no idea what had transpired. I woke during the night to find my belly wet. At first I thought it was blood. Without disturbing my brother, I crept from bed and found a flashlight. Where had the strange substance come from? My parents told me nothing of sexual change, and I was too naive to relate my own seminal flow to that of farm animals. My fevered psyche interpreted the incident as a warning from Jesus that I must be baptized.

I resolved to go to mass the next morning, Palm Sunday. My parents approved—though not without some hesitation that I might turn Catholic. . . . I hoped to remain anonymous, so I decided to attend a later mass.

I dallied along the road, examining pools for frogs' eggs, throwing sticks and stones into a swirl of rusty water emerging through a culvert near Mud Creek, and admiring a grove of juneberry trees loaded with blossoms. Twice I turned and started back for home.

By the time I reached St Joseph's Catholic Church, the second mass had ended, and there was no other. Jesus, I felt, had arranged this timing for some umbrageous reason of His own, sheltering me from Catholicism. Services were about to begin at the Christ Evangelical Church across the street. On the steps were Eileen Ewald and her parents. I had had a crush on Eileen ever since she appeared in second grade and said "sugar." It was not the word itself, but her cultured tone in saying it that struck me as special. I ached to be in love with her.

I followed Eileen into the church and sat in a pew at the very back. I was entranced by the pale oak altar with its pastel plaster crucifixion. The organ music, the first I had ever heard, was splendid. All through the sermon, by the Reverend Joseph Krubsack, I sat in a daze. Jesus had directed me here!

I lingered until Rev. Krubsack was alone and told him of my wish for baptism. He promised to baptize me and my family on the Sunday after Easter. But I would not become a full Lutheran, he warned, until I had passed instruction.

PLOUGHING AND SEEDING

For five dollars, my uncle hired out his team, Bill and Bess, for plowing. I was a coward near horses, and when Dad asked me to drive the team while he steered the plow I refused. Horses would suddenly shake their necks and bare their teeth.

My uncle was a hard driver. I had seen him beat Bill with a club while the horse was tied in his stall. In pain, the horse broke free and ran from the barn toward Minnow Lake, with my uncle in pursuit. I followed and saw him corner Bill, who waited docilely while my uncle, his wrath spent, grabbed the broken halter and stroked Bill's neck with surprising gentleness.

Eruptions of violence always dismayed me. In a recurring dream, Osmo Makinnen threatened to attack. When I sought to defend myself, my arms froze at my sides. Usually I woke in a sweat. Why my impotence? Dad had given me pointers—and he had boxed at carnivals. To support my ineptitude, I found the Bible useful. If you followed Christ's example, you simply turned the other cheek. I found the violence of men far worse than any violence of horses. A man enraged by a horse unleashed an enormous force few men could hope to restrain.

One lasting image is of my father beating Lady. I had been told to graze her in timothy along Sundsteen Road. Since she was always docile, I went to the house for a drink of water and lingered talking to Margie. When I returned, Lady was not where I had left her. Shortly, I heard my dad's angry voice—the cow was in the cornfield. When he flung stones at Lady, she sped crazily across the potato field. Dad cornered her near a fence, grabbed a tree branch, and beat her. She stumbled and fell, quivering, her belly swollen with calf. I grabbed the branch. Dad was shaking with rage. I flung my arms around Lady's neck. I felt her blood on my face. Slowly, she righted herself. I told Dad it was my fault. "It's all right," Dad said. "Take her to the barn. Give her water."

TIMBER

On weekends I accompanied Dad to Buckotaban Lake, where we peeled logs for the Wisconsin-Michigan Lumber Company. Dad and a friend, Marion Briggs, were hired to strip bark from the logs and pile them so that sledges and tractors could reach them for easy hauling. Briggs was a tall, husky man in his thirties, with a small daughter. He had been abandoned by his wife, reputedly a Spanish dancer. His mother raised the girl, keeping her in homemade dresses of an ugly Victorian style. Briggs was a violinist who, under mysterious circumstances, had given up his career. Only rarely would he consent to perform. He encouraged Dad to play instruments. They earned thirty cents for each log trimmed of branches and debarked. By working hard, they could finish six or seven trees an hour. My job was to peel logs Dad had trimmed and slashed along one side. I used a "spud," or tire iron. Pine bark came off easily. The spruce were difficult though. On these I used a drawknife, a blade with two parallel handles, scraping free the obstinate bark without gouging the wood. Since I was slow, Dad worked most of the spruce himself. The best logs would be sawed into lumber, the remainder pulped. Our clothes and hands were coated with pitch. Only kerosene would cut it.

Briggs worked by himself, creating his own piles of timber. One afternoon he walked over to me, chatted briefly, and then whipped out his penis. There's a protocol for relieving yourself in the presence of other males: either you turn your back or you stand beside them, facing the same way; neither of you gazes at the other. Briggs's member was almost equine; I had never seen anything like it. Dad came over and spoke curtly to Briggs, who never displayed himself to me again.

THE JOLLYS

By traversing Ewald's forty and our own, we reached Perch Lake, the best of all nearby lakes for swimming. Minnow, nearer our house, was thick with bloodsuckers. And wading was impossible—you were soon up to your knees in muck. Perch Lake had a wide sandy shore and a sandy bottom. To get to the beach you had to cross a large potato field owned by a bad-tempered bachelor, John Simon, the town grave digger, whose house was invisible from the lake.

A grassy bluff with scrub Norway pines overlooked the beach. By getting a good run, you propelled yourself into the water. We had contests to see who could jump the farthest. For a swimsuit I wore old jeans cut off above the knees. My sisters had one-piece suits from Sears. Nell, only four, rarely went with us. My cousin Grace's breasts had already formed. George Jolly delighted in flashing his rear at Grace—"mooning," he called it.

I enjoyed going to Perch Lake with the Jollys. George was my age, Bill a year older. They lived at the opposite end of Sundsteen, a mile and a half past the school. I thought nothing of walking the distance to meet them, and since there were no telephones, there was no way of knowing whether they would be home or not. They came from a huge family of ten children. Bill and George loved fishing and often went to Columbus Lake.

The Jolly house was a two-storey affair covered with gray shingles. It had the usual spread of outbuildings—a barn with lofts for hay, a henhouse, a pigsty, and corrals for cows. The father and the oldest son worked for the Wisconsin-Michigan Lumber Company. Mrs. Jolly was an ebullient woman with huge breasts who wore the same dress for months, until it turned to shreds. All of her dresses were of the same magenta Rit tint, the hue rubbed dull by grease and child-soil.

The downstairs living room doubled as a bedroom. Here the parents slept in a single bed with the three smallest children. Upstairs, the four boys shared another bed, as did the girls, Margaret, Helen, and Lucille. No rooms had rugs or linoleum. Bill and George would lie on the floor directly over the dining table, collect bed fluff, wood slivers, and mouse turds, and drop them through a crack into a pan of baked beans below. Daily, Mrs. Jolly baked bread and cinnamon rolls. She gave me thick slabs of hot bread smeared with bacon grease and peanut butter or wildcherry ("pincherry") jam. There was never enough silverware. The family ate at a rectangular oak table in two shifts, the older girls feeding the younger children. In the center of the clothless table, near a platter of fried pike and perch, stood the blue roaster full of beans. Bread, homemade jelly, butter, lard, fresh milk, coffee. To help yourself to food you simply reached into the roaster and then wiped your fingers on some bread. No plates matched, and most were cracked. Only the parents used spoons and forks. Cinnamon rolls. Fresh gooseberry pie.

At school Bill and George often took my part against Osmo Makinnen. Bill, blond, short, and muscular, was quieter than George, who had black hair like mine and was always mischievous. Both were good students. The three of us would start high school together. Bill later died at Monte Cassino in the early years of the war.

From the Jollys I learned how to fish, and they taught me the little I knew about sex. They seemed wiser than I, perhaps because they had older brothers, perhaps because they were raised far more permissively; their mother hardly had time to linger over their nurturing.

For our night swims in Perch Lake, Bill would bring matches, and after we swam, we'd rustle up wood for a fire. Bill had already reached manhood, but George and I lingered in late adolescence. One evening, George and I, naked, were horsing around, grabbing one another. Bill squatted near the fire watching. When George wrestled me to the sand, pinning my shoulders, Bill came over. His penis was hard. He started to play with it. George also began masturbating. I sat hunkered with my head on my knees, amazed, excited, yet vaguely embarrassed. Out in the lake, hundreds of toads swam toward our fire. As they hopped frantically ashore, we beat them with sticks and threw them into the flames. Then we doused the fire and left the beach.

Columbus Lake

I met Bill and George Jolly one morning at their house at 6 A.M. Their seventeen-year-old brother, John, a freckled, husky youth, was still asleep on the bed the three of them shared. He was lying on his back and his sheet had worked up across his chest, revealing a sizable erection. George settled a noose of fishing line around John's penis and dropped the loose end of the line out a nearby window. "Watch," he laughed, running downstairs.

The black thread moved with delicate tugs. John grew even more erect. George yanked harder, and John awoke, cursing. "That's George doin' it again, right?" Keeping the string taut, he went over to the window and urinated. George yelled, ran back upstairs, and proceeded to wrestle his naked brother to the floor.

Later, while George ate breakfast, I helped Bill dig night crawlers. They loaned me a cane pole; they each had casting rods. They jammed some bread and cheese into a bag, which would serve also for bringing fish home.

To reach the lake we traversed a superb stand of virgin timber—pine, hemlock, and cedar, with some yellow birch. Partridge flew from thickets. When we reached a floating bog, I matched my footprints to George's. One misstep and you were up to your waist in muck. As it was, on any portion of the bog your feet were under water. The trick was to leap to the next clump before the mass sank deeper under your weight. The vast lake was visible a hundred yards off. We soon reached high land and a rapid creek that flowed into the lake.

We dropped our gear on the sand and stripped to our underwear. The shallow water was rife with pickerel weed. Beyond was a drop-off where Bill planned to fish. We tied fish stringers and a small bag of worms around our waists. George showed me how to bait the hook.

Bill hooked two walleyes and some bass and bluegills. George caught a pickerel, which he threw back, saying it was too bony, and nearly a dozen bass, bluegills, and large perch. My catch consisted of six bluegills and three smallmouth bass.

Robert Peters, age eighteen, holds his sister Jane in the family's living room. Courtesy of Robert Peters.

We stopped for lunch, stripped, and had fun swimming and splashing. When we were thirsty, we simply scooped up handfuls of water and drank. A doe and a fawn appeared. A black bear, fortunately without cubs, spied us and waddled back into the forest. While Bill continued fishing, George and I lay stretched out on the sand, absorbing sun and talking about girls. He claimed that he "did it" with Alice Carlson. She was the oldest of a brood of children left motherless when their mother had died giving birth. I knew George was fibbing, yet I chose to believe him, enhancing his prowess, fearsome and mysterious to me. Perhaps I had a crush on George, of the kind youths have on one another. I don't know. The more masculine—and crude—he was, the better I liked him. I wished for the afternoon never to end.

IMPREGNATION

Charlie Mattek had staked his Guernsey bull in the north pasture, waiting for Lady. When I led her to the gate, the huge Guernsey caught her
scent, grew aroused, reached the end of his tether, and pawed the ground.
While he grew frenetic, his penis dripping, Lady seemed oblivious of him
and kept munching grass, well beyond his reach. When Charlie pulled Lady
nearer, the bull began licking her, his penis a hot rod of meat ready for
penetration. He shuddered and withdrew, lowing. Strings of semen dripped
from Lady. "That should do it," Charlie said. I led Lady home. I was to
bring her back if she remained in estrus.

CARNIVAL

The carnival took place in a field at the junction of Sundsteen Road and
Highway 17. I walked there before opening day to help erect tents and
booths. Brightly painted vans were arranged in a row at the back of the
field. Barred wagons, badly in need of paint, held a lion and a gorilla. Some
booths were already up. There would be a ferris wheel and a merry-go-
round. The carnies looked rough, most of them unshaven, some stripped
to the waist. The women among them dressed like men.

A large tent was splayed over the dirt, ready for hoisting. Half a dozen
men were driving stakes into the ground and tying guy ropes. "Don't just
stand there!" a voice shouted. "Get to work." The man, in his mid-twenties, wore red trunks and was tanned a savage brown. His biceps were huge
and flexed as he stood before me. His accent was strange. "He'p get this
tent up and you'll earn a silver dollar."

I held the guy wires taut while he secured them to stakes. The crew
raised the tent, working a large center pole upright. We erected shorter
poles. The pungent odor of crushed grass blended with the snake-like smell
of canvas.

We set up platforms for a trapeze and surrounded an area of painted
boxes and hoops with a circle of wire, where the lion and gorilla would
perform. Near the center pole stood an ornate calliope, which received
power from a noisy generator.

When we broke for lunch, the carnival man invited me to his wagon.
His name was Brik. He was from Georgia, and traveled with the show for
half the year, moving north during the warm season and moving south
when it got cold. He bossed the crew.

The interior of his wagon was set up like a living room, complete with small sofa and an embroidered, brightly colored pillow saying "I LUV U MOM." A small dinette contained a couple of chairs and an icebox, and a mattress and blankets were on the floor. "Like liverwurst?" he asked. "Sure," I said, sitting at the table. He brought out milk and pop. "Milk keeps my muscles big," he said. "I suppose you noticed."

"I want to look like you," I said, feeling stupid as soon as my words were out.

"You've got height, lad. Here, stand with your back against mine. You'll see."

His buttocks flared against mine. He tightened the muscles of his back.

"I was right. You're taller." He faced me. His chest was covered with curly black hair. "You'll have hair, and it'll be as black as mine." He laughed. "And you'll get muscles." He had grown up on a farm. "I like ramblin'," he said. "I could never be like my dad, married to some woman, with kids tying me down."

He smeared liverwurst on slabs of soft A & P white bread, piling the sandwiches on a paper plate. "Two's plenty," I said. His bare knees touched mine. He spread his legs. I felt giddy, swallowed milk, and finished my sandwich. A magnetic current from his knee jolted me. There was sweat on my lip.

"Well, let's get on. There's more work to do." If I stayed, in addition to the silver dollar, he'd see that I got a pass for the big tent show. "I wish you was older," he said. "I'd ask you to join this here carnival, and live with me."

Later, I went to his wagon to collect my pay and found him on his couch stark naked. "Don't get upset, lad. You've seen a man naked before. I have to wear my 'public duds' for tonight." I stole a look at his penis. It had an enormous foreskin. He pulled some dress pants on, felt in his pockets, and withdrew a silver dollar. "Don't see many of these around," he said. "Plenty in Colorado, though." He gave me a piece of paper saying "Tent Show: Admit One."

I thanked him. He told me that if I helped tear down the tents the next night, I'd earn another dollar.

All the way home, I heard his accent. In a trance, I milked the cow. I'd go anywhere he wanted, do anything he asked.

I plastered my hair with brilliantine. I regaled Margie with descriptions of the tiger (in actuality a defanged beast) and the gorilla. She would use my show pass; I'd sneak under the tent.

The Big Show was exciting, particularly the aerialists, billed as The Flying Godeckes from Poland. Spangles barely concealed the runs and tears in their tights. Glimpses of peach-colored flesh glowed whenever the woman balanced on her head and spread her legs and the trapeze turned.

The aerialist doubled as a lion-tamer, while his partner put the gorilla through hoops and loops. A scrawny elephant, tuskless, performed listlessly with a girl dressed as a ballerina with glittering tiara sitting on his head. A pair of clowns pretended to throw pails of water at the audience; the water was feathers. During the show, Brik circulated, supervising the erection and removal of props.

I treated Margie to cotton candy and a sideshow featuring a fat woman with a second head growing from her side, a midget missing all fingers except for his thumbs, and a mummy, reputedly the body of John Wilkes Booth, stolen from its grave. Most fascinating of all was a lady geek. Once a night, so the hype went, she required a feast of hen's blood, Black Orpington, to be precise. We paid our fifteen cents and crowded close. A nervous hen was tied by its leg to a stake in the ground. Harsh recorded music, in scratchy violins, heralded I-Zelda's appearance. She undulated forth, painted like a gypsy and dressed in a gaudy skirt and layers of beads. "A good fat hen holds one pint of hot blood," a tout exclaimed. "For your admission, you will observe I-Zelda, Princess of Turkey, bite this here black hen's throat. It will cost you another fifteen cents to see her suck out the life, killing the chicken dead!" He motioned us closer. "Anybody with a bad heart, leave now. What you are about to witness ain't for the squeamish!" No one left. Margie looked puzzled, then horrified.

With ceremonial gestures, I-Zelda smoothed her hands over her body, jangled her bracelets in a brief dance, circled the hen (now positioned between two large lighted candles), took up the fowl, and began sucking its beak. She pulled a scarlet scarf from her cincture and wound it about the hen, securing its wings. Taking the bird firmly by its feet, she placed its entire head in her mouth. The bird struggled. I-Zelda withdrew the head. Trickles of blood were visible on its throat. I-Zelda's mouth was bloody.

Margie was sick. We pushed our way through the crowd and started home. This incomplete act, like so many in a lifetime, assumed a mystical force. Was she a sorceress, or merely another desperate human performing an outrageous act of survival?

I did not return to Brik the next evening. I stayed in the field all afternoon gathering and husking corn. I chopped wood. After supper, I lay in bed praying for Christ to quiet my turbulence. He approached with palms extended, the wounds visible. He smiled, His robes wafted by an aromatic breeze. As He neared, I saw that His face was the carnival man's!

FIGHTS

To stifle the numerous quarrels Margie and I had that summer, my mother would declare, "Just wait till you get to high school. Those guys are tough. They'll knock your block off."

My worst quarrel with Margie occurred a week before high school, the week after the county fair. To play pig family we formed a circle of kitchen chairs on the grass. Our conflict was over which of us would play the sow. Margie felt that a male should always play the boar, lingering at the back of the pen digging up roots while the lucky sow lay on her side squirting forth piglets. For a convincing porcine look, we wore Dad's heavy winter coats.

I would, for once, be the sow! I grabbed the coat my sister preferred, put it on, and flopped down in birth throes. I loved the delicious sensation of birthing. Squirt. Squirt. Squirt. When I turned to lick the piglets, Margie kicked at me and yelled. I fought back, spraining her hand. She announced she would drown herself in the lake.

I called her bluff, waved good-bye, and took the coats and chairs back into the house. Half an hour later, I began to worry, filling in time with some desultory hoeing in the flower garden. I started for the lake, near panic. No signs near shore of her shoes or clothes, no footprints, no evidence of a drowned person in the water. If she had indeed jumped, she had drifted into the cranberry marsh, out of sight.

I returned home. As I passed a hayrick, crying, Margie jumped out laughing. "Served you right," she said. I felt both angry and relieved.

From this point on, we played few childhood games. Within a few days her menstrual cycles began. Mom was in the Rhinelander Hospital having her goiter removed. Dad sent Margie to Aunt Kate to explain the facts of life and chose the occasion for my own sex education—or at least he tried. He explained "monthlies" and said it was time I "fucked" a girl. I should cross the road and take Celia Kula into the woods and "do it." I was shocked. The paradox of women as both citadels of purity—this is how I saw my mother, and how my father conditioned me to see her—and licentious whores was painful.

GYM

I dreaded gym class, so I delayed the perfunctory physical examination for weeks, hoping I would contract a disease rare enough to excuse me from class. Not only was I inexperienced at games, but I dreaded showing myself nude to strangers. The ball we had played at the Sundsteen Elementary School was for kids. Even then, I could rarely catch a ball, and my balance was terrible—I had never ridden a bicycle. The only thing I did well was sprint over the rough terrain of those gravel country roads.

The principal, Mr. Kracht, known for his violent temper as "The Bull of the Woods," demanded to know why I was not attending gym. He was unimpressed when I said I lacked money for clothes. His ultimatum: "Attend on Monday! I will personally see you do!"

While the other students suited up, I stalled, removing my shirt as carefully as if it were glued to burn scabs. The locker door hid my lower body from view, and I faced the wall, preferring to show the world my rear rather than my privates. Once in the gym, I stood about with my arms awkwardly folded, intimidated by the prowess and agility of the other boys, especially those from town. When it came time to choose up sides for games, I was always chosen last. I avoided showers until the gym teacher threatened to strip and scrub me himself. "We don't want you stinking in class," he said. Again, I lingered, disrobing slowly, waiting for the other boys to finish. Draping my towel in front of me, I'd make my way to the end of the shower, face the wall, and bathe. Weeks elapsed before I was able to linger and enjoy the hot spray, a treat indeed considering our primitive bathing conditions at home.

Eventually, one of the flashiest town boys, Augie La Renzie, took an interest in me. I helped him with Latin declensions. He was curly-haired, funny, incredibly agile, and popular with both girls and boys. In his freshman year he made varsity basketball. During free periods, we would meet at the gym, where he gave me pointers on basketball. I was soon fairly adept at free throws. Augie also gave me health advice: Never wear someone else's jock strap; keep the venison out of your teeth; stop using brilliantine. He grew up to marry the county judge's daughter and became a World War II ace and a commercial pilot.

Henry Bauer

Henry was born at home in 1932 on a rented dairy farm near Money Creek, Minnesota, a small town in Houston County in the southeastern corner of the state. The second oldest of four children, Henry has an older brother and a younger sister and brother. He is retired from teaching and was living in a city in southeastern Minnesota at the time of our interview.

EVERYTHING I DISLIKE in myself is from my German side. My dad's family was German and my mother's family was Norwegian. A lot of the things you hear about the Germanic culture were true of the men on my dad's side. They were aggressive, arrogant, boastful. My Norwegian side is more docile and placid. But when I was growing up, we were closer on my father's side; they were adamant about getting together for holiday reunions. I came to realize that I didn't like that aggressiveness and arrogance, but since it was what I grew up with, it was my idea of what a man was supposed to be.

According to his older sister, my dad was raised to think that all the obnoxious things he did—which he continued to do all his life—were cute. He was the oldest boy in a German family, and spoiled. His father bought him a new car when he was only fifteen. He quit school after the eighth grade, never mixed much with other people, and never learned that he couldn't always have everything he wanted. He never got over demanding to have his way, and he used any method necessary to get it.

After my older brother was born, my father desperately wanted a daughter. Then I came along, and had the misfortune to be a boy. I've never regretted it, but Dad certainly did. When my sister was born a year after my younger brother, I overheard my grandmother say to my aunt, "I'm sure glad Ted finally got a girl. He was so disappointed in those other two." By the time I was four years old, I knew that he didn't like me. When we were sitting around listening to the radio, I often wanted to sit on his lap, but he would never let me. If I climbed onto his lap, he'd say, "Get off! I'm tired." One time, when I was twelve, we had a houseful of Dad's relatives visiting. There was no place to sit, so I sat on Dad's knee and he flicked his hot cigarette ashes down my back. I left the room crying, hurt and humiliated.

Threshing Scene, by Jeff Kopseng, based on a photo courtesy of Henry Bauer

When I was about four years old, I just loved some of my dad's friends. They were so nice, and gave me attention. One man especially, a neighboring farmer, was so pleasant; he always smiled and was always happy. I remember thinking what a beautiful man he was. He was good-looking, but it wasn't his looks. I liked him because he was so darned nice. I didn't think men were supposed to be nice.

My older brother worked outside with Dad. He was kind of Dad's buddy and I was Mother's friend. I must have been kind of effeminate when I was little, because I wanted my hair curled, and my mother curled it for me one time. I played house a lot, and my mother would come and pretend to help me. She made it fun and often made me laugh. I liked dolls when I was four, five, six years old. Nobody seemed to be too upset about that, not even my dad. I remember him saying a few times, kind of as a joke but not real put-down, "Henry should've been a girl."

Once a year, black singers from a college would come to sing in the local church, and my aunt always had them over for coffee. One time, I sat on the lap of one of the black women. She was large and plump, so warm and nice, I liked her very much. After that I wanted a black doll. In those days everyone called it a nigger doll. I got one for Christmas and I loved it.

About the time I graduated from college, just before entering the Army, I was really hurting, troubled by homosexual thoughts and feelings I couldn't control. We didn't hear anything about homosexuality back then. The late forties and early fifties were the dark ages of sex. What information you could find was awful. I read in a book or magazine that masturbation was bad for you, so I tried to stop.

I went to the Mayo Clinic in Rochester and saw a psychiatrist. Apparently, the official position of the clinic was that if you worked hard enough and wanted to badly enough, you could change from gay to straight. I told the psychiatrist about having homosexual feelings and he said, "Well, you don't have as much of a problem as you think you've got." I was delighted, because this was what I wanted to hear. He said, "Now, I want you to do some dating and, a few months from now, write back and tell me how things are going." The idea was that if I would just date girls, I would get over my fear of them. Homosexuality was regarded as a fear of the opposite sex. In our rural culture, we believed doctors were the ultimate experts, next to gods. So I tried dating and thought I was doing just fine. I even wrote the psychiatrist a card telling him so.

In the army, in Korea, two or three months before I was due to come back to the States for discharge, all my defenses wore out. It was nip and tuck every day. I thought, can I hang on, or am I going to lose control? I didn't want to have a nervous breakdown over there, because I'd be put in a military hospital and God only knows when I'd have gotten out. I was quite religious then, having been raised a Methodist in a very conservative culture, so I would repeat to myself a couple of Bible passages I remembered. One was, "Trust in the Lord with all thy heart, and lean not unto thine own understanding." The other was, "You shall know the truth, and the truth shall make you free." I had no idea at that time what the truth was going to be, because I was so totally denying my gayness. I still accepted the idea that I was straight and only had to conquer my fear of girls.

I got a teaching job in a small town within easy driving distance of Rochester, because I knew that if I was going to get help, I had to be able to see a psychiatrist. For seven years, three days a week, I left school and went to Rochester for psychotherapy sessions. I paid it all out of my own pocket because I had no medical insurance. I didn't even dare to take my legal tax deduction, for fear somebody would find out. At that time, seeing a psychiatrist automatically branded you as crazy.

I wanted desperately to change. There had been a guy in Korea everyone knew to be a homosexual; the other guys would joke about him. I didn't want to be known as one of "them," so I worked and worked. After lying on the psychiatrist's couch for a whole year, all of a sudden, one day, I realized I was very angry. It scared the shit out of me, because I didn't know the anger was there, I had buried it for so many years. I had a hell of a time learning to deal with it. That was in the days when psychiatrists wanted you to get it all out at once—just go into a rage and spit it all out. I couldn't.

After seven years of this—and, of course, the psychiatrist was encouraging me to date again—I still hadn't figured out I was gay. He pronounced me cured, said I was fine and I didn't need to come back anymore. I believed him, but I noticed when we shook hands the last day, he didn't look at me—he looked at the floor. Later I realized he knew better, but didn't know where else to go. He was under the gun of his superiors and didn't dare say, "Look, Henry, accept the fact that you're homosexual." And if he had said that, I might have freaked out.

Things started to go really bad. I'd send for pictures of gorgeous young men and then get pissed off at myself, tear them up and throw them out. I was a little over thirty years old and horny as hell.

I saw another psychiatrist once a week for four years. He was shrewd and nonjudgmental. He just let me talk and pointed things out occasionally. I spent a lot of time putting myself down, since I thought I was completely worthless because of my homosexual desires. I was convinced I was rotten, that there was nothing good about me. One day, after about a year, he zeroed in on me. He pointed out things I had said I'd done that were good, and then he insisted that I say out loud, "I'm a good person." I felt like I was being strangled. It scared the shit out of me. I tried every trick in the book to avoid admitting there was anything good about me, but he wouldn't let me out of it. This guy was a tough old fart. Finally I said it, and after saying it I almost started to cry, but instead I started to giggle like a little kid. I couldn't stop giggling.

That was the turning point, when I started to get better, though I still considered myself straight. I saw him for another three years, and whenever I would get into my self-deprecating mode he would turn the screws. I couldn't get out of it. He never told me, "Look, you're homosexual, accept it." I think he knew I was so paranoid about it that if he had just told me to accept it, I would have freaked out. He let me discover for myself. I was shaving one morning, looking at myself in the mirror, and all of a sudden I realized I was seeing beauty in my arms. I was never a physical specimen, but it didn't matter. I was beginning to see some beauty in myself.

After four years with him, I began sneaking up to the Twin Cities on Saturday nights. I would go to the Hennepin Baths—this was all before AIDS—and I'd watch the queers. I'd go in the steam room and of course they'd come in. They obviously wanted to do something, but I would ignore them and feel horrible about it. Then I heard about a different bathhouse, went there, and started getting into sex. It was very exciting, but I still had the guilt and still considered myself straight.

I started going to a bar called the Gay Nineties for about the last hour on Friday nights, just to watch the queers. But one night, a little voice in me started saying, "These are my people." That voice kept on coming again and again, "This is where I belong, these are the people I belong with." I was still rejecting being gay, but the voice wouldn't stop.

When I was forty-four, on Thanksgiving weekend, I was at a gay bar in La Crosse called the Down and Under. When I saw two very macho-looking guys sitting at the bar, I thought, this bar can't be gay, they're not gay. When they started kissing passionately, I was shocked. After all this time, I still thought all gays were nellie queens. Then I thought, boy, if they can be gay, I can too. That was the moment I threw in the towel— that was my coming out. I saw a gorgeous guy dancing by himself in the middle of the floor, so I went out and started dancing with him. Why was I spending twenty-five dollars a week on the psychiatrist, when I could be spending it on myself, having fun? The next week I told my psychiatrist, "I'm gay, I realize now. I don't think I need to see you anymore." He said, "That's fine," we shook hands, and he wished me luck. I can never describe the weight that was lifted from my shoulders. At forty-four years old I felt I was just beginning my life.

I got ungodly promiscuous for the next four years, and thank goodness it was all before AIDS. I think when anyone first discovers his sexuality, he's going to go crazy for a while. There were two bookstores in Rochester. Going into them probably wasn't very wise for a public school teacher, but I wasn't the only teacher going. We could sneak in the back doors off the alley and somehow there was never a problem. They had glory holes, and young straight or bi guys would come in wanting a blow job. They were horny and usually a little drunk and hadn't been able to pick up a girl in a bar. Sometimes I would bring one home—gorgeous men. Those were the ones that always turned me on, more-or-less straight or straight-acting guys.

I've never had a relationship and I've never wanted one. I suspect that I'm not capable of it, or maybe I fear it. I've had some wonderfully exciting sexual experiences and still do occasionally, but AIDS has scared many young guys away from even the safest sex. I like being independent, free to come and go. I just met a neat guy about my age at a picnic in Minneapolis. We had good conversation, but I could see he was also very interested in me sexually, which is not what I want. I want to be friends with guys my age, but I don't want to get into sex with them. I prefer to have sex with a younger guy or not at all.

Coming out to myself and other gays didn't make me instantly at ease with being gay. If anything, it made me more paranoid. I probably would have been fired from my teaching job had my gayness been discovered. There were plenty of good Christian teachers and administrators who would have seen to that. I'm still not ready to come out publicly. In this town, gays and lesbians who are open about it get hate calls and death threats. I'm fine with being out to a few good friends and supportive relatives.

My dad would make a sexual joke and then laugh lasciviously. He regarded sex as very dirty and nasty and funny. My mother regarded it as very dirty and nasty and not funny. A young neighbor girl in the little town of Money Creek had gotten pregnant and Mother said, "Well, she got *herself* in trouble." Her eyes got big, which made me think it was really bad.

Until I was about ten years old, anytime I was walking upstairs in front of my dad, he would goose me all the way up the stairs. Apparently, this gave him some kind of thrill. When I was about ten and protested, he didn't do it anymore. He was verbally abusive, and he played mind games with all of us. We never knew what to expect—sarcasm, insults, anger, or a putdown joke, all of which we were expected to accept with grace. Dad's temper was one of the most intense I've ever known, and expressing anger was perfectly acceptable for him. For us kids, however, getting too angry meant getting punished, sometimes severely.

I have suspected that my dad may have been a closet homosexual, given his extreme frustration with life. He didn't have the access to therapy I had, so I suppose he dealt with it in the only way he could. He hated homosexuals. As Shakespeare said, "He doth protest too much." But he also seemed to hate women. When television came out and we'd see entertainment shows with a woman in skimpy clothing, you'd think a heterosexual man would have enjoyed it. But Dad would say, "God, she thinks she's smart." He always put women down, treated my mother like dirt under his feet. Outside the family he was a very popular man, as abusive people often are, but inside he could be cruel.

My relationship with my mother was infinitely better, but there were things that weren't right. She gave me too many enemas when I was little. I think she got some jollies from that. Kids were given enemas a lot then—people thought it did them some good when they were sick—but I got enemas when I know I didn't need them.

Church played a great role in formulating my guilt feelings, because in those days the church controlled people by making them feel scared and guilty. And of course it still does, especially the religious right. I was quite religious until I came out of the closet and started reading the gay underground news, such as *The Advocate*. Since I've learned how the church has discriminated against gays and many other groups in the name of Christianity, I've become very hostile toward the Christian religion.

When I was about thirteen, going to a country school, I discovered masturbation. There were three of us boys in the eighth grade—that was the entire grade. One day, one of these boys and I were walking home and a little white terrier dog was following us. We took the dog to a secluded spot down by a little stream and my friend beat it off. Within the next few days, I tried it myself. That's when I became aware of sexuality.

I was a real good friend of one of the other boys in my grade. He kept asking me to stay overnight at his place. Naturally, we would have slept together. I never went, because I was sexually attracted to him and was afraid that once we got to bed I would grab his cock and start playing with it, and that would be unacceptable. I had this fear instilled in me about the awfulness of any kind of sex.

I was always interested in wildlife and conservation, so in 4-H I built wildlife shelters to place along the edges of our fields, and another one which I demonstrated at the county fair. If I were to get a blue ribbon there, I would go on to the state fair. I knew all the boys had to stay in a dormitory at the state fair, and I was afraid of what I might do, or what one of them might want to do with me, so I purposely did a poor job at the county fair.

My worst fear in high school in Winona was having to take phy. ed. and be in the locker room with the other boys. I suppose I was afraid I'd get a hard-on, even though other boys did frequently, much to my fascination. But more than that, I think it was the competition—playing football and basketball. I didn't know how. We didn't play those games on the farm. During basketball season, the teacher would come in, take roll, toss out the basketball, and go have coffee for the rest of the hour. I was glad when he left us on our own, so we farm kids could go over to a corner and talk and stay out of the game.

There was something horrifying about phy. ed. and I hated it. When we played basketball, we had to dribble down and make lay-up shots. That was the most foreign thing in the world to me. The city kids had no mercy and would chew us farm boys out royally when we did something wrong. Very often, I would get sick and stay home on the day I had phy. ed., especially if we were going to be wrestling, which I hated most of all. I don't think there was ever a day I was sick that wasn't a phy. ed. day.

Joining choir in my sophomore year got me out of phy. ed. one day a week. I loved music anyway. I loved singing, and choral music is still one of my favorite forms. I also wanted to learn to play piano, and bugged may parents until they finally let me take lessons. For some reason, my dad hated music and didn't want one of his sons being a musician, even though many of his relatives were. Joining choir was probably what caused me to end up majoring in music in college, because I discovered the beauty of great music that I might not have otherwise.

When I was about a junior in high school, I tried to screw a cow. I had gotten up on a bushel basket, ready for action, when I heard my dad and the farm owner coming to the barn door. So I never consummated my act of love with the cow and I never tried it again. Another time I was going to fuck a sheep, but the sheep was so dirty it wasn't possible. I tried to have a calf suck my cock once, but one lick ended that. The calf's tongue was so rough, it was extremely painful.

I never heard the word "homosexual" until my senior year in high school, when I was trying to put the make on a friend of mine. To keep me away he said something like, "There are three kinds of homos—homo sapiens," and homo something else I can't remember, "and homosexuals." That's the first time I knew there was a word that described my sexual feelings. The words gay, faggot, and queer weren't passed around like they are now. Some guys I knew were effeminate queens, but I didn't think of them as having sex with other guys. I didn't like them, felt embarrassed in their presence, and avoided them. I'm still embarrassed to be seen in public with guys like that.

During my senior year, I drove my dad's car to school and gave a ride to a neighbor boy who was in the ninth grade, a real cutie. Sometimes in the wintertime, when it got dark early, we would sit and talk at the place where I let him off. One time I got him to sit on my lap and I beat him off, but I felt so guilty about it I kept him at arm's length after that. I know he wasn't gay, but I'm sure we could have had some exciting times had it not been for my guilt.

I put myself through college by playing in a dance band. There was a high school kid who was in the band also, and within the next two years he and I got to be pretty good friends. Oftentimes when we got back from a dance job I gave him a ride home. We'd sit out in front of his house and talk about sex, if I could get him on the subject. Sometimes I jacked him off and sometimes he did it for me, but we never took our penises out of our pants. It was very erotic. He was straight, as far as I know.

During my years in college, I began to get more and more bothered by my homosexual feelings. I'd assumed this was a natural phase boys go through—maybe I'd read it somewhere—and that by the age of eighteen it would change. I tried to do some dating and to force myself to have fantasies about girls when I masturbated, but it didn't work. By the time I was a senior in college I was becoming a nervous wreck about all this, so I was staying away from sex, for the most part. Just after I graduated from college, I went to Rochester to see that first psychiatrist, the one who told me to do some dating.

Our farm was in a valley and we had pastureland that extended into the woods on the sides of the bluffs. I was in heaven when I was in the woods; it was an escape. In the summer, it was my duty to get the cows home for milking. Frequently, they were back in the woods. I usually went early to give myself time to explore. I loved the wildflowers I would see there. Often I would drop my pants and jack off back there, sometimes with a cow or two watching curiously. It was very erotic. I still love the southeast Minnesota forests and go hiking in them occasionally.

I have always believed that growing up on a farm builds good character. My mother and I didn't like farming, but as a teacher of thirty-four years I always knew that the farm kids were my favorites—wholesome and decent and clean-cut. They were more honest, more down-to-earth, more reliable; they knew the value of work. In that way, I appreciate my upbringing. But I was pretty isolated.

When I was fifteen, the milkman who came to get our milk was beautiful. This is when I was really getting horny to do something with another guy. I waited every day for him to come. There I was, a fifteen-year-old kid standing around wondering how to get at this guy's body. I couldn't even talk to him, couldn't think of anything to say. I just stood there, watching him, wondering if he knew why. If I had grown up in a city where I had the freedom to get downtown, to be exposed to more city influences and gay men, I might have come out a lot sooner. I feel certain that if I could have been seduced by some gentle, understanding man when I was fifteen or sixteen, I would have avoided a lot of pain.

Harry Beckner

Harry was born in his grandparents' bedroom on their farm in northeastern Nebraska, Wayne County, in 1937. He and an older sister grew up on three rented farms in that area. Harry was an elementary school teacher for thirty-seven years, was married for twenty-seven years, and is the father of two children. He lives on an 80-acre farm in western Iowa with his partner, Bill Hogan, where they raise cattle, hogs, turkeys and chickens, and put up their own hay.

I'VE LIVED A heterosexual life, but it was a facade. In 1957, I wanted to get away from home. What do you do? I got married, which was the appropriate thing to do in that day. On the wedding night, I was wishing I was going home with a man instead of a woman. I looked at all the guys in the wedding party that were sexy as hell and I would've gone home with any one of them, except that wasn't the way it was supposed to be.

There was an empty farm place between the two country schools where my wife and I taught, and there was another gal that taught a mile up the way. I was in hopes that I could get another guy to teach close by, and the four of us would live in that house. We two guys would sleep together, and the two women could sleep together. I thought it would've been just neater than hell, but it never came to be.

The first few years of being married I was fucking every night and jacking off in-between because the fucking didn't satisfy me. I relished nights when my wife went out and I stayed home and took care of the kids. I'd get out my jug of wine and drink till I felt pretty dang good, and then I'd go to the bathtub and do all kinds of things with little toys that I'd invent, because I didn't dare have anything around. I'd have a sex orgy with myself, and dream about other guys.

In the sixties, *Life* magazine had a story on the gay life of San Francisco. It showed guys leaning up against lightposts and trees, waiting to get a trick. I dang near wore it out reading it, thinking oh god, I wish I was in San Francisco.[1] Some of my wife's relatives had just gotten back from California, and several of the people they had gone out there to see were no longer couples because, as they said, "Her husband left her to live with a guy. Can you believe it? They call it 'gay.'" I thought, god, that's what I am.

I was married for twenty-seven years, but I was always out playing around, having sex with men and being sexual with my wife on the side. The hardest part was saying, hey, I'm gay—I can't live on both sides of the fence. Now I'm very open with my family and they all accept it. I'm still Dad and I'm still Grandpa, like I was when I was straight or whatever.

I've always been interested in guys, and it's never been something that I felt dirty or guilty about doing. It was such a part of me that I accepted it as being natural—I did it because it was an urge, and I satisfied the urge. I assumed that everybody did it, because *I* felt so comfortable doing it. I never thought of myself as homosexual and I knew of no one that was. I read about homosexuals in health books, but I thought you had to be some kind of a fruit loop to be one. I was as normal as the next guy. I knew I liked guys, but didn't everybody?

There were two women that lived together in our town, and they were accepted by the community. Mom said, "Well, one of them's got to be the man." So I realized as a kid that women did that, but there weren't any men that I knew of. There were two guys, two miles from us, that lived together for years and died together, but as a kid I just passed that off. When Dad needed help at harvest time he told me to go get them, because they didn't have a car. Everybody said they were brothers, but they didn't have the same last name.

The first farm we lived on was only eighty acres and not that productive. We were very poor, so we made do with what we had—one tractor and horses. Dad said that if I did the work, then he wouldn't have anything to keep him busy. So until I was in high school I did very little farmwork except walking through the corn and cutting out all the cocklebur, a pesky weed. I did that from the time I was big enough to carry a hoe.

House and garden and chickens were things that Dad said I could do up until I was fourteen—"Stay around the house and help your ma." I had to help plant and take care of the garden. We never had to worry about mowing the house yard because the chickens ate all the weeds and the grass. I always had a batch of my own chickens to raise every year, from the time I was big enough to take care of them. I think I've raised just about every kind that they make.

My grandparents, my mother's parents, lived about two miles from us. You could stand in our door yard and see their place. I saw them almost every day. My grandmother used to say, "Learn how to sew, learn how to cook, learn how to bake—you don't know what that old lady that you marry is going to be like. You may have to do those things." I did a lot of cooking. I couldn't wait for my mom and dad to leave—in those days they didn't go much of anywhere—so I could have the kitchen to myself and stir up something. Usually it was pies or cake or something that Mom didn't make.

People used to just drop in to visit, which they don't do anymore. If there wasn't anything in the house to serve for lunch, I'd be out in the kitchen whipping up a lunch while my parents were in the living room talking with the guests. I even made ice cream and baked a cake both while they were having a chat. When they got done chatting, I'd say, "Come have lunch!" One Sunday we had a family gathering of all the aunts and uncles and cousins. I was flying around there helping serve this, that and the other thing, and one of my uncles said, "He's going to make somebody a good wife someday," and I thought, hmmm.

When I started high school, we moved to a farm that was 240 acres, three times the size of what we'd had. In 1950 that was a pretty good size. We had two tractors, so I got worked in real well. We always had cattle, hogs, and corn and oats. In the spring, I would take off days from school to help plow and disk and plant oats. By the time we got to planting corn, school was out. When it came harvest time, we were the only ones in the area that still had a threshing machine. My dad, two neighbors, and myself was our crew. Another guy and I would load up all the bundles, haul them over and pitch them off, then go back out and get another load. Most of the other farmers already had combines. Dad thought it was a waste to use a combine, because he wanted the straw instead of leaving it out in the field.

I preferred milking by hand, so I usually did that while somebody else used the machine. We took our cans of cream to town on Saturday night and sold it to the creameries. That was our paycheck for the week, what we bought our groceries with.

Dad was thirty-nine when I was born, so I always felt that he was an old man. He was kind of a loner and I was more outgoing, so we didn't have a good close relationship, but we always got along. Mom and I were always real close. If I got anything at school when I was a kid, like a candy bar, I waited to share it with her when I got home. She was always so happy to have it. I took every paper home from school to show her.

My sister and I went to a country school a quarter of a mile from our house. One day when I was in kindergarten I asked the teacher if I could go to the bathroom. I wanted to go to the outhouse because I'd noticed a hole in my pants, in my crotch, and I was afraid everybody was going to see my underwear. I didn't go to the outhouse, I ran home. It was snowing something fierce, the wind was blowing like crazy, it was below zero, a blizzard. I didn't put on my mittens, I didn't button up my coat, and the snow was deep already.

When I got home, I was crying because my hand was frozen from holding my coat shut. Mom and Dad had just butchered a hog, and they were working on it in the kitchen. Mom said, "What's the matter with you? Why are you home?" I said I had a hole in my pants, and I was afraid someone would see. Mom told Dad to go tell the teacher where I was. I stayed home because Mom said I would just run away again. She thawed out my hand in cold water, and then I got to have some cracklin's from the fryings of the lard.

This is weird, but when I was four years old I thought it would be neat to be able to go out to the cemetery and walk around underground and play with everybody's cock. I knew that they wouldn't care, and I could get an assortment of them. I had never been to a cemetery, but I knew there were cocks out there and nobody would care if I played with them.

Dad was quite a sexy man. Mom did the puritanical thing, like so many women did back in those days. Sex was taboo. We'll do it if we have to, but we aren't going to talk about it. Dad was interested in presenting himself. I used to watch him stand in front of a mirror when he got dressed. He'd reach in his pants and make sure his cock was in just the right place so it would show. He'd see if it made the right impression on his pants, and if it didn't he'd rearrange it.

When I was five, Dad had a friend come home from work with him for supper one night. The guy was single, and he had just gotten back from World War II, and he was cute. I went into my bedroom and arranged my cock in my pants so that it would show, hopefully, so that he would take an interest in me. Then I came out with something to show him, but he didn't seem to notice my cock. There probably wasn't anything *to* notice, but I went back to my room and rearranged it, got something else to show him, and came back out. I kept doing that till my mother told me to quit making a nuisance of myself and go play.

I always wondered if Dad played both sides of the fence. If my mother and sister and I were gone for some reason, he always got one of his older brothers to sleep with him. This brother was about ten years older, and he and his wife hadn't slept together for years. I've been interested in sex since I was old enough to know that there was a difference, so these things made a mark on me. I thought it was a little queer.

Dad had another brother, a year or two older, that never had married.

"I always felt fortunate to be on a farm, that it was the best place to be." Harry Beckner at age thirteen. Courtesy of Harry Beckner.

Uncle Fuzz used to come for the Fourth of July and Christmas. If he came at Christmas, he might go home by Easter, because he worked seasonal jobs for farmers. He would stay with us until he ran the battery down on the radio, then go on to the other relatives who had electricity. One of my uncles had seven or eight girls, and Uncle Fuzz would let them—or ask them to—paint his fingernails and toenails, and he'd always have a necklace or something on. No male wore a necklace in those days. I started thinking Uncle Fuzz was just a little bit queer, but it was okay as far as I was concerned.

In high school you had to fit the mode or you were queer, so I played the straight line. But I wasn't interested in girls. I wore extra-tight pants because I wanted the guys to say, "Look at his cock," and they did. One time I was sitting in the car waiting for my sister and a guy said, "I've got to see that big thing." He came over and stuck his hands in the window. I let him unzip my pants and take it out. Once he got it out and it got hard, he left.

My best friend and I were born on the same day. Our cocks were so identical that if you put them in a sack you couldn't tell which was whose. I always wanted in his pants. He was of the Catholic faith and said, "If I play around, I've got to go to confession in the morning and tell them I had sex with a male, so I don't want to." One night he said he had to take a leak, and I said I had to. So we got out of the car. I said, "Somebody's coming!" and it scared the heck out of him. He got in the car and didn't zip up, so I grabbed his cock and played with it. I did that two or three times with him and it always worked.

Another night we had been up to the next town. He had a girlfriend there, and she had a boyfriend in the town. We were outsiders. We'd gone up to the girl's house, and her boyfriend found out about it, so we got our hind ends chased out of town. We had a tire that was darn near flat on a gravel road, and we were just flying along to get the heck out of there and save our necks. When we got out to the farm he had to pump up the tire, and then we sat there in the car. I reached over and—he was very cooperative—unzipped his pants and took his cock out and banged him off. "You son of a bitch," he said. "Now I've got to go tell the priest in the morning."

I was involved wholeheartedly in Future Farmers of America.[2] But driving the tractor through the field in the summertime, cultivating corn, it was hot, and I was so sleepy watching the corn go by. I would think, I'm not going to farm anymore. I'm going to get me a big, fancy, high-falutin' city job. Yet, deep down inside there was that part of me that loved the farm.

My best friend and I were chosen by our FFA chapter to go to the national convention at Kansas City when I was a senior in high school. Fred, a student teacher, went with us for the week, and we all slept in the same bed. Fred must've read me like a book. At night, he and I would sit on the couch and talk. One night he laid his head in my lap and said, "Well, this is nice, but there's something hard underneath." He banged his head up and down. "Oh, it's got to be your belt buckle. Undo your belt buckle." So I undid my belt buckle. "There's still something hard." I was a minor, so he didn't touch it. But, god, I wish he would have.

That fall I started teaching in a country school and sent Fred an invitation to the Christmas program. He said he was going to stay with me that night. I was exhilarated and didn't know what to expect. It was colder than hell and we slept upstairs in an old farmhouse that had no heat upstairs. We had covers on till the cows came home. We talked in bed for a couple hours, and Fred said, "Let's lay side by side so we can keep warm," so we snuggled up real close. He slipped his hand over onto my thigh and inched over, little by little, until he touched my cock. It was harder than hell, just ready to jump up and down. I grabbed his and we had one heck of a rendezvous. That went on for several years.

One of the guys I went to high school with was a cheerleader, and when a guy was a cheerleader, he was a pussy. We both started teaching that fall right out of high school. I suggested that we stay together in a hotel in

Norfolk for teachers' convention. In the middle of the night he rolled over and his cock was hard as he rolled onto my hand. I grabbed ahold of it and started banging away on it, and about the time that he was ready to shoot, he reached over and grabbed ahold of mine. Man, did he ever thrash it! He shot his load and rolled over and went to sleep, and there I laid all primed and in trouble. But it was worth it, because I always wondered what he had.

Bill and I have been together for over seven years. We met in Carter Lake Park in Omaha, looking for tricks. I'd taken the whole day and gone to town to see how many I could do in a day. Bill and I had times together for several years before we got together. Now we're both pretty well settled; we're monogamous and have been since the summer we started.

One Saturday that summer, Bill was digging the septic tank hole on his piece of land. I saw his car parked there and he was down in that hole throwing dirt out. He had carved steps into the dirt, so I walked down—about ten, twelve feet. All he had on was a pair of shorts, and I yanked them down and gave him a blow job. He asked me if I wanted to get off and I said no, because I still wanted to tear around. A couple weeks later he called me up and asked if he could come see me Saturday night. He brought me a gorgeous bouquet of iris. It would've taken a bushel basket to hold them all. We put them in bouquets, and I asked him if he could stay all night. We've been together ever since. If I'd have looked for somebody high and low, I would never have found anybody as compatible.

When Bill started to live here with me, he used to say, "Why don't you clean out the stuff from around those trees down there?" I've got all kinds of stuff in those trees, from treasures to junk. I said it was because I might need it someday. That was one of the things I learned: You don't throw anything away, because if you throw it away you're going to need it and you'll have to buy it. In the years that Bill has lived with me, he's used more out of those trees than I have. He'll drag something up to the house—"You mind if I take this? You got any use for this?" In the city, if you don't have, you don't have. What are you going to make do with? On the farm, there's always some way to come up with it. If it's food, you can grow it or raise it. If it's heat, you can go cut it down and chop it up.

Usually farm people are more down-to-earth, not pie-in-the-sky, and accept things for what they are. I always felt fortunate to be on a farm, that it was the best place to be. You've got a lot of freedom that you don't have in town. I used to look at my cousins in town and think, jeez, how awful! And I still feel that way. When spring comes in town, so what? The grass gets green and you've got to mow it. On the farm, spring is the most exhilarating time of the year. Everything starts to come to life, new baby animals and time to start planting.

Someday, Bill and I are going to build a house on Spencer's Mountain, south of Missouri Valley. He would like to build it today, but I'm not ready to quit farming yet. Bill has two-and-a-half acres and has got the blueprints all drawn. It's out in the country, so I could handle that. There's a cemetery just west of the property, where Bill has bought three lots. That's where we're going to be buried someday. You can see Omaha from there. It's about sixteen miles from Omaha, perfect and beautiful.

NOTES

1. Harry refers to an article, "Homosexuality in America," in the June 26, 1964, issue of *Life* (pp. 66–74, 76–80). The photograph he recalls, of a man leaning against a lightpost, actually showed "a policeman in tight-pants disguise wait[ing] on a Hollywood street to be solicited by homosexuals cruising by in cars." The article, by Paul Welch and Ernest Havemann, reported on the gay world's recent emergence from the shadows, consequent conflicts with law enforcement, and perspectives on this "affliction" from legal, religious, and scientific viewpoints.

2. Future Farmers of America (FFA) is an organization for students in grades seven through twelve, to help them prepare for careers in farming and farming-related businesses. It was founded in 1928 in Kansas City, Missouri, where the national convention is held each year. Members of local FFA chapters participate in varied activities, including livestock and crop judging competitions, and are eligible for various degrees and awards.

Jim Cross

Jim was born in northeastern Iowa in 1938, where he and his parents and older brother lived with his grandparents on their 160-acre farm near the small town of Westgate, in Fayette County. His parents bought their own farm nearby when Jim was about four years old. Two sisters were born after that. Jim and his lover, George, live in Madison, Wisconsin.

WHEN I HEAR some of the stories people tell of their childhoods I think, my god, I must have been really protected. Maybe I missed something. My parents were very open, very nurturing, tried to let us have as much rein as we dared before they would pull us in if they saw us going off the deep end. They were always very supportive of us learning how to do different things. For many years I didn't realize what good role models they were.

My mother's mother died when she was five, so she was raised by an aunt and uncle. We lived with them when I was a young child. After that, we still saw them a great deal. They were like grandparents to me, always supporting me in whatever I wanted to do, and praising me if I did something good. They gave me a real sense of who I was, and of feeling good about myself. They were very strict people, but at the same time they were very progressive for their time.

Even after gas and electric stoves were popular, my grandmother insisted on keeping her wood-burning cookstove. My grandfather would sit by the stove, by the cob box, and I would sit on his lap and he would read to me—Mother Goose tales and other children's stories. There were always books in the house. And Grandpa would hitch up the two-horse team to the flatbed wagon and take my brother and me down to the creek bed to get a load of sand for our sandbox. We had the hugest sandbox in the country.

When I was about four years old my father bought his own farm, where I lived until I graduated from high school. It was a smaller farm, 120 to 140 acres, two miles from my grandparents' farm. We lived about a half mile off of the main gravel road, and the road to our place was just dirt. Certain times of the year the mud was so awful, we couldn't go back and forth in a car or pickup. We went on the tractor from our house down to the corner, where my father would leave the car. I always got dirty riding the tractor, and it made me mad, because then I didn't look good when we got to town.

We had hogs and Black Angus feeder cattle and chickens running about. Washing eggs was a daily chore—if the eggs made it to the house. One day my father went out to the chicken house carrying two buckets of water. While he was there, he gathered the eggs. He had one bucket of eggs and another that still had water in it, and when he came out of the chicken house he decided he was going to throw the water out. But he didn't pay any attention to which bucket he picked up, and there went the eggs. We were lucky enough that we got to see it happening.

We had a pot-belly stove, and my brother and I had to get wood from the basement, bring it up and pile it in the woodbox by the stove for overnight, so that we wouldn't freeze to death. I was usually the one that helped in the house because I liked doing it and I was the youngest. My brother was enough older and stronger that he could help Dad do the outside stuff. When the first of my sisters was born, I was delegated to the house to help mother so that meals were ready when my father and brother needed to come in and eat. I was glad, because I enjoyed cooking and all of the things that go along with keeping house. I learned to appreciate a lot of the things that farm women do and most farm men take for granted.

My brother and I got along real well as young children, but we started drifting apart. I realized that I was more prone to keeping house and I enjoyed it. I think in some ways he was resentful because I was able to do that, and I still could do outside work if I wanted to or needed to. I never felt like there were real boundaries. My parents never pushed us into those slots, where a guy had to do this, a girl had to do that. It probably explains why they were very supportive and accepting, from the very beginning, when I came out to them. I think they already knew, in their hearts.

I did a lot of cooking and baking—pies, cakes, cookies, most everything, the basic stuff that farm people eat. And there was always canning. We had a very big garden and we all worked in it. My mother and I would do the canning and freezing in what they used to call a washhouse, a little shell-type building with cooking and laundry facilities that we used pretty much all summer and into the fall. A lot of cooking and canning happened in that little building.

My father was always appreciative of anything that I did to help him. If he didn't like the way I was doing something, he would say, "I think you'd find it easier to do it this way. Let's try it this way." At the time I thought, oh yeah, sure. But in the long run he was usually right. Working with my father was quite regimented and routine—you fed the cows at this time of day and you fed the pigs at this time. The long blocks of time that my mother and I spent together were a lot more spontaneous. But I was close to my father and I really admired him. He was a very hard-working person, a very simple, common person, and extremely well-liked. There wasn't anyone that he couldn't talk with.

My brother and I were always watching the farm animals do what they do naturally, whenever the mood strikes. And my folks were certainly aware that my brother and I were sexual and sometimes played out sexual fantasies with the neighbor kids. The first time I got caught having sex I was ten or eleven years old. It was with the neighbor girl, and we were in our hayloft and lost track of time. We were both stark naked, feeling each other and doing all those things that kids do. We were interrupted when my father came up to throw hay down for the cattle. Fortunately, he didn't throw us down with the hay. He just told us to go in the house and behave ourselves—didn't make a big issue of it. When we talked about it afterward, he didn't chastise me or say that my hands would fall off if I touched that thing again. We had neighbors that would tell their kids that if they didn't stop playing with themselves, their hands would rot, they'd go blind, all sorts of awful things.

Maybe six months later, there were two neighbor boys a year and two years older than I. The three of us were in the barn and of course we had to experiment. I was already attracted to the male gender rather than the female, and I was real curious to know what other boys looked like. I initiated it, but it was a mutual thing, they didn't fight it. They were from a very big family and told me that they had done this kind of thing with their brothers and sisters. We were getting pretty serious, playing with each other's genitals, when both my mother and father walked in and caught me with my pants down. They said, "Get your clothes on and go outside and play like you're supposed to play." I thought, what does that mean? I didn't understand what they were saying much of the time. But they didn't get really wild. Some parents would have started beating their kid.

I finally wised up and realized that there were lots safer places, so it happened many times after that. Our farm sat at the edge of a heavily wooded area, twelve to fifteen acres. Oftentimes we'd just hike into the woods. That was real safe, because there were lots of places where nobody would find you. We made a number of little hideaway places. We'd get a bunch of leaves and make it like a bed.

We did this for two or three years. We were performing oral sex on one another, and anal sex a year or two later. Then it began to fade, because

"My brother and I got along real well as young children, but we started drifting apart." *Left,* Jim Cross and his brother, about 1940. Courtesy of Jim Cross.

they were getting to the age where that kind of behavior was not accept-able for them. I always felt fine about it and enjoyed it. I knew it was en-joyable for them, but I knew that I enjoyed it a lot more than they did. When it finally ended, it was real hard for me and I didn't quite know how to deal with it. I felt like they were rejecting me as a friend.

I grew up in a pretty religious household, Missouri Synod Lutheran, one of the strictest of the Lutheran denominations. There was no grey—it was all black or white. I went to parochial school in seventh and eighth grade, took catechism, and was confirmed. By this time I knew where my sexuality was headed, but I was still uncertain. At the parochial school I had a teacher who was a dirty old man. He was always coming around,

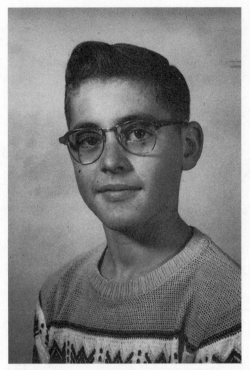

Jim Cross as a junior high student: "By this time I
knew where my sexuality was headed, but I was still
uncertain." Courtesy of Jim Cross.

touchy-feely. One day during class he was talking about a particular Bible
lesson and he brought this word up, homosexual, and my ears perked up—
that's a word I don't think I've heard. At home that night I looked it up
in the dictionary, and then I started going to the school library and finding things with that word in them. I was very curious and learned quite a
bit about it just by reading.

My freshman year of high school, I saw this guy and I knew that he
was watching me too. Tom was a year ahead of me. I worked on the school
newspaper, and he was one of the editors. At first, the attraction was more
like questioning—he was wondering where I was at, I was wondering
where he was at—until we had spent enough time together and finally realized where we were both at. Then things began to happen. We got to
know each other and spent more time together, and one thing led to an-

In his early teens, Jim Cross plays the cigarette girl for his parents' friends and neighbors at their Saturday-night card club, about 1952. Courtesy of Jim Cross.

other. Tom was old enough to drive and had a car. We were sexually active during my sophomore and junior years in high school.

Tom and I worked together on the school paper for three years, spent a lot of time together, and had a lot of fun. We would go to ballgames and dances with a group of friends, guys and girls, and when the evening was ready to wind down, Tom would give me a ride home. We would sometimes park on one of the roads and sit and talk. It felt real good having someone that I was that close to, but it wasn't a real heavy thing. We never talked relationship talk. We wouldn't have known what that was all about, anyway.

I dated in high school, but dating to me was just a fun time. I didn't harbor any great thoughts of getting married and having kids and living happily ever after. My parents would have liked that to happen, but they didn't ever put a lot of pressure on me. There were times when they would say, "Why don't you date her? She's really nice and you're so cute together." But I never went out with high school sweethearts with the idea of going to bed with them. I always thought it was gross. After a while, I think my folks realized that I probably wasn't ever going to seriously date a woman and get married and settle down. Perhaps that's one of the advantages of having an older brother—he kind of took care of that.

The jocks—the real macho guys, the big brutes—gave me the hardest times in high school. I was pretty small, rather petite, and they would get on my case about being a real femme. They used to call me "Nellie," and I'm not sure they knew fully what it meant. Once in a while I would hear "fag" or "homo." It used to make me really angry, but I knew that I couldn't do a whole lot about it. There were three or four of them, twice as big as I was, so I wasn't about to pick a fight.

My high school years were the toughest, because I was realizing what was going on with me. It was a small school and everybody knew everybody, so you couldn't get lost; you were always out there, for whatever that was worth. Toward the end of my junior year, my folks realized that I was having some difficulties in school and asked me what was wrong. I told them that I was being harassed by a bunch of the jocks. They talked to the school principal and things kind of leveled off in my senior year, so it wasn't as bad. But I had a lot of fun in spite of all that. I had some really good friends.

After high school, I was in the Army Medical Corps for three years. I was sexually active the whole time I was in service, but I really came out after I got out of service in 1960. I lived in California for two-and-a-half years and spent a lot of time going out and partying. Then I moved back to the Midwest, where I've lived since.

My family is pretty comfortable with my sexuality and how that weaves into the family circle. I've been in a relationship for close to fifteen years, and my family is very supportive of it. They're also very fond of George. He's like a member of the family, and it's been that way for a long time. I've been in other relationships where it was very similar. They weren't as long-lasting as this relationship has been, but they were always accepted.

Growing up close to nature, close to all those things that you see come to life, gives you a completely different perspective on how you deal with other people as well as yourself. Seeing life becoming life, respecting that, watching that happen, watching things grow—I kind of did the same thing with myself. It was totally uncluttered. I didn't have to deal with a lot of people. I had lots of time to think my own thoughts and to process those thoughts. Doing that made me much more respectful of others and of everything in the universe.

I loved being in the country, but sometimes I would get lonely and would crave seeing other people. It was nice to have company or to go to the neighbors' and visit with them once in a while. And I never really liked the farmwork part of the farm. I saw my mother and father work very hard for many years and I made up my mind that I didn't want to work that hard.

But the farm is where my foundation was laid, and it's taken me a few years to realize how strong that foundation is. Just the fact that I was able to grow up in a healthy home taught me a lot about how to deal with everyday things. I feel like I can relate to all kinds of people, and on all different levels. Being aware of and sympathetic to people who aren't as privileged, caring for your fellow humans—we used to hear those things a lot from my folks. And just being proud of what one has accomplished or is still accomplishing.

I've never regretted any of the things I've done, and I've done lots of crazy things, probably just because I *am* gay. I'm sure I wouldn't have done them otherwise. I'm real satisfied with where I'm at at this point in my life, what level I'm at with my own people and with everybody. I don't feel real uncomfortable, no matter where I am anymore. I won't allow that. I can hold my own as a human being, and should have the same rights as anybody else. I'll do what I have to do to get those rights.

Dennis Lindholm

Dennis grew up on a 160-acre farm in southwestern Iowa, Montgomery County, between Elliott and Red Oak. Born in 1940, he has an older brother and a younger sister. A high school teacher, Dennis has lived in the Madison, Wisconsin, area since 1966: He lives on a small piece of land near Cottage Grove, Wisconsin, where he gardens extensively.

I FEEL VERY angry and bitter toward society for robbing me of much of my life. I spent so many years denying and subordinating and hiding the fact that I was gay. A lot of unhappiness and some severe depression were the result of that. Until I came out, I didn't realize what I had been doing. I can see now that I have been gay all my life, but I didn't always know it, or at least I didn't admit it. There wasn't the option to be myself.

I was married in 1963 and divorced in 1970. I have no regrets about the divorce, but I am angry that I felt forced to marry. There wasn't any alternative, there weren't any other role models. It wasn't fair to my wife either. I loved her, but by the end of our marriage I was having sex with her because I had to, not because I wanted to. The kids were four and five years old, so the divorce was difficult and painful. In those days women always got custody, so I didn't even fight it. But they were too much for her, so she was very happy for me to take them whenever I would, and I was very happy to take them. Basically, I built my life around the kids—I took them at least twice during the week, every weekend, and all summer.

After the divorce I just drowned myself in work. I was a workaholic, still am, and moving out in the country gave me plenty to do, because this place takes a lot of work. I was teaching full-time and spending basically full-time with the kids as well, so I didn't have much time to think about other things. At least that's how I kept myself from thinking. I didn't come out to myself until 1985. Oh, Christ, if I had known, I could have had those fifteen years that I isolated myself. I had several affairs with women, but it didn't occur to me that I could have affairs with men.

Seeing *Consenting Adult* on TV is what really got me to come out. This kid told his mom that he was gay and she kind of accepted it, after a while anyway.[1] This was in early 1985, a really rough time in my life. My friends were moving away and my kids were graduating from high school. I had devoted the last fifteen years to raising those kids, and they were leaving, so I was getting panicky about what was going to happen.

I called the gay phone line in Madison to get a psychiatrist, because I thought I was sick. I decided to try this because I was going to commit suicide anyway. I had it all figured out, so it wouldn't hurt to try. I got ahold of Tony, to whom I shall be grateful for the rest of my life. He spent about forty-five minutes talking with me, and suddenly I didn't think being gay was such a sick thing anymore.

I had been conditioned to believe that the things homosexuals did were very sinful, sick, and dirty. I had gone to an X-rated bookstore a couple of times to look at erotic films. When I saw people standing around in the dark, waiting for other people, I put them in the category of perverts. I thought that was what it meant to be gay, and that was not me, so I concluded that I wasn't gay. I didn't know about the gay community. I knew there were gay people in Madison, but I didn't know where to go, I didn't know that it was okay, that a normal person could be gay.

I went to the Gay Center in Madison and found out that there were gay bars in town, that it was all right to go to them, and that there were different activities available. These people weren't child molesters and perverts. Everything happened so fast once I made the first step. I started going to a coming-out support group, and one night I went to a meeting of gay men over the age of thirty. It was a potluck, so I made something real special, and I was about a block from the place when I said to myself, "Dennis, what in the hell are you doing? Go home where you belong." But I went and, as it turned out, they were normal people. This was all so earth-shaking. You just can't believe what happened to me inside. When I came out and that weight got lifted off my shoulders, Jesus Christ, I was flying ten miles high for so long. I haven't thought about suicide since.

I came out to the kids in the summer of 1985. Once I finally got the word "gay" out, it wasn't so bad, but getting it out was just horrendous. I don't really know what their reactions were, because I avoided looking at them. I tried to reassure them that just because I was gay didn't mean they were going to be gay, and all the other things that my gay fathers support group had told me to tell them. I said that I had tried my darnedest over the last forty-five years to change, but I couldn't, and I was accepting it myself for the first time.

Farming was a hell of a lot of work. It was hard work and it was hot work, and it was always pretty iffy how it was going to turn out. I hated farming and couldn't wait to get far away from it, I was just so bored and always alone. Morning and night, we had to feed and milk the cows, feed the pigs, and feed the chickens. I had to take the cows down to the pasture every morning before the school bus came, and go get them every night. We milked about ten cows, from which we sold the milk until the state put in sanitary regulations that we couldn't meet. Then we sold just the cream and fed the milk to the pigs. I carried the milk out to the hog lots after we separated it up at the house. We used the cream and egg money to buy our groceries when we went to town once a week. We were fairly self-sufficient and didn't buy anything we didn't have to buy.

All summer we had to put up hay and harvest oats. Haying was the worst because it was always so hot in Iowa, and when the hay was ready it had to go in the barn whether it was 110 degrees or not. We worked with the farmers in the area, and had bought a baler together. The baler would go from farm to farm and all of us would follow it, putting up the hay at one farm, then moving on to the next.

We very rarely did anything other than work. We had a large garden and Mom did most of that. I would help when it came time to do things like pick beans and shell peas when she was canning. Mom wore the pants in the family, made all the decisions, and Dad just worked all the time. He never slept beyond 4:00 in the morning and was up and gone by the time we got up, so we had to go out and help.

I was in 4-H for years, an officer in our local club and on the county level, and went to camp a couple of times.[2] I raised and took care of my own steer and pigs and dairy cattle. I liked working with the animals, but when your 4-H project was over you sent the animals off to the slaughterhouse. That was just the way it was.

On Sundays we went to a Methodist church. In Sunday school they really drilled into us how lucky we were that we weren't Catholics. When Kennedy was running, that was a big thing, to have a Catholic as president and have the pope running our country. I was very religious in high school and went to a religious college for two years. I was president of the local and district youth groups, so that took a lot of time. On Saturday nights, I helped put the church newsletter together. On Sundays I helped the minister. For several years, I did everything in the Sunday service except the sermon.

I got into embroidery in my early teens. I liked doing things with my hands, and I liked embroidery because you had colored threads, nice pictures of flowers and little animals, and when you got done you had something that was real pretty. Dad didn't like that I was doing it—it was sissy—so I didn't make a show of it. My mother bought it for me in the first place, so it must have been okay with her. One time I told a kid from school

Dennis Lindholm with his yearling holstein heifer, Candy, at the beginning of the 1956 4-H club year. Courtesy of Dennis Lindholm.

that I would let him see my embroidery if he promised he wouldn't tell. I showed it to him and the next day in school he told everybody, which was disastrous. I didn't do embroidery again. I became very conscious of what male things were, of what one does and doesn't do. I've always been envious of women who could pull out their knitting and do that while they're talking or watching television.

I started collecting insects when I was in junior high. I would go down to a creek that ran through the farm, where I could find a lot of insects. I don't think Dad particularly liked that either—there was something sissy about collecting butterflies and those kinds of things.

We were pretty isolated out on the farm, but Sunday was visiting day when people would just drop in. That's one thing I really miss. We would get home from church and have a big dinner and be lying around, and someone would say, "Let's go for a ride," and we would just go. We would

"I started collecting insects when I was in junior high. I don't think Dad particularly liked that either—there was something sissy about collecting butterflies and those kinds of things." Dennis Lindholm, about 1957. Courtesy of Dennis Lindholm.

stop in and see if somebody was home and they would always be glad to see us. We would go in and stay for a while—play cards and talk and have a good time. "Why don't you stay for supper?" And lots of times we did, but we always had to get home because the cows had to be milked.

People would come to our place, just out for a ride, and they would stop in to say hello. "Why don't you stay for supper?" "Oh, no, no." "Come on in. We've got plenty." "Oh, well, okay." Those were just the most fun times. Sometimes kids were along, but it didn't make any difference, because they always included us kids in playing cards.

My sister and I played together because there weren't any other kids that lived close enough to do anything with. My brother had his friends and I was always in his way, so I was just somebody to beat up on. In high school, I was a real pain for him because he had a driver's license, and my folks made him take me along to spare them from having to take me to wherever I had to go to. That's probably one of the reasons my brother didn't like me. Another reason was that we had to share a bedroom.

My brother showed me how to masturbate. One day he said, "This is what boys do." I hadn't done it before that. I understood what the birds and the bees were about, because of the farm animals, but sex was something you didn't talk about. Masturbation was a sin. I was tormented by guilt, and prayed myself to sleep at night so I wouldn't touch myself.

I was the outside one in the family, and felt that I never really belonged. My folks and the neighbors all thought that my brother was a great person, so I was just his brother and not a person in my own right. I was very insecure and tried harder than everybody else. I was really trying my darnedest to be the best little boy ever. I was a big wheel in school, did all kinds of stuff, but I was discouraged because I was too small to be good in sports, which was the only thing that really counted.

I knew I was different, and I knew it was stuff that I couldn't share with anybody. I was very much taken with good-looking boys, and thought that a couple of the high school senior guys were so big and attractive. I was attracted to a couple of my classmates; we were best friends, and my best friends were all good-looking boys. I suppose I was in love with them. I certainly built my whole life around them, as far as getting together on Saturday nights. The big thing was to go into Red Oak to drive around a lot and go to the movies—there wasn't much else to do.

It was so awkward when we couldn't get together because they had a date. I was envious of them, and jealous, and I fantasized about them having intercourse with their girlfriends. I couldn't wait to go to church camp every summer—god, there were some knockouts there. I would dream about them for months, about them being with girls. I never dreamed about being with those boys myself. I didn't know one could do that, or even dream about doing it. I knew two men could masturbate one another, but it never occurred to me that two men could sleep together.

The worst thing you could be called in high school was a homo, but kids threw that word around without knowing what it meant. I was very careful not to wear yellow on Thursdays.[3] The messages that I got about homosexuality were all very negative, and in the back of my mind I was afraid that someday somebody was going to find out that I was like that. Every once in a while the newspaper would have an article about a purge in Washington, about how they had found homosexuals in the State Department or wherever, and all of them were dismissed. One time, a hundred and some were dismissed under Eisenhower.[4]

Dennis Lindholm as a college student in 1962. Courtesy of Dennis Lindholm.

Things just happened and I kind of stumbled into them. I stumbled into teaching because I was a history major and there wasn't anything else I could do with it. I stumbled into marriage because that's what you had to do. I'm just waiting for retirement, to do all the things that I *want* to do. There are three big milestones in my adult life, three major steps that I have taken that have saved me. First was the divorce, because it liberated me from a very stifling situation. Second was moving back to the country, so I could get back to the soil. Third was coming out.

My sister and I get along real well, so I've tried to come out to her. I would never tell my brother. We still don't get along, and he's the exact opposite of me—he likes guns and golf, he's a Republican. After I came out to the boys, I asked them if they wanted to talk it over with their mom, because if they did I said that I should be the one to tell her. They said they didn't want to, and she still doesn't know about me. The boys and I are good friends. I'm certainly an influence in their lives and I am definitely their dad. I was always around. Coming out to them was rough, but we got through it and we're very close today. I love them more than anything in the world.

I'm very closely tied to the land. Living in the country is tremendously important to my self-worth and satisfaction. I would love to farm, but I wouldn't want to have to make my income from it. My one-and-a-half acres is really all I can take care of, and I want to stay here as long as

I am able to take care of it. It isn't farming, but it's more than just a garden. I'm not afraid of work, and I'm not afraid of getting my hands dirty, so I get a lot done. I'm pretty self-sufficient, both in terms of doing things for myself and living off the land.

I've become very domestic and I like it. When I was married, my wife did the kitchen work. I had to teach myself cooking and canning and all the other things that I do. Sometimes people make comments about how I'd make a good wife. That kind of stereotype just infuriates me. But I *would* like to get married again—this time to a man—and I do mean married. We should be able to get a legally recognized marriage and everything else that goes with it. I don't know if we ever will, but that's my political goal.

My social life is entirely gay-oriented, but I'm not out at work, so I still lead two lives in that respect. I belong to several gay groups that meet once or twice a month, and I get together with friends. I'll probably always be at the edge of gay life, because I have an awful lot of social conditioning to overcome. I bought into everything they fed me all those years and I know a lot of other people who have not overcome that internalized homophobia. I'm not sexually active, partly because of the health thing, but also because it's just something you don't do, it's dirty. I've gotten over a lot of that, though. My therapist told me, "Dennis, you've got to have anal intercourse with somebody so that you know what you're talking about. Then if you don't like it, you don't have to do it." So I did it, and I thought it was great. But I've never been a bottom yet, and I'm a bit worried about that.

What did I do for my midlife crisis? I changed my sexual orientation. Really, I just admitted it. If I could take a pill today and change from being gay, I wouldn't take it. I wouldn't even consider it. Up until I came out, I would have said, "Give it to me!" So I've come a long way. Basically I accept that this is the way I am, and it's all right. Besides, I like men. In fact, I love them.

I've been involved with religion all my life, rejected it a couple times and gone back to it. I'm in a stage of rejection now. I converted to Catholicism after I got divorced, and was very sincere about it. I tried hard to lose myself in it, went to mass every day for years. That was one way I got through fifteen years of being alone. I even thought about joining the priesthood. But when I came out I realized how anti-gay the Catholic church is. Intellectually, it's easy to reject religion, but when I get into periods of having to cope with loneliness, it's a crunch. I'm basically a romantic, a backwards-looking one. I like the romantics, I like their philosophy. A lot of the German romantics converted to Catholicism and then committed suicide. That was my thinking for a long time.

NOTES

1. In "Consenting Adult," a 1985 television movie based on the novel by Laura Z. Hobson, a college student reveals to his parents that he is gay and a respectable family is devastated.

2. 4-H stands for Head, Heart, Hands, Health. Earlier agricultural clubs in the Midwest grew into the 4-H movement during the 1910s and 1920s. The national 4-H program was developed by the U.S. Agriculture Department to reduce the social isolation of rural youth and to instruct them in modern farming and homemaking practices as well as good citizenship. At local 4-H club meetings, members recite the 4-H pledge: "I pledge my head to clearer thinking, my heart to greater loyalty, my hands to larger service, and my health to better living, for my club, my community, my country, and my world." 4-H projects are exhibited at local, county, and state fairs. Some 4-H members show cattle or other livestock at these fairs, entering into competitions in which their animals are judged on health, appearance, carriage, etc. Junior leaders are 4-H youth who assist adult program leaders after completing several years of 4-H work.

3. Variations on the "wear yellow and you're a queer" theme are evident in several men's stories. This phenomenon may be related to a meaning of the word yellow from the early decades of the twentieth century. In that era, to say that someone was yellow, or that he had a yellow streak or a yellow belly, was to say that he was cowardly, lily-livered—a contemptible, worthless person. This connotation may have been extended to the queer-baiting schoolyard jabs of adolescent males. The color pink seems to have acquired similar connotations in recent years.

4. Throughout the 1950s, the Eisenhower administration pursued government clean-up agendas related to those of Senator Joseph R. McCarthy and his associates. Individuals deemed to be communist or homosexual were denied government employment.

James Heckman

James was born in 1941 in east-central Indiana, where his family lived on three rented farms during his childhood. He had an older brother and has two younger sisters. James was married and is the father of two children. He lives in east-central Wisconsin, where he is retired from a career in farm livestock health.

I WAS FOUR years old when my brother Richard was killed getting off the school bus. I liked him very much, we were good buddies. One evening we had our pajamas on and were playing together. The next day he got off the school bus at home and a car hit him. From that time on, my childhood felt very lonely. Both my parents went into a state of depression. It seemed like my mother was always crying or in bed. My dad just kind of disappeared. He went out to work early in the morning, came back for meals, and went back and worked until dark. He was never much for words when things got difficult.

My brother became the perfect child in everybody's eyes. According to my uncle Al, Richard would have been the greatest athlete, an all-star in basketball, baseball, and football. According to my dad, Richard would have been the best farmer and the hardest worker, and according to my mother he would have been such a handsome young man, the idol of every girl's eye. My grandmother said Richard was such a good little boy, Grandma's boy. He became an angel in everyone's eyes, as it so often happens in old Catholic families. Because I was a survivor, I didn't get all those praises, so I tried to emulate Richard. He had played with marbles a lot, so I tried to get into that, and he'd had a habit of chewing on his shirt collar when he played marbles, so I chewed on my shirt collar.

Several months after my brother was killed, I got quite sick with rheumatic fever. I know the thought went through my parents' minds that they were going to lose another son. I was their only child at the time. Lying there in bed, I felt a keen closeness to them. My dad had a sad, empty look on his face, and my mother started to cry. I thought, I better pull through this for my parents, and I better behave.

My dad's family was all German Catholic and had been farming as far back as I know. My dad was a high school dropout, but he was highly respected in the community as a very good farmer and as being honest, hardworking, fair, and always willing to help out. When there was a need on another farm, if there was a death or illness, he was always there. That's the way my parents were. They were very Christian people. Not that they were always saying prayers, but they were just very involved and got along with people. My mother's family was Irish on one side and German on the other. Farming was all they were ever involved in. My mother was an outstanding cook. She baked lots of pies and cakes and was always showing them off at the county and state fairs, where she got a lot of blue ribbons and big prizes. She was a 4-H leader, very active in Extension Service and home demonstration work.[1]

Our farm was 250 acres, primarily a hog operation, but we had a few dairy cows and chickens and beef cattle. The land was very productive and we cropped almost all of it. With the livestock and the fieldwork, there was always a lot to do and I was involved in all of it. Saturday mornings, I hauled manure. I was up early every morning doing chores, and I really couldn't get involved in school activities because I had to go home to feed and put bedding down for the cattle, or take care of the hogs. We housed a bunch of hogs in some buildings that didn't have an electric water pump. Every day, before and after school, it was my job to hand-pump water for those blasted hogs. It probably took only about a half hour, but it seemed like an eternity.

Come the spring of the year, I liked to fly a kite in one of the outer fields, or go down to a creek that ran through the farm. But as soon as I got home from school, if I didn't have my clothes changed in ten minutes' time, my mother was yelling at me to get out there on that tractor—some plowing or other fieldwork had to be done. If I was lucky I would get back to the house in time to do my homework.

In the course of eleven years of 4-H club work, I completed about 120 projects. My mother insisted on all these projects so that I would stay busy all summer. For eleven years, I showed beef cattle. I always had one or two steers at the county fair. For seven or eight years, I showed hogs. I always had a pen of barrows or gilts at the fair. For five years in a row I showed grand-champion poultry. I was in the corn project, the electric project, and forestry, and I did gardening for four or five years. I was an officer of the local 4-H club, and then got involved in the county junior leaders group. That was my biggest social outlet during junior high and high school. It was the thing to do, and it was the one time I could get to be with other groups of people. My extended family was very close-knit. We always got together for every birthday, every holiday, plus I don't how many other times.

"I always had one or two steers at the county fair." *Above,* James Heckman trains a beef animal for showing at the 1951 fair. *Below,* he washes the animal in preparation for showing. Courtesy of James Heckman.

"For five years in a row I showed grand-champion poultry." James
Heckman displays his 1956 grand-champion chicken. Courtesy of
James Heckman.

My uncle Al was a rather arrogant guy. He thought he was the best
farmer in the neighborhood. He did it bigger and better, and always had
new equipment, the best available. Al never married. He was extremely
handsome and in a lot of ways I really admired him. He had been a naval
aviator in World War II and was a nut on sports. To hear him tell it, he
was the greatest athlete that ever lived. I helped him out a lot on his farm,
morning till night. In the summer months, we did a lot of custom hay baling. If we weren't baling hay, there was corn to be cultivated, and then the
wheat harvest started. Al would go on tirades—calling me a sissy and yelling at me about not playing sports well enough, I would never amount to
a hill of beans because I couldn't play basketball, and I didn't know how
to drive a tractor properly. I could drive it as well as any other kid my age.
Everybody said, "That's the way Al is." They just let it happen. Now I re-

alize he was a very frustrated and miserable person. There's not much doubt in my mind that he was a latent homosexual, and it was never possible for him to be his real self.

My grandfather, my mother's father, was a gem. He was wonderful, kind, loving, gentle, and he never put any demands on me. He was Al's father and took a lot of abuse from his own son. I used to work a lot with him. Whenever I could, I was helping my grandfather and my uncle on their farm, plus working on my parents' farm. They were about four miles apart. I would jump at any opportunity to be with my grandfather, and we would get lots of things accomplished—fieldwork, work on the livestock. Of course, according to Al, we were doing everything wrong. Every so often, my grandfather and I would sit down and talk—just small talk, or what the weather was like. He was very good to me. When I would go to town with him, he always knew everybody on the street and had all kinds of friends.

About the sixth or seventh grade, when I was showing cattle in 4-H, I would see other guys and really wanted to be close friends with them. And I just loved to look at guys. I would go to basketball games to see those muscular players out there in short pants. I was lonely and very much wanted to be good friends with those guys. Anything sexual I just put out of my mind. I never looked at anyone naked, I didn't touch my private parts, and I made darned sure I wore pajamas to bed.

Sometimes, when my parents were gone, I would admire my mother's clothes and put them on—undergarments, corsets, girdles, dresses, the whole works. I would put makeup on too, and fantasize that if I could dress like this, maybe some of those guys would be attracted to me. It really turned me on; I would get an erection. In my early high school years, I had dreams about being like a woman for the purpose of attracting guys.

I had a lot of friends who were girls, and got along very well with groups of girls, but dating was very difficult. I always felt like a complete dud. But there were guys I would have given anything in the world to be with. One year, the only reason I asked a girl to the prom was because we got to double with her best friend's boyfriend. I was just in a fog that he and I would be sitting at the same table the whole evening. He was the only person I wanted to impress that night. When I was a junior in high school, I was selected to go to Hoosier Boys State.[2] I loved it because there were only guys there, so it was okay to develop friendships with them, but I could never quite do it.

From the third or fourth grade through high school, I seriously thought about going into the priesthood. Priests were not supposed to have girlfriends—that was my defense. I would sometimes have dreams about being with a bunch of guys in a monastery and not having any undergarments on underneath my cassock. In some of the dreams I had physical contact with them. But the idea of the priesthood began to fade away, and I decided I would just have to work hard, do well in high school, go on to college, get a good job, and get myself established. Someday I'd find the right girl and fall in love. That's what was supposed to happen.

My mother was rather strict and her emotions could fly apart at times, and my dad was always difficult to reach. Except for my grandfather, I never felt any intimacy, and I never felt my parents understood me. They loved and cared for me, but I sensed that I was not living up to their expectations. Early on, I began to sense there was something different about me. I didn't know what it was, but there were things that I couldn't relate to them.

Often I wished I could be at my mother's side to cook and bake and sew, but in German Catholic farm families only girls did those things. When we would go visiting, I was very interested in how the house was decorated, what type of food was on the table, how well-dressed they were. Needlework, knitting, and crocheting fascinated me, and I really wanted to do them. But had I done them, I would have been ridiculed for being such a sissy. My uncle would have started it and it would have spread out from there. Even my grandfather would say, "Oh, you don't want to do that. That's girl stuff." My grandfather would never do anything domestic, and washing dishes was the only thing my dad would ever get involved in.

When I was in the seventh or eighth grade, there was a very nice and attractive young man who lived on a farm not too far from us. He was a junior in high school and a very good basketball player. In Indiana, basketball is king. It shocked the community when he shot himself, committed suicide. They talked about the fact that he didn't go out with girls. I admired him and felt like I understood him. He too felt that pressure to be the square peg in the square hole.

On the farm, I was able to bury myself in so much work that I was tired at night. I couldn't think about going out. I was exhausted, and I was so busy with the 4-H club and with my projects. In high school, the kids in town would go to the swimming pool and mess around at the drive-in restaurant. I never had time to be there. Through farmwork, I buried a lot of fantasies. I became very caring towards older people and was a darling to a bunch of old ladies. I think I was doing this to find relationships.

The drawings on restroom walls was where I got my sex education in high school; penises, the female organs, that's where it goes. One time when I went over to a neighbor boy's place after school, I saw his bicycle by the chicken house. I peeked inside and saw that he had an erection and was having intercourse with a chicken. He must have ejaculated, because he was really going at it. When he came out the door, I had stepped away and acted like I had just arrived, and nothing was said about it.

I would see bulls and boars mounting cows and sows and I would wonder, what makes them do that? How do they know what to do, where to stick it? I would wonder how a man and woman could get together to have a child. What arouses them? I never felt that, and I thought maybe it was because the human race had advanced beyond those animal instincts. At Purdue, I had a course in the physiology of reproduction in farm animals. The professor was rather blunt and to-the-point, and it wasn't until then that things really began to go together. I was so naive, I didn't even know about the female anatomy.

I was twenty-two or twenty-three when I began to masturbate, and had my first sexual experience when I was twenty-five, in graduate school. A guy approached me in the library rest room and we went to his dorm room and had sex. I loved it, but I was so scared I was shaking. The old-time Catholic church was wonderful at teaching guilt. I went to a priest immediately afterwards and cried uncontrollably. "Don't worry about that, it will pass," he told me. "It happens to a lot of guys. You'll meet a fine girl and you'll have some kids."

Two or three times after that, the same guy approached me. When I said I couldn't do it, it wasn't right, he tried to tell me it was okay if it was what I really wanted and if *I* felt okay about it. I had a couple of experiences with a married guy in graduate school who followed me into my room. I didn't like that, because he was forcing himself on me—although I have to admit there was a little bit of it I liked.

I was twenty-seven when I got married, in 1968. I thought I would grow into it, because that's what the priest told me. It was time to get married, and she was a fine woman. I think one of the reasons I married her was that she was a few years older than I was, like my brother, and she seemed to be the type of woman he might have married. It sounds strange, but in many ways I looked at her as being more of a sister-in-law than a wife. And because my brother would have had children, I had children. There was a time when I thought of my own children as my brother's children.

In our early years of marriage, sex was okay. I could do it as long as we were having children. But when my wife had a hysterectomy, sex became impossible for me. My wife knew something was wrong. I was in pretty bad shape, very despondent. I had decided to suppress my homosexual feelings, and that I would end my life if they ever came to light. I would never accept it, and became very much a homophobe as a defense. I knew all the dirty jokes about fags and queers. Then, when I was about thirty-four, I met a guy—gay and good-looking—and I fell head-over-heels in love.

I couldn't handle it anymore. I went out to the piece of farmland that I owned, drove my car into the barn, and made a serious suicide attempt. There was no reason why it failed, except maybe the grace of God. The vent came loose from the tailpipe. I kind of lost consciousness, rolled out of the car, and found myself on the ground when I came to. After wandering around the farm for a while, feeling like the biggest failure ever, I went home and my wife took me to the hospital. She kept telling me that whatever the problem, she would be willing to accept it. When I got to my third stay in the hospital psych. ward, I told her I was homosexual. She was hurt, but there was never a thread of anger. She was so relieved to know what the problem was. I'm not sure I would have pulled through, had it not been for the way she accepted it.

I called my parents to ask them to come to see me in the hospital. It had gotten to the point that I wouldn't even talk to them. They were calling and sending letters, saying they cared about me and were praying for me—whatever my problem, they wanted to know about it and would accept it. But I knew they felt absolute disgust about this issue. When we had a little family conference in the hospital, I told them I was homosexual. They reacted negatively, said it was just so disgusting. My wife told them that if they wanted their grandchildren to be a part of their lives, they would have to accept their son for who he was. They've never talked with me about it since then, but they've accepted it. I love them and they love me, and they see how happy I am. My dad and I have gotten closer. The last few times we've seen each other, we've actually given each other a hug.

I told my children when they were in high school, and we have very amiable relationships. My daughter had a lot of anger toward me, but is accepting things very well. My son is having a tougher time dealing with it and is not real comfortable being around me. He has always been kind of the macho athletic type and is terribly paranoid that someone is going to find out. I think in time he'll be okay.

On the farm, I learned to appreciate nature, and for me being gay is a very natural thing. Some cornstalks do not bear ears of corn, some gilts do not have babies. Normally when you raise breeding stock they reproduce, but not everything fits into place perfectly. On a farm, you accept that some things are out of the ordinary. That has helped me to accept being gay. One time, a neighbor had paid a lot of money for a bull, but it wouldn't breed any cows. It's a natural thing—it happens in nature. I wonder what would have happened to that bull if it had been with a bunch of bulls?

Living alone as I do, there's a degree of loneliness. Farmers are that way too. They have neighbors and friends, but on the farm they're out there working alone. You learn to accept and appreciate the quietness. I love being alone sometimes, but not all the time. I like having a lot of friends. I don't have a lot of real close friends, but I have a lot of good acquaintances. I don't feel compelled to jump in and out of relationships. I was involved in a relationship for six or seven years, and for five of those years I was pretty much monogamous. But I don't feel the need for a relationship now. I would probably be much more promiscuous if it weren't for this whole AIDS situation, but there are ways to get around that. I've had some wonderful experiences in the past sixteen or seventeen years, since I really accepted things.

Farming taught me the value of hard work. I love that good old rugged work ethic. But realizing that I was different and that I was having trouble fitting in, I engrossed myself in long hours of hard work, covered up all of my problems with work. It wasn't all bad, because I got well established and achieved a lot in a few years. I did well in school, and had I been out in the open about understanding my feelings, I'm not sure I would have achieved as much. I don't regret not knowing that I was gay when I was growing up. When I see young kids at the bar, I sort of envy them, that they're able to be themselves, but I feel sorry for them in a way too. They're not going to appreciate life the way I appreciate it. It was a lot of struggle and very lonely, but a lot of what happened to me has made me appreciate what I am today.

Farm people are perceived to be conservative, not the activist type, not as vocal. When it comes to economic issues, I tend to be very conservative. But when it comes to social issues, I'm a liberal. I'm still a Catholic and I'll probably be one all my life, but I take sharp issue with how the Catholic church has been so detrimental to the acceptance of homosexuality. I go shopping for the right priest to talk to. But faith is a very personal thing, and my Catholic faith is still a strong part of me. I'm active in the church and attend on a fairly regular basis, although I'm not as hung up that it has to be every Sunday.

I love to go to New York City periodically. I have a friend there who says I should live in a larger city, where I could have more of a social life. There's a part of me that agrees with him, but agriculture is my life. I like working with farm people, although they don't really understand me. I love their character—their sincerity, their down-to-earth honesty, their love of nature, of things in the open. And I admire good business people, and good farmers are good businessmen. I think the people I work with have a pretty good image of me, but most of them don't know about my personal life. I can't share that with them now, but when I retire I want the word to get out to the people I've worked with—the dairy producers, the veterinarians, the feed salesmen, the guys at the co-ops. They're going to be shocked, but their eyes are going to be opened.

NOTES

1. The Cooperative Extension Service is a national program of agricultural education sponsored jointly by the U.S. Department of Agriculture and state and county governments. Consistent with an emphasis on learning by doing, personal demonstrations are one of the methods used to promote innovative practices in farming and homemaking among farm households.

2. Hoosier Boys State is the Indiana version of an annual program of citizenship training for boys of high school age who have demonstrated leadership qualities. The Boys State program originated in the Midwest in the 1930s and is directed by the Americanism Commission of the American Legion.

John Beutel

John was born in 1943 and grew up on a succession of six rented farms near Monroe, in Green County, south-central Wisconsin. He has four brothers, two older and two younger, and a younger sister. John lives in the country near Stoughton, Wisconsin, where he is a high-school music teacher.

THE FIRST TIME I fell in love with a man, when I was twenty-six, I realized that I wasn't going to walk down the aisle with a woman. Through my late twenties and thirties I had a lot of friendships with men that I thought were relationships, but I was insecure and wasn't capable of focusing. I would lose interest and have to stray and have more sexual partners. In my early forties, during a period of considerable depression, I went through a couple of years with a psychiatrist and pulled some things together, but I still didn't get relationships.

In the last few years I've come to the realization that a large part of my identity has been as a teacher. Every bit of energy I had went into my teaching, to the point that I ignored relationships. And my self-esteem wasn't very high. I'm exceedingly shy and non-aggressive. I still like teaching, and work hard at it, but it isn't the definition of me anymore. I'm beginning to understand who I am and I've gained a lot of self-confidence, whereas before I was just trying to blend in and be nice. For the first time, I'm able to have friendships on an equal footing, and I try not to worry so much about what other people say. I'm more likely to go to the bar and wear what I want to, rather than what I could wear to blend into the wall. This is sort of hackneyed, but—I am what I am. The first time I heard that song in "La Cage aux Folles," I cried and cried.

Now I'm very much up for a relationship. I think I'm ready to talk about the things that need talking about. But now that I'm ready, I'm having trouble getting one off the ground. There are times when I don't like living in the country because I'm alone, and it's lonely for me. But there's also a part of me that says, well, you can be lonely in the middle of New York City. So I've been back and forth about whether to move or stay here. I really like it here—the privacy is very attractive to me—but I still have a longing to live in a large city. But I'm pretty much set in my job right now, and it's very difficult to move. I have the great fortune of being

103

able to travel, and that has made up for not living in a city. I don't want to teach in Chicago, but I think I would love living there. Some of my friends tell me I would come running back here after two weeks.

My father came from Germany with his parents in the 1920s, when he was twelve years old. From when they were married until I was three, he and my mother lived and farmed with my grandparents. My first memory is when I was two years old. We had a housewarming party and all the relatives were there. My great uncle Otto played his accordion, and everybody danced in the living room. I sat alongside the rolled-up carpet and whenever my grandma got the broom they did a German broom dance, and everybody would laugh.

The farms we lived on were all mainly dairy farms. Early on, when my parents started farming on their own, they had just three kids and things went quite well. Riding into town to grind the feed with my dad, we'd sing together—"You Are My Sunshine" and "Bell Bottom Trousers." We had a wonderful rapport and I loved being with him. He had an upbeatness and spontaneity that he lost after a while, as the family grew and times got harder. From early on, before I was in school, I was often out helping my dad do the chores in the morning. I would shake up the bedding for the cows, feed them ground feed, feed the chickens and gather the eggs. Every Saturday, we bartered our eggs for groceries in Monroe. We had work horses until I was eleven or twelve years old, and I would drive them for mowing hay, making hay, and cultivating corn.

Everybody pitched in and accomplished things together. My mother and my older brothers or I would do the milking if dad was with the threshing crew or, later on, if he was working off the farm. From early on, Mom worked jobs outside of the house for extra money. I never knew we were poor. I knew we didn't have a lot of money, but we always had something to wear and great food on the table. No matter what, we would eat together two or three times a day. If Dad was out in the field, we waited till he got there, then we sat down.

Many evenings in the summertime the whole family would play softball after milking, and we played horseshoes and croquet a lot. Every Saturday night we took baths in a big galvanized tub on the kitchen table. Until I was in fifth or sixth grade, we didn't have a bathroom. I was third in line to take a bath and dry off in the middle of the kitchen. Every four weeks, Dad would give us a haircut.

I loved going to country school—the individual attention, the nature walks, putting on Christmas programs. When I was in sixth and seventh grades, I got to help the teacher and I loved it, so I decided that I was going to be a teacher. My plan was to go to Green County Normal School, the two-year teachers' college, and then teach in a country school. However, when I was graduating from high school they were closing the country schools down.

By the time I got to high school, I wasn't real crazy about farming. I never sluffed or got out of doing chores, but my interest was in other places. I really took to music, and my mother liked that very much. She was almost doting at times, and my father was proud too. When I did well in high school, my parents were both very pleased and supportive, which was a source of friction with my brothers. They were sort of rowdy in high school, so my being serious about school and everything was seen by them as my playing the favorite, particularly of my mother. She and I were always very close and we got along very well. There was a certain ebullience and buoyancy; everything was upbeat.

The accordion was really important to me. In my whole life, it is probably the thing that I was best at. I started lessons when I was ten, and practiced a couple of hours a day. I was just in heaven, and my parents loved to hear me play, particularly my mother. Once I was out on the back porch playing, and my mom got a phone call from the cheese factory up the road a tenth of a mile or so. They requested the "Red Raisin Polka." In music, I could be myself and I could lose myself. My teacher said I didn't have to practice seven days a week, but I did. Even when we were making hay all day, I would find time for playing and practicing. If I didn't practice at least five times a week, I was almost distraught.

My aspiration was to be a professional accordionist. I entered a lot of amateur contests around south-central Wisconsin. First prize was fifty bucks, and I thought that was big bucks! For two years in high school I was state champion, and competed in the *Chicago Tribune* Chicagoland Music Festival. I played classic overtures—"The Marriage of Figaro," "The Barber of Seville"—and Mendelssohn piano concertos and a lot of other pieces that were transcribed for accordion. During high school, I was in a pop combo, The Rhythmaires. We had an accordion, trumpet, trombone, tenor sax, bass, and percussion, and would play at school dances and community functions. We did "Moonglow" and "Ja-Da" and "The Darktown Strutters' Ball."

Grandma and Grandpa Beutel were educated to about eighth grade, but they had a real wisdom that probably had the greatest influence on my life. It was such a thrill when Grandpa would let me hoe in his garden, and I always mowed their lawn. Grandma would ask me to help her clean the house, and I got to sleep on their porch. I would get to help Grandpa

"The accordion was really important to me. In my whole life, it is probably the thing that I was best at." John Beutel in 1962, playing for company at home. Courtesy of John Beutel.

decorate the Christmas tree, and if you know Germans, the Christmas tree is *it*, every piece of tinsel. Grandma would often say little rhyming phrases in German, then try to tell me what they meant. She always said, "A house is not a home without flowers." I spoke German almost exclusively with my two older brothers until I was three.

Grandma was sort of like a mother hen, but it was more than that. She and I just clicked on all cylinders together. When she wanted to send letters to my brothers in the army, she would have me sit down at the table, and I would write them for her. At times I felt a little uncomfortable doing that, but Grandma wanted it done, so that mattered. She would say, "This is what I want to say. You make it right and write it down." One of my older brothers loved the accordion, so I made a tape and mailed it to him in Germany.

My grandpa was Prussian and had been a lieutenant in the German cavalry, in World War I, but he was very gentle and soft-spoken. My grand-mother was in the Women's Christian Temperance Union, but not really hard-core. She told me that she would get in trouble at her church women's group, where they would spend more time planning the fall bazaar than studying the Bible. She said, "I'm not very popular there. I told them today, 'I'm here for Bible study. You can talk about the bazaar some other time.'"

My parents were not regular churchgoers, but I was. I went to church with my grandparents when I was in the upper grades and in high school. Church was so important to me that when I was in high school I almost committed myself to being a teaching missionary. Church was a source of comfort, a place where I got positive strokes. I went to church camp in the summer until I got to high school, and then I was active in the youth fel-lowship. I read my Bible, I was confirmed, I tried to be a good person. That's what I thought church was about. We belonged to a relatively con-servative church, Evangelical United Brethren.

When I was four or five years old, I knew there was something different about me because of the things I liked to do. One day, after my dad and I had taken the cows back to pasture, we picked a bouquet of apple blos-soms. And in the spring I would go out to the woods every other day to make sure I saw the first violets. The side of a big hill where I played was covered with blue sand violets and shooting stars, and the woods were sprinkled with Dutchman's-breeches. I thought those flowers were the most beautiful things, and I never heard my brothers talk about them. I had some dolls and a tea set and spent a lot of time playing with one of the neighbor girls. That was the subject of considerable scorn and teasing from my older brothers, but my mom seemed to think it was all right.

Our menus were set—meat, potatoes, salad, vegetable, dessert. Farm staples. I didn't do a lot of cooking, but I liked baking and had a knack for it. I made a lot of jelly rolls and cookies, and I can't tell you how many two-egg cakes I made. I helped a lot with the house cleaning, too. Mother was very tidy, so the house was cleaned every Saturday, whether it needed it or not. I loved to iron and we ironed everything, even the bed sheets. The stuff I did was considered girlish by my older brothers, but it never bothered me enough to keep me from doing it.

We would pick bushel baskets full of peas by 7:00 in the morning, shell them by 11:00, and have them in the freezer by early afternoon. I became the major canner and freezer, and loved helping can peaches. Mom would get two bushels of them at Brennan's Market in Monroe, and when they got ripe we would have a peach canning afternoon. The same with chick-ens and tomatoes we raised. I arranged all the jars according to color so they looked nice on the shelves. There was something about salting things away—you were able to preserve those colors for the winter. I became an excellent pickle maker. We made them in the old crocks, layered them with dill and vinegar, and soaked them in salt water for so many days. When we did our own butchering, I would saw pork chops and wrap them up for the freezer, and help my mom make sausage.

Wherever we moved, we spiffed up the place—threw some sunflower seeds along the barn and mowed the weeds and whatever grass came up. In high school I got heavily into gardening and we had huge, spectacular flower gardens. We lived along the main highway, and people would stop and ask if they could walk through the garden—we had forty or fifty kinds of annual flowers. The *Farm Journal* would occasionally have articles on flower-arranging, with little projects to do. I really got into that, to the point where I entered open-class at the county fair and won best-of-show twice. I would have twenty to thirty entries—stem specimens, arrangements for dining table and coffee table, a basket of mixed garden flowers. I was competing with about fifteen elderly ladies and one other young man.

The old ladies there thought I was a darling. It was a badge of honor, something I did really well without any training. I loved doing it and just did what came to my head. When we cleaned house on Saturday, I'd go out and gather flowers so we would have six or eight flower arrangements in the house for the weekend. If I liked an arrangement, I would make a drawing of it so that I could do it again. I was ridiculed for doing it by my older brothers and my brother just younger, but it wasn't enough to make me quit doing it. I had the approval of my parents and my grandparents, and that held up.

Until I got to high school, I was pretty confident of myself. When I was in country school, everybody played softball, and we would play other schools. I went through elementary school being a really good ball player— I was able to hold my own in games and physical things. But adolescence kicked it out of me. Partly because of my brothers, I lost confidence in my athletic ability. Phy. ed. in high school was probably the worst punishment I ever had to endure. I felt so self-conscious and uncoordinated, and resented having to take it.

As a child, I didn't maintain friendships for very long because we moved so much. I didn't have very many friends in high school because I lived in the country, and at Monroe High School there were the city kids and the country kids. Even some of the teachers talked down to the country kids and were very insensitive. I had a couple shirts that I thought were really pretty, so I wore them to school, and was quite severely heckled by several guys in my class, who gave me the nickname of Wop. I had no idea what it meant, but it really pushed me down. I was very self-conscious and had the beginnings of an inferiority complex, partly because I was from the country. I became very much a people-pleaser, to compensate for what I thought were flaws.

Neither of my parents ever spoke one word to me about sex, and there was nothing taught in school, so I ended up being really ignorant about it. I've heard my mother say that she felt that on the farm we learned about it from the animals. I realized that the bull was let out in the pasture with the cows at certain times, and I knew about cows being in heat, but I never really thought much about it. On occasion I saw penetration, and I helped deliver calves and would see pigs being born. That was about it—not much to go on.

In fifth or sixth grade, I was fascinated by pictures in the *World Book Encyclopedia* of statues of Greek and Roman gods. I drew pictures of them, without fig leaves, and forgot to take the drawings out of my pocket when I got home. When my mother found them, she confronted me and gave me a swat and said that I shouldn't do that anymore. I went into puberty very early, and it was scary because I didn't know what was happening. Hair was coming out from places that I hadn't had hair before. The first orgasms I had were when I was sled-riding. Coming down the hill, I'd do belly flops on the sled and think, whoa, is this great! I didn't know what it was, but I knew there was a big, uncomfortable wet spot on my long underwear.

During high school I started to see interesting magazines and books at a shop in Monroe, where we got our Sunday newspaper after church. The first time I ever read anything about homosexuality was in 1959 or 1960, in a magazine called *Sexology*. It was basically heterosexual, with questions and answers and diagrams, but it did mention homosexuality. I would go into the shop and very carefully read parts of it. There was a new one every month or two, and eventually I even bought a couple of them. Two other magazines, *Young Physique* and *Demigods,* were basically photographs of men in posing straps.[1] I bought a number of them. How I got the courage to do it, I don't know. One day I bought one just before a youth fellowship meeting and sat through the meeting with the magazine hidden under my shirt. When I got home the ink was all over my stomach, but it was great. I would also buy *Playboy.* I found the nudity sensuous, not necessarily the women.

Later in high school, I'd hide my stack of magazines under bales of straw in a shed, and would go out there in the afternoons to take my pleasure reading them and masturbating. Masturbation was a very scary thing for me. I would never do it before a big musical performance, because I thought it would wreck all my notes. One time I masturbated the night before a band concert, and I was just petrified that I wasn't going to be able to play well. I thought that I might be punished by God. I had incredible guilt, and masturbation made me feel more guilty than the fact that I got off on same-sex pictures.

In one of my magazines was a drawing with an arrow sign that said, "To Fire Island."² I started thinking that there must be other people like me, there must be something going on, but I still had absolutely no idea. There were several people in my high school class that I thought were effeminate, and there was always, "Wear yellow on Thursday and you're a fairy," but I still didn't really comprehend being attracted to males. Until I got to college, I didn't know that there were other gay people.

College was the best four years of my life, because I had no labels. I wasn't a farmer, I was just another kid, and we had a great band, a great music department, and I had the time of my life. The first time I was together with a guy, I was twenty or twenty-one years old, working at a supper club in Monroe. I took this guy's order at the bar, and the chemistry was all there. He talked to me a lot and asked me what I was doing later. After I got off work, we drove around and talked. God, my blood was racing hard. After about an hour we had traveled just about every road around Monroe and he got up the nerve to touch my leg. Then everything just sort of happened. When I got back to my car, I thought lightning might strike me. I was petrified.

For a couple of years now, I've been wanting to tell my family that I'm gay. It has caused me a lot of pain, and I'm hoping for courage. The number one thing is my fear of rejection. The other thing is that I don't know how much they understand. My family is very conservative and not particularly sophisticated. I sometimes think that I could come out to my sister, because we can sit and talk for hours. On the other hand, she and her husband are so conservative, her husband particularly. But for all I know, she'd say, "Well, everybody knows." I've had a number of friends who have come out to their families, and they've said everybody knew about them for years.

My dad and I are quite close, but I don't have a lot in common with my family any longer, so I don't know how to relate to them. I did get a cat so we could talk about cats, but I don't have kids, and that takes care of quite a bit of conversation in the family. All four of my brothers were in the army, but I had a teaching deferment. And I'm the only one in our family who has a college education. It has taken my older brothers a long time to deal with that.

Being gay has been a source of considerable pain, but in some ways I think that pain offers something greater. It's sort of a conduit to get to another place. Being on the outside, struggling, has helped me as a teacher. It has given me more compassion for the underdog, the ones who are having problems. I think I serve as a great example as a gay man, in my teaching and in the way I live my life. I try to be a good person, an honest and moral person, down-to-earth. I just don't know any other way to be. Two years ago, when I came out to my pastor, he said that I could only be accepted as a good Lutheran if I abstained. I'm not going to accept the church's definition of me. God made me, God loves me, and I'll duke it out with God when the time comes.

NOTES

1. Until the late 1960s and the 1970s, when explicitly gay-oriented pornography became widely available, physique magazines such as those John mentions provided gay men with erotic depictions of the male body. Many of these publications were produced to look like magazines for body builders and physical culture enthusiasts, but their intended audience was well defined.

2. Fire Island is a narrow, 32-mile-long barrier island just south of New York's Long Island. Gay men and lesbians from Manhattan began creating a summer community on the island in the 1930s. By the 1950s, Fire Island had become an underground gay mecca. The reference to Fire Island that John encountered in a physique magazine alluded to this.

Myron Turk

Born in 1944, Myron grew up with two brothers on a 160-acre dairy and hog farm near Black Earth, in Dane County, south-central Wisconsin. He married at age twenty-five and came out at thirty-eight. He lives on 5-acre hobby farm near Madison, Wisconsin. In this brief narrative, Myron describes seeing his own childhood being relived by his nephew.

MY DAD USED to tell me I was a mistake—that I was supposed to have been a girl, but something went wrong. Since I was treated like I was supposed to have been a girl, I was really confused about what I was supposed to be and how I was supposed to act. Dad spent all his time with my older brother, teaching him everything. I just couldn't work with the machinery well enough to please Dad, and he was not subtle in letting us know if we didn't do something right. I was relegated to being Mother's helper, except when they needed help with things like milking cows, cleaning barns, or haying. I took care of the chickens and the family vegetable garden. We had a big garden and did a lot of canning and freezing. I also took a keen interest in cooking. My mother was very encouraging and supportive of my endeavors, so I was willing to try almost anything.

Dad would make cruel remarks about my brothers and me in front of friends or relatives or other people who came to the farm. He and my brothers were all very slender, while I took after my mother's German side and tended to be heavy. And probably because I was unhappy, food was a consoling thing in my life. Dad would make remarks like, "You got tits just like a woman." I can remember that like it was yesterday, and it's been thirty-five years. I became so self-conscious about my body I almost refused to take phy. ed. in high school, and I would never go swimming or take my shirt off. Even if it was one hundred degrees, I would melt before I would expose myself to any more comments like that.

Mother did the best she could to compensate for Dad's behavior. It's a pretty lopsided world when you're starving for affection and about the only place you're getting it is from your mother, but I'm thankful I got it from somebody. My dad didn't allow my brothers and me to have opinions on anything. We were told what to do and what to feel, and we were

"We weren't that far from town, but I felt isolated and lonely. That's why the animals have been my friends. It was always a great reward to have something alive that you could pet on the head and it would love you for what you were and wouldn't give you a bunch of grief." Myron Turk, age sixteen, with newborn calf, October 1960. Courtesy of Myron Turk.

never allowed to be angry. It was bad to be angry. Dad and I were distant until I got to be fourteen or fifteen, and then it became hostile. I just got tired of being treated like I wasn't even a person, verbally abused and slapped around, so I got back at Dad by being smart-mouthed. It didn't solve anything, but it gave me some increment of satisfaction to outwit him sometimes.

I can see my brother doing to his son what Dad did to us. My nephew is extremely good at breeding dairy cattle and keeping farm records and that kind of thing. But my brother and Dad have ruined him as far as driving farm machinery, because they just belittle him when he makes a mistake.

Now he refuses to drive machinery at all. Although my nephew is supposed to take over the farm, I'm not sure he'll ever get around to doing it.

It's pretty sad—like my whole childhood is being played out in front of my eyes. But my nephew's got it even worse, because he's an only child. My brother isn't physically abusive, but he does a lot of the same things to my nephew that Dad did to me. And Dad goes to the farm every day to help my brother, and ends up doing these things to my nephew, too. Then my mother and my sister-in-law try to overcompensate, suffocating my nephew with attention and protection. I can see so much of myself in him, it's scary. I'm afraid he's going to have many problems before he's found his way in life. I hope he can persevere.

My nephew is seventeen, a big kid, intelligent, effeminate, and pretty lonely. I think he's going to be gay. For years he got dolls and Susie Home-maker kitchen sets for Christmas, and he's so campy it scares me. I feel it would be out of place to broach the subject with my sister-in-law, but I would like to be there if my nephew feels like he has no one to turn to. If I had known somebody who was gay when I was growing up, a positive role model, or had had access to a counselor, I might have accepted myself for what I was and not pretended to be straight and gotten married.

Norm Reed

Norm was born in 1945 in northeastern Ohio. Until he was seventeen, he lived on a small family farm in a Mennonite farming community between Massillon and Wooster, in Wayne County. Norm grew up with two older sisters, an older brother, and a younger brother. He was married for five years and is the father of one child. He lives in the Cleveland, Ohio, area.

GOING TO CHURCH was my own choice. For a while, my father was basically a drunk, and my mother was a run-around whore. It was us kids who felt the need to get involved with church. It was kind of a haven, a nice place to be on Sunday mornings, away from the fighting that Mom and Dad were doing at the house. My parents were very anti-church and would have nothing to do with the little Mennonite community. We weren't Mennonites, but every summer I would go to Bible school for two or three weeks at a Mennonite church. Sundays I would go to a United Brethren in Christ church, sort of a branch of the Mennonite church.

When I was seven years old, I got very involved in praying and reading the Bible and learning as much as I could by listening to every word the evangelist or minister would say. I decided when I was in third or fourth grade that I had to be a minister. When I was ten or eleven, Mom and Dad got interested in going to the United Brethren church. I never had any intention of getting them involved or trying to help them get their lives straightened out, but eventually they kind of got it together as a result of being more visible in the church community. Groups of people would come to our house to have prayer meetings in the backyard. All through high school, I was involved with groups like Youth for Christ. We would hand out tracts at school, inviting kids to come to church. In college I studied Christian education, preparing to become a missionary. After college, my wife and I became heavily involved with church work. We taught in a Christian school for three or four years, and were married for five.

Dad worked in a factory full-time, but had grown up on a truck farm where they sold vegetables for a living. We had only about six acres. We always had four or five cows, barnyards full of chickens, and rabbits. By the time

115

I was seven or eight, it was my job to get up around 6:00 and milk our cows. Then we would have breakfast and go off to school. I milked in the evening as well. Our neighbors about a half mile to the west were Mennonite, and every night when the woman would go out to feed their chickens, she would sing church songs. During the winter her voice would echo across the fields, and sometimes we'd go outside just to hear her sing.

We butchered chickens and rabbits every Saturday during the summer. We would clean and pluck five or six chickens and Mom would use them during the week, mainly for Sunday dinners. She would invite people in— neighbors, other farmers, but the majority were people from the church. After church, there were at least twenty, twenty-five people there for dinner. And during the week there were always lots of people there, a lot of commotion. It seemed like our house had become the center of neighborhood activities.

We had maybe three acres of strawberries and raised our own vegetables, so we all did a lot of work in the gardens. We had a tractor but we didn't have a lot of the equipment that the larger farmers had, so we would go out with scythes and sickles to cut hay. On occasion, Dad would loan his tractor out, or I would drive the tractor to help cut the farmers' fields for them. Our farm sat in the middle of larger dairy farms, and during the summer we would work for the neighbors, give them a hand with baling hay, taking care of their cows, cleaning out stalls, and anything else that they might have to do. It wasn't because we wanted the money, it was because that was the way things were done. If a neighbor was sick or in the hospital or couldn't tend his farm, I would volunteer to take care of his cattle, do the milking. And my dad had a way of volunteering me to do things when I didn't want to.

Grandma and my younger brother and I slept in the same bed for a number of years, and my older brother was in the same room. Everybody wore everybody else's clothes, and I always got my older brother's rags. We did not have running water; we had a pump in the cellar. I always wanted to get away from the farm. My grandmother on my mom's side lived in town and I often asked her if I could come live with her. Sometimes I'd go in on Friday night after school and spend the weekend with her, go to church with her on Sunday and then back home. I'm not sure I liked being with her as much as I liked not being on the farm. Dad was such a mean bastard, nobody ever wanted to be around him. He was always very demanding, rather brutal, and things had to get done his way. He and Mom fought all the time, and he would often take it out on us kids. By the time I was born, my parents had gone through the Depression and the war, and Dad was supporting a family, trying to keep up a small farm and his own job. I think he felt a lot of pressure and was very frustrated.

Mom, on the other hand, was always supportive, pretty much no matter what we wanted to do. And anything that we were a part of, Mom was there—church youth group, Cub Scouts, school band. She was a volunteer cook and room mother, so she was at school every day with me and my little brother. She wasn't overly protective, but she just had to have that grip on us. She didn't want us taken away from the farm or the house too much. I think getting involved with our involvements was her way of showing how much she loved us without communicating much verbally. As far as sitting down and talking and sharing feelings, we never did that.

On Saturdays, Mom would root us out of bed around 5:30, 6:00 so she could rip the sheets and covers off and get her laundry started. My sisters helped her with the house chores. We had two great-uncles—old bachelors, just awful old biddies—who lived maybe eight miles from us. We often had to clean their house, and every year Mom would make me and my little brother clean their darned wallpaper. We always had to be busy doing something. We could never just sit and read a book, and we didn't have a TV. I'd watch Grandma crochet and I wanted to learn how to do that, but Mom didn't want me to learn. She didn't know how to crochet, and maybe she thought that was something she could not be a part of. But Dad said, "Oh, it doesn't matter," so I learned how to crochet, and that was my hobby.

Every Saturday, the neighborhood would get together and have a ballgame. We had a very nice ball diamond in one of the neighbors' fields, and the fathers got together to put up the poles and a net. Some weekends everybody played. There might have been as many as twenty-five, thirty people up there. We always met at our house, then up to the field with our bats and balls and gloves. On occasion, while the fathers were playing with their kids, the mothers would make ice cream. When we were through playing, we'd all get together and have ice cream and cake and pie at our house. My mom had grown up with a friend who was blind all her life. Mom would sometimes go pick her up and bring her over to the house. She loved my mom's fudge, and on an occasional summer night Mom would make a big batch and we'd all sit out in the yard on blankets, eating fudge and talking.

We had so much commotion and no privacy whatsoever in the house, and Mom always had to know what we were doing. I just lived for the days when they would go to a church meeting or somewhere and leave me alone in the house by myself. Those times came infrequently. I used to take long walks, just to be alone, and I loved ice-skating and would often go skating at night by myself on a neighbor's farm pond. On Saturday nights I would meet a friend at the railroad tracks, because his house was a madhouse too. We would flicker flashlights so we could see each other coming, then walk the tracks together for maybe twenty, twenty-five minutes and go our separate ways. One of my friends in grade school lived about two miles from us, so on occasion we'd meet at the pond or do something together in the evening. But his parents were very strict on him too, he had to be home, and they always questioned where he was going. All the parents in that community had such a grip on their kids. You could never leave the house without saying, "I'm taking a walk," or, "I'll be back in an hour." You had to be always in the presence of your parents, for some reason. I think it was just that they had to control what they had.

When I started school, I was kind of a mama's boy. But one thing I made sure I knew how to do was to tie my shoes. My sisters drilled me till I got it right. When we had gym in first grade we played in our stocking feet, and I knew how to tie my shoes, but a lot of the cute little boys didn't know how. If it was a good-looking boy, I would make sure that I was the one who helped him put his shoes on. I'd put his foot in my crotch and tie his shoe for him.

We were never allowed to mention anything relating to sex or pregnancy at home. One morning when I was about ten years old, I was lying in bed rubbing myself, and it felt so good. I ejaculated and I was so scared about it. I thought I was real sick, that I had done something wrong to my body. The next day I said, "Mom, I don't know what happened, but white stuff came out of me." She just said, "Oh, really?"

A lot of times I would take walks so I could masturbate. It wasn't like I could go in the bathroom and close the door, because we had no door on the bathroom, just a curtain. I couldn't do it in bed, because my brother and my grandmother were lying right there. It was just such a hassle; I couldn't be alone to do anything. We were always so afraid of getting caught at anything we did. Mom or Dad or somebody might be watching. And then, because it was such a hush-hush thing, I felt guilty for doing it.

Sometimes, when Mom and Dad would go away for a couple hours, I would go up in Mom's closet and dress up in her high heels and dresses. I wasn't five or six, trying to play mama. I was twelve or thirteen, and I thought dresses were so comfortable. I did that for a number of years and most of the time they didn't know anything about it, until I began wearing her outfits to work in the fields sometimes. It was no big deal. "Oh, Norm's got Mom's dress on again." Once we were out in the field spreading cow shit, and there I was in Mom's high heels, her white gloves and a dress, with my pitchfork. They just kind of accepted it, except one day when I was down by the barn in one of her better dresses. A damned goat started chewing on the dress, and I thought, oh no, Mom's going to really be pissed, so I backed away and the goat ripped it right off of me. But other than that, no one ever said anything about it.

One day I was down at the barn fooling around and a calf started butting me. I thought, oh, this could be interesting. The inevitable happened, but I didn't know what damage I might have done—if it was good for the calf or not, or if it could kill him—so I didn't let him suck me off very often. There was one guy in high school—a drum major—and maybe three or four times we met in the bathroom between classes and jacked each other off. He was tall, thin, and very attractive. I think that was just a sexual outlet for him, but for me it went a little deeper.

I think Mom always knew that I was gay, but it was never mentioned. If we ever sat down and talked, it was always about, oh, this person's doing this, or the grandkids are doing that, or the neighbors, or her church activities. It was never heart-to-heart. In high school, I was going through this turmoil; I wondered why, if I'm a Christian and I believe in God, do I feel this way towards other guys? There were a number of times I would just stand at the kitchen window and stare out. Mom would come up behind me and put her arm around me and say, "Norm, what's wrong? Talk to me." But I could never talk to her. I would just say, "Oh, there's nothing, nothing wrong." I didn't know anybody who was gay. In that community, they would as soon shoot somebody that was like that as they would a mad dog. To them, it's just part of the Devil.

I met the woman that I married in high school, and we went to the same college. She fell in love with me, and I truly loved her. I was still going through the transition from adolescent to adult, not knowing that anybody else like me existed, but regardless of how I felt toward other guys, I wanted a family. The only right thing to do at that time was to get married and have kids and become the missionary that I wanted to be. In my college psychology courses, homosexuals were just briefly mentioned, with no definition. Most of what was in the library was written by very religious-type people, who damned it as very abnormal behavior that could be cured with counseling, and said that there was no excuse for being homosexual.

I got married when I was twenty-two. I had read in some book that the best thing for a person to do if he thinks he's a homosexual is to get married, because the homosexual feelings will subside. Within a month or two, I knew I had made a mistake, because what I had felt toward my wife subsided and my feelings toward men increased. I felt guilty whenever it happened, but every now and then, if there was an opportunity, it was very discreetly handled, and she never knew about it. One day we received a letter from a friend that we had both known in college. In the letter, he revealed that he was gay. I think she was kidding when she said, "Norm, since the two of you were such good friends, does this mean that you're a queer too?" I looked at her and said, "I didn't know he was a homosexual, but I know that I am." I wasn't going to hide anything from her at that point, and she just went nuts. Three years later, we got divorced.

I always tried to be so prim and proper in the eyes of other people. When the divorce came, she ruined my prestigious endeavors in the large church in Cleveland that she and I had belonged to. The minister came to me and said, "There's a law on our books that if behavior like this takes place with any of our members, we have the power to ostracize them." He was not at all willing to talk it through with me. He saw the Devil in me, and if you are a Devil they don't want anything to do with you. He said, "The only way you can enter our building again is if you present yourself to the deacons and confess your sins before us. If we decide to forgive you and we feel that you have made an honest repentance to God for your sins, then you would need to confess your sins in front of the congregation and they would vote on whether they still want you in the church."

It made me so angry, I never went back. I thought, holy shit, why put me through all of this just because I'm gay? To me, being gay didn't mean that much. I had already gotten to the point where I felt it was wrong, but then I felt, hey, this is me. Whether it's right or wrong doesn't matter. It's nobody else's concern. The biggest turn-around for me was how angry I was at those hypocritical church-going people whose husbands were cheating on their wives, or whose wives were having their boyfriends in during the day, or whose little kids were screwing in the church parking lot. These were the church leaders, religious fanatics who have ruined the lives of very good people because they have ostracized them or made their lives guilt-ridden by cutting them off.

Eventually I met some other gay people, got involved with some of the activities downtown, and started going to bars. I'd never been inside a bar. The first gay march we had in Cleveland, I was right up in front, carrying a banner down Euclid Avenue screaming for gay rights, because it just made me so angry to think that I had given my whole life up to that point—I was twenty-seven—basically to God, to the church. Every time the church lights were on, I had been there, picking up kids for Sunday school, Bible school. My whole life had been wrapped around Christian addictive behavior. One night at the baths, a very prominent person in our church walked up to me and said, "Well, Norm, don't be surprised. I'm not." He and I became very good friends. He was also a very religious Christian believer, and he was married and had children. We spent hours on the phone, sharing experiences and how we felt.

As I was finally coming to terms with being gay, my younger brother came home from college and lived with me for a while. I could see that he was definitely gay. "You can't be any different than I am," I said. "You're gay and you're not admitting it." He said he didn't think so, I said I'd prove it to him, and that night I took him to the baths. After that, he and I became even closer and were able to discuss things. He didn't have a hard time accepting being gay, because he never felt guilty, never liked church, never held much stock in any of that. I don't think he ever questioned whether it was right. He was so relieved to find out about himself, he was telling everybody. He told my parents and my older sister about himself, and he mentioned me in there too. He had a big influence on my being forced to better accept it within myself.

There is no explanation for my being gay. The Lord and I have an understanding, and He's just going to accept it the way it is. I have a lot of faith in the Lord and the Bible. I believe the Bible as literally as I can understand it. I've never felt punished by the Lord for being gay. I've been punished tremendously by religious fanatics who thought I was the perfect person, but ostracized me when they found out I was gay. I still believe the same way I did. I just don't practice it by going to some social club that they call church and Sunday school. The attitude that I have now towards fanatical religious-right-type people is probably the attitude my dad had when I was growing up.

I grew up believing that God was very vengeful, and at the same time I was taught that God is love and Jesus forgives. Maybe that's how I finally accepted that there's no problem with my being gay. Until the divorce and the horrendous thing at church, I felt guilty. This is not what the Lord wants; God would not condone this sort of thing. Then I thought, well, I'll just take Him for His word, that He does forgive and that He is a loving God. I believe so much in God's love and in the grace that's sufficient for all of us through Him. He's the one that created me and gave me these feelings. I've accepted this now for eighteen years or so, and I'm happy that I am where I am at this point in life. I'm not afraid of anybody finding out I'm gay, and I don't have to feel guilty or try to hide anything.

I've felt some resentment toward my mom for not telling me that she knew. I feel she should have said, "Norm, I know you prefer being with guys rather than women. There's nothing wrong with that—there's a lot of people like you. Let's talk." It was up to her to acknowledge to me that she knew, not to just keep asking me, "What's wrong?" Had I realized I was gay, I would never have gotten married. I have a son who's twenty-two now. I would never undo what has been done, but it would have prevented a lot of heartache, as far as the divorce and child custody. About a year and a half ago I told my son that I'm gay. He said that he had suspected for a long time. Then he hugged me real tight and held me, and thanked me for feeling comfortable enough with him to let him know. Now we can talk about anything.

I'm so glad to be away from farming. I had my fill of all the animals and the commotion. I think that's why I live alone today. It's so peaceful. I kind of feel bad for people who are growing up in the country, but then in another way I don't, because it's a rich life. We ate well, had good neighbors, overall people were rather kind. In meeting really good, honest, genuine people, I would say I've met the best of them by growing up in that area. Some of those old-timers just cannot be beat. Even though they're anti-homosexual because they don't understand it, they're still wonderful Christian people. If some of them found out I was gay, they would say, "I think I had a cow that was something like that once." It's no big deal to some of those old-timers, and they don't even know what it means anyhow.

It was important that the cows got fed by six in the morning. It was important that they were milked by a certain time at night. It was important that church was attended every Sunday. Everything was important to everybody; you had to be where you were supposed to be at all times, and you had to be there on time. We grew up trusting everybody. Bums would come down the road, and Mom would invite them in and make a big meal for them, give them some extra bread, and send them on their way. I'm very trusting and giving, and I don't expect anything in return. If you need it, fine, take it. If I can help somebody out, I'll do it. That's the way that community was.

My interests were always on things other than country things. When I was maybe fourteen, I had an opportunity to get involved in a local theater where I had gotten a part in a summer play. My dad thought that maybe it was too worldly, so he wouldn't let me be in it. It really makes me mad when I think about the opportunities that I was not allowed to have because it just wasn't right, or it was too far away, or it would cost too much, or it would take me away from the routine of everyday farm life. Other kids grew up in better homes than I did, where there was maybe a little bit more fun and laughter. It was never any fun at home, except those nights when Mom made fudge or when all of us kids would get to throw buckets of water on each other, or just play games. Dad was always there telling us how to do it, or that we weren't doing it quite well enough. And Mom was always there, not necessarily domineering, but just being there.

We never had TV and it was a sin to go to movies. Years later, when I visited a church where I had gone as a kid, I was wearing a tie. A woman came up to me with scissors and said, "You either take that tie off or I cut it off." It was a sin to wear a tie to church—too worldly, putting too much emphasis on yourself. God doesn't want that sort of thing. I just cannot stand organized religion, to have some minister up front befooling everybody from the pulpit.

My mom passed away about six years ago. In her memory, I thought the whole family should get together, and we've been doing it now for six years. When we get together, at least once a year, we have such a good time. Every April, towards May, we meet on my older brother's place in southern Ohio and we have a mushroom fest because, growing up on the farm, we all went out with our bags to hunt mushrooms. There might be forty of us, all the grown kids and their spouses and their kids and their kids. My younger brother brings his lover with him. They've been together for about eighteen years.

I would love to have a lover like my brother has. Maybe ten years ago, I was down at their place and at 5:30 in the morning I heard all this laughing and giggling going on out in the kitchen. I was still in bed and I thought, jeez, they're having a party out there. So I put on my bathrobe and went out and peeked around the corner, and there's the two of them sitting at the table just laughing and telling jokes. They've been doing that kind of thing for the last eighteen years—just like two little magpies. That's the kind of companion I'd like to have. But most people whom I've gotten involved with, there's always something that I have to criticize. Either they're not neat enough or they're not clean enough, or they're too— I don't know. I like things a certain way, and if it's not that way it's just no way at all.

Ronald Schoen

Born in 1947, Ronald grew up with two sisters and one brother on a small dairy farm in Dakota County, southeastern Minnesota. He lives in Rochester, Minnesota. In this brief narrative, Ronald describes why he is willing to "walk a tight-rope" as an elementary school teacher in a rural district.

I ENJOYED living on the farm, but I absolutely hated all the work that was involved. My father still jokes that when he would come in one door of the barn, I would go out the other door, heading out to the woods or down to the river. By my late teens, I had made up my mind I was going to teach elementary school. At that time, very few elementary school teachers were men, but my parents never questioned it. They allowed us to be who we were and to do what we wanted to do, within the confines of Catholic doctrine.

By my second year of college, I was sure I was a homosexual. This realization frightened me, as I felt it would jeopardize my career choice. It had been instilled in me that being a homosexual was incompatible with teaching children. The next three years of college were full of emotional turmoil as I faced one decision after another concerning my sexuality. I read everything about homosexuality I could secretly get my hands on in the college library. I decided that I would never admit to my homosexuality and that I would never practice my true sexual preference. I also decided never to marry, as I considered that to be living too much of a lie. Masturbation became my savior.

After college, I began teaching, got my first apartment, and started to buy pornography. I had my first homosexual intercourse at the age of twenty-four, when I was picked up by an older man on the streets of Rochester. For the first time I said out loud, "I'm gay," but my obsession with the incompatibility of being gay and being a teacher was still overriding. Everything I did had to be methodically thought out as to how it would affect my standing in the eyes of the rural community in which I was teaching. I was certain that as a teacher I could not expect to discover a true, loving gay relationship. That belief left me feeling empty and rather worthless, so I threw myself into my teaching and devoted myself to my students. Fortunately, a two-and-a-half-year relationship in my late twenties helped me open up to love and take pleasure in my sexuality.

I've never wanted to lose myself in a large city or lock myself into a ghetto. My sexuality is a very important part of my life, but it's not the only thing. My profession is extremely important to me. I teach sixth-graders in a rural school district, and one of the reasons I've chosen to stay there is that everybody knows everybody else. It's kind of a family—that close-knit, midwestern sense of home and community. Former students of mine who have graduated and married now have sons and daughters in my classroom.

My sexuality has me walking a tight-rope. The more open I've become with my gayness over the years, the harder it has become to live in this self-imposed closet and be satisfied with my existence in the straight world. On the other hand, my involvement in the straight world, both professionally and socially, prevents me from becoming more involved or open in the gay community. So I'm isolated from both communities.

Even though my profession continues to prevent me from announcing my sexuality, I've become more relaxed in recent years. I no longer feel the desperate need to keep the secret. The number of colleagues who know I'm gay has grown from two or three to eight or nine. Last year, when a colleague began gossiping about my sexuality, I took the direct confrontational approach rather than running scared. It probably didn't stop the gossip, but it did a whole lot for my self-respect.

One day during the summer of 1988 I received a phone call from one of my former students who was then in the eighth grade. He asked me to meet him at a local park. After an hour of discussing minor adolescent problems I asked Chris if there weren't larger problems he wanted to talk about. He then proceeded to tell me that he was gay, that he wanted to tell someone who would be understanding and not offer any condemnation. His two previous attempts to tell someone had failed; one adult had told him that he was just going through a phase. Another had been very affirming until homosexuality was mentioned, then offered Chris a reduced rate on counseling sessions given by his wife.

Our conversation in the park that day lasted for more than three hours, and during the next four to five years I became a mentor to Chris. I helped him establish a pen-pal connection with a gay youth in Minneapolis, and helped him find music by gay artists, adolescent novels with gay themes, and materials on gay history, gay organizations, and current events related to gay issues. AIDS was a regular topic of conversation, as were his social involvements, his crushes on classmates, and his plans for the future.

Once Chris gained his driver's license, it became easier to maintain contact with him. When a gay youth support group was established by the gay/lesbian community in Rochester, he began attending weekly meetings. Chris was in frequent contact with me during his freshman year of college, as I allowed him to call collect whenever he wanted or needed to talk. He came out to most of his classmates, joined the campus gay organization, and had his first serious relationship with another man.

As Chris has matured and developed his own life, our contact has become less and less. It has been almost a father-son relationship as I have watched him grow into an intelligent, articulate, and talented young man. That I was able to help him through the uncertainties, fears, and isolation of his adolescent years is an unparalleled reward. This experience has pointed out to me the importance of rural and small-town gays. So instead of taking my frustration and loneliness and running to a large city, I continue to walk my tight-rope here in rural Minnesota—hoping not only to make a difference in the lives of my students but also, someday, to fulfill my need and desire for the warmth of a love relationship.

PART 2

Coming of Age Between the Mid-1960s and Mid-1970s

Boy in Farmyard, by Jeff Kopseng, based on a photo courtesy of Tom Rygh

Introduction

THE BLOSSOMING of America's sexual revolution and counterculture movements represented the beginning of the end of what Henry Bauer referred to in his interview as "the dark ages of sex." *Life* attempted to shed some light in a 1964 article, "Homosexuality in America," which declared, "A secret world grows open and bolder. Society is forced to look at it—and try to understand it."[1] This article, in a popular photo-news magazine that was a fixture in many rural homes, presented homosexuality as a seamy and unfortunate kind of life. Nonetheless, it served as an important eye-opener for fifteen-year-old Doug Edwards, growing up on a farm in central Indiana, and for Harry Beckner in Nebraska, who was twenty-seven years old and married with two children.

In 1967, CBS television aired a similarly dismissive special report on "The Homosexual."[2] Newsweek described the efforts of an organization of San Francisco clergy to overcome the Bible's "heterosexual bias" in their ministries.[3] Also that year, the television show "N.Y.P.D." became the first network series to portray gay characters.[4] "Where has Hollywood's sudden vivid interest in homosexuality come from?" *Time* asked in 1968. "It comes from what's happening all around," replied John Schlesinger, director of "Midnight Cowboy," a movie about a male prostitute. "Everybody does more or less what he wants to these days, and no one says anything about it." However, *Time* observed that Hollywood's chance to enlighten the public was undercut by the fact that "most of the homosexuals shown so far are sadists, psychopaths or buffoons."[5]

In 1969, *Time* reported that a federal task force headed by psychologist Evelyn Hooker had concluded that "homosexuality presents a major problem for our society largely because of the amount of injustice and suffering entailed in it." *Time* observed that "the report comes at a time when homosexuals are more visible and assertive than ever. . . . Americans can now recognize the diversity of homosexual life and understand that an undesirable handicap does not necessarily make everyone afflicted with it undesirable."[6]

Also in 1969, *Time* published a major article, "The Homosexual: Newly Visible, Newly Understood." It gave the reader a glimpse of the diversity of gay and lesbian lives, included a range of views on whether or not homosexuality was a sickness, and acknowledged the inconclusiveness surrounding the "what causes it?" question. "Homosexuals have never been so visible, vocal or closely scrutinized by research," *Time* stated. "The militants are finding grudging tolerance and some support in the 'straight' community." The article stated that "homophobia is based on understandable instincts among straight people, but . . . also . . . innumerable misconceptions and oversimplifications. The worst of these may be that all homosexuals are alike." The article concluded that America was challenged to come up with ways to discourage homosexuality without making life miserable for "those who cannot be helped, or do not wish to be."[7]

The first television drama to focus on homosexuality from a non-homophobic perspective was "That Certain Summer," a made-for-TV movie that aired in 1972. However, television shows in the early- to mid-1970s also portrayed gay men as sexual predators and lesbians as murderers.[8] Farm boys who liked to read and could get to a library or bookstore might have discovered such gay-positive novels as James Kirkwood's *P.S. Your Cat is Dead*[9] and *Good Times, Bad Times*,[10] Gordon Merrick's *The Lord Won't Mind*,[11] or John Reid's *The Best Little Boy in the World*.[12]

Compared to the men who went before them, those who came of age between the mid-1960s and the mid-1970s generally had less difficulty coming to terms with being gay. A more liberal social climate lessened the pressure to marry, which made it more likely that a gay man would figure out that he really *was* gay before he found himself hitched. And America's sexual revolution increased the likelihood that he could envision a life apart from the heterosexual mainstream. Though limited in scope and usually negative in tone, the growth of gay visibility in the mass media helped to foster the idea of a distinctly gay way of life. But it was apparent that this kind of alternative lifestyle would have to be lived clandestinely, or as part of a fringe community in a large city, and neither of these prospects seemed feasible to many men. An empowering sense of gay community and a more open, mainstream gay identity were just beginning to develop.

David Foster gives a candid account of the emotional and sexual passions and frustrations of a highly romantic adolescent. Some may be repelled by his descriptions of bestiality, but his story is an important illustration of how a socially isolated teenager found an outlet for his sexual urges. In contrast, wet dreams constituted Doug Edwards's only sexual outlet until he learned to masturbate at age eighteen, and masturbation was his sole outlet until his first sexual encounter with another man at age thirty-nine. The insularity of German farm communities figures prominently in what Larry Ebmeier and Martin Scherz say about the ways in which their childhoods have influenced their lives. Richard Kilmer examines the comfortable middle ground he has found between rural and urban; Tom Rygh ruminates on the assets and privations of his small-town life.

Mark Vanderbeek reflects on his efforts to achieve, as an urban professional, the solid self-identity and support he felt as a Nebraska farm boy. Abusive parents are the focus of Heinz Koenig's and Frank Morse's accounts. In contrast, Bill Troxell celebrates his grandfather's gentle influence. Dale Hesterman and Everett Cooper, both recently divorced, examine their hard-won gay identities and the hurdles they faced—for Dale extreme social awkwardness and a poor body image, for Everett the blinders and baggage of a rigorously fundamentalist religious upbringing. John Berg, never so burdened, recalls with fondness his first date—with another teenage farm boy.

NOTES

1. Paul Welch and Ernest Havemann. "Homosexuality in America." *Life:* June 26, 1964, pp. 66–74, 76–80.

2. Described in *The Alyson Almanac*. 1990. Boston: Alyson Publications, pp. 28–29.

3. "God and the Homosexual." *Newsweek:* February 13, 1967, p. 63.

4. Described in *The Alyson Almanac*. 1990. Boston: Alyson Publications, p. 28.

5. "Where the Boys Are." *Time:* June 28, 1968, pp. 80–81.

6. "Coming to Terms." *Time:* October 24, 1969, p. 82.

7. "The Homosexual: Newly Visible, Newly Understood." *Time:* October 31, 1969, pp. 56, 61–62, 64–67.

8. Described in *The Alyson Almanac*. 1990. Boston: Alyson Publications, pp. 32–33.

9. James Kirkwood. 1973. *P.S. Your Cat Is Dead*. New York: Warner.

10. James Kirkwood. 1968. *Good Times, Bad Times*. New York: Fawcett.

11. Gordon Merrick. 1971. *The Lord Won't Mind*. New York: Avon.

12. John Reid. 1973. *The Best Little Boy in the World*. New York: Ballantine.

David Foster

David was born in 1948 and grew up with four brothers, two older and two younger, on a grade-A dairy farm in Manitowoc County, in eastern Wisconsin. He lives in Sheboygan, Wisconsin.

I LOVE TO go to straight bars, but I don't cruise per se. I just like to look at guys. I usually run into somebody that I know from work and that makes me feel confident—if anybody is wondering why I'm there, he'll see that I'm talking to one of the gang, so I'm okay. One time I met two really sweet guys from work at Ten-O-Two, a popular bar in town. I asked, "Are you guys married?," meaning were they married to women. One of them laughed and said, "No, Dave, we're just buddies." I thought that was kind of cute. He was answering me in a gay context, so I knew that he knew I was gay. Usually if we're drinking, things come up and if there's a private moment here or there they'll ask me questions about being gay. They're curious, and sometimes it's to my advantage.

When I'm with buddies from work, I'm very conscious of how I talk and conduct myself. I believe in blending in, maybe because I have to in my job and in this size community. I don't go for guys that are trying to prove a point by holding hands and walking through the mall, saying "We have as much right to hold hands and kiss in public as straight people do." I just don't like that public display, proving to the world that you're gay. I would never take part in a gay pride parade. If I see somebody being ostentatious, earrings galore all the way up the ear or something like that, I think it's too much. I believe in being yourself, but there's a proper time.

I've met some gay people from the bigger cities, and I think there is such a thing as coming out too early. Coming out later is significant in getting a broader aspect of the whole thing. I think I'm more concrete-thinking on a lot of things, not so flitty. You're older when you're learning about things, so you think a little more and can make better decisions, like about doing drag or taking it up the wazoo. I don't do risky things, like public cruising.

132

Mom cleaned the milkhouse every day and did many other farm chores. I helped her with the house-cleaning, gardening, and cooking, while my two older brothers helped my dad with the farm chores. I preferred to work with Mom, but when my two younger brothers became old enough to help her, I was forced into doing some of the farm chores. What I did, I did very well. I've always been a very thorough person, very organized and clean. I did farmwork that way too, cleaning the barn and sweeping the feed into the cribs. I loved side-raking hay, transforming the field of cut hay into neat rows. When I followed the row of hay, it would bug me if I missed any. I'd get off the tractor and take a fork and throw the hay in on the corner. I would wash the glass block windows in the barn after whitewashing. Nobody else would do it, but I just thought it wasn't finished—there was whitewash sprayed on the windows and it didn't look right, so I washed it off before it cured. Once it cured, you couldn't get it off. I was complimented for things like that. My mother would say, "David's the only one that sweeps it that clean." My dad liked my working for him. I never lost my temper, I never complained. We were up at 4:30 in the morning, went out there and did chores, then washed up a little bit and changed clothes. We undoubtedly smelled like the barn when we went to school, but *we* didn't know it.

We had to wear the same pants and shirt to school all week. In high school I was a little self-conscious about that, so I would try making it look like a different outfit by wearing a sweater with the shirt. But everything was ironed, and there was no way that four boys in school were going to change shirts every day, plus all the barn clothes. It was just too much work. Sunday nights the kitchen table went way to one side, and Mom set up the stuff she needed to start right early in the morning washday Mondays—the old wringer washer, and the three washtubs for rinse and bluing, and a scrub tub with the washboard in it. She did the socks and the handkerchiefs on a scrub board before throwing them in the washing machine, and then everything went out on the line.

When I was little, I was such a mama's baby, always hanging onto her leg, that she'd finally just slap me one and say, "Sit down and play." With some of the gifts that I wanted for Christmas, Mom or Dad would say, "Oh, that's for girls," but I still wanted things that other boys wouldn't want, like an Indian bead craft set, a loom to make potholders, a little aluminum tea set, and a Betty Crocker baking set. I had a big Gilbert erector set with a real electric motor, and I really enjoyed that. I loved to watch *The Wizard of Oz*[1] every year. It bugged me because it would start at 6:00 in the evening and I had to go out and milk cows at that time. I was pissed off—they could at least let me watch the beginning when the tornado comes.

David Foster, age thirteen, with Skipper. Courtesy of David Foster.

We were a fun family and had a lot of fun times when cousins and aunts and uncles would come. We had food galore under the big shade tree, and played croquet. I was good at that. We got together at every meal. Supper was when things were talked about, and we were all at home in the evenings. We were tired. We all had chores to do before supper that started as soon as we got off the school bus. We'd get into our farm clothes, feed the chickens and gather the eggs, throw straw down for bedding, put hay down from the mow. Putting the milking machines together was always my job. After supper we'd go out and milk the cows, and that lasted sometimes till 8:00. We'd come in and do school work around the kitchen table under a buzzing fluorescent light, watch a little TV—"The Ed Sullivan Show," "Gunsmoke"—and then we all went up to bed about the same time.

Our clubhouse was originally a chicken coop. I would keep it clean, and asked Mom for some old curtains, ran a stick of wire through them, and put them on the windows. When Mom threw out an old rug, we even had carpeting in there. Aunt Clara lived in Milwaukee and would bring all kinds of old dresses and purses and hats—even little bottles of

"Putting the milking machines together was always my job. After supper we'd go out and milk the cows, and that lasted sometimes till 8:00." *Above,* fifteen-year-old David Foster helps with milking. *Below,* he pours a pail of milk into the bulk milk tank in the milk house. Courtesy of David Foster.

cologne and old lipsticks. My younger brother and I would put this stuff on and parade around. I made a hoop skirt with binder twine and rings from a barrel, and put a big skirt over it. I had heels and nylons and a hat. It was wonderful. My brother liked to dress up in an old suit and put on little wire-frame glasses. He had a cane and walked like an old man, and we'd walk around arm in arm. My parents would laugh and take pictures.

Sometimes people would stop in to buy eggs. I was the guard when my mom would wash her hair at the kitchen sink, where she could use the sprayer. She would take her blouse off and had a bra on. "If anybody comes to the door, tell them to wait." I was a good boy. We were all good boys. We didn't get into town much, and even in town there wasn't anything really bad going on. My older brothers went out for football and track, but I just wasn't into that. I liked gardening, and my mom would let me order some gladiolus bulbs or something different. One year I raised First Lady snapdragons from seed. I started them in an old dresser drawer full of dirt, with plates of glass over it, and I set that by the house at the southern exposure. I nurtured those little transplants, and stuck them all in a big row in the garden. They were beautiful, one of my achievements in my teens. I was good in the garden. The care was there. I looked at things every day to see how much they had grown. We always had a big garden—a big row of raspberries, strawberries, always a big potato field, and a big patch of pumpkins.

Once I asked my dad what the rooster was doing to the hen, standing on top of her with her neck feathers in his beak, pushing his tail feathers behind hers. He told me that it made the hen lay more eggs. As for breeding the cows, Dad used artificial insemination—and even that was a mystery. We had to leave the barn when the breeder man arrived, so I grew up thinking that *he* fucked the cows.

My younger brother and I would play around with our cousins, Linda and Ruthie, in the empty corn crib, showing off how far we could pee, much to their delight. I kind of had a crush on their father, who was very open about taking a leak in the barn. My dad was very prudish. If we'd walk in on him when he was taking a piss in the gutter, he'd quick put his hand there to cover it. My cousins' father would whip it out anywhere. He had a big cock, and he'd just take a piss, and it kind of turned me on. Once in a while he'd come out and help my dad do farmwork. Fixing the chopper, laying there on the ground underneath it, his shirt would ride up and I'd see his belly. It was erotic.

On summer nights it was almost dark before our chores were done and my oldest brother would drive us down to Cedar Lake. On a hot night it felt wonderful to jump into the lake. We would meet other farm boys there, and we had a big tractor inner tube with all our names painted on it. I painted my name close to Rick's, a cute neighbor boy. There were some very romantic nights out there, as it got dark and the crickets were chirping. When I was old enough to swim out to the raft, we would stand around there and get really close. I would go home and fantasize about Rick. I'd kind of wish I were a girl and that he would love me and I could just hold him and kiss him. Once my younger brother said, "David has a crush on Randy." Randy was a neighbor boy who was in high school. If I was in the garden or mowing the lawn when he drove past our place, he'd toot the horn of his hot rod. That just made my nipples hard—I mean, that he would bother. He was just a doll, a heartthrob. In the yearbook it said, "Handsome is as handsome does."

My dad rented out a barn to a man who wanted to raise pigs. Paul was a slob and he smelled like pigs, but he was young and he was always shirtless, and he had a gorgeous, black, hairy chest. I had a real bad crush on him. I think my brothers knew that too. Once in a while I'd be helping my dad milk cows and Paul would stop over in his junky car with a 500-gallon drum barrel of whey to feed the pigs. He'd come in the barn and sit there and scratch his chest and spit in the gutter. It was just so erotic to me, I wanted to grab that guy and pull him into a corner someplace.

I was jacking off before my teens, before anything could come out. My older brother asked me once, "Dave, when you do it, does that white stuff come out?" I looked at him curiously and said no. I imagine he was a little worried, but when it finally happened to me at least I knew I wasn't going to die. I usually jacked off in bed at night and would catch the white stuff in a handkerchief; we all had to keep one under our pillow. One day as Mom was ironing she said, "Boys, whatever you're doing to the white hankies, please stop. I can't get the stains out." So we all started keeping red and blue farmer hankies under our pillows.

Skipper was a beautiful German Shepherd. When he was just a pup, I would take him in the clubhouse and lock the door. Then I'd get naked and lay him on my crotch. He would lick my cock, and when I shot my load he would lick that up, too. Skipper and I played like that all the while he was growing up. When he got a little older I would play around with his cock. He would be standing over me as I lay naked, and squirt his semen in my crotch. It was clear and watery and very pungent. I would jack off at the same time and he would lick everything up, which saved me a lot of trouble. We did this a lot up in the barn among the bales of hay, even in winter. One day Skipper was hit by a vehicle on the highway and his back was broken. I wept as Dad took him up the lane for a ride in the truck, along with a deer rifle and a shovel.

The easiest sex on the farm was blow jobs from the calves. They're always ready when you are. The best blow jobs were from newborns. They were very gentle, but they're born with teeth on their lower jaw. Sometimes I would put two fingers over their teeth. Butch was a Hereford bull, just a darling, with big brown eyes and a white curly head. He was my favorite pet, and all the while he was growing up I played with him secretly. I let him suck my cock when he was little. When I would come in his mouth he probably thought, "Well, finally this teat is putting out." Butch grew into a beautiful, handsome bull. Before running around with the heifers, he was kept in a stanchion. He was used to me touching him all over, so he never kicked when I fondled his balls. They were heavy and solid, and soft as velvet when I rubbed them against my cheek. I would stroke his belly where I could feel his cock still inside him. When a little bright pink carrot came out of the hole in the middle of his belly, I grabbed it. It was wet and hot, grew to be about twenty-four inches long, and increased in thickness to about two inches. I was stroking the length of it with both hands when he shot his clear, watery semen. It all happened very quickly. Then I would go around to the front of him and rub my hands on his nose. He would roll his upper lip back, hold his head high, and make heavy breathing sounds.

Sunday afternoons when I was home alone I did risky things. My older brothers had left home already, and my folks and younger brothers had gone to visit relatives. One Sunday, I walked into the barn and called, "Butchie," and he came walking in from outside almost immediately. I'd heard lots of stories about how bulls can take a mean turn without warning. I put some ground feed in his manger, then hopped over the fence, walked behind him, and fondled his balls. He kept right on eating, so I went all the way with him, jacking him off. I would go in the pen with Butch whenever I got a chance. I would take all my clothes off, except for my shoes and socks, and ride him like a horse. One day, before getting his rocks off, he turned around and started to nose around with my cock, then put his big, wet nose on my chest and started to lift his front legs. He wanted to mount me! I yelled at him and got the hell out of there. He could have killed me. Soon after that, Butch was moved to another farm to run among the heifers and breed them when they came into heat.

Before my affairs with the bull, I was playing around with heifers and cows. When a cow stood in the gutter, it put her cunt at a perfect level to my cock. I would wash her cunt first, then just gently play with the outside of her and talk to her. When she allowed me to finger-fuck her without stepping out of the gutter, I took the final step. After a while I could fuck her as long as I wanted and she wouldn't step out of the gutter. Sunday afternoons in winter, when it was absolutely safe, I would get completely naked except for socks and shoes. I would stick my cock and balls inside of her, then lay my chest against her back, holding her sides with my arms.

One time, when I was in high school, I got caught in the act when my older brother walked into the barn. He just looked at me and shook his head and said very calmly, "Dave, don't do that," as though he had done it, too. And one time I walked in on my younger brother, who was sitting on the barn floor behind a cow that was lying down. He got up quickly and walked away from me. Anyway, I got the idea to fuck a reclining cow, so the next chance I got I cleaned her up and laid a few burlap bags on the floor behind her. If it was pretty risky, I'd leave my pants on—pull them down to my ankles and lay sideways behind her, with her tail over my hip. When I had more time, on Sundays, I'd get naked and sit behind her, straddling her with her tail over my right leg. I had a favorite cow for doing it this way; she would moan a little with each breath she took. One time I sucked one of her teats and after a bit I was getting mouthfuls of milk.

There were men that came to the farm to sell farm products—Watkins products, herbicides, petroleum products, seed corn—and I always found these men attractive. The inseminator I found attractive, the milkman I found attractive. If I was home alone when the milkman stopped in to get the milk, I would fantasize about going up to him and saying, "Would you mind if I played with your cock? Would you come in the clubhouse with me?"

When I was a junior in high school, I had a terrible crush on a very athletic senior. Kevin was adorable and much more mature than the other boys. He had a brown furry chest already. I wrote a love story about Kevin for English class, and I kind of put me in the character of the girl. It was about the prom—"The Infinite Prom"—and they were killed on their prom night in a car accident. I read it in front of my English class. I used Kevin's first and last name, and had to build up my confidence to ask him to sign a document that gave me permission to use his name. I typed it up real nice: "I, Kevin Moore, do hereby give James McKaye, alias Dave Foster, permission to use my full name in this piece of literary work. . . ." He signed it for me, so I had his autograph.

I had such a crush on Kevin that I thought I just had to have him, or I had to tell him how I felt. He obviously knew how I felt. I was just a stupid, silly queer with glasses. I didn't go out for any sports. I was intelligent, but not real intelligent. We had a small plot of woods with gray, smooth-barked trees. On one of them I carved, "In the midst of life, we are in death"—something I had read in a short story. I planned at one low point that I would go there and commit suicide, and they would find me by this tree. On a nearby tree I carved Kevin's name.

They were drafting really heavily when I graduated from high school in 1966. I worked one year on the farm, but I didn't like farming that much, so I went to work at a factory nearby and lived at home on the farm. One summer night, when I got home late, I heard familiar bellowing coming from the barn and knew my pet heifer was in heat. Heifers were skittish, but I had a favorite one that was a little older and liked standing in the gutter. I walked down to the barn. Everything was easily visible in the moonlight. She swayed her back low and swung her tail to one side. I took off all my clothes, she backed down in the gutter for me, and I had the greatest fuck from her ever.

Within less than a year I was drafted. My first lucky break was that I went to military police school instead of infantry. The next lucky break was that I was sent to Japan. I was twenty years old when I had my first experience with a man, in Japan. Guys talked about a fag bar called the Peanuts Bar, and of course I had to check that out secretly. And then it all came together, that there was more of me around than I thought. After I got back from the service, when I was twenty-two, twenty-three, I got ahold of a gay guidebook. I looked up Sheboygan and there was nothing. Milwaukee wasn't too far, so I ventured down there. A lot of the places in the book weren't there anymore, but I did find one, 1000 East, and they had a list of all the current bars and restaurants. Then I knew there was a whole 'nother facet of being gay.

I fell in love with Keith when I had just come out. I had been futzing around with so many guys that I finally felt like there's got to be more to life than this. We got married, exchanged rings and everything—went down to Page Jewelers at the mall and picked out the same band. We were really bold about that. We had a little ceremony by ourselves with a lobster dinner, and I wrote something up—"I promise you this and promise you that"—and it went very well. We had eight or nine years together. But I didn't want to be committed to one man and I tried to bypass the fact that it wasn't great sex, because I liked every other aspect of it.

I fell in love with a straight man and out of love with Keith. Jerry had a little bit of a drinking problem. The first time he came over to our house, it was a hot summer night and I had invited a bunch of the guys from work over. I had lots of beer in the fridge, so we had a party. It got to be dawn, the robins were singing, everybody else had left, and it was just Jerry and me sitting in the kitchen. I put my hand on his and said, "Jerry, do you know that I have a terrible crush on you?" He said, "Yes, I know, and I think you're a hell of a nice guy to party with." I asked him to come upstairs with me. Jerry started to come over a lot and spend the night. I loved to see him, at all hours. Guys like that will go out drinking and then all of a sudden they're alone at the end of the night. They know where to call, they know I've got beer in the fridge. I loved him, and I wasn't going to say, "No, you can't come over. It's three in the morning and I'm here sleeping with Keith." I wanted to see Jerry, he needed a friend, and I knew that with him in that condition I could get away with murder. Keith and I tried to work it out, living as roommates in separate bedrooms, but that worked only for a while.

Keith and I see each other every weekend; that friendship is still there. And he's a big part of my family. They know I'm gay, but we don't talk about it openly. If I get invited to a family function, they'll say, "You can ask Keith too," and he's more excited about it than I am. He's a very lovable sweetheart. Keith is HIV-positive. It was very heartbreaking, but that was at least eight years ago. He sees a doctor two or three times a year and he's doing fine. He just kind of takes it in stride, and I hope he'll continue to go on like that. He's redoing his house, and I'm helping with that. There's a little decorator in me, like all of us.

I get tested once a year, because I've been with a lot of sex partners in the course of a year, but I do play safe. Every time I pick a guy up in a straight bar and he stays overnight I think, if I had a lover I couldn't do this. As long as I can go out and catch one and have a good time, I don't miss having a lover. I can do exactly what I want. But I don't know if that's really good for a person. When you live with somebody, it's give and take. You have to listen to their music once in a while, even if it's solid Barbra Streisand for three hours or "The Sound of Music" twice a year, which was Keith. My aunt has been single her whole life, and she's just a bear to get along with. I'm wondering if that will happen to me.

We always went to Sunday school and church and Bible school. I just went along with all that stuff, but I always doubted any kind of deity or afterlife. I believe that when you die you die, just like a rabbit or dog or cat—it's just all dark. I don't think that's necessarily bad, because you try to get more out of life. I want so much out of life. I've always been an adventurer. I would dream of far-off places, the Peace Corps and going to India, and urban places had an allure. I think Milwaukee is a great town. Other people would like to be away from it all, in a little house in the country or in a cottage up north someplace. I want to be where people are—the symphony or the opera or festivals. I want to be part of it. Sometimes it bugs me to be here alone, climbing the walls. So I go out, just to be with people. I look forward to going to work, because I have good relationships with a lot of guys there.

I've always been a romantic. I get misty easy, and I can sit here and cry over an opera. I'm collecting videos of operas, and they're all the same—love and death or murder or something—but I find every one of them fascinating. I'm sitting here crying as they're belting out the songs. I've never been to a live opera, so I'm going to try it. It's going to be a little difficult to go by myself, but once you're in there and the show starts, it's okay. A lot of things in life you don't do because you wait too much to do it with somebody. I don't know that any of my friends in Sheboygan would go to an opera with me, and I don't know anybody in Milwaukee. But maybe now I will. Maybe I'll see them, or they'll see me. Maybe I'll recognize somebody from the bar, and they'll know that we both like opera, and we'll start seeing each other. Maybe I'll say, "Come up to Sheboygan sometime."

NOTE

1. In the 1939 movie, *The Wizard of Oz,* Dorothy (Judy Garland) goes on a fantastic journey that begins and ends on a Kansas farm. Whether the story is viewed as a fable of being different and wanting to escape, or simply as a fascinating adventure, the annual television broadcast of this classic movie was a special event for David Foster and gay boys everywhere.

Doug Edwards

Doug was born in 1949 and grew up on a 560-acre grain and livestock farm in Hendricks County, Indiana. He grew up with three brothers, two older and one younger. Doug lives in the Indianapolis area, where he works with the state environmental agency.

MY EXPOSURE to gay life has been limited, but I've been around and observed enough that I've drawn some conclusions. One is that a lot of what people perceive as gay personality—lispy talk, faggoty manners—is affectation. Guys are that way because they're around other people who are that way—people who, for whatever psychological reason, want to flaunt their differentness. And if anything has held us back, that has. I know some people who are naturally that way, and they're the sweetest people, and I have no qualms whatsoever about being known as their friend and hanging around them. There are also a lot of guys who obviously behave that way out of affectation.

I've had a couple of boyfriends who started out acting real butch, real regular, and doing a good job of it, and when I got to know them better they slipped into that habit. One I met just a year ago seemed like a regular guy, but the more intimate we got the more he let his guard down and slipped into the lispy speech. It bugged the shit out of me. I really don't think it was his natural way. Of course, others probably view me in much the same way. I'm accused of being butch. And to what extent this is a pose, I suppose *I'm* not in a position to judge. But this influence by association is something gay people really need to grow out of, because it does stigmatize us.

If anti-gay movements proliferate and there is a fascist backlash against homosexuals, I will become an activist and I will come out. I wouldn't do it before that. I think it serves a better purpose to be a regular person and not rub other people's noses in your sexuality. That's one of the big things I have a problem with in the gay rights movement historically. That's probably been more of an impediment than it has been a boost to progress for gay people. Homosexuality is natural for those of us who are this way. We are just as regular as anybody else, because we didn't choose to be who we are, like a black person didn't choose to be black. The prejudice remains, and that's what you have to assault frontally. But first you want to try to persuade people before you clobber them over the head and subdue them.

I don't like this separatist way of thinking. It's at the crux of the problem that society has in comprehending human sexuality. When you think of yourself separately, as a minority, you've ghettoized yourself. We are not separate. Homosexuals are a cross-section of the entire population, and the only thing that makes us any different is the fact that we have different objects of sexual passion. As long as you think of yourself as part of a separate group, I don't think you have any right to complain when other people treat you that way. I am gay, that's a fact of life, and I do not wish to be different from what I am. But I don't think being gay stamps me as special in any way. That kind of self-absorption pulls us down more than it builds us up.

My dad was thirty-six when he married, so he was well into his fifties when he had his last one. I think he made a conscious effort to minimize his sons' involvement in the farm, mainly because we were just tenant farmers. It was not a farm that would be handed down the family, so Dad didn't want to see us nurture the idea of staying on the farm. I think it also had to do with his perception of the social and economic status of the farmer. I think he felt a little inferior by it and, like most dads, he wanted something better for his kids. So he saw to it that we all went to college and took a few steps up on the economic ladder.

Dad farmed in partnership with his brother, but Dad was the brains behind everything, and he was pretty much a man who did it his way because it could be done better his way, rather than having someone else do it and screw it up. I had kind of a reverential attitude toward my dad. In some respects, he was as close to a saint as I think I'll ever know in this life. He was a very quiet man, extremely shy, but very intelligent, someone who could have done a lot more with what God gave him than he had the chance to. But that didn't matter to him. I loved him in a way, but it was not a close emotional type of love. Ours was not that kind of family. My relationship with my mother was a little more difficult. She was very short-tempered, and since oftentimes Dad was in the field working when I was a little squirt, I was around home and more exposed to her. My mother was a very devout Christian, but my dad was an agnostic free-thinker from a Quaker background.

We were a pretty insulated family. The folks were too absorbed in eking out a living to get out and socialize much. I was a solitary and self-sufficient child. Up to about the age of eight or nine, a lot of my time was spent building little model cities in a sandlot or somewhere where the earth was friable. I liked building my own little world. Since we never had much money I didn't have many toys, so I was always improvising with blocks of wood and pieces of pipe. One day I saw a doll house in a toy catalog and I thought, there you have a nice little house, you have little furniture, and you can set it on a street. So I asked for a doll house for Christmas, and Mom took me to Danner's 5 & 10 down in Danville to look at doll houses. She didn't act embarrassed by it, and at the time I didn't *know* to be embarrassed by it. It's not that I liked dolls; I liked models. My oldest brother made a big deal out of that, and for years I was ridiculed as the little brother who asked for a doll house for Christmas.

For a while I wanted to learn to play a musical instrument, so I lobbied my folks, and in my early teens I started taking voice lessons. I also started getting teased rather mercilessly by my oldest brother about this sissy activity, and after three years of it I finally just adamantly refused to go to my lessons. I really didn't like the discipline of practicing, but deep down a lot of it had to do with being pegged as a sissy.

As a five-year-old, I had a crush on a cousin who was in the navy. One summer he was home on leave and came over to help us bale hay. Ryan was a young, good-looking man, and the first time I saw him he was in his navy uniform. When he was there, I didn't want anyone to fool with me except him. I sat in a high window in the dairy barn where we were putting the hay in the mow, refusing to let anyone else lift me down except Ryan. That feeling for Ryan stayed with me for many years.

When I was seven or eight, my older brothers had some friends that would come over occasionally, and they'd usually end up having tag-team wrestling matches in the haymow. Being a little squirt and always feeling left out, I'd try to dart in and get involved. Of course, they'd always try to get me to scram, but I'd keep darting back in. I wanted to be paid attention to, and I was attracted to one of their older friends. I liked to latch onto his leg and I wanted to pull his shoe off. I wanted to see his naked foot.

One of the first sex lessons I got was when I was about eleven or twelve. The cow pasture was right next to the house, and I was looking out the window, just daydreaming, when I saw one Angus mount another. I asked Dad what they were doing, but he was preoccupied and acted like he didn't want to be bothered. I wanted an answer. "Why are they doing that, Dad?" He said, "Well, they do that to make babies." I said, "Is that what you and Mom do?" Snap. He lost it right there, and told me I was not to bring it up again. He was very curt, which was uncharacteristic of Dad.

The first time I knew how it was actually done was from a brother and a neighbor kid who was much more world-wise than I was. One day they told me that the boy sticks his dick up the hole in the girl's ass. I was incredulous. I knew girls had holes, but I didn't know much about it. I said, "They don't do something disgusting like that!" and for the longest time I thought, oh god, how can I ever do that when I grow up?

One day in early November of '64, just out of the blue, I suddenly realized I was gay. I was a sophomore in high school and had a crush on a guy in my class. He was the high-school jock, the best football player the school had ever had, perfect build. I'd had little crushes on teachers and never comprehended them for what they were, but this guy I became fixated on. This was about the time that *Life* magazine ran its famous article on homosexuals. It was a ground-breaking thing that was quite shocking and controversial. *Life* was one of the few magazines we took. I was inordinately interested in it, but I don't think I realized that what they were talking about was me. One night after I went home from school and was up in my bunk bed doing lessons, it suddenly hit me like a ton of bricks. My attraction to this classmate, why I never seemed to have the same feelings for girls that other guys did, why I seemed like such a social misfit, why I was so miserable. Suddenly that night I knew I was homosexual, and from that day forward I knew I would never change.

I was having wet dreams and I didn't know what they were. I was kind of ashamed of it. I would just get a hard-on during my sleep and shoot, and wouldn't know what happened till I woke up. Later in high school, I would spirit away Havelock Ellis's ancient tome, *The Psychology of Sex,* to my little hideout in the haymow. There was a copy of it in my uncle's house that my dad got through a book club when he was younger. It had chapters on masturbation and homosexuality and premarital sex. And that's where I learned about bestiality. I didn't learn it from the animals— I learned it from Havelock Ellis.[1]

The only kind of friend that I had in high school was a fellow who was older than me, a bright fellow, also a farm kid. I got to know him through 4-H. One reason there seemed to be mutual attraction was that intellectually we were on a similar plane. But there was more to it than that; he was a particularly good-looking fellow. But he didn't have a real sense of humor, so he wasn't the kind of a guy that you palled around with. Our friendship was kind of a prim, intellectual palling. But there were a few times where I was aware of some sexual tension between us. Even though I wouldn't think of it explicitly, I knew that I wanted to get in his pants, and he was probably feeling the same thing. What I wanted him to do was seduce me. At the county fair there were a couple instances of horseplay where he momentarily let his defenses down. But he came from a very religious family, so god knows he probably didn't have any experience either. It was the blind leading the blind.

A few other times with guys that I had some attraction to, there would be fleeting comments or gestures, but nothing that would lead to anything. God knows, if they'd tried I would've shut it off, because I was scared of myself as well as other people. But if someone had seduced me I could've been had. In junior high and high school, I often had daydreams about one of the neighbor farmers. I'd go out in the back lot sometimes when he was out in the field nearby, and I'd daydream about him seeing me, getting off the tractor, coming over, saying hi, shooting the breeze. Before you know it, I'm nailed against a rock.

I had read about wet dreams, about coming, and about masturbation, but I did not relate them all. I didn't discover masturbating to orgasm until I was eighteen. One summer afternoon I was up in my hideout in the haymow. There was a little wood-slat chicken coop up there that I'd draped a throw rug over, and the rug just happened to have a hole in the middle of it, about two-thirds of the way down one side. Quite a few times I'd laid on my stomach on that thing and stuck my dick through the hole— didn't whack it off, just stuck it through there because that's what you do with it. I guess at least that much was instinctive. This one day, I must've been fantasizing something particularly vivid and humping away, my dick sticking through the slats of the chicken crate. I got myself so worked up that I did finally orgasm, and I instantly connected that to what happens when you have wet dreams. So I sat there and got an immediate hard-on again, and I jacked off. That's when I discovered I could do it at will. I didn't need to hump a chicken crate, I could just sit there and use my hand. That was wonderful. Talk about freedom, being imprisoned for so many years and finally being free.

My dad had a good friend who was a farmer in another part of the county. Along about the time I was in high school, the story got back to us that his oldest son announced that he was gay. His father, who was already being pummeled by a financial dispute in their family, was devastated. One day they found him hanging from a rafter in the barn; he'd killed himself. I was only vaguely aware of this story, even into my college days, but I began perceiving the dangerous ground I walked on. Not that my dad would have done anything like that. But it would've been real difficult for everybody if I'd had the courage to announce it. We simply didn't talk about feelings, we didn't talk about ourselves. God knows, you didn't admit something that you weren't quite sure of about yourself, especially if it was sexual in nature.

Boy with Angus at Fair, by Jeff Kopseng, based on a photo courtesy of Doug Edwards

Through my college years and my twenties I dated girls regularly, and tried to get in their pants a few times. I never succeeded, but I knew I could get it up for one, and if she had dropped her pants I would've hooked her, and I probably would've liked it for two or three minutes. Marriage was out of the question. I never conceived that I could hide in marriage. Girls scared me, frankly—the idea of what I would do if a girl got me in bed and wanted me to have sex with her. In my late twenties I realized I had to get off this merry-go-round of dating. It wasn't fair to the women and it wasn't fair to me, so I quit. I began to see more and more signs of depression, and I knew it was from loneliness and the pressure of not dealing constructively with my sexuality.

About the time I turned thirty, I started almost annual trips west for hiking, and one of the first trips I took was with a fellow I knew through work. He was two years older than me and also unmarried, a good-looking fellow, an outdoorsman, interested in a lot of the same things I was. We had done some hiking and canoeing together locally before we took a three-week trip to the northern Rockies. Even before we embarked on the trip, I started to fall for him. We camped at a particularly beautiful location in Wyoming and one morning, waking up, I was laying on my back and he was on top of me. He wasn't laying on me, but he was on top of me looking square in my face. Just as soon as my eyes opened he went back over on his side. The sexual tension was so thick by the end of the trip, we were at each other's throats. I fell in love with him. Infatuation is what it was, but that was a first for me. God, I was thinking about him all the time, and didn't know what I could do about it. A few weeks after that trip, I got the nerve to tell him that I loved him, but I didn't reveal that I was homosexual. He had a hard time taking that; he was dating girls, and it was just left at that.

That winter, the depression got quite a bit worse and I didn't know where to turn for help. The year before that trip, I'd had major surgery, and my doctor in Danville had been very aggressive at getting at that problem and getting it taken care of. I thought he would know how I could connect with other people like me. The day I saw him, I told him flat out, "The reason I'm seeing you is because you handled my other problem so aggressively, got right to it and got it solved so I'm physically okay now. Well, I have another problem—I'm homosexual. I'm a non-practicing homosexual." The doctor looked shell-shocked, absolutely flabbergasted, and kept asking me, "What do you mean, non-practicing?" I could not have anticipated his reaction at all. I thought this guy, having gone through medical school so recently, would know how to handle something like this. I told him, in the most specific way I knew how, what I was hoping he would do: "I've got to talk to someone who can help guide me." He mumbled around some and asked a few questions. Finally he said there was an M.D. that he thought could help me.

Dr. Dooley practiced in Broad Ripple, a little artsy community in Indianapolis. At my first appointment, his questions made me uneasy right from the start. "Was your father weak? Was your mother domineering?" I knew I was in trouble when he went down that road. He told me that it was going to take quite a few sessions, but he knew he could help me. "I can make you heterosexual. My brother-in-law used to be homosexual, and I treated him, and now he's married to my sister." Among the techniques he used was aversion therapy. I knew what that was, and I told him, "Excuse me, Dr. Dooley. You're trying to get me out on first base, and I'm already on third." I didn't go back to him.

Two years later, I attempted to come out to a guy who I'd considered my best friend in college. We'd been roommates and I had been best man at his wedding. He was also a farm fellow. I hadn't been much in touch with him for quite a while, but I still considered him a good friend and I needed to tell someone. His wife had a cousin who was openly gay, and they'd talked about him a lot, so I knew he was a little uncomfortable with it, but he didn't seem to be totally put off. I put it to him as delicately as I could. "You talk about your wife's cousin? Well, I need to tell you something about myself. I have something important in common with that person." He knew instantly what I meant. He was rattled, but there was no outburst, and we just left it at that.

A couple months later I was in his part of the state again. I hadn't heard from him and I wanted to find out whether or not anything was left of our friendship, so I called him and asked if I could stop by for a brief visit. He said he was going to be working in the field, but they would be around the house at noontime, so I could come on over then. I hadn't even gotten out of the car when he came out and met me. His dad and grandfather and a lot of other people were at the house. We greeted each other and he said, "You can't come into the house." I didn't even ask why. I saw his wife at the door and his dad peeking around the corner of the house.

There's not much to say about my sexual life between 1982 and '89, just more bouts of depression that I dealt with by myself. I didn't know about cruising in adult bookstores or health clubs, and the thought of going to gay bars scared the shit out of me. I did make a stab at meeting some guys through personal ads, regular guys who had similar interests to mine. All but one of the respondents were not genuinely interested in outdoor stuff, but seemed to be looking for someone to fulfill a flannel fantasy. The one who *was* interested turned out not to have any particular interest in me, but wanted me to turn over the responses of all the other people and get us together for an orgy in the woods. I didn't want to have any part of that, so I went back in the closet.

When I was just shy of forty, I was in a retail bookstore in Castleton one day. The salesman that helped me I'd seen in there before—a very masculine, hot-looking guy. He was real friendly, had a big sunny smile, and we quickly found out that we had similar interests. Watching him write out the special order for me, I saw his nice big angular hands and I thought, god, I'd love to have that hand around my cock. He was just a regular guy, and that's one of the things that I found so appealing about him. He said,

"You want to join me for supper?" So he clocked out and we walked across the parking lot to a restaurant. I began to sense that maybe something was happening, but I was not versed in the game of nonverbal communication. I was still averting my eyes, concealing my interest. I was scared.

TV monitors suspended from the restaurant ceiling were showing a wrestling match, and at one point, in the middle of our meal, a guy got up in the ring and took off his robe. He had a wonderful body, and we both happened to look at it and then saw each other's unguarded reaction. We finished our meal and walked back across the parking lot. I really didn't want to leave it on that loose end and obviously he didn't either, because he finally said, "Doug, do you mind if I ask you a personal question?" I knew what was coming, but I loved the way he put it. "Are you straight?" We made a date and a couple days later was my first sexual encounter. That's when I lost my virginity, thirty-nine years old.

A lot of the problem I've had in coming out, in connecting with people, has been a personality problem—being very backward, shy, scared of people, like my father was. I had to wait till I was thirty-nine to discover what most guys take for granted when they're fifteen. It's a sad story, but the first time was good. I'm grateful that it happened that way instead of at a rest park, or at the hands of my father or an uncle. In all those years I never even came close to having an opportunity to mess with a guy. Why is it that I never got into a situation where I could've been propositioned, or where someone could've just flat out come on to me? I probably did too good a job of concealing my interest, not just acting straight and butch like a good, manly, farm kid should, but avoiding eye contact, avoiding anything that even hinted I was interested.

Later that year, I stumbled onto cruising. I'd gotten a new mountain bike and was riding it around a park on the south side of Indianapolis. A fellow stopped me and we started chatting, and he complimented me on my legs, and smiled. I suddenly became aware of solitary men sitting in cars looking at me. I went back to the parking lot and just sat there and started watching. For months, I would go to that park and just sit and watch, never talking to anybody. I was too scared. Then everything started falling into place. About a year and a half later, I screwed up the courage to go into a gay bar. Several married encounters had told me that the 501 was the place I should go—the Levis and leather bar. I still go to the bars fairly regularly, but I'm pretty much an outsider. I don't talk easily to strangers, and there are some people I simply don't want to have anything to do with.

I started doing volunteer work for the Damien Center in Indianapolis a year ago, paired up with a person with AIDS in a buddy program. My

PWA has lived the life of a street person for many years. He's somewhat retarded, he looks bad, and has real social problems. He likes to go to a local mall to play pinball and shop in record stores, so I knew that would be one of our major activities. One of my brothers recently moved into a house nearby and works nearby. I knew he would see us out somewhere sooner or later, and it would shock the hell out of him to see me with someone like that, so last year I decided I'd better tell him what I was doing and why. I also felt it was time that someone in the family knew that I'm homosexual; I've never liked the word gay. He handled it okay, and said he had suspicioned it.

No way I'll ever give my oldest brother the satisfaction of knowing for sure, even though he's called me a queer ever since I was in junior high school. He's pretty sure of it, but he has not a shred of evidence and I don't want to give him that satisfaction. I hope he goes to his grave not knowing for sure that I'm a queer. If he finds out, that's fine—I'm not going to slink away from it—but he doesn't need to know from me. My other brother it wouldn't bother at all. I'm sure he suspicions, and I imagine his wife does too, but there's no compelling reason for me to say anything to him, so why bother?

Since Dad died and my mother is in a retirement home, I have the majority of the responsibility for looking after her needs. Our relations are cordial, but there's a distance and a tension there because of differences in religious and social outlook. I have a respectful regard for her—a parental love, not an emotional love. My dad in certain respects was the kindest, broadest, most generous-spirited man I ever knew. But he had his blind spots and his narrowness.

Every Sunday afternoon I would go out to my folks' house for dinner. Mom went to a conservative Christian church, and every week the preacher was ranting and raving about some issue. A year before Dad died, the issue was AIDS being God's retribution on the unholy, and that came back to the dinner table. Many other times, I had rebutted things Mom brought home from her preacher, but this time I didn't say anything. Dad stayed silent until finally he just said, "I don't think I could stand to be in the same room with a homosexual." I don't know if it was just a lack of exposure, a lack of compassion, or uncomfortableness about something inside himself. Dad came from a family of all boys who, with the exception of one, were all late to marry. Their excuses were always economic, but money doesn't keep a man from marrying till he's in his late thirties. If you really want to live with a woman, you do it regardless of your circumstances. What my dad's problem was, I don't know, and of course I'll never know. It's not important now.

NOTE

1. Havelock Ellis (1859–1939) was an English psychologist and specialist in human sexuality who called same-sex attraction "sexual inversion." In 1936, his multi-volume *Studies in the Psychology of Sex* was published by Random House, making it available to the general public for the first time since it was originally published in the late 1890s. Until 1936, its sale had been restricted to doctors and lawyers. The volume on sexual inversion was the first book to present a comprehensive and sympathetic perspective on homosexuality.

Bill Troxell

Born in 1950, Bill grew up with one sister on a beef and grain farm operated by his extended family in Clinton County, Indiana. He lives in Indianapolis, but is still involved in raising registered livestock. In this brief narrative, Bill reflects on how the gender roles of his childhood have influenced his identity as a gay man.

ANYTIME I NEEDED to get away to think my own thoughts, I'd go walking through the woods. Often the cows would be in the woods somewhere, and part of my wandering was to connect with them. When I'd eventually find them, over a ridge or down in a hollow, I'd sit down and be with them. I was a part of the herd as far as they were concerned—they were used to me. Off in the woods, lost in my own little world, I felt like I belonged. A lot of my problems were solved sitting on a tree stump in the woods with the cows.

I never wanted to be a tractor jockey, but I could never get enough of working around the livestock as a boy. My dad didn't spend a lot of time with the livestock, but I learned a lot from my grandfather and my uncles. In the springtime, when everybody else was busy doing fieldwork, I was much more at home with the cows—counting them and keeping records on who was bred to who and when they were going to calve. In the summertime I was showing cattle and going to rodeos, where I was belt-buckle-high to a lot of cowboys. That was a great attraction.

At the International Livestock Exposition in Chicago one summer, when I was twelve or thirteen, I was introduced to a couple of steer wrestlers. I couldn't take my eyes off of them. In a moment of pent-up excitement before they competed, one of them grabbed me from behind, lifted me off the ground, and rubbed his big knuckles into my crew-cut head. Watching him compete and slam his steer into the tanbark, I got excited thinking about how playfully rough he had been with me earlier.

I've never been close to my father, but my grandfather on my father's side was like a father to me. He was a tall man, strong and rather quiet. He usually didn't have a lot to say, but when he did, everybody would stop to listen because it was very significant. I had a lot of respect for him and felt a great bond between the two of us. He, like some of my uncles, was the strong yet gentle and unassuming kind of man that is now the kind of guy I'm sexually attracted to: tall, clean-cut, sleeves-rolled-up, suntanned.

My father's side of the family tended to be less demonstrative of their feelings, but my grandfather would do something my father never did—sit down and talk to me. My grandfather always had time for me, and it felt good to touch him and to have him touch me—grab my shoulder, pat me on the head, kiss me goodnight. One time he leaned down to give me a kiss and I could feel his beard stubble on my face. I'd never been that close to a man before, and I thought, wow, that really feels good! Sleeping in my grandfather's room one night, I was awakened when he came in to go to bed. With intense curiosity, I watched him get undressed. After that, whenever I stayed at my grandparents', I would pretend to be asleep so I could watch my grandfather get ready for bed.

I've absorbed the influences of many good people in my life and made them a part of me. I've been influenced not only by strong, clean-washed men with rolled-up sleeves, but also by women with flour on their hands and aprons around their waists, standing behind the screen door and waving at me when I got off the school bus. I identify strongly as a man and I am not effeminate in any way, but I feel like I'm comfortably in balance with both aspects of my family in me—my masculinity, and those parts of me that feel more nurturing and caring.

Larry Ebmeier

Larry was born in 1950 and grew up in Gosper County, south-central Nebraska, on an irrigated crop farm near Bertrand. The oldest of four children, Larry has one brother and two sisters. He lives in Lincoln, Nebraska, with his partner, Donald Freed, where he works as a pharmacist and writer. This brief narrative describes how German Catholic farm culture shaped Larry's identity.

WHEN I WAS thirteen or fourteen, Mom and Dad took my brother and me into one of the bedrooms at the far end of the house to tell us some of the facts of life. In this particular lecture, they told us that situations existed when two men would want each other and get together and have sex. I couldn't imagine how two men could have sex, but they made it very clear that this was one of the most heinous things that could ever happen, within the vast realm of sins categorized by the Catholic church.

Mom was a staunch Catholic and I was very proud to be a Catholic. I enjoyed being an altar boy; I loved the rituals and the structure and the rules. It made me think I was involved with something that was good, a big family. But the church was kind of frightening, especially when I started to understand who and what I was. I was taught, as many Catholic boys were, that the only honorable reason to have sex was to have children after you were properly married. To do it for any other reason was very sinful, and any kind of masturbation was very wrong. I knew it was going to become harder and harder for me to keep in line with not sinning.

I accepted that I was gay very early on, but I didn't really accept it. What I accepted was that it was a fact of my life. But how was I going to work around it? I knew it was something I would have to get control of and make sure that I kept under wraps. I consciously did not want to get intimate with anybody, male or female, so when I was a teenager I ate quite a bit and became quite fat. I wanted to be unattractive and sort of neuter, a sexually anonymous object.

From growing up with a very strict set of rules in the Catholic church, I thought there was a certain way people should be, even though I knew *I* wasn't that way. In my early twenties, the people I hung around with

156

"Being the oldest, I basically was the example when we were growing up, and I pretty much ruled the roost. I tended to lord it over [my brother] Pat and my sisters." *Left,* ten-year-old Larry Ebmeier and siblings in the family's living room. Courtesy of Larry Ebmeier.

were all heterosexual, and I did quite a bit of joking at the expense of gays. Then I fell in love with another young man, and was affected the way an adolescent might be with his first love. But there was a lot of turmoil about sinning—I would go from masturbation to confession to masturbation to confession.

In my mid-twenties it started to catch up with me. I would draw pictures of naked men, and one evening I wrote on one drawing that I had to feel another man's body. I didn't know how I was going to work it out, but it was something I just had to do. It took a few more years, but slowly I started to seek out various local agencies. There wasn't a whole lot in Lincoln in the mid- to latter-seventies. I had my first experience when I was thirty years old, so I was a late bloomer.

After I started to come out and get acquainted with the gay community in my late twenties and early thirties, it seemed like I was the peg that didn't fit. I wasn't a queen; I didn't like to dish. I always tended to feel more at home with some of my non-gay friends. I still feel that way, but less so. It was somewhat of a dilemma, because I knew I was gay but I didn't enjoy the banter, I wasn't into the style, I wasn't into the things they did.

People that I've come into contact with in the gay community tend to be more outgoing, more talkative, less introverted than I am. I wonder if there aren't other people out there who are like me, more quiet and private, not like the gay mafia that you see so much of—the outgoing, outspoken, socialistic, activist, flamboyant and fast-paced, dishing, camping-it-up type of people who seem to dominate when gays come together in urban areas. I know there are a lot of people like me in the gay community, but I never meet them,—maybe because, like me, they're at home stewing over something.

I tend to be on the liberal side of things, but it seems like so much of what goes on in the political arena with gays is a lot of blind following. I'm not a big activist, and I disagree with some of the tactics of the more outspoken gay rights groups, like Queer Nation and ACT UP. I was not behind the civil rights marches back in the sixties, nor did I burn my draft card, even though I was against the Vietnam War. I don't think those kinds of tactics accomplish much, except for a lot of counterproductive things like rioting and bad publicity. You need some noise, but I think that quiet diplomacy and steady laboring behind the scenes is going to get a lot more done.

The gay community could be a lot more effective if they would stop demanding "gay rights" and start demanding "gay opportunities." When we start talking rights, the other side always says, "Why should you have rights I don't have?" I don't want more rights. All I want is the same chance. I want the same chance for a job, the same chance not to be beaten up when I walk down the street, the same chance to get insurance for me and my partner.

If I had been in the heterosexual mainstream, flowing with society, I would have been the first to settle down and marry and have a family. I'm not a drifter or a rover, I'm not a free spirit who goes wandering into the mist and climbs mountains. I'm a play-by-the-rules type of person. I like the idea of having a house, a stable relationship, and a steady job.

When I went through adolescence, I was very much not a part of anything and I developed no identity. That had to come later, and it came in a confusing way and it's still coming. Not that everybody doesn't learn about themselves all through life, but I feel like I'm ten years behind everybody else. I'm not sorry it has turned out this way, though. Had I been heterosexual, I would not have had any reason to question who and what I am. My gut feeling is that I'm a lot more in tune with myself and other people and why they act the way they do, simply because I've had to be.

A large amount of my energy has always gone into wondering what others are thinking. It's almost a curse sometimes. I catch myself doing it and I think, don't you have something better to do with your time? It has tended to make me very aloof and distrusting of friendly overtures by other people, gay or straight. I'm very private and guarded, so I have to rely on my own resources a lot, spiritually and otherwise.

On the other hand, it has made me settle down and be organized and do some things that were probably good for me. It has made me want to be perceived as a stable, solid citizen and a professionally upstanding person. It has made me tend to be monogamous and to put value in a household. Despite all of the negative things I've had to contend with, I'm generally an optimist. If you work hard enough and are organized enough and do the right things, you can make a reasonable life for yourself, which is what I feel I have done.

Martin Scherz

Martin was born in 1951 and grew up on a 160-acre farm in southeastern Nebraska with an older brother and sister. A writer, he lives in southern Wisconsin.

WHEN I GO back home, I feel a real connection with the land—a tremendous feeling, spiritual in a way. It makes me want to go out into a field and take my shoes off and put my feet right on the dirt, establish a real physical connection with that place. I get homesick a lot, but I don't know if I could ever go back there and live, and the place that I remember doesn't really exist anymore. I can go back in my mind easily enough, but when I go back on short visits it doesn't feel like home anymore. A place that was lived in up the road is now nonexistent; the trees and buildings are gone. It's all corn. What I would like to return to really isn't there in a lot of ways, but some of it is. I could probably be happy going back to find those pieces, but it would take a certain amount of compromising on my part, and I'm not sure I'm up to it. I feel alienated in a lot of ways, and it's not the kind of place that would welcome me if I lived openly, the way that I would like to live. I would be shunned.

I'm sure my parents know I'm gay, but I don't think they care to talk about it. I'm pretty sure they view it as something that's my life and not really theirs. We're a family that minds its own business in a very extreme way. What you do is your own business and nobody else's—a real western kind of attitude. You don't ask people about their money or their sex life or anything like that. You wait till they come to you for help, and then you help. I feel that way about a lot of things myself.

My sister knows, but it's just that old "we don't talk about that kind of thing" going on. I suspect that sometime, probably soon, I'll be talking with her about it. Every time I see her we kind of edge up to it, and I would like to. My brother and I don't have a whole lot of contact and our lives have always been so different. We really don't have a lot to talk about. My parents know that I have to live my own life, and they've always recognized that I'm an independent son-of-a-bitch, and I'll do what I want to anyway. I was running away from home when I was three. I wasn't mad

160

about anything; I just wanted to go off. I got all the way to the top of the next hill, which was about a quarter mile. Our neighbor came over the road, stopped and asked how far I was planning to get that day, and brought me back home.

Our place was in the uplands, away from the river bottoms. It was land that was not seen as real desirable when the country was opened for settlement in 1854. The German immigrants, who came over after the Yankees had come onto the bottom lands, got what was seen as the poorer country up on the hills. A lot of the farm was grassland, with scrubby trees along the creek boundary, and some nice timber as you got closer to a larger stream—lots of oak, some hickory and wild walnut. We were on the edge of the Great Plains, so it was rather treed for Nebraska. The farm sloped down to a small creek running through the middle of the land, and there was a lot of rock here and there—limestone and glacial boulders. I spent a lot of time playing by myself down in the creek, building dams and little cities made of mud and sticks. It reinforced the idea that I was somehow alone in the world.

My father operated a bulldozer as well as farmed. During the summer he would often be bulldozing somewhere, building waterways and dams and terraces. When I was little, he was working down on the Missouri River bottoms, clearing trees, and a tree fell on him and crushed his leg. He was out of commission for about a year. We had crops in when this happened and when they were ready to be harvested, all of a sudden one day, the farm place started filling up with vehicles—cars, pickups, tractors, corn pickers. All the people from the neighborhood, from church, from wherever, came and got our crops in that year for nothing.

In the sixties we started to rent more ground as farms got larger. We raised corn, alfalfa, milo, wheat, and every once in a while we put in a crop of rye or oats. Year in, year out, we had cows to milk, and we had a lot of chores. Taking care of the calves was my main responsibility. I had to feed pigs once in a while, but I tried to let my brother do that because the hogs were noisy and I didn't like their behavior. I liked the bovine qualities a lot more. During the summer we spent a lot of time putting up hay, and I was always assigned jobs painting, making fence, and digging russian thistles from the pasture. In the fall we would spend several weekends making wood down in the timber. We built our own sheds for calves and hogs, and in the wintertime we would build gates to use in the next year's fencing.

I did a lot of stuff like any other farm boy would do, but I was always kind of a clown and a cut-up. I liked to make a farce out of everything. I wasn't serious when I should be serious sometimes, and I'd always screw up. I felt like a damn fumbling idiot around farm machinery. My older brother was good at that kind of stuff, and that made me worse by comparison. When I would screw up, my dad would say, "Oh, go up to the kitchen with your mother." I think it was his way of saying that I had to decide whether I was going to be a sissy or whether I could really help on the farm. I think fathers can somehow read that their sons are gay, before their mothers do even. They don't see the whole picture, they just see a part that they're afraid of, and they use a type of fear to try to steer the kid the other way. Lots of times, instead of going to the kitchen, I just went off somewhere. I had books and magazines—history and adventure stories, mostly—stashed in places around the farm, and I would go off and read.

We shared work with aunts and uncles who lived close by. An aunt and uncle lived next to us, another pair lived just up the road a half a mile, and yet another pair lived down the creek about three miles. I didn't like field-work and preferred to work with livestock. I never did cultivate corn. That's like growing up in New York City without seeing the Empire State Building. My dad would've had to take the time to teach me how to do it, and he'd already taught my brother, so why should he teach me when I wasn't going to farm anyway? I think from an early age my parents had a good idea that I wasn't going to farm, and my brother had first say of what he wanted to do, and he wanted to farm.

When we bought the farm in the early sixties, several immediate changes came about. We built a dairy parlor, with stanchions and automatic milking, and thus upgraded to grade A and increased the herd substantially. We got a central furnace—before then, we heated with a wood-burning stove and an oil burner—and we got a refrigerator. We had been using a canister made out of galvanized tin, called a "coolerator," that we lowered into the ground to keep things cool. And we didn't have a television till the sixties sometime. I was twelve years old when they bought that place, and that was about the same time I had my first wet dream. I knew I was living through some big changes, both internally and externally, and was always impressed that things coincided like that.

We were real poor until the sixties, so we did a lot of hunting and fishing and ate a lot of game—squirrels, rabbits, pheasants, quail, and also deer once in a great while. I hunted birds and small game, but not real enthusiastically. An uncle of mine shot a dog that I was very attached to, and killed the pups. My brother and my father were accomplices. That was a traumatic experience and it was just senseless. There was a lot of violence, which I think was one of the reasons why I knew that I wouldn't be farming. I saw a lot of wanton brutality—like whacking animals on the head with whatever was on hand, to drive them. And I wasn't too old before I found out where the cattle were heading when we would load them onto a truck. At an early age, I came to associate Omaha with death, so I didn't want to go to Omaha. I thought I was never coming back.

There was a period when I was in third or fourth grade where I shunned people as much as I could. I would not go to football games with the family. I'd scream and kick and hold onto things to not go. I guess I was really feeling my loner oats. If I had my preferences when I was growing up, I would rather have been with an older person. I grew up with old relatives around all the time, and was always interested in hearing their stories. I spent a lot of time with my paternal grandfather. He lived close to the school, so I would run over there after school was out. We would putz around in his garden, and he would take me down into the cellar and show me the wine he was making, and sometimes we'd sample it. He taught me how to swear, which I always loved him for.

At family gatherings, I would talk with great aunts and great uncles, of whom I had many on both sides of the family. I would ask them about what they did when they were little, and how they did things, and why were we related to them? In high school, I spent a lot of time with my Great Aunt Sophie. I had a deep sense of being rooted in that place and was real interested in family history, so I asked her lots of questions. She had known her grandparents pretty well—my great-great grandparents—so she was a living link with people who had settled in that area in the 1850s.

When I was nine, ten, eleven and didn't have to do stuff at home, I would walk the two miles into town, go into the taverns where the old men were playing cards, and sit and talk with them. I did this until I left home for college. I would spend Friday and Saturday nights in the company of men ranging in age from their mid-fifties to their eighties. The tavern was a community center, a gathering place for families in a European sense—a place to get something to eat, to see your neighbors, to play cards. Otto was one of my real close friends when I was growing up, even though he was an old man. He taught me a lot of little stuff that adds up—how you do something, or how you used to do something, or how you say this in the dialect that he spoke, or jokes or stories or whatever. And there were a lot of other old men that I would just sit and talk and play cards with.

I was aware of an outside world, but I didn't pay much attention to it because it didn't seem to matter in our little community. We were very insular. A lot of the people were from the same villages in Germany and were all related for the most part; cousins were marrying cousins way back, but not necessarily first cousins. I don't think we were too imbecilic. Most of the community was Lutheran. There was one Lutheran church and a small Methodist church right in the village. Out in the countryside there were six Lutheran churches, each within a couple of miles of each other. At least two of them formed because somebody couldn't stand somebody else, so they split, and so did the congregation. It was a contentious little place in some ways.

There were family grudges that had gone on for decades. I knew of one that started around 1900, because of a fence dispute, that still went on when I was growing up. There were grudges between the different groups of Germans. The people from Hanover thought that the Frieslanders were idiots and told them so on numerous occasions. And there was a general distrust of all things from the county seat, which was a large town for that area, about 3,500 people. This town had Catholics and it had Irish and all sorts of other groups. There was distrust of a neighboring village that had a strong French population. And there was a little community of Alsatians between the French and the Germans, just like in the old countries.

There was dislike of people from the cities for the most part, and the word "nigger" was used all the time, and not with any kind of familiarity; there were no black people in our community, and maybe just two or three in the county who lived over on the river. We saw black people coming through to hunt quail and pheasant in the area once in a while, down from Omaha or up from Kansas City. When they stopped in town for lunch they would be extremely talked about by both adults and children. Lots of nigger jokes, Rufus and Liza jokes.

When I was in high school, there was a parade to celebrate the village's centennial anniversary. Among the groups in the parade was a marching corps from North Omaha, composed entirely of black kids. The parade wound around town and ended up in front of the American Legion Hall, and kids were going into the hall to use the bathroom. When a couple of black girls started to go in, the Legion commander charged up to the front door and stood with his legs spread far apart and his arms folded across his chest. "We don't let no niggers in here." The girls kind of shrugged and walked away, and somebody told them they could use the bathrooms at the church down the street. That's when it really hit me that this kind of thing was for real. There had been race rebellions in Omaha in '67, '68, which I was aware of, but I really didn't know what was going on.

It was a sexually naive community, even though it was an earthy community in a lot of ways. What one mammal does with another was all around us. You'd see a bull mounting a cow, you'd get a feeling in your pants, and by a certain amount of rude extrapolation you could figure out that that's what you were supposed to do too. On the other hand, you had this deep Protestant current working against it. You were taught to be a good little Lutheran and to abhor your body, even though it was supposed to be a temple.

Sexual things mystified me for a long time. When a cow would go into heat, my dad would say, "Go out and check which one of the cows is bullin'." We had to separate them and cull the cow and keep her till a "suit-case bull" got there—an artificial inseminator. For years, I was trying to figure out what was going on. At a 4-H meeting when I was about nine, somebody was talking about barrows—gelded male hogs—and I said, "Dad, what's a barrow?" He wouldn't answer me. And I was agog when a couple kids were cornholing in front of everybody in the locker room in fifth or sixth grade.

My brother and I slept together till way too late—till I was about twelve and he was seventeen. He was the first person I ever had any kind of sex with, and not at my initiative. By that time I knew what a hard-on was and I had my first wet dream. I had a vague awareness that sex was something real powerful and that it was something that adults and parents in particular didn't approve of for kids. But then I discovered that I liked it and that kind of complicated things. My brother would act as though he were sleeping, and I felt guilty because I thought I had somehow tempted him and was the one responsible for it. He never fucked me, but there was a lot of other stuff going on for a couple of years. It stopped when he went to college.

When I was about thirteen, I was kind of in love with a boy my age. We would go camping once in a while down by the pond on our place. I was really tempted to have physical contact with him, but we never did. When the weather was nice I would go to my secret spot to jack off. It was on the very back of the farm, a half mile from the house, in a little wet-lands with huge old willow trees. In the middle of the trees was a large, flat stone that my grandfather had dragged out of the field. I would lie on it on my back and look up at the sky.

In high school I spent hours and wasted a lot of gasoline looking for the devil after midnight, as my Sunday school teacher put it—driving around and drinking and making out. My last year in high school, I had sex with a girlfriend from a neighboring town and enjoyed it immensely. We exercised a certain amount of caution, because my sister had become pregnant when she was in high school and my parents were mortified that there were going to be two of us who had to get married. Once or twice they said, "Now, you aren't going to go out and park, are you?" and I'd say I didn't think so, thus avoiding the lie. Beyond that, they never talked about sex and we had no formal sex education in school. It was a matter of trial and error and discovery of oneself.

I knew that I was different somehow, but I didn't ever hear anything about being gay. In high school there was queer day, where people would wear something yellow, but it was just a stupid fad because nobody knew what a queer was, really. In January, 1970, I was a freshman in college and we took off on the winter choir tour. Riding a Greyhound bus at about thirty-five degrees below zero, we hit such points as Emmetsburg and Strawberry Point, Iowa, and Albert Lea, Minnesota. I was tremendously attracted to my choir tour roommate, Richard. We slept in the same bed several times on tour and I was real tempted to initiate something, and I think that he was too, but nothing ever happened. Instead, I wandered into a drug store somewhere in northern Iowa and saw a book, *Good Times, Bad Times*. I saw the word homosexuality and picked it up. I also read a lot of Yukio Mishima in college because I was taking some Asian literature courses, and discovered the homosexual themes in Mishima.[1] I sublimated it to a great degree by smoking a lot of dope and dropping a lot of acid for a couple of years. Then I started drinking again.

After I got out of college, I had a rather torrid affair with a woman for a couple of years. One night I was in a bar, pretty drunk, and the bartender said, "You better not drive home—why don't you stay at my place tonight?" I said okay, no argument at all. When he started rubbing my leg, I thought, oh, I never considered this possibility before, but now that it's happening I think I'll go along with it. I went to bed with him and we had a very nice time. I was drunk but I knew what I was doing. It was really enjoyable but it scared the hell out of me because I didn't know what to think of it for sure. I was shaking like a leaf. We got together a few times after that, and then I left to go to graduate school, where I steered away from sex with men.

Roger and Bill were bachelors who lived together on a farm in our community. There weren't many bachelors who lived together around there, and in high school I had a feeling that something was different about them. "They're war buddies," was the excuse. They really were war buddies, from the Korean War; one of them had rescued the other. Bill was a native of the farm where they lived and had inherited it from his parents. They had beef cattle and did some farming. They also had a ranch out in Colorado, where they spent part of the year.

When I was about twenty-five, I took off from graduate school and moved back home for the summer, the last summer I spent on the farm.

One night I was in town drinking and Roger was there. By that time, I had a pretty good idea that he was gay. We started drinking together and then he said something about going to his place. Bill was away and Roger and I ended up having sex. I saw it as kind of one last fling with a man before I got married. I was dating a woman then who would become my wife a year and a half later. Roger and I never slept together again but we saw each other often in town. He was a real good-time person. I would ask him, "So who's gay around here?" and he would say, "You don't want to know." I think it meant that there were a lot of husbands around there who had been friends of his.

I knew that I liked being with men, but I wasn't sure that was how I wanted to spend my life. I had been brought up believing that to lead a fulfilled and happy life you got married to a woman. I never really considered other possibilities and never considered what a profound effect it would have on me to put blinders on and try to lead a heterosexual life. In 1985, I came out to my wife. She asked me to see a psychiatrist and at that time we were trying to stay together, so I agreed. He really helped me to just decide who I was and what I wanted to do. I realized that my preference was for men and I decided that I needed to live as a gay man. My wife didn't deal well with it, which I can understand, so we were just kind of moving on down the road to separation and divorce.

I was having a couple of drinks with an old college friend, who I later found out was also gay and married. He said, "You heard about Richard didn't you?" I said no. "He's dead." I'd lost contact with Richard—my old choir tour roommate—quite a while before that, and it turns out he died from AIDS. That spurred me to quit living a lie. I decided that night that I was going to set a date to get out of my marriage. A couple of months after that I moved out and started coming out.

There's things I probably would do differently but I'm not going to see that time again so why bother thinking about it? I tend to do something and not look back, which I inherited pretty well from a grandmother of mine. I'm still attracted to women once in a while, but I haven't acted on that in a long time. I guess I'm happy preferring men. I do admit to being a little envious of, let's say, a flaming queen growing up in East Overshoe, Iowa. He knows that he's going to get out of town after high school and that he's going to wind up in Minneapolis or New York or wherever. People like that seem to have things a little more predestined. Having come from the other side of it, where things were so nebulous for so long, I would rather have had them clear-cut. If I would have fallen in love with a guy when I was sixteen, maybe it would have saved me a lot of trouble. The thing I mainly learned is to be flexible—to roll with the punches.

There are things you can't control and there are things you can. Everybody's life has some winter in it and you can't control that, but you can control what you do about it.

A part of me would really like to farm, but I'd have to do it on my own terms. If I had the wherewithal, I would go back to more traditional farming, such as using horses for certain things. I can envision myself doing organic farming, and I would explore the possibilities of truck farming, with the metropolitan areas of Kansas City and Omaha relatively close. In the area where I was raised, the old patterns of farming are disappearing year by year. You don't see nearly as much pasture and livestock. All you see is corn and soybeans anymore. I don't like the direction that farming has taken, the increased industrialization and reliance on corporate power and corporate structure. Bigger farms might mean more production, but the cost in human lives is far too great to be a good thing.

We've lost a lot of the independence of small communities such as the one I come from. For the most part, they continue on a blind descent into some kind of modern hell. The patterns of rural life have disintegrated into a cheap imitation of suburban life. The kids are involved in the same shit that the urban and suburban kids are. They don't have much of a sense of community anymore. They lose their grocery store, they become just a collection of old people living off what years they have left and wondering what their kids are up to a thousand miles away. There's a center of life that has disappeared, and I'm not sure what anybody can do about it anymore. Bring in some Amish? I tend to be a romantic, I guess. The Amish have a good way of life in many ways, and a lot of people could learn a lot of things from societies like that. I admire them, although I recognize that Amish culture can be oppressive to nonconformists.

You wouldn't have to scratch far on me to find out that I grew up on a farm. There are a lot of inferiority complexes bred into rural people and I have them too, but I think growing up on a farm is an advantage in a lot of ways. I tend to be phlegmatic, and I'm not too impressed by things that impress people who grew up in suburbs and cities. I tend to be real cautious and conservative, not politically but in a sense of not desiring to change radically. I'm pretty old-fashioned in a lot of ways. I've always kind of admired village eccentrics and cranks, and I think I'd make a good one. If I did go back it would probably be in the guise of Old Man Scherz. I'd show up at school board meetings and give them hell and speak against censorship. Why aren't you letting them read *Tom Sawyer* and *Huckleberry Finn* anymore? I'd probably start going to church again, just to be a pain in the ass. You have to find your frontiers wherever they exist, and if it's a Bible study group, it's a Bible study group.

NOTE

1. In James Kirkwood's 1968 novel, *Good Times, Bad Times* (New York: Fawcett), the special relationship of two boys at a private school is threatened by the headmaster, a man deeply shaken by a homosexual scandal at the school a few years earlier. Yukio Mishima (1925–1970) was a prolific Japanese writer. His first novel, *Confessions of a Mask*, introduced the theme of homosexuality, which recurred in many of his works.

Richard Kilmer

Richard was born in 1951 and grew up on a 200-acre dairy farm near Wonewoc, a small town in Juneau County, in central Wisconsin. The third of seven children, Richard has four brothers, two older and two younger, and two younger sisters. He lives in Madison, Wisconsin, where he works as a pharmacist and collaborates with lesbian friends in raising his son.

IF I HAD stayed on the farm, I would have never dealt with being gay. I would have probably gotten married and had sex with men on the side. I think a lot of gays don't leave the farm, so there's probably a lot of people out there who are doing that. So many people there are alcoholics, and I think that's what a lot of gays gravitate towards, to kind of deaden their feelings. The mode of socializing and entertainment around there is either the church or the bars or television. There's not much else going on. It would have been very lonely and stifling. I feel lucky that I had the ability to leave and to deal with being gay. I know how hard it was for me, and I'd been to college, I'd traveled, I'd been around people who had very different values than what I'd grown up with.

For a lot of people in the country, there's basically a lot of hard work and not a lot of time to philosophize about their sexual identity. And there's not a lot of resources, not a lot of people around to talk to. Nothing gave me even an inkling that there were gay people out there. Being gay was beyond most people's comprehension. They heard little dirty rumors, but nobody would talk about it, even though probably half the families there had children who moved away who were gay or lesbian. Now it's kind of whispered about. "So-and-so's daughter, she's in Madison, she's one of *those.*" Maybe it was whispered about when I was growing up, but I never heard it. My father's attitude is similar to a lot of people's in those communities. Anybody can be your buddy, friend, neighbor or whatever, as long as they're not too open about what they are. I'm really open about being gay, but my family kind of hides it from people.

"I'm nothing but a dumb farmer" has been my father's theme throughout his life. He always had another job besides the farm; otherwise we prob-

170

ably would have had a poverty-level existence. He worked as a mechanic, so it was pretty much up to my mother and brothers and sisters and me to run the farm while he worked during the day. Maybe it was from listening to my father, but I always felt there was a stigma attached to being a farm kid. Some of the kids I hung around with were from town, so I just didn't feel with-it. I would milk the cows in the morning, and if I didn't have time to take a shower I smelled like the barn at school, and they would make comments on that. And our clothes were a little different.

The people who lived in town seemed to be more sophisticated. They had more money and nicer things. My parents were very frugal. Other kids would talk about going to movies, but it was really uncommon for us to go to a movie. They would talk about going out to eat, but I was sixteen or seventeen before I ever ate at a nice restaurant. Once or twice a summer we would go to a drive-in for a hot dog or a hamburger, and then we'd have to share with our brothers and sisters. They'd all be divided into pieces. I couldn't have a whole one myself because my mother knew I wouldn't eat it all.

When we were younger, we had to do the housework because my father was at work and my mother did the milking. We took turns washing the dishes and cleaning the house. I liked doing that. When we were done, we were expected to help with finishing the milking and washing the milking equipment. As we got a little older, seven or eight, we were milking cows. That was one of my favorite jobs. Eventually we were milking thirty-five or forty cows. I felt like I could understand the cows more than anybody else could. I could kind of sense if a cow was sick; there was just something off about the way she would stand or move. Anytime my father would beat a cow, I would have trouble dealing with it.

I kept records on the cattle and was always upset that my parents weren't more interested in keeping better records or getting registered cattle. For me, it was easy to know every calf and every cow, to know who their mother was and who their offspring were. I would say, "That cow's mother was so-and-so, and that's why she's such a good cow. How do you know which ones to keep if you don't remember who their mothers are? You want to keep the ones that are out of the good cows, not the ones from the cows that are mean or don't milk very well." Every year, my father would sell half of the heifers before they had their first calf. I would say to him, "Take those five heifers and hide them somewhere so the cattle buyer doesn't see them. They're out of your best cows. He's going to pick your ten best ones, and you're going to be left with the ten that are okay but not great. You're not helping your herd by doing that."

We went to the neighbors one day when one of our heifers was missing. They said, "Well, if you can identify it, we'll give it to you. Otherwise, it's ours." I said, "Well, it looks just like this . . .," and sure enough it did. It amazed my parents that I could describe every animal to a tee, but it was just a given that I would know those things. It was the same in school. It was a given that I would get A's and my brothers would get mediocre grades. My older brother would say I was always the favorite of my parents, that everything I did was wonderful and everything he did was not. It's just that I really enjoyed doing the work; I really cared, and he didn't. I was fastidious. "No, that's not clean enough, you've got to clean those better. And this is a mess, you've got to pick this up." I could be a little bossy about things, just a little tyrant.

If a Catholic married a Lutheran, it was a scandal. You married in your church or you didn't marry. People were so conservative and so racist, making comments about niggers all the time. We even had a priest who would make comments about how black people were taking over the world. He wouldn't preach it from the pulpit, but he would preach it in people's homes. They had no experience with blacks at all, except maybe through relatives who lived in Chicago or Beloit. All my uncle would talk about was how bad the niggers were in Beloit. From six or seven on, it was sickening to me. One of my cousins would say, "Why do these people hate like that?" Everybody else seemed to be oblivious to it.

I felt like a fish out of water, because I had such different ideas and feelings about things. Why would I think it was wrong, from early on, that people made racist remarks? Maybe it was because I felt I was different and didn't fit in. From my earliest memory, I knew I was gay, so I always had this part of me that I had to hide. I thought if people knew, they would never think I was this wonderful person, so I overcompensated by being a dutiful son—getting good grades, being polite, not drinking, doing the things I was supposed to, going to church and being the altar boy. I felt it wasn't fair that my mother would be out working on the farm and then she would have to come in and cook the meal while everybody else sat around. So I became her helpmate, setting the table and doing those kinds of things, even as I got older.

We kids would play for hours in the woods, building dams and forts, and we had secret spots that we would go to—rocks and caves and streams. We liked to play on cliffs that overlooked the stream. It was a big drop, and we would be crawling all over them. We had a secret trail that couldn't be seen because the trees covered it. We could duck behind the trees and there was a narrow ledge that would take us down to the stream. It felt like kind of a magical spot. We built a little cabin on top of the cliff, under a ledge that was the cliff above it.

From fourth or fifth grade, kids were using the word queer. If you wore white sox, you were queer. Of if you wore a certain color shirt on a certain day, you were queer. But sissy was the word they would use more often. I would be called a sissy when I played with girls, but I didn't let it bother me. My older brother used to call me the little woman when he was mad at me. "Your eyes are too big. You're like a woman." I think he was jealous because I was well-liked and I always did everything right. He was drinking at fifteen.

If you're under ten or so, it's pretty normal for a boy to be doing house-work. But if you're over ten, you'd better be out doing men's work, driv-ing a tractor and that kind of thing. I wasn't real thrilled about driving tractors—it was just too overwhelming—but I liked doing the things that I could kind of daydream while doing, like raking hay. I did the harvest-ing work, but it was messy and smelly, with all the machinery and the fumes and the noise. I'd be covered with dirt and chaff, and it would be down my back.

In Future Farmers of America, I showed and judged cattle, and I was involved with 4-H for quite a few years. It was good for me because it was based on farm projects, but it was also social and broadened my horizons. When my younger brothers came into 4-H with me, I pushed them to do more than they would have probably done on their own. When I got se-lected for Badger Boys State and for Trees for Tomorrow camp, it was not because I had anybody pushing me to do it. I drove myself to do the things I did. My parents were supportive but they weren't encouraging. Unless I did something bad, whatever I did was okay. With a little more push, I think I could have accomplished more.

My grandpa, my mother's father, was really into tramping through the woods. We'd go on long hikes and he would tell far-fetched tales about In-dians and whatever. I really liked hanging around and going fishing with him. My aunt Evelyn broadened my view of the world. She encouraged me to become a pharmacist, and I think part of it was because she's a hy-pochondriac. She had kind of wild ideas about things, and people thought of her as eccentric. She was interested in bird-watching and other things that people around there had no clue about.

My father was disappointed that I didn't take over the farm, because none of my brothers showed the interest that I did. But I just didn't think it was for me. I needed to get away and see what else was out there. I was going to college and I wanted to travel. I knew that it would be really hard for me to live on the farm, but in another sense I wanted to. I really wanted to be a veterinarian, so I could be involved in farming but have an education and be more mobile. But there wasn't a vet school in Wisconsin, so I went to pharmacy school. That way, I figured, I could live in a rural community, have a hobby farm, and travel.

Later, in high school and in college, I decided I should make a concerted effort to start dating women. I really liked some of the women I dated, but the sex was not satisfying and I always felt I had this thing that I was hiding from them. When I got out of college, I started a commune near a little town I worked in. My friends from college moved out there and it was a lot of fun for three years. We had horses and all the pets that I had wanted as a child. The town was very religious and family-oriented, and they thought we were very strange, all these men and women living together.

In 1977, I took a year off and went on a bicycle trip around the United States and Canada. At the end of the trip I came out. I'd heard that gay people lived in big cities, mostly San Francisco and New York, so I moved to San Francisco. My plan was that I would get in contact with my family eventually, and if they came to visit I would pretend I was straight. There was no way I could integrate being gay into my life as it was. I had to leave my former life and start this new life. My sexuality was like another person, it was not me. To me, being gay was just sex, and it was a total revelation to me that gay people in San Francisco were having relationships, not just sex. I was blown away by all the gay people, and the whole scene felt so threatening. I was looking desperately for somebody to talk to, and that's when I got involved with the Unification Church—the Moonies.[1] They were willing to invite me over and listen. I was looking for this ideal life where I wouldn't have to deal with my sexuality.

When I wanted to go home for Christmas, the Moonies said that if I left, I'd never come back. I said that was a chance I'd have to take. Back in Wisconsin, I was talking with my brother about the Moonies and why I was going to go back out there, when it dawned on me. "You know, Chuck," I said, "I've decided I'm *not* going to go back to the Moonies. I'm going to deal with being gay instead." He said, "Oh? How do you know that?" I said I'd always known. My parents were pretty freaked out that I had joined the Moonies. When I went to see them on the farm, I told my mother that I had decided I wasn't going back, and I wasn't going to get married either. I was going to deal with being gay. She was real calm about it and said she had always known. She said I needed to tell my father, so we told him. He was totally numb, and for the next few weeks he wouldn't talk about it. My mother was so upset, that's all she *could* talk about. She went to a priest that we had when I was a kid, the racist pig, and he said that I was going right to hell and that there was no hope for me.

My mother said that my father cried all night the first night, and that he said he would sell the farm and use the money if it would make me better. I said that was not what I needed or wanted, and that it didn't work that way. My mother talked to another priest they'd had. The rumors were that he had to leave town because he had an affair with a woman. He said that if I hadn't lived in Madison, that bed of sin, I wouldn't be that way. She just needed to pray for me. In desperation, my mother turned to the parish priest they had at that time. She didn't want to do that, because she didn't want people in Wonewoc to know. He said that if God hadn't wanted her son to be that way, he wouldn't be that way—so that's the way God wanted it to be. Then my mother was okay with it, and not too long after that my father said to me, "You are the way you are. You need to do what you need to do. But I don't want to talk about it, okay?" I said that was fine.

All of my boyfriends have been very well-accepted by my family. I was involved with José for seven years, and the first time we went to visit my family on the farm we camped, because we didn't want to stay in the house. The next time we visited, we were going to camp again, but it was raining, and my mother suggested that we sleep in a bedroom that had only one bed in it. After that, when we would visit, that was our bedroom. But José was very religious. "We can't have sex in your parents' house. That would be sacrilegious." I said, "Oh, come on! Either they expect we're going to do it, or they assume that we wouldn't. One way or the other, it's not going to matter to them." The next morning my mother came into our room after milking the cows, sat down on the bed, and started talking to us. It was such a shock!

José and I lived in New York City for a year. That was a mind-blowing experience, living on West 48th, about six blocks from Times Square. I felt claustrophobic, like there was no way I could get out. There was a little community garden where I'd spend my free time. It was really hard. I felt so far away from the country. José said, "You know, you're really not happy here. Maybe you should go back to your parents' farm for the summer." The next day I walked into work and gave two weeks' notice. I came back to Wisconsin and spent the summer on the farm, then got a job and moved to Madison. My aunt and uncle wanted to get rid of their farm, which is a half a mile from where I grew up, so I bought it on a land contract. If I ever want to go back to the farm, I have a place.

My father has liked all of my gay friends because they've always been

Right, Richard Kilmer with his parents and two brothers in the spring of 1956. Courtesy of Richard Kilmer.

interested in him and what he was doing. He takes it as a good sign if people don't treat him like a dumb farmer. He would have difficulty dealing with them if they were talking about being gay or showing any affection in front of him, but if you don't speak about it or make it obvious, then he's fine. It's the way he deals with a lot of things in life; "I just don't want to know about it." My older brother is not real supportive, but it doesn't bother me. One of my younger brothers says I wouldn't have to be this way if I didn't want to be. But I'm not going to change his mind, so it's not worth arguing about. My other brothers and sisters have all been real supportive. They all came to Madison for the first Gay and Lesbian Visibility Alliance march.

A couple of friends had been to the 1987 march in Washington, D.C., and they wanted to do a march in Madison.[2] Their enthusiasm swept me up, so I helped put together the first march, on May 6, 1989. I think there were seven thousand people. We worked for a year and a half to get it together. There was a lot of publicity, and I was very open about being in the news. The Madison newspaper comes to my parents' town, and there

"When I got out of college, I started a commune near a little town I worked in. We had horses and all the pets that I had wanted as a child." Richard Kilmer and Merry Legs in the autumn of 1976. Courtesy of Richard Kilmer.

was my name. I wanted a lot of people to march, not just lesbians and gays but also families and friends, so I asked my family to come and march. I told them how important it was to me, and they came. My older brother didn't, but the rest of my family did, and we all marched together. I was totally shocked that my father came. He was very uncomfortable, but he did it. The weather was very cold and the speeches were a little long, but it felt very good. It was kind of an affirmation of my life.

I could go live on my farm, but I don't. I would probably be supported in the community because I have roots there, but I still have some under-lying fear. I know there are lesbians and gays living around there, but they're very isolated. One of my cousins is gay and he still lives there. He works at a cheese factory and is very open about being gay. He has been harassed on the job, but he gets along pretty well. In rural areas, people who are openly gay are shunned by the other gays and lesbians. They won't associate with them because that points the finger at them, and they want to keep their identity hidden, even though everybody probably knows all their little secrets anyhow.

Madison is so accepting, in certain ways, even more accepting than New York City. In New York you could do what you wanted, everybody was anonymous, but it felt oppressive. Here in Madison, people know each other. It feels like it's kind of the in-between spot for me. I can have a garden here. It would be wonderful if I could have chickens and a goat. It's not living on a farm, but I don't want the isolation of the farm. I like having lesbians and gays around me, having that sense of community. So I'm kind of on the fence, not a farmer but not a city slicker either.

Being from a farm, I always felt kind of different, and that seemed to give me strength to deal with being gay. It's that same sense of not quite belonging. In certain ways, growing up on a farm and then moving to the city was like being from a different country and moving to the United States. I feel like I grew up in a different culture. It seems like gay people who grow up in urban areas are better off, better educated, and better able to function in the world. The city is their territory and they're more familiar with it.

There's something about the way you order your life that's different on the farm. This time of year you need to do this, and this time of year you need to do that. You don't think about anything broader, you just go along with the flow. You're more isolated and think about everyday kinds of things. You know that there are certain times of year that things need to be done, so you can't go and do other things. There's a little bit more responsibility and a more rigid schedule. You've got to be there twice a day to do the milking, even if you want to go do something else. You watch the temperature and you watch the seasons. Rain means something different to me than to somebody who grew up in the city. I think of the farms and the land, and I think, oh my goodness, we really need the rain. Somebody who grew up in the city thinks, oh shoot! I wanted to go to the beach today.

I want to be looked upon as a very good citizen—all of those things that I want people to associate with being gay. Some gay people want to flaunt and be really outrageous. That's just not me. It may bring about some change, but in the long run the people who plod along are going to make more long-lasting change. Everybody who's lesbian and gay should be as open as they can. People need to know that we're out there. I definitely don't agree with people who stay in the closet and lead dual lives. In that way I'm more radical, but I consider myself a moderate. I know people in the radical fairy movement who think I'm pretty yuppie. But I grew up in the hippie days, I started a commune, I was a Moonie. I'm not even close to being a yuppie.

Since I came out, my goal has been to share my life with somebody in a forever kind of monogamous relationship. My dream was to be in a relationship with a farmer, or somebody who really wanted to be on a farm. In that situation, I think I would have really enjoyed living in the country, working outside, and being around animals. Dairy farming would have been very fulfilling. But to do it alone would be too lonely, and once you're isolated there you don't meet people. I've been in one relationship for seven years and one for two years, and I've dated other people. Being gay gets in the way of a relationship, because you have to deal not only with your own feelings about being gay but also with the other person's feelings. José grew up in a Catholic family, and then became a born-again Christian. He had a lot of stuff to deal with about religion and being gay, and it had a huge effect on our relationship and the way he felt about himself.

My son Micah is with me two days a week. I agreed to donate my sperm and to be co-parents with his mothers, lesbian friends who I love like my family. My major concern at the beginning was that he wouldn't recognize me as his father because we would see each other so seldom. But we have a wonderful connection and we get along very well. He's a very bright and confident child. He may get a lot of grief from other people about my being gay and his mother's being lesbian, and I have a little concern about how he'll deal with it. But he's not going to get any more grief than I did. He's surrounded by so many people who love him, and he's got so many opportunities. Maybe I indulge him a little too much. "You want a big hamburger? Fine. You only eat three bites? Fine." When I grew up, I had a third of a hamburger when we would go out to a drive-in.

At Micah's age, I was climbing in a tree or playing in the creek. I could have fallen off a cliff or been washed away by a flood. My parents were working away somewhere and had no idea where I was. I don't even like Micah to be in the backyard by himself. I want to know where he is every second. I'm thankful for growing up on the farm. It felt very free to have all those wide open spaces, and I hope Micah can get some feeling of that freedom from going to my farm.

NOTES

1. In the Unification Church, founded by the Korean evangelist Sun Myung Moon, the religious and political conformity of "Moonies" was strictly enforced.

2. The second national March on Washington for Gay and Lesbian Rights was held in October, 1987. Hundreds of thousands of people gathered in the nation's capital to draw attention to the need for gay civil rights and for more action against AIDS. It was the largest gay and lesbian assembly up to that time, as the first national march had been in 1979.

Heinz Koenig

Heinz was born around 1952, the sixth of six boys, and grew up on a Wisconsin farm. He lives in the Minneapolis area. This brief narrative is adapted from a letter sent anonymously in which Heinz stated, "An interview is impossible. After all these years I am still a victim of being a gay farm boy." Heinz recounts being rescued from abusive parents by a gay man.

DAD WORKED US so hard that all my brothers had run away from home or joined the army by the time I was sixteen. My sixteenth birthday was marked by a demand from my dad that I drop out of school and help him on the farm. Since school was my only pleasant time, I begged him to let me continue. He said I could, as long as I could get all my chores done. I got up at 4 A.M. so that I could finish chores by the time the school bus arrived, then came home at 4 P.M. and worked until 8 before I could begin my schoolwork. I didn't have any time to cultivate friendships and envied those kids who did.

One day my guidance counselor, Lloyd, called me into his office to talk about college scholarships. When I asked my dad to sign the applications, he tore them up and told me in no uncertain terms that college was for queers and draft-dodgers. When Lloyd called me into his office a couple weeks later and asked about the papers, I told him what had happened. I began crying and told him about my life at home. He embraced me and held me as I sobbed. It was the first time I could remember anyone showing me physical affection.

When Lloyd took me home to talk with my parents, my dad struck him and threw him off the farm. I was then taken to the side of the barn where I was tied hands above my head, my pants were pulled down, and I was beaten with his wide belt until blood oozed on my back, buttocks, and thighs. When my screams became too loud, he stuck his bandanna in my mouth and tied it in place with a bit of rein. I was left tied up outside all night, only to be cut loose at 4 A.M. and told to get to work. He threw me a pair of overalls and told me to get used to them because that was all I would be wearing from now on; my school days were over. My mother kept her mouth shut, having been abused by him for years.

180

My blood stuck to the overalls. By that evening I was too tired to do anything but sleep, so I went to my room and he locked me in. I set the alarm for 2 A.M. and woke before it went off, climbed out the window, and got to Lloyd's house by 5. He called the police, who took pictures of my condition. Lloyd pressed charges and the police arrested my dad. At the hearing, my father said that Lloyd was a homosexual who had beaten me to steal me away from my family. My mother was afraid to dispute his word and agreed that Lloyd was filling me with all sorts of notions. I told the truth and Lloyd told what he knew. One of my brothers told how dad had abused him too. The court said that I should be placed in a foster home until I was eighteen, and the judge okayed Lloyd's request that I be allowed to stay with him.

As it turned out, Lloyd *was* gay, but he didn't force anything on me. In the evening we would watch TV or I would do homework and he would kiss my neck and tell me how proud he was of me. I slept with him almost every night—not sexually, but for security. When I got a scholarship to the University of Wisconsin, Lloyd paid what it didn't cover. In Madison, I began to trust people and settled into a good lifestyle. That was in 1970. Lloyd is dead now, but my parents are still alive and I still live in fear of them. I lead a life that is very closeted.

Tom Rygh

Tom was born in 1953 and grew up in southern Wisconsin on an 80-acre farm near Argyle, in Lafayette County. His grandparents, who migrated from Norway, came to the farm in 1912. Tom grew up with two older sisters, an older brother, and a younger brother. He lives near Monroe, Wisconsin, and works as a psychiatric social worker and a writer.

SOME GAY MEN from the farm want to completely erase that part of their lives. I've been through that phase. After high school, I couldn't make tracks away from the farm quickly enough. I didn't even tell people where I was from. I thought that the only way you could have any class was to be urban. My big goal was Madison or Chicago. I thought anything having to do with being gay was going on in the city, in a gay ghetto. Sometimes I still feel that way. But when I came back to the farm and got weaned away from the city, I started to appreciate the feeling of elbow room, being out and away from the city, sort of sitting on the sidelines observing life. But it's a really ambiguous feeling. There are some things that I like about being out here in the boondocks, and there are some things I hate about it, and there are still some times that I really wish I were back in the city.

If I had grown up in the city, I'd have probably been happy to stay there and maybe life would've been easier. It's much easier to make contact and network there, and there's more social support. I sometimes feel like I'm missing out on a chunk of my identity, but I'm not sure I want to go back to living in the city. I'm not sure I'd know how to integrate. Even though I'm living in a predominantly straight rural community, I feel very comfortable with my sexuality. And in some ways I feel freer out here, in terms of being my own person. I'm not sure how much I identify with the gay mainstream, whatever that is. Politically, I'm quite liberal and progressive, but the bar scene is kind of difficult for me. It's been probably a couple years since I've been in a gay bar. When I'm out mingling, even though I'm enjoying myself, I feel like I'm missing a beat now and then. I get nervous and feel intimidated. I don't feel part of it somehow—I feel kind of like it's them and me. But then, I don't know how much I identify with any group.

If you grow up in New York or even Madison, you're probably a little more street-smart. You're more social, you have the right haircut and the right things to wear, and you're always hip to what's happening. That's something I never will be, and at one time it bothered the hell out of me. When some gay people find out that I live in a hick small town an hour outside the city, they don't want anything to do with me. Many city people never venture out into the country, but growing up on the farm, you sooner or later have contact with the city, so you get both worlds eventually. It gives you a full circle of experience.

The farm seemed to be steeped in history. It was the first place in the New World for the family, where everybody learned the American ways. There was a big, elegant, old-fashioned house up on a high hill looking over the Pecatonica river valley. My grandparents hadn't added running water, electricity, or central heating, and we lived like that for several years before my father slowly added those things. Before we put the plumbing in, I carried water into the house from the outside pump. Splitting and carrying in wood for the furnace was another of my chores. Walking over the hill to play with the neighbor kids, there was a feeling of freedom and elbow room. And there was a profound sense of security. You never worried about anything. You had the whole world at your feet, playing along the river, with all these places to hike and explore.

My grandmother on my father's side lived with us for a while. She spoke Norwegian, and she spoke so little English we kids kind of held her in awe and were afraid of her. She certainly wasn't mean to us, but she was very stern. If we'd say the wrong thing, one glance would be enough to put us in our place. She was kind of mysterious, sort of a paragon but unattainable completely. She looked worldly—like something from the outside world—and she was the epitome of grace under pressure. In Europe she had been a city woman, and even here she always looked sophisticated compared to the other neighborhood farm women. She dressed nicely, and she didn't talk or act like them. I think that's where my father got his haughtiness from. On the one hand, he was very liberal. "We don't care what the neighbors think, we'll live the way we want to live." But there was another part of him that was like my grandmother. The neighbors had to think the best of us. We always had to be prim and proper and in our Sunday clothes, so to speak.

We had beef cattle and pigs, and we raised corn and hay for the livestock. When I was really young, my father and his brothers would do all the fieldwork and the heavy stuff. As I got older, my father and I did most of it. Being very stoically Norwegian, my father didn't talk much, and that

"Being very stoically Norwegian, my father didn't talk much, and that was how we were supposed to be." *Left,* twelve-year-old Tom Rygh on the farm with his father and younger
brother. Courtesy of Tom Rygh.

was how we were supposed to be. But when my brothers and sisters were
helping out, we would kind of turn it into a party, laughing and joking.
My father was kind of a perfectionist, and things had to be done on his
schedule, so I really didn't have much say-so or flexibility. Whatever had
to be done, I just did it. As I got into my high school years, farmwork became a pain in the ass. It was drudgery. Day after day, you'd get up in the
morning and never see the outside world. But in the summer I liked being
outdoors and getting the sunshine and fresh air.

I went to a one-room country school up through eighth grade. All
those years, I had only one other person in my grade, my cousin. We were
all little white Protestant kids and one Catholic kid. The twenty-nine or

thirty of us kids would be in the schoolhouse and, on stormy days, it would feel like its own little world. In first grade, I did a lot of bicycling, hiking, and exploring with two boys, my best friends. We would explore old live-stock pens, climb up in the trees, lick little blocks of cow salt, and end up taking off our clothes and examining each other, looking and touching. After that, I went to a different one-room school, so I got split from those two boys until high school. Three or four years later, I took the cousin that was in my grade out to the chicken house and asked him to take his pants down so we could look at each other. He did it very hesitantly and was very uncomfortable, so that was the end of that.

I saw my parents kiss maybe once, and not much touching beyond that. Sex was a taboo subject. Once, for whatever reason, my older sister had typed the word "fuck" on a piece of paper and thrown it into the waste-basket. My mother found it, and the whole house went into silence and shock for three or four days. When I was in first or second grade, we kids found a stack of dirty magazines that somebody had thrown by the rail-road tracks that ran behind the farm. That was just like a gold-mine find. They weren't so much pictures, but writing, describing sex between a man and a woman. We took them home and I read them over and over. Anything like that I could get my hands on, I latched onto. When the Sears Roebuck catalog would come, I'd turn right away to the underwear pages.

We went to church almost every Sunday, and confirmation and Sun-day school and Luther League. I was raised believing in God and the scrip-tures and all that, but when it came to the things I wanted to do or was doing with other boys, it didn't even cross my mind that it was against the Bible or that I was committing a sin. In confirmation, I read the chapter on sexuality over and over again, just to read about the body parts.

I went through grade school with Brian and got along with him very well. He was a year or two older than me and I always thought he was kind of hot. He told stories about going home with this guy and that guy, and humping each other. When I was thirteen or fourteen, my older brother and I went to Boy Scout camp in northern Illinois. One night, all the boys were crowded around the tent that Brian was in because he was jerking himself off and producing semen. It was fascinating.

My older sister had a novel called *Compulsion*, a crime mystery drama, and the back cover said something about two of the main characters hav-ing some kind of homosexual involvement.[1] I sneaked it out of her room and thumbed through it and found a couple of scenes where they stum-bled into bed with each other. It described pretty basically that they had sex together. There was one other chapter which I laboriously went through and finally found where they invited a third guy into bed. He wouldn't, but then it described what the other two did. Every chance I got, I read those chapters over and over.

I hated high school and got involved in as little as I could—just went through the motions for the whole thing. I had this feeling of always swimming upstream, going against the grain. I was a tall kid, so I was expected to do the basketball thing in high school. We didn't have all that sports stuff in country school, and I hated basketball, so I didn't do it. I don't think my father was too happy about that. Our high school was typically small-town, a lot of hoods. My first day, a guy came up to me with brass knuckles and said, "You're about to start the worst four years of your life." Any chance he got, he threatened me. It was really stifling.

In high school, I got reunited with my friend Jim from first grade. Once during phy. ed. we were both sitting out while the other kids were playing, and he was stroking the hair on my leg. I knew that there was stuff going on among some of the guys, both in the locker room and when they'd go home with each other. I'd had a couple invitations that I turned down because I didn't trust them. I was afraid if we did something, they'd spread it around school. Jim and I were pretty close friends through high school, and he was always inviting me to come home with him. I'd never seen a condom before he showed me one. One day during a study hour we did this big fantasy thing, how we were going to take a boat to Europe and sleep together. I was really aroused. I was disappointed when some of these boys started drifting the other way, dating girls. My oldest sister had a book about adolescent sexuality, and the chapter on homosexuality said something about growing out of it as you get older and you date. I wasn't upset when that didn't happen.

There was a wooded glen in the back part of our farm, a long way from any of the neighboring farms. You had to walk up on the high hill to get there, and from the top of that hill you could see for miles. My father took us kids up there once and pointed out barns where people had killed themselves on five different farms. I spent a lot of time back there by myself. Sometimes I would take my clothes off and jerk off, fantasizing about one of the neighbor boys stumbling along and finding me in the act and joining in. A neighbor boy talked about their hired man who would have the calves suck him off. I never could figure out how he dared do that, for fear they might bite. My fantasy was to sneak down there and watch him.

By the time I was a sophomore or junior, I hated farming, I hated the rural community, I hated the bigots and the hicks, I hated having any identity with it. I was ready to go any day. Loneliness was what I was feeling— I'm the only one out here, everything is happening in Madison or Chicago. It was hard to get the free time to go anywhere, because I had to farm seven days a week. By senior year, I had a couple of good friends that were in college in Madison, so I got a weekend away now and then to go stay with them. That was around 1970, '71, and there was all kinds of stuff going on there, the anti-war stuff, the pro-gay movement, and everything. I got to go to campus and see all these good-looking men, and by that time I knew what it was and I wanted it. I had a million fantasies, and I imagined living in an apartment in a city, having lots of friends, being very social, having a good job, no more smell of the farm.

College was a very liberating experience, but my father was getting into failing health, so I went back to help on the farm after college. It was really depressing at first. I was lonely, I was away from everybody I'd gotten to know, and it was back to the drudgery. Through a mutual friend, I met this guy named Jake. He was about twenty, living with his parents and farming. He called me and said he wanted me to go to Madison with him, to shop for some jewelry for his fiancée. We went out for drinks afterward. He knew that I was gay, because our mutual friend had told him. But he was straight. He told me that up one side and down the other. We had a couple of drinks, and somehow we got onto the subject of our bodies. "Do you have hairy legs? Do you have a hairy chest?" I was very aroused by the conversation and I'm sure he was too, although he didn't let on. On the way home he talked about how he wasn't having sex with his fiancée because he was a good Catholic and couldn't do that till after marriage, but he had never done anything with a man and never would.

We got together several times after that and nothing happened. One day he called me, and I told him my father and I had been out putting a new roof on one of the sheds. He said, "Oh, I can just see you out there without your shirt, getting all brown." I got really horny, but he gave me these really mixed messages about being straight, and I bought it. This went on for several months until our mutual friend, who supposedly was gay, was getting married. Jake and I were both in the wedding party and had to spend the night in a motel. After the wedding, he went out and bought a bottle of sherry and brought it to our room. I was getting a little suspicious. Between the two of us, we drank the whole thing, and we started talking about each other's bodies again. I was wearing just a T-shirt and a pair of undershorts. He had on undershorts and a long nightshirt, and I came out of the bathroom just in time to see him slipping the shorts off. Then I was really suspicious.

Jake said he wanted to see what I looked like. Would I take my undershorts off? I said I would if he would. He said he wouldn't, but I knew he already had them off. By this time I was raring to go. I was very attracted to him, and I hadn't done anything in months, living out on the farm.

One thing led to another, and we ended up on top of each other. He didn't have an orgasm, but I most certainly did. Driving home the next day, we talked about it quite a bit; it was never going to happen again. He was going to get married in a year. A week later he was back at my place, and that time he did have an orgasm.

I thought that Jake wouldn't get married, and it hurt me very much when he did. I thought that he would buck his parents and buck the church and buck society, and that he and I would farm together. Two or three weeks after he got married, I started seeing him again. His wife was working days, so he was home alone and invited me out. I would hide my car in his garage and go in the house, and he would always be conveniently in his nightshirt, just getting out of bed. This went on for seven or eight years, and we had sex every place imaginable—in the house, in the car, in the hay barn, between the corn rows, in the trees—even when his wife was around. I felt guilty about it sometimes, but I figured *he* should be worrying about it.

After Jake and I developed a relationship, being back on the farm was much better for me, but even that had some hardships. Our relationship had to be top-secret. He would always put on this super-straight act whenever we'd be out together. I kind of would too, around the small town, but I wouldn't go out of my way to be super-conciliatory like he was. That really aggravated me, and I didn't have any control in the situation. With a married man, your schedule revolves around his. I'd be sitting home waiting. If she's going to be busy tonight, that means we can get together. After three or four years of that, enough was enough. I still see Jake, although not nearly as often. On some level, we still love each other and we have a very good, mellow friendship. I've gotten over the desperation.

My younger brother is gay and has been in a relationship for ten or twelve years. He sort of came out to me when we were both on the farm, but I don't know that I was much help to him. I think I inherited an awful lot of my father's genes; it's hard for me to talk about stuff like that. But we're pretty close. We usually talk at least once a week on the phone, and I go to visit with them quite a bit, or they come down here. We get gossipy about men that we know in common, and there have been times we've double-dated. When he and his lover are having problems, he'll confide in me. We don't do a lot together, because they'll often do things with other couples and it gets into a Noah's Ark syndrome—everyone's paired off and I'm old Noah.

My mother knows about my brother and his lover, because it's so obvious, and she has no problem with that at all. I'm sure she knows about me, but I've never come out and discussed it with her, I think because it's such a taboo to discuss anything sexual. But my mother's very liberal and very tolerant. It wouldn't bother her in the least. She lives downstairs and I live upstairs in the same house, so she knows various men that I've dated. They stay over and we sleep together, and she welcomes them in. I have a very close platonic female friend—we've been friends for fifteen, twenty years—and now and then my mother will ask if the two of us are ever going to get married. I think she sees me as bisexual, but I don't really hide anything from her. We just don't discuss it.

Before I went back to the farm, when I still lived in Madison, I'd go to bars and do a one-night stand here and there. A relationship wasn't anything I thought about. With Jake, it was the best of both worlds. We didn't live together, so we didn't have to put up with each other full-time, but we got all the other benefits. Now I think I'm ready for a relationship and would like to get my hands on something like that, but I don't know quite how to go about doing it. I have some good role models, like my brother and his lover, and two other friends who live near here, who moved up from Chicago. They've been together for twenty years and have just adopted a child. I would want a monogamous relationship. I'm a little bit jealous, and I would like my partner to be a little bit jealous about me, a little bit possessive. Maybe I'm too much of a romantic. Maybe I'm thinking about something that could never exist. But I'm like my grandmother in that I'm going to hang onto that ideal anyway. I'm going to aspire to it, and if I don't find it, I don't find it.

In some ways, I think relationships have a better chance out here than in the city. There's not this constant bombardment. When the whole AIDS thing started, I was having my affair with Jake and we were monogamous for many years, so I completely avoided all that. I was really nervous and paranoid about getting back into mainstream sexual relations, so that further reinforced me to go into hiding. In some ways, that's what I think I've done, and maybe am still doing. I live very isolated in this community, sort of hidden, kind of the way I was in high school. Many of my friends are in Madison or Chicago.

All those laborious, freezing mornings, shoveling shit, it felt like the whole rest of the world was going on out there, and there I was all alone, and nobody knew I existed, or cared. It made me patient and tolerant and gave me an ability to step back. Maybe that's part of my Norwegian upbringing; you've got to suffer a little to be happy. Maybe that's a Protestant thing, but I do kind of believe it. I don't willingly believe it, but it seems to be a part of me.

Something about rural deprivation sort of excites me. Everything is so easy and available in the city. If you want to have sex, you can find it anywhere—in the bookstore or the bar or on the street corner. In the country it's more of a challenge. You're horny, and you're looking for this other person, and when you finally find him it's just incredible. It's still sort of a sustaining myth for me—discovering somebody that I've known for a long time, and we never knew that about each other, and then something happens. I've developed crushes on so many men who were straight as arrows and had no interest whatsoever. After a few months of being alone, I would read all kinds of stuff into any little movement they made. Maybe it would be a store clerk that would help me try on a pair of pants. Any little touch was a big enough thread of hope to go with.

There's a little bit of a gay community around here, but it's really hard to network. People are very cautious. Two lesbians run a bed and breakfast in town, and there are transplanted Chicagoans looking for the rural life. I know of a couple of gay farmers who have been running farms together for years, but I don't know how I would ever get to know them. Somebody once said that farm boys can never be one hundred percent happy. When they're in the city, part of them will long for the country, and when they're in the country, part of them will long for the city. I think I will always feel that split. There is life out here in the boonies—a little bit more stable, a little less revolving around heading for the bar on Friday night, a little bit more self-reliant. But it works a lot better if you've got a partner.

NOTE

1. *Compulsion* is Meyer Levin's 1956 novel (New York: Simon and Schuster) based on a 1924 Chicago murder case in which two homosexual men, Nathan Leopold, Jr., and Richard Loeb, were found guilty of murdering Robert Franks, a fourteen-year-old boy.

Dale Hesterman

Dale was born in 1954 and grew up with two brothers, one older and one younger, on two farms in east-central Ohio. The first was a 70-acre crop and dairy farm. When Dale was about ten years old, his family moved to a 300-acre farm five miles up the road, where they raised sheep, beef cattle, and pigs. Crops included hay, wheat, oats, and corn. Dale was married and is the father of one child. He lives in Ohio.

ON THE FARM, there is a different sense of life that has more depth and understanding to it. You see animals born, you see them die, you butcher a cow and that provides meat on your table—and that's okay. When you ride on the tractor with your dad, cutting the hay in the field, and you cut into a rabbit's nest, you feel badly about that—but it's okay. There's a sense of life going on, that you and I will live and die but that won't really change anything. Seasons will still change and flowers will still bloom and die.

We were on a big hill and could see for miles, and there wasn't another house in sight. As far as we could see, we owned it. There was one spot in particular over by the barn, where the bank sloped down and the wind was forced up through the intersection of the bank and the overhang of the barn. On windy days you could stand there with your coat open and just lay against the wind. Behind the barn, where the bank sloped off, there were thousands of rock fossils. As long as the bull wasn't in that field, it was fun to sit and look at those fossils. I would roam the fields and the woods with a dog I grew up with, my best friend.

Even though we could see for long distances, we could always hear cars coming before we could see them. You could hear the wind. You could hear yourself think. Nobody came that way, no one paid any attention. I miss that privacy. I felt like I was invisible wherever I went, that I could do and be and think whatever I wanted. Now, I could spend a week in my apartment and never walk out the door. It's very much a refuge for me. That sense of freedom is kind of exciting. It pushes everybody out farther, and I can say who can come in closer.

My dad hated his factory job, but he stuck with it until he retired because he couldn't make enough on the farm. The three of us boys all had daily chores and helped with harvesting the crops. I hated it all. We were always land-poor, so there wasn't much money. The house was never fixed up very well. Farming was too hard a work for too little return. My dad was not one to teach you things. He would tell you to do something, and if you did it wrong he would get disgusted. "God damn it, I should have done it myself!" We all worked in the garden, and I usually did the yardwork because I liked doing it—mowing, planting flowers, doing the trimming. My room was always neat and clean while most of my family was very cluttered, and I got great pleasure out of tidying things up. I would go through and clean the house periodically as a favor to my mom.

When I was maybe five years old, I crawled up on my mother's lap to kiss her. She turned away and said, "Don't ever kiss me on the lips." I have no recollection of my mother ever kissing or embracing me, or saying she loved me. And I certainly never had any of that from my father. I had a strong sense of neglect, that my parents didn't really care and weren't interested in me. I was very close to my grandmother, my father's mother, and spent lots of time with her, weekends and summers. From her I learned about touching, hugs, and kisses.

My parents never had much comment for us on what we did, but it was clear I had brains and that was a source of pride for them. They gave me a dollar when I got straight A's. That was the only sense of uniqueness I had. I wanted so badly to be different, to stand out. Through the sixth grade I went to a country school and things were clicking along. I had all these buddies of mine from school at my sixth grade birthday party. We had those little horns with the thing that unrolls and rolls back up. All of us were standing under the light in the center of the room blowing them at once and they all shot out and got tangled up with each other, and we just laughed and laughed.

Everything fell apart in seventh grade, when we merged with other schools in the area and went to a different school, where the country kids met the city kids. I felt awkward, didn't fit in, didn't make friends easily. My freshman year of high school we merged again, and they put us in tracks. I went college prep and most of my elementary school friends went vocational, so we split up and I was kind of a loner. The high school was twenty-five miles away, an hour bus ride in the morning and an hour at night, so it was hard to go to many activities.

My parents didn't go to church but they were always willing to take us, so I went regularly from probably the fifth grade on. I would go to Sunday school and vacation Bible school and all the Christmas things. Those were the only opportunities I had to socialize with other kids until my sophomore year, when I started an encounter group that a local church was doing. The group met for six or eight weeks, and I did two years' worth of maturing in that period. I had been very naive, unaware of what other people thought of me, unaware of puberty. The group opened me up to a lot of things, but it was devastating. I became aware that I was different from everybody else, I was a sissy, people were making fun of me, I needed to grow up. I was despondent and embarrassed about how immature and unsocialized I was.

The minister took an interest in me, so I felt like there was somebody who cared. One night, I left a note for my parents and ran away. I was going to go stay with the minister and try to work things out. But he lived twenty-five miles away. I'd walk by farmhouses and mean farm dogs would start chasing me, barking and growling. I was scared to death. Finally I'd walked five miles and got out to the blacktop highway, but there was no traffic at two in the morning. It was terrible. I kept walking and walking and thought I'd never get there. So I stopped at a house, woke them up, and told them my car had run out of gas way down the road. Could I call someone to get me? I called the minister, he took me to his home, and I went to bed. The next morning he made me call my parents to tell them I was okay. My mom was real upset. She'd called my dad home from work. Of course, they wanted to know where I was. When they came to get me, the minister talked with them, tried to get them to understand that they should show me some attention, talk to me. My mom stared straight ahead and was kind of shaking, and looked like she had been crying. The only thing my father said was, "Look what you've done to your mother." They took me to school, I went home at the end of the day, and it was never mentioned again. I vowed to myself never to hurt them again.

When I was sixteen, I was working at McDonald's so I couldn't go camping one weekend. Our family did a lot of camping together, and this was the first time I didn't go. There was a note on my desk when I got home from school that Friday: "It's really sad to go on this trip without you. We have always enjoyed going with you. I know you can't always understand, and I don't tell you much about my feelings for you, but everybody has to guard their heart in their own way. Just know that I always love you. Mother." I realized then that my parents did care. It was just that they couldn't show it in ways that I needed to see or feel it. My father's father died when he was five and his mother had to raise four boys in the Depression, so there wasn't a lot of time to give him the things he needed. He was alcoholic in my early years, quit drinking when I was about six. My mother was raised in a very strict environment with seven younger brothers whose father had been raised in abusive foster homes.

I picked up some friends in the encounter group, but just when that was feeling good we moved and I started my junior year at a different school, where I had trouble making friends. That summer I went to a church camp that turned out to be kind of an evangelical, quasi-fundamentalist camp. I got saved and my world turned around. I became this wonderful person. I wasn't sulking anymore, I wasn't prone to depression, life felt better. I made a lot of friends in a Christian youth group and became a youth leader in the church. I really had a good time my senior year of high school with my Christian friends. We would have wild prayer meetings at the house. Thirty youth would come over and we'd be on our knees whooping and yelling and all praying in loud voices at the same time. My parents would be sitting in the other room smoking cigarettes and drinking coffee, wondering what the hell was going on, I'm sure. But they were just thrilled—I was a good kid, a model person in the church. I visited the shut-ins and carted them all over.

When I stayed with my grandmother, my uncles had magazines like *True Confessions,* only geared towards men. I never read the stories, but the sketches that went with the stories had very masculine men—hairy chest, shirt open or maybe off, muscular, tanned, rugged. In high school I would see guys and wish I looked like them—a tall slender guy who had gorgeous hair, the football guys, or the jocks who were good looking and very masculine. I was probably physically attracted to them but I rationalized that I just wished I looked like them. In a health book we had in the house, the section on homosexuality talked about studies that had been done, and one had found that men whose right testicle hung lower than the left were more prone to homosexuality. I looked at mine and, doggone it, the right one *was* lower than the left.

I went to a Christian college in Kentucky and was again very much a loner. Late in college I had my first awareness that maybe I was gay, but I didn't linger on that thought. After I'd finished college, I stopped at an adult book store one night on my way to work, but I couldn't get the nerve up to go in. A week later I got the nerve up, went straight to the rack of gay male pornography, bought a magazine, and shot right back out the door. If there was anybody else in the place I never saw them. I looked at the magazine in the car and threw it in the trash before I got home.

About four years ago I was finishing up my Ph.D. program and thinking, I am gay, I am married, I have a child. I have made my bed and I have to lie in it. A year later I was thinking, there's a support group for people who are coming out, maybe I should check it out. Flakiest group of people I ever met! They all had some bizarre quirk about them, and after about four sessions I decided if this is being gay I think I'll pass. A year later I had the chance to move to San Francisco. I wanted to go and my wife didn't. I was feeling like, this is it—do it or die, come out now or you might as well kill yourself because it's no good living this way. I felt I couldn't put it off any longer because it wasn't fair to my wife for us to get out to San Francisco and for me to come out to her there. So I came out to her.

Two years ago, when my wife and I decided to separate, I came out to my parents and my brothers. I sent my parents a letter and they called me the day they got it. "You're our son, you'll always be our son, that will never change." But it has never been discussed since. I brought it up again when my parents came to California to visit. We had stopped at McDonald's and when I brought it up my dad said, "Well, coffee's gone. I guess we should get back on the road." My mom asked me when I first knew. I told her college was probably the first that I was made aware of it and didn't suppress it so much, but I didn't let myself be fully aware of it until two years ago. I'm hopeful my mom and I can talk some more about it.

My parents' best friends were at my dad's funeral. They've been best friends since my parents were married, and this woman is my mom's closest friend. We received a flower arrangement from this woman's son, but it was from the son and his roommate, a man. I said to my mom that it was odd that his roommate would send the flower arrangement, too, and she said, "Oh, he's been with him quite a while now." I said, "Do you think he's gay?" and she said, "Yeah, I think he probably is. I've always thought that."

I asked her if she and his mom had ever talked about it, and she said, "Oh, no. I would never bring it up in case his mom doesn't know. I don't want to be the one to tell her because she might not accept it. I know his father wouldn't accept it so I figure it's just best not to talk about it." I said, "That's kind of odd. Here you've been friends all these years and you both have a gay son and you've never talked about it," and she said, "Well, it's not my place."

When my wife and I told my daughter we were separating, we told her I was gay. In the months leading up to that, I had bought her several kids' books on the issue and we'd read them together and talked about gay people. She had grown up with a lot of lesbian friends of my wife, so she had no problem with me being gay, but she had a problem with the fact that her parents' marriage ended because I was gay. The same holds for me. If I weren't gay, I'd still be with my daughter on a daily basis. That's been the most painful for me. If there's anything I resent about being gay, it is that. Sometimes I sit and cry and say over and over, I'm sorry, I'm sorry, I'm sorry.

But what I did I would do over again. Congruence in life is really important to me. I do have times where it's like *The Best Little Boy in the World;* if you could take a pill and be straight, would you? He says no way.[1] I can't say that all the time. I like finally being who I am, and if I think of me in this place, inside this apartment, I'm fine with who I am. But the minute I step out of here, I'm reminded that I was never one of the guys, and I think maybe if I could have taken a pill and been straight I would've been one of them. It's definitely a straight person's world out there and it would be a whole lot easier to function in it if I were straight. Or when I think of my daughter, I think maybe all this pain wouldn't have happened. On the other hand, if I could have come out a lot earlier maybe I would never have married and I wouldn't have had to go through all the pain of divorce and loss.

My former wife and my daughter are my strongest support system. I talk with them at least twice a week. It's a little difficult in that I know my former wife still loves me very much. I don't think she harbors any misconceptions about us getting back together, but I know if I find a partner it will be a second round for her. He will become my best friend and I won't talk as much with her. I'm thinking maybe I should pull away a little bit and not share as much with her. If I do that gradually, I think it will be less painful if I find someone else.

I became very good friends with a guy I met in California, in a support group for gay men who had been married or were currently married. He and I had a lot in common, and about nine months later we had sex on the beach at night. I have never felt anything like that. It was wonderful, incredible—like circuits got plugged-in that had never been plugged-in before. For the first time in my life I felt normal. And then about a month later I met a guy who swept me off my feet. Not only was it an incredible sexual intimacy but I also felt an emotional intimacy. He told me he loved me, he loved this and that about me, and we had so much fun. He said and did all the right things. I found out a few months later he didn't mean any of those things, but it was the first time in my life I ever felt loved in a whole way. I have no doubt about my former wife's love for me—the depth and the greatness of it—but it never felt whole.

It's this odd paradox within me, to want to be unique and different on one hand and on the other hand to want to be like everybody else, to feel like everybody else feels. I always have felt badly that I was never one of the guys. I was never athletic, I never hunted, I never understood the thrill of talking about pussy and tits. Now, as I try to become part of the gay community, I still feel different. Most of the gay men I talk to had early sexual experiences, as often with male adults as male teens. I didn't even know anybody who was gay. And when gay men talk about sexual activity of a casual nature, I haven't done that. Part of it was morality and part of it was that from high school on I've had an extremely negative body image. I feel okay about my face, but I think my body is very ugly, almost grotesque. I have not had sex with very many men, in large part because I can't imagine anyone would find my body attractive.

When I went to bars in San Francisco, a lot of the guys wore very skimpy shorts, and ninety percent of the younger ones would have their shirts off and had well-developed chests and great tans. I finally quit going to those bars because I would be so depressed. If I'd grown up in the city and been part of a group of guys, maybe I would have developed more of a sense that everybody has different bodies, they come in all shapes and sizes, and that's okay. The locker room was the only exposure I had to boys' bodies, when I cowered in a corner, quickly changed for gym, and always avoided taking a shower.

Outside my office is an expanse of lawn, and in the summer lots of guys go there and play ball or frisbee. They're in shorts, shirts off, very attractive. Some gay guys love to sit and watch them, but I don't. It's depressing to me, like the bar scene. I wonder if that's related to growing up where it's not part of your experience to look at other people. In the city or suburbs, people sit on their porches and watch their neighbors. They ride buses and trains and stare at others. We never did that, and it's uncomfortable for me to do it now or to think of somebody doing it to me. When I'm home, the blinds are closed if I think anybody can see in.

I've spent much of my life working very hard at being a sociable person. I often get down on myself because I wish I was more gregarious. If I go into a group where I don't know anybody, I'm very much a wallflower. When I get together with a few close friends, I'm the life of the group. I wish more of that part of me could come out in other social settings. If I'd had more opportunity to learn about developing friendships and relationships, not being shy and backward, I might have come to grips with this sooner. It has just been within the last two years that I've turned my self-concept around. Body image is still a problem, but I feel good about the kind of person I am. If they could meet me and get to know me, I think a lot of people would be interested in me, not just in terms of a relationship but friendship too. I would like to meet somebody just like me. That's how good I feel about me.

What I face now is the same issue I grew up with—how do you meet people? The frustrating thing about being in this small community is that there aren't many opportunities, and after a while you feel like you've met every gay man in town. I'm not comfortable with the bar scene, although I don't mind going out with a group of guys for a good time. I love observing, and there's something about being with a bunch of other gay men that's really thrilling. There's something about the chase that goes on in the bar that's fun, but nine times out of ten I'm not part of the chase. To go to a bar and never get hit on is devastating to my almost futile effort to build up my body image. But my friends always say it's hard for anybody to hit on me because I won't give them a chance. Somebody could stare at me for half an hour and I'd never look at them. There's still that sense of feeling awkward, not knowing how to relate socially and meet people. And there's a fear that I haven't figured out yet. What am I afraid of?

NOTE

1. John Reid. 1973. *The Best Little Boy in the World.* New York: Ballantine.

Frank Morse

Born in 1955, Frank was one of seven children on a small livestock and crop farm near Poynette, in Columbia County, in south-central Wisconsin. He was married and the father of one child. At the time of our interview, Frank lived in Milwaukee, Wisconsin. He died in 1993 from AIDS-related causes.

The farm where Frank grew up had very rocky soil. For several weeks each spring, Frank and his siblings had to pick the rocks from the fields, load them on a flatbed wagon, and haul them to a ditch. Many wagonloads of rocks were dumped in that ditch each spring, and the dulling, oppressive nature of that work haunted Frank for many years. In the last few years of his life, he made a kind of peace with that rock-picking and all that it represented by selecting colorful rocks from the farm of his childhood and hauling them to his home in Milwaukee to create borders in his backyard garden.

This brief narrative describes Frank's relationship with his father.

MY FATHER WAS a section foreman for the Milwaukee Railroad, so he worked away from the farm five days a week. After work, he'd go to the bar. As far back as I can remember, Mom would wake me up early in the morning to go out and do chores before school. After school, as soon as I got off the bus, I would do chores again until dark. And the whole summer was farm work. I was very angry about being charged with all those responsibilities, but Dad was off at the bar drinking, so I just did the work. I didn't have a choice. If I didn't do what had to be done, there would be physical reprimand.

I grew up in a very dysfunctional, alcoholic family. I would cower in my bedroom, afraid that Dad was going to come up with his five-foot leather strap with a big brass buckle. He'd hit us with that a lot. Mom was always the enabler. She would not make any judgments about Dad. He knew how to discipline us boys and keep us straight. She was protecting herself, making sure she didn't get reprimanded or physically assaulted.

All through high school I liked to keep the garden and lawn nice, and Dad didn't think I should be spending as much time on that as I was. He would bitch me out and tell me to get my ass out in the fields. Then he would be very critical of the way I did the farmwork, even though he wasn't there to teach me or to supervise. He'd tell me I wasn't feeding the hogs

"I grew up in a very disfunctional, alcoholic family." Frank Morse, age four, sits on his mother's lap, next to his father and sister. Courtesy of Joy Morse.

enough, I wasn't keeping their pens clean enough, I wasn't cultivating the corn right. He demanded that I cultivate a big field of corn when I was only eleven or twelve years old. When I fell asleep on the tractor and drove through a fence, I was beaten. When I started talking about going to college, Dad was very much against it. The day I actually packed my car to leave for college, he finally understood that I really was leaving, and we got into a fistfight. I beat the living shit out of him and drove away.

In college, I got to be a very heavy drinker, and when I was drinking I could be just like Dad. A few years ago, I gave up alcohol completely. I was very conscious that when I was angry or sad, I'd stuff all those feelings down myself with beer. As a child, I was very angry about my dad's drinking. I yearned to have him recognize my performance and my achievements, but it never happened. In high school, he never attended my football games, track, wrestling, or plays. He never said, "You've done a good

"All through high school I liked to keep the garden and lawn nice, and Dad didn't think I should be spending as much time on that as I was." Ten-year-old Frank Morse kneels in the family vegetable garden. Courtesy of Joy Morse.

job," or "Thanks for doing that," or "I'm proud of you." Part of my yearning to be with a man is yearning for that kind of recognition. I want a man in my life who will give me that.

One day, in 1981, while my father and I were talking about the farm, he had a heart attack and died in my arms. For me, there was no grieving; it felt like the right time for him to go. Now, sometimes, I miss him and feel a need just to be with him, or to say, "Hey, Dad, look at all the achievements I've had in my life." I know he would be proud of me, and I know that he probably wouldn't say it. What if he had found out that I'm gay? Part of me thinks he might have been very accepting. I think, deep down, that's one of the things he struggled with—that he wanted to be with a man. Since I've found out that one of his drinking friends was gay, I've wondered what went on.

Mark Vanderbeek

Mark was born in 1955 and grew up with two older sisters and a younger brother in southeastern Nebraska, near Adams, in Gage County. The farm was predominantly a grain operation, with some livestock. At the time of our interview, Mark lived in Kansas City, Missouri, and worked for a printing company as an electronic prepress specialist and Macintosh consultant. Mark killed himself in 1994 in the midst of what he described as "an ongoing struggle with clinical, hereditary depression." In this brief narrative, Mark describes how his rural and small-town roots continued to shape his achievement-centered identity.

MY BROTHER DAN is the heir to the throne of the family farm, and he can have it. I have a feeling my parents would have been pretty thrilled if I had wanted to farm, since I'm regarded as more of a perfectionist. According to my dad, when we went out to do fieldwork during planting season, I knew how to prepare the fields just perfectly for him. But Dan is pretty much a perfectionist now, too. Some people might think he fell with his proverbial ass in the butter, but I'm not envious. Dad is supposedly retired, but even in retirement he lives and breathes farming. He goes out to the farm every day, come hell or high water, and kind of manages and manipulates things. Dan has had to learn to finesse that and sometimes has to undo my father's damage.

It was pretty well-known, maybe even from kindergarten, that I was going to be an artist. I just exhibited that talent and it took root. God, the number of times I grumbled about being out on that fucking tractor going back and forth over the fields. And the number of times I grumbled about getting dirty with grain dust. My mom says that's why I didn't become a farmer. I don't like to get dirty. My parents indulged me when I'd put up resistance after three weeks straight of going out to the field. Then it was time for me to do something else for a couple of days. But that doesn't mean when there were emergencies I didn't pitch in. It was a group effort, and I still feel a part of that effort today. My parents haven't the faintest idea what I do in my career, but it's kind of expected that I will keep up with the price of grain, and how much rain they get, and I do keep track of that stuff. It's second nature, something you never lose.

Even though I didn't grow up in Adams, I considered myself an Adams person because I went to public schools there, and I had a very strong sense of community—of contributing and sharing. Sports, academics, and everything were very competitive, and when you did something, you did it as much for the glory of Adams as for your own enhancement. In my class, peer pressure and cliques were virtually nil, and the pecking order was minimal. We all tolerated each other's idiosyncrasies and respected each other's space. The teachers instilled that in us.

In high school, anyone who had any athletic ability went out for football and basketball, because it was important for Adams to have outstanding teams. Not being a jock, I still felt a part of all that. I was student manager for the football team all four years, the right-hand man to the head coach. And I made posters that went up around the high school building the week prior to each basketball game, to help build up enthusiasm. They purchased special poster-making supplies for me, the whole nine yards. It was regarded as a significant contribution, and that's quite a big deal for someone who's not a jock.

It wasn't until I was a senior, second semester, that I actually had a study hall, because I always had every minute of school filled up with something. I often had to split band and art classes because both sides were saying, "Mark, we need you!" I saw myself going to school to prepare for other things, not knowing specifically what, but it was all in preparation for something else. Mrs. Harrold, my trig and geometry teacher, could be a feisty, unyielding person to other people, but I always thought of her as someone who would not accept less than your best. Mrs. Knowles, my choral teacher in high school, was a godsend. Under her wing, I got my love of classical music—my first and last love—and the sense that you are what you set your mind to be.

I lived a totally celibate life in college, and I have a certain amount of regret about that. I was so dead-set on getting that 4.0 GPA that everything else was out of the picture. I just hammered away at it, relentlessly. I might have been dodging the issue too—kind of like I needed to resolve one issue at a time. The first issue was my career, or purpose in life, and after I got my first job I was permitted the freedom to pursue the other aspects of my life. That's one thing that's been out of sync in my life—the ability to juggle several things at one time.

A lot of gay people spend their lives just grazing the surface. Then there are the over-achievers, who have a subconscious need to prove their worth

Mark Vanderbeek, age three, and his sisters, *left*, Sandy, and Pat.
Courtesy of Sandy Coorts.

in society. I tend to be an over-achiever. At times it's a blessing and at times it's a curse, but I don't want anyone at work to ever have reason to say, "Not only is he gay, but he doesn't do above and beyond the call of duty." You can call me a faggot, you can call me any slur you want to, but don't ever call me a sluff-off or someone who doesn't put out 110 percent. It's definitely a trait I picked up from my father. He would say, "Count your blessings for every day you can work."

Growing up in a small community, I had a strong sense of identity—the farm, the small town, the small school. I've heard other people say that when they realized they were gay, they felt like they must be freaks of nature. But being gay never really caused me great inner conflict, because I've always had a fairly strong sense of who I am. I'm an Adams kid, I go to Adams school. When I was in doubt or turmoil about something, I had those things to prop me up and tell me, "Hey, you're okay. This issue will be resolved."

I grew up in quite ordinary circumstances and the most "wholesome" of settings. I always knew I was gay, I've always been comfortable with it, and I certainly have no regrets about it. I've taken my lumps like everyone does, straight or gay or whatever, and I wouldn't trade places with anyone. I've gotten this far to understand who I am. I would just as soon stay on track and find out what's ahead. Despite what people in New York or Los Angeles might say, I don't consider Nebraska the middle of nowhere. I think the Midwest is a wonderful place to be. Omaha is like a second home to me, other than Adams. It's very much a sense-of-community type city, the focal point being Omaha, with the suburbs looking to it. I feel a little lost in Kansas City, with the core city kind of languishing and the suburbs taking over. Not having that core to identify with is kind of baffling to me.

Everett Cooper

Everett was born in 1957 in southeastern Indiana and grew up on a dairy farm in that region. He has one younger brother and three older sisters. Everett was married twice and is the father of three children. He lives with his husband in Wisconsin and works as an optician.

DADDY WAS ONLY too happy to finally have a son, but I think there was something about the gentleness of my nature that frightened him and he just pushed me away. I was a model child, really responsible. It wouldn't have occurred to me to back-talk my parents or not do something I was told. When I was quite small, my dad's younger brother would throw me up in the air, and I was just terrified. It was a great game of teasing, and jesting between my dad and his brother, what a sissy I was. It was communicated to me very strongly that I was somehow inferior as a male.

My brother Andrew was appropriately macho. He was the hunter and the trapper, so Daddy thought he was wonderful. By the time Andrew was nine, my father had given him a real .22 rifle to hunt with. When our parents were gone, Andrew would get the loaded rifle out and keep my sisters and me just terrified, teasing us. Daddy was so approving of Andrew that nothing was ever done about it.

My earliest recollection of my father is being beaten with a belt when I was three or four. I was crunched down in a corner, trying to shrink away from him, and my mother stepped in between us and told him, "You're not going to do this to him anymore." I spent all of my growing-up years trying to do things which he would approve of, but none of it was ever quite enough to make him move back towards me. When my father's raccoon-hunting cronies would come over, he would tell them about Andrew's hunting exploits and accomplishments. There was no mention made of me—I was just an afterthought. It just wasn't in me to be macho and tough, so Daddy couldn't approve of me. It was appalling to me that Andrew actually took pleasure in killing animals.

Before we had real horses, Andrew and I rode stick horses. They didn't even have heads, come to think of it. With no television, we had seen only a few cowboy shows at other people's houses, but with that bit of inspi-

206

ration we had invented some cowboy games. There were no girls to be damsels in distress, so I would play the damsel and then play one of the cowboys as well. Andrew refused to ever be the damsel. I would put my mother's and sisters' discarded nylons on my head for long hair, and wrap a cloth around me for a dress. When Andrew was nine and I was about twelve, the cowboy games gave way to real live horses.

I became involved in the dairy operation because both my parents had outside jobs. A hired hand had been taking care of the milking, but he wasn't doing it to my dad's expectations, so he fired the guy. I could see that my parents were in a bit of a pinch, so I volunteered to do it until my dad could find somebody to take over. The entire dairy operation became my responsibility at about twelve or thirteen, and I milked the cows morning and night until after I graduated from high school. There were times we had as many as seventy head of cattle on the place, but we never milked more than maybe fifty at a time. I was out milking the cows at 5:00 every morning, and after school I got on the bus and went right home to do the milking. It was an awful lot of work, and restricted me from being involved in much at school. By the time I got to my senior year of high school, I was getting pretty tired of that much responsibility. Daddy sold the cows as soon as I went away to college because he couldn't depend on Andrew to take care of them.

In addition to working in factories, my father was a part-time pastor of a small church. Our home and church life was very fundamentalist evangelical—Church of the Nazarene. We went to church probably three times a week, and we had spring and fall revivals where we went two weeks straight every night. We had hellfire and damnation preachers who came in and thundered at us. I believed everything and took it very much to heart. Everything was so structured within the framework of right and wrong as defined by the church. We purported to love "fallen mankind," but we really didn't. We saw ourselves on a plane above them, and they were the riffraff who deserved to "die in a Devil's hell," as the evangelists put it. We were prejudiced against anyone who wasn't Christian, to our definition. We purported to love the sinner and hate the sin, but that wasn't reality. A favorite topic was, "He that looketh on a woman and lusteth after her in his heart has already committed adultery." So I made good and sure that wasn't going to happen to me.

We had no television, because it was sinful, and my dad didn't like for us to listen to radio music. In those days, my mother was happy enough that she sang a lot of the time. I picked up on this, and from the age of four or five I would get up on an old seed separator that sat out in the barn lot and sing at the top of my lungs. We were three-quarters of a mile from the nearest neighbor, and a few times they called and asked, "What's that noise over there?" They couldn't identify it as singing. They thought somebody was screaming. "Everett is out on the seed separator singing again." Hymns were all I knew—"Rock of Ages," "Amazing Grace." By the time I was ten years old, I knew almost all the hymns in the book and could sing them word for word, without a book in front of me.

The first time I sang in the first grade of school, the music teacher stopped the whole class and said, "My gosh, you really know how to carry a tune, Everett." From that day forward, nothing could stop me. I sang at civic events, at weddings and funerals, and at hootenannies. I was the first person from my high school to win the All-State Choir Award. My mother saw that I had this claim to fame, and arranged for me to take private voice lessons during my high school years. I even had a contract from a recording studio in Tennessee that was going to put me on the road. Then I made the mistake of getting married, and the rest is history.

Once when we had a calf born, Daddy said I could have it. From day one, I let April suck my hand. She grew up and had calves, and even as a cow she and I were really close. To me, the cows weren't the numbers on their chains around their necks. They all had names and very definite personalities. If I'd be really upset, I could go out into the pasture where April was, and lie down, and just bawl my eyes out. She would look around at me like, "It'll be okay."

Mother would be there for me if I needed to talk. She was very aware that my father and I didn't have a closeness, so she tried to be more to me. When I was fourteen or fifteen, she told me that Daddy was so excited when a son was finally born, but then not very long after it was almost as if he became jealous of my relationship with her. We were very close, but she wasn't the smothery type. She would make a big deal out of my accomplishments at school—singing, playing the piano—so that I felt like there was something I had done well. A couple of times when my mother made my dad come to open house in grade school, he would tell my male teachers, "If Everett does anything wrong, be sure and give him a good paddling board, and be sure and send a note home with him and I'll take care of it again when he gets home." That just didn't make any sense, because I wouldn't have dreamed of getting in trouble.

My teacher in third and fourth grades was the first male teacher I had. I absolutely adored him because he was the first man who reached out to me and said, "Gosh, you've got it on the ball—you're a great student, you participate well, you're intelligent." He said those things to me, not in so many words, but by the way he treated me. I needed that, because I was missing it so much from Daddy. I needed a man to say, "You're worth something." Sometimes I wonder what would've happened to me if that one man hadn't given me a sense of worth.

As we got older, I became more Mother's boy and Andrew became more Daddy's boy. My oldest sister and I were more Mother's children, because we were model kids. Andrew and my second sister, Sally, were the two renegades, and they were my dad's kids. Before Andrew was born, Sally and Daddy were so close that he referred to her as his Little John. She was the tomboy of the three girls, the one who rode the tractors with him. She started calling me "queer" at about seven or eight. I had no clue what it meant, but I knew it was derogatory. My mother would become insane with anger and slap her in the mouth.

In the first grade, the school building was so archaic that the restrooms were concrete shanties at the back of the playground. I had gone to the restroom in the middle of class one day, and I heard somebody come in behind me. When I turned around, an older boy was standing there fully exposed from his waist to his knees. That was the first time I'd ever seen adult-size genitalia, and I was absolutely mesmerized. But I was scared, and when I ran out of the restroom he tried to cut me off.

I saw *Tarzan* on TV when I was seven, eight, nine and I thought his body was so beautiful, and that I'd like to touch him. Sometimes at the end of a day of baling hay, my dad and brother and I would skinny-dip in the pond to clean off before we came home. I thought Daddy was absolutely gorgeous and would like to have touched him, but I knew from what I *didn't* hear from everybody else around me that what I was feeling was not quite normal somehow. After I went into puberty, all the boys were laughing in groups and talking about kissing girls. I had girlfriends too, but I recognized that I really would like to be holding hands with a boy. I was excited about being in gym class, because I knew we were all going to be in the shower together. But I was concerned that I might be embarrassed by an inadvertent erection.

My mother introduced us to Zane Grey novels, and I really got into them. I always found myself identifying with the heroines, wanting to be where they were, in the hero's arms. My mother told me how disgusted she was by a book she was reading about two guys who met in the war. One introduced the other guy to his sister, and when they came home from the war, the sister and the guy got married so the two guys would be available to each other.

Andrew and I and a friend who was a year older than I found a place we called "the cave" in a very secluded woods. There was a waterfall, and back under it was a large eroded area that had the appearance of a cave. We camped out there a few times. Where the waterfall came over, a pool had collected where we would go skinny-dipping. We played erotic games, grabbing each other. Around the time I turned thirteen, our friend introduced Andrew and me to masturbation. He didn't let us see him masturbate; he just brought the semen over in his hand after he'd done it. We were mesmerized, just couldn't believe it.

Andrew became especially interested in the changes that happened to me when I went into puberty. We slept in the same bed and when I was fourteen and he was eleven we began to masturbate together—ourselves and each other. There was a lot of rivalry and antagonism between us by day, but at night it was almost as if we were lovers. There was a very definite Jacob and Esau scenario going on. My brother initiated most of this sexual activity, under cover of darkness, and we never spoke about it. We did this almost every night until I left for college.

When I was somewhere between thirteen and fifteen, we were at my grandma's and there was a news report about gay men in a park somewhere in California. The family got all up in arms, saying "Kill the perverts," and that kind of stuff. At that point I realized something happened between men, and it smacked of what interested me. I knew it was called Sodom and Gomorrah from the pulpit, but I really didn't know what it was.

Until my junior year of high school, I felt really guilty about masturbation—that I was going to lose my mind or God was going to kill me or something. I began to get away from that when I had my first major crush on a guy, my best friend during my junior and senior years of high school. God, I was so madly in love with him I would've sold my soul. For one of our English classes we had to keep a journal, and he would let me read his. He was involved with a girl, and was having sex with her every weekend. I kept his journal till I was twenty-four years old—not because I cared what he had been doing with a girl, but because I was in love with him.

When I was sixteen, I was dating a girl and I thought I might want to kiss her. I knew Andrew had kissed girls, so I asked him—when you kiss, do you suck or blow? I don't remember that he was really able to answer my question. But I never tried to kiss anybody else until I went off to Olivet Nazarene College in Kankakee, Illinois, where a girl from Pittsburgh taught me how to kiss. Dating was the thing to do, so I dated girls that first year of college. It was the first time I didn't have to worry about my parents watching or about having to go home to milk the cows. There were a fair number of gay men at this fundamentalist college. A friend showed me a picture he had found of his roommates, ministerial students, in a sexual setting. He and I had much the same type of religious upbringing, and when we looked at that picture we looked at each other and it was like a light went on—oh, okay, this really does happen. He and I never did anything, but I wondered if he was gay.

When I went home at Christmas that year, I was dating a black girl. I told my parents I was dating a girl. Could I bring her home sometime? Sure. During the course of the conversation it came out that she was black, and my dad went totally berserk. It upset me so much that when I went back to college I collected my things and ran away to New Mexico for six months, where I lived with my older sister. She had a television, so I would see the news and *Phil Donahue* and other shows where homosexuality was talked about. I began to put the pieces together, but I still couldn't make a transition, so I went back to Indiana, got together with my high school sweetheart, and got married. That was what you did in that culture, and I guess subconsciously I thought getting married would validate that I was okay, and all this stuff would just kind of fall away.

Within a couple of months after my first son was born, his mother and I had a conversation in which I told her that not only was sex between us not anything like I expected, it was terrible. She wasn't satisfied, and I wasn't satisfied. I told her about what had gone on between my brother and me, and she was so frightened by it that we never mentioned it again. We were only nineteen, for heaven's sake.

We went ahead and had two more children, and the whole marriage was really bad. It was crazy that we were together; all we ever did was argue. Maybe she didn't know how to get out. And yet she was bright enough to figure out what I couldn't. She called everyone in my family and told them, "He's gay. That's why I kicked him out." It was vicious and vindictive. Other than the conversation we'd had years before, she had nothing on which to base that. I was married to her for seven years and never had sex with a guy. Whatever fantasies I had were with men, but I didn't have anything except the masturbation experience with my brother to go on. My family believed her, so I turned around and got married again, partly, I guess, to convince them—and myself—that I wasn't gay.

After my second wife and I were married, I found out that men meet in parks, public restrooms, and bookstores. I had heard this years before, but didn't have enough sense to act on it. Then, driving through a park in Colorado Springs, it dawned on me—there were all these single guys driving around, there must be something going on. I started sunbathing there and a guy came running by and stopped and looked at me. I made some inane comment and we started talking. The first time we made love, it was like—this is it! This is what lovemaking is supposed to be. God, it was wonderful. We wound up falling in love with each other and had a relationship for two-and-a-half years. I didn't know what it meant to be in love with somebody—to eat, sleep, breathe, and think about them twenty-four hours a day. I was twenty-eight, twenty-nine, and he was maybe thirteen years older. He was married, too.

I want to come out to my family, although my mother has said on more than one occasion that she would rather one of her kids would die than tell her they were gay. The thing that keeps me from telling them is not that I have any guilt or bad feelings. I could quite happily go in and say, this is what I am—take it or leave it. And it's not that I think my mother couldn't deal with it, not even the fear that she might tell me to get out. It's just that my mom has had so much sorrow—my brother's alcoholism and his being in jail, and my sister Sally, who has driven her insane for more than a decade with vicious, hateful stuff. I don't need to come out to them to validate me to me. I'm okay with who I am. But it would just crush the life out of her—one more great big sorrow—and why would I want to do that to my mother?

There are people at work I've come out to, but with some of the people in my family I wouldn't be surprised if they would pick up a gun and shoot me. So I'm just playing it by ear. My dad could get real deadpan and order me out of the house, or he could beat me to a bloody pulp. He has in recent years, without even looking angry, hauled off and punched people—knocked them down and hurt them. If they all find out inadvertently, or suspect, it won't bother me. But I know I'm going to tell my brother. He turned to drugs and alcohol when he was still in high school, and when he was in the marines he brought home pictures he took of guys in his platoon that could be described in no other way than homoerotic. And methinks he doth protest too much sometimes. It's important to me to talk to him about it. He could pick up a gun and shoot me, but I don't think he will. He may deny it outright and tell me I'm disgusting, or he may open up and say, "Yeah, let's talk about it."

So much of the time during junior high and high school, the pressure to conform, to be masculine, ate at me a lot. If I'd had an inordinate amount of teasing on any given day, I would get real melancholy, and would sometimes go out in the woods to cry or to fight things out inside myself. And I enjoyed riding my horse in the openness and expanse of the fields. It was almost a gift to be able to get away and think my own thoughts—to ride free and unrestrained. I often wondered if my school friends in town were ever able to get away from everything and get in touch with themselves.

And I've often thought what a pity it is that my own three sons haven't had the privilege of growing up on a farm.

This summer, my oldest son asked me how I felt about something with reference to homosexuality. I gave him my opinion, and he just looked at me kind of funny and said, "Daddy, are you gay?" I was not expecting the question, so instead of answering it I asked him, "If I were gay, would that change how you feel about me? Would that change the openness of our relationship? What would it do to you?" Next summer, I'm going to tell the boys. In the event that any of them are gay, they need to have role models, to understand that it's okay. It's very important that they know this as early in life as possible. And in the event that none of them are gay, maybe they'll reevaluate the prejudices and biases they're picking up from other people.

I have some frustration and anger about the friction between my religious upbringing and coming to grips with my sexual orientation—about being forced to be stuck in a lie, about the unfairness I've experienced in disentangling myself from my most recent marriage, about being thirty-five and just now coming out. And by god, I'm so sick of other people dictating. Trying to come to terms with my own sexuality, I've had to shed almost all of my religious beliefs; they just won't fit with it. The farm has given me another backdrop, something else to move back to. I think of myself as a Christian deist at this point, with a real appreciation for God's creation, as opposed to just worrying about religious practices. I believe the true religion is to be as kind as you can be to others. With so much hurt and hate in the world, why do we want to inflict more on each other?

When my second wife and I started going through the process of divorce, we told close friends and our pastor and his wife that I was gay. At no time did anybody say, "Wow, this is interesting. Tell me more about it." They just put up walls. I have a real deep sorrow that people don't want to know. It's not a matter of, "Oh, I didn't know that—that's neat to know." It's, "Don't tell me, because I don't want my mind changed. I'm comfortable being antagonistic and prejudiced against you." It makes me very sad that a lot of people think we're all a bunch of perverts running around. And not only do they think that, but they *choose* to think that—they choose not to know the other side of it. I would like somehow to become politically forceful in changing that perception.

For a long time, especially in my adolescent years, there was such a lot of guilt, and then when I was married there was a lot of resentment. Why can't I be normal? Why did this have to happen to me? Once I was able to shed my fundamentalist beliefs, I came to realize that whether you're straight or gay, you're made in the creator's image. I'm put together pretty amazingly, and as different as I am to so many others, there's nothing wrong or bad about the way I am. Now that I've stopped worrying about what if and why not, I look at the beauty of the relationship I had with the guy in Colorado Springs. I think in some ways same-sex partners are far more capable of being real in a relationship, because they understand more closely where each other is coming from. The physical love and spiritual communion I have had with other men have been far superior to what I have observed in heterosexuals.

If I could snap my fingers tomorrow and become straight, I wouldn't do it. I'm very happy the way I am, and I want to find somebody to share that gladness with. I don't want anybody right this minute, because I need to spend some time with myself. But if the right person came along six months or a year from now, I could see myself making a commitment to a relationship. I would like a monogamous relationship because I think it makes sense in terms of one's health, but I would like a relationship more than I would insist on it being monogamous. I wouldn't want a relationship that was real clingy and where I had to be constantly affirming the person. I've been through that with both of my marriages. But I would like to have somebody to do things with, to go to bed with at night and curl up and cuddle with. I'm real cuddly.

John Berg

Born in 1957, John grew up on 300-acre mixed livestock and crop farm near New Ulm, in Brown County, south-central Minnesota. His older sister and brother were grown-ups during his childhood. John lives in northeastern Iowa and works as a librarian. This brief narrative describes how he responded to his emotional and physical attractions to other males, from grade school through high school.

WATCHING THE TV movie of *Cinderella,* with Lesley Ann Warren, I was very taken with the handsome prince and thought how lucky I would be if I were Cinderella and could land him. Sometimes when my parents weren't around, I would get into my sister's wardrobe and put on her bridal gown and veil, pretending I was getting married, walking down the stairs with the long gown trailing behind me. Sometimes I would go outside with my sister's dresses on and pretend to be a woman visiting the city. I'd sit on one of the farm implements and pretend I was driving somewhere. The pole barn would be a restaurant where I'd have lunch, and then I might go to the chicken barn to visit with the girls and do some shopping.

It was typical for my mother and father and me to go for a drive on Sunday afternoons. As we drove around they would look at other farmers' fields, chatting and listening to polka music on the car radio. My father was always very interested in seeing how his crops compared to other farmer's crops. I would sit in the back seat, day-dreaming and waiting for the ice cream that we would stop for about mid-way through the trip.

On our drive one Sunday, when I was twelve or thirteen, my mother had to return some dishes from Ruthy and Les's wedding that had taken place the day before. It was the first wedding I had ever gone to and I was very happy about going. Both the bride and the groom had dressed in white, and Les was stunningly handsome in his white tux. He was a farmer, so he was very sunburned. His face and hands were ruddy and his hair was slicked straight back. Watching him during the ceremony and the reception, I thought how lucky Ruthy was to have a nice man like that—a man like I wanted to have. When they left for their honeymoon, I was almost jealous that she was going to be the one with him. Sitting in the back seat

215

of the car, looking out the window, I was day-dreaming about what it would be like to be alone with Les. He would be driving the car and I'd be sitting right next to him, like a boyfriend and girlfriend would do.

Kevin was a couple years older than I and lived on a farm maybe ten miles away. The summer before my sophomore year in high school, I saw him doing some field work. He was shirtless and very tan. After that, I would ride my bike past his farm, hoping to see him. That fall, Kevin's sister and I were working on a school project with two other students. I planned it so the group would meet at her house, and maybe I would get to see Kevin. After we finished with our project we were sitting around in the living room and Kevin's mother served us bars and soda. It was harvest time and apparently Kevin had been working pretty hard that day. I was hoping he would get in from the field before I had to leave.

Kevin came into the living room shirtless, wearing tattered, snug-fitting jeans. He usually worked shirtless and always wore long pants. He was a little taller than I, very slim and muscular, blonde hair, blue eyes, and very tan. He kicked off his boots, pulled off his socks, and reclined on the couch to watch TV. This was my first chance to talk to him. Seeing that he was interested in farming, I geared my conversation to that. How was the work? Was it pretty hot? How were the bushels running? Kevin seemed to pay pretty close attention to me and made good eye contact, so I went home fantasizing about how wonderful our conversation was, and hoping we would meet again.

A few weeks later I had built up a bit of nerve to ride my bike to Kevin's place and invite him over to my farm. Much to my surprise, he said, "Sure, let's get together tomorrow." I had our date all planned. I needed to get Kevin upstairs to my room so my mother wouldn't be able to horn in and become the focus of conversation. The next day, waiting for his arrival, I cleaned up my room, getting everything as spotless as I could. I dusted my dressers and even refolded all the clothes inside. I planned a menu of finger foods—crackers and Cheez Whiz, popcorn, and a selection of soft drinks. I had a phonograph, and wondered what kind of music Kevin would like. I had David Cassidy, Bobby Sherman, and one country-western record.

Trying to figure out what to wear, I went through four or five changes of clothes. I settled on a newer pair of jeans and a nice shirt, but not too dressy. We had a long driveway and I sat on the front steps of the house watching each car go by. Finally, Kevin turned into the driveway and I felt faint. I didn't know what to do—should I run out and meet the car, or sit casually on the steps and look macho, farmer-like?

After Kevin and I had talked in the driveway for ten or fifteen minutes, my parents came out of the house and we visited with them for a short time. In order to break away from them, I invited Kevin to go for a walk around our farm. We had just built a new farrowing barn, my father's pride. I explained all about the stainless steel pens and the slat floors, and the whole process from breeding to farrowing to working with the feeder pigs. Kevin was quite taken by this new building, so I showed him some of our other farm buildings and we walked through some fields.

After an hour or two of looking around, Kevin said it was about time for him to get home. That was not my plan, so I suggested we go up to my room to listen to some records. We sat cross-legged on the floor, the hors d'oeuvres on the floor next to us. My emotions were running very high, but I tried the best I could to make eye contact with him. When I put on a David Cassidy record, I said, "You might not like this," but he said he was a Partridge Family fan, too. In no way did he mock or tease me. He ate my munchies and listened to my records and we had a good time. I wanted him to really like me and to come back a second time.

There was an electric energy. I wanted Kevin to touch me and to hold me, and I wanted to touch him. I was really thirsting for that kind of attention and affection from another male, but I didn't know if it was appropriate or how to get it. I was certainly drawn to how Kevin's jeans fit him, but I think what I really wanted was his attention and validation— for him to see me as a male on an equal level with him. When it was time for Kevin to leave, I walked him out to his car and told him how much I had enjoyed the evening and that I would like to do it again. We never did, but there has always been a fondness in my heart for Kevin and my first date with a man.

PART 3

*Coming of Age Between the
Mid-1970s and Mid-1980s*

Feeding the Calf, by Jeff Kopseng, based on a photo courtesy of Gary Christiansen

Introduction

THIS ERA SAW major mass-media attention to homosexuality, in print and on television. Sergeant Leonard Matlovich's discharge from the Air Force after he made it known that he was gay became a *Time* magazine cover story in 1975. Superimposed on the cover photograph of Matlovich in uniform were the words, "I Am a Homosexual," in large, bold type. In addition to detailing Matlovich's case against the military, the article described "the gay drive for acceptance" and America's response to gay people coming out of the closet. It provided a snapshot of urban gay culture, the diversity of gay lifestyles, as well as legal, medical, and religious perspectives. *Time* concluded that civil rights protections for homosexuals made sense, but that the "anything goes" attitude that fostered tolerance of homosexuality threatened our society's well-being.[1]

The main event of the decade was Anita Bryant's 1977 campaign to "save our children" by repealing a county gay rights ordinance in Florida. Her efforts and the reactions they provoked generated unprecedented discussion, debate, and gay community organization nationwide. In Rhode Island, Aaron Fricke's determination to take his boyfriend to the high school prom generated nationwide publicity in 1980. Several major-studio movies with strong gay and lesbian images appeared in 1982, including *Making Love, Personal Best,* and *Victor/Victoria.* Also in 1982, Wisconsin became the first state in the U.S. to institute a wide-reaching gay rights law. This period also saw the election or appointment of many openly gay and lesbian individuals to local, state and national offices. By the mid-1980s, AIDS had become a powerful force for gay visibility in the mass media. This was exemplified by the jolting announcement in 1985 that actor Rock Hudson had AIDS.[2]

Meanwhile, at the library or bookstore, farm boys in search of themselves might have happened upon Patricia Nell Warren's gay-positive novels, *The Front Runner,*[3] *The Fancy Dancer,*[4] or *The Beauty Queen.*[5] In addition, James Kirkwood's *Some Kind of Hero,*[6] Andrew Holleran's *Dancer from the Dance,*[7] and Armistead Maupin's *Tales of the City*[8] presented homosexuality in a way mass-market publishers had never done before. Also appearing were informational books about being gay, some written for gay men and lesbians, others for their parents, other family members, and friends seeking understanding.

For many of the men whose stories are presented here, coming of age between the mid-1970s and the mid-1980s meant that they would come to grips with being gay between their teens and mid-twenties. Very few of them would marry, and these marriages would be short-lived. "It took me till I was twenty-five," Rick Noss lamented. "I wish I had come out when I was younger." Yet many men only fifteen to twenty years older than Rick would have considered themselves fortunate to have been able, in their twenties, to figure things out and proceed forthrightly to continue creating their lives as gay men.

These younger men were generally more inclined than those who went before them to inform their parents and other family members that they were gay. In many cases this revelation was provoked rather than self-initiated, but in all of these cases the response was a matter-of-fact statement of being gay. "When I realized I was gay, I didn't try to run and hide from it," said Gary Christiansen, who sent a coming-out letter to his parents and siblings when he was twenty-five. "Even though I knew my parents weren't going to like it, I knew that was just the way it was."

Those who were not open with their families about being gay seemed to be in unspoken but mutually "agreed-upon" standoffs on the issue. Todd Ruhter: "I'm sure [my parents] probably have a good idea, especially as I get older and I'm not marrying, but they don't bug me about it. . . . As long as they don't actually know it, it's not real." Connie Sanders: "I suspect that on some level everybody in the family has an inkling. My parents are probably doing major denial." Richard Hopkins: "How can they not know I'm gay?" None of these men was attempting to camouflage his life in order to appear to be heterosexual; they simply had not yet taken a proactive approach to revealing their homosexuality. That they intended to do so someday was often apparent. Unlike those who had been gay farm boys before them, these men were more likely to be empowered by a sense of gay community and by being able to envision and create a more open, mainstream gay identity for themselves.

David Campbell plans to move back to the country, in pursuit of the large garden, animals, and isolation that city life does not allow. For Jahred Boyd and Steve Gay, country life is already a reality. Rick Noss describes his strong sense of belonging—both in Omaha's gay community and back home on his parents' farm. After years of "lies and lies and lies," Richard Hopkins contemplates telling his parents that he is gay and HIV-positive. Lon Mickelsen describes his ongoing task of reshaping a life of approval-seeking conformity into something more healthy and fulfilling. As the wounds of a defiant and abuse-filled childhood continue to heal, Steven Preston finds fulfillment in hobby-farming with his husband.

Connie Sanders ruminates on the incongruity of the southern Illinois farm culture of his boyhood and the gay culture of his Chicago community. After years of striving to be a parent-pleasing son, Ken Yliniemi credits his ex-wife with helping him develop the stronger self-identity that led to his coming out. Randy Fleer and Clark Williams reflect on the influence of anonymous sex in their lives. Joe Shulka embraces gay activism, both in Minneapolis and in his hometown, while maintaining close ties with his family. For Todd Ruhter, being openly gay is incompatible with the family and hometown ties that are so important to him.

NOTES

1. "Gays on the March." *Time:* September 8, 1975, pp. 32–37, 43.

2. Events of 1977 to 1985 described in *The Alyson Almanac.* 1990. Boston: Alyson Publications, pp. 35–41.

3. Patricia Nell Warren. 1974. *The Front Runner.* New York: Morrow.

4. Patricia Nell Warren. 1976. *The Fancy Dancer.* New York: Morrow.

5. Patricia Nell Warren. 1978. *The Beauty Queen.* New York: Morrow.

6. James Kirkwood. 1976. *Some Kind of Hero.* New York: New American Library.

7. Andrew Holleran. 1978. *Dancer from the Dance.* New York: Morrow.

8. Armistead Maupin. 1978. *Tales of the City.* New York: Harper and Row.

David Campbell

David was born in 1958 and grew up on a farm in central Ohio, with two brothers, one older and one younger. He lives in the Columbus, Ohio, area where he is co-owner of a floral business.

ANYBODY WHO KNOWS me knows I'm a mommy's boy. Sometimes I rebelled against what she'd tell me, and we fought, but for the most part it was a good, close relationship. My mother always had a large vegetable garden, and flower gardens, and I was always so happy to be out there helping her. I preferred doing that over some of the other things that had to be done. One year I had chicken pox when she was planting the garden. I stood at the kitchen window, watching her and crying because I couldn't go out there.

I know my daddy loved all three of us and my mom. He was a big, handsome man, very nice, always working and very involved in the community. He was on the library board and the county board, and we were all very involved in the Methodist church where he was a lay minister. He loved watching Ohio State basketball games at night, and when I'd hear him cheering I wanted to be out there watching TV with him. But we had to be in bed at 9:00.

Until my father died when I was nine, we farmed about eight hundred acres and had about one hundred head of Holstein dairy cattle. Except for one hundred acres and a few head of cattle, my mother sold our share of the farm to my uncle and grandfather who had been in partnership with my father. We farmed that hundred acres and raised a few steers for our own use and to make a little money. My brothers were more involved with the equipment and the plowing and planting, and I was more involved with feeding the livestock.

The night my father died, my aunt was staying with us at the house and my uncle had taken my mom to the hospital. My father had a brain tumor and had been hospitalized for a couple of months. He was thirty-four and my mom was two or three years younger. I looked out the bedroom window and saw my uncle basically carrying my mom into the house. She was devastated, but she came in and talked to us. In a way, his death made us all a little stronger, and it made us very aware of money. We never wanted for anything, but we never had a lot. Everybody pitched in at the house—cooked and did dishes and the laundry. I cooked more than my brothers did because I enjoyed it, and Mom relied on me to do that.

In high school I weighed 285 pounds, so I wasn't involved in sports at all. I was too big to play anything other than football, and I was really too fat to play that. I was class officer, Future Farmers of America president, band president, on the student council. My brother was an officer in FFA, and I was expected to follow in his footsteps, as he was expected to follow in my father's and uncle's footsteps. A lot of things were expected of us in a fairly small community, and in a family where everyone was always involved in the community and the church.

I need to write a letter to my FFA advisor to tell him how much he helped me. I hated him but loved him because he pushed me to do so many things that I never would have done otherwise. He pushed me into public speaking, pushed me to run for office, to be on all kinds of judging teams and apply for all kinds of awards and scholarships. I never wanted any credit for anything. He pushed me to run for state FFA treasurer, which I was and enjoyed very much. I loved traveling all over the state, speaking at banquets and presentations.

After my first year in college, I went on a diet and lost one hundred pounds. I started feeling better about myself, and started running and swimming a lot. At the gym one night, a man approached me. It was very exciting, because I realized there were other people who had the same feelings I did. I enjoyed what we did and I wanted to do it again, but I was very embarrassed and felt cheap. I would flirt with men at the bars here in Columbus, wanting to have sex but afraid to go home with them.

I had just graduated from college when I met Cal at a bar and we started seeing each other. He went with me to the farm a lot; he enjoyed gardening too, and Mom would always set an extra place for him at Sunday lunch. She assumed he was just a friend from school. Cal and I were together for three years. Not too long after that I met Michael, and we had a relationship for seven years.

When Michael and I broke up I moved home for about a week till I could find an apartment. Mom found a card I had saved that was signed, "Love, Michael." She showed me the card and said, "What does this mean?" I told her she didn't want to know, and she said she did, so I told her he was my boyfriend. She said, "You were right. I didn't want to know." But she wanted to talk about it, and she wanted me to see a psychologist. I said, "Fine, I'll see a psychologist, but I think you need to go with me, because I don't think there's anything wrong with the way I'm feeling."

The psychologist told my mother, "If David doesn't want to change, there's nothing I can do to change him, and there's nothing you can do to change him. You'll have to accept that." And he said, "I think I'm finished seeing David, Mrs. Campbell. You can come back as many times as you feel necessary."

The whole family always gets together for Sunday lunch at my mother's. By now they all know I'm gay, but I don't flaunt it and we don't talk about it. If I bring a guest to lunch on Sunday, they don't say anything about it. I don't think it's that big of a deal to them. We're all very accepting of each other, to a large extent. My mother doesn't approve of my being gay, but she says she wants me to live my own life and be happy. She has asked me periodically if I'd consider dating women, and I say, "No, I don't want to, and I don't ever care to." I say it kind of snippy, not to be disrespectful but only because I've said it so many times.

Everybody in my family is pretty much goody-two-shoes. I've always wanted to be accepted and liked by everyone, so I've always been kind of a middle-of-the-road person. In growing up, I was always just agreeing with people and doing what they told me. I would never say anything real controversial, because I didn't want to be an extremist, I didn't want to alienate anyone. I didn't like confrontations, and I never *was* in a fight. When I've been in arguments with somebody I've been living with, I've always ended up crying.

Keeping a clean public image is important to me. I try to be just a person, rather than an openly, politically gay person. I think I'm a lot more responsible than a lot of gay men. I'm not somebody who goes flitting in public, advertising the fact that I'm gay. I don't think of myself as a barfly or a very effeminate faggot who walks down the street. I don't think I'm a butch person either. I just think of myself as a person. I don't wake up every morning thinking I'm gay, I don't read gay publications, I don't surround myself with gay things, but I'm comfortable with being gay. For the most part, I just live my life day-to-day, and the gay part never enters into it.

Here in Columbus, I don't worry about telling people that I'm gay, but back home it's an issue. I go home a lot, but I avoid going into town so I don't run into somebody at the grocery store and have them ask, "Are you married? How many kids do you have?"—all those kinds of questions that people you grew up with tend to ask you. But that hasn't kept me from going to high school class reunions, which I've enjoyed very much. The first time I went was my tenth year. I really wanted to go because I was one hundred pounds lighter than I was in high school and I felt good about myself. No one knew me when I walked in, and I just talked to the people I wanted to talk to.

When I went away to college, I came home on weekends and during the summer. I still have a huge garden out at the farm every year. I go out there at least three or four times a week in the summer. Once I was off the farm I didn't think I'd ever want to go back, but now I would love to live out in the country again. I've always enjoyed having animals, and I like being away from a lot of other people. As soon as I get this house finished and sell it, I'm going to build out there. I'd like to have animals and a huge garden, raise all my own food, build a fifteen-foot wall around the entire thing, and let no one else in, ever, unless I invite them in—and that would be very infrequently. I'm serious about this—my self-sufficient little commune.

I don't want to be by myself forever, but I don't want somebody around just to have somebody around. I want companionship and a feeling of love. Sex would be fine, too, but that's not a big concern. My life doesn't revolve around sex like I think a lot of people's lives do, straight and gay. I would love to find somebody who has the same interests I have. I can go out and work in the garden from sun-up till sundown, never see anybody, never eat, and just be so happy. I lose all track of time, and I get mad because it gets dark and I can't keep working. It would be great to work in the garden with somebody else right beside me who felt the same way. But I don't think that will ever happen, as strange as I am.

Jahred Boyd

Born in 1959, Jahred grew up on a mixed livestock and grain farm in north-western Minnesota. He lives on a small hobby farm near Webster, Minnesota. His partner of nearly ten years, Terry Bloch, died in 1992. In this brief narrative, Jahred describes what it means to him to be gay and rural.

I'VE LIVED IN the Twin Cities, and I think so many gay men's lives there are so superficial. They are so concerned about things that don't really matter, like where they live and what they wear. I'm real content with where I live, and if I have a clean tee-shirt and jeans on, I'm fine—I don't feel awkward at all, no matter where I go. I guess I'm more down to earth, very common, and when I go to parties where it's all urban people I feel like I'm the country boy. Once I went to visit my friend Alan in San Francisco. He had invited people over, and then we were all going to go out to eat together. Alan was a little uncomfortable introducing me because I'm midwestern, from Minneapolis, just like Mary Tyler Moore; we don't know anything! When all these hardcore city people started talking about where we were going to eat, they asked me if I liked sushi. I said I'd never had it. You've *never* had sushi? It was as if I'd said I had grown up in Antarctica. It didn't bother me at all, but Alan was uncomfortable, like they were thinking I was just a hick. So I asked if any of them had ever had lutefisk, and not one of them had even heard of it.[1]

I decided as a kid that I was going to live on a farm when I grew up. I hated the mechanical stuff with a passion—vehicles, tractors, machinery—but I enjoyed taking care of the animals. I did all the livestock chores, and if an animal was sick, I gave the shots. With the heifers, ewes, and sows, I was good at delivering the young ones. When I was three or four years old I would deliver lambs by myself, and when the ewe would knock me down I'd get right back up to take care of the lambs and get them to suck. If a sow had pigs outside in the winter, we'd bring them into the house. Mom says that when she'd get up in the night, I'd be up taking care of them.

It takes a special kind of gay person to grow up in a rural area and want to stay there, and I'm more that kind of person than my partner Terry is. He could be a city person very easily. Terry needs to have people around

228

"I decided as a kid that I was going to live on a farm when I grew up." Jahred Boyd takes a walk with the pups in the spring of 1994. Courtesy of Jahred Boyd.

a lot more than I do, like most of my friends and acquaintances who live in the Cities. I enjoy having company, but I also enjoy being by myself. A lot of the people who stay in rural areas are like that, and it's real hard for gay people who grew up on the farm and want to live on the farm to find someone who also wants that. My friend John says that when he goes out with someone and brings them out to his farm, he can tell by how they act the minute they get out of the pickup if it's going to work or not. Most gay people from the city think living in the country is isolating, and they just can't handle it. It *is* a simpler life on the farm, but whether you're on the farm or in the city you have to come to terms with the fact that you've really only got yourself in life, and if you don't make yourself happy someone else isn't going to make you happy. Too many people clutch onto someone else, looking for security and acceptance.

I think I would have been a real good farmer because I really enjoy just going out and doing the chores. I thought about going into dairy farming when I bought this place. I could buy my hay and feed and just take care of the animals. What a good life that would have been. To me, farming is real relaxing and doesn't even seem like work. But I'm kind of a workaholic, and I think that comes from growing up on a farm. It's hard for Terry to get me to go anywhere on a vacation because I just don't trust other people with the animals. They're my responsibility, and if something happens I feel guilty. No one but Terry would put up with that. Someday I'd like to have a farm or ranch for young gay runaways and gays whose parents have kicked them out, an oasis where they can get away and not worry about straight people or being closeted. They could stay here and Terry and I could be surrogate parents until they're able to get on their own feet. They need positive role models, and they need to see that relationships can last.

NOTE

1. A staple of Scandinavian cuisine, lutefisk is dried cod which is tenderized by soaking in lye, and then rinsed before cooking.

Steve Gay

Born in 1959, the ninth of ten children, Steve grew up on a dairy farm near Waterloo, in Dodge County, southeastern Wisconsin. He lives and farms up the road from his parents' place with his lover, Jim Lawver. Steve and Jim's life as a farm couple is the focus of this brief narrative.

MY MOM AND dad are from the old German straight-and-narrow school of thought. I haven't had much of a relationship with them since my oldest sister took it upon herself to tell them I'm gay. I talk to them, but I don't get invited to holidays or anything with the family because they don't want Jim there. I let it be known that if Jim was not welcome to come along with me, I preferred not to come at all. Jim has pretty much come out to everyone in his family, and I've been included in every one of their holidays since we've been together. His whole family comes to our place for Easter every year, and last year they were here for Christmas too.

Jim and I have been together for eight and a half years. We were introduced by a mutual friend at Rod's, a gay bar in Madison. We were probably in lust when I asked him to move in with me after a couple of months. It wasn't until about a year later that we really started to get to know each other, so we've had a lot of rocky roads. I think the way my family reacted probably made us stay together more than anything. After my father found out about Jim and me, he said, "How long do you think this is going to last anyway? You know, gay relationships don't last very long."

At one time, Jim and I were the gossip of Waterloo. "There's two gay men living outside of town." In a small town it spreads like wildfire. Being as open as I am, it doesn't bother me that everybody knows and thinks it's their business. In a small town that's what you've got to put up with. Maybe a year ago, there was some gossip going around that Jim had AIDS. How that got started is beyond me, but I guess everybody's got to be talking about something. I think they're done talking about us now. Hell, there are lots of gay people living in Waterloo that they don't even know about.

Jim and I used to go to a pub near town—kind of a rough and tough bar that gets a lot of farmers and roughnecks. I think most of them knew we were gay. A couple times when we've been there and heard things said about us, I've looked right back at them. There's one idiot who was a year

"I always had a thing for stuffed animals." Steve Gay, age five, with his growing collection. Courtesy of Steve Gay.

behind me in high school who was really drunk one night, and he was saying things like, "Hey, Gay, why don't you come over here and suck my cock?" When I looked right at him, he looked the other way. I thought, you're just a drunken asshole—but I couldn't believe that the other people there who knew me didn't tell him to shut his mouth. A couple of them were fairly friendly with Jim and me, but they just sat there and let him say what he wanted to.

I've always wanted to farm, but not driving tractors or milking cows. I enjoyed working with livestock, and I really liked hogs. When I graduated from college in 1981, I came back home to the farm because my dad had a good opportunity for me to get started. For me, hogs are a pleasure to work with, at least for another fifteen or twenty years. Jim works for me and has to take orders from me when we're working outside. We're together twenty-four hours a day, which is very stressful at times. Sometimes we want to wring each other's necks, but it's nice, too, because we're on the same schedule so when we have time off we can go and do things to-gether.

It seems like a lot of our gay friends put Jim and me up on a pedestal. They think so much of us and of the fact that we're on the farm and that we've been in this relationship for so many years. We don't feel like we're anything special, because we know everything we've had to go through to get here. Through a lot of hard work and dedication, this is what we have. Fifteen, twenty years ago, I would never have imagined that I would be as happy with my life as I am now, and that I could be the way I am. We can be something society says we can't; we can act like we're married and have a total life together. When a farm feed company holds a meet-ing, the invitation is usually addressed to the producer and his wife. Most of the time, my invitation is addressed to Steve Gay and Jim. They prob-ably have an awareness that we're gay, but it's never talked about and I never make a big deal out of it. I just kind of let things go as they go, and people can think what they want. As open as we are about it, I don't know how many people really know.

Our gay friends think it's just wild that we're pig farmers. There are probably more gay farmers than we realize, but most of them aren't open about it like I am. I guess it's just the strong-willed part of me that some people have and some don't. You've got to say, hey, my life is going to be what *I* want, it's going to make *me* happy. If other people don't want to contribute to that, well, then they won't. If they can't handle it, that's too bad. It takes a lot of will and self-determination to go against your family and friends—to make people see you differently than they used to. It takes some gay people a long time to build up to that. They have to feel so much torment and depression to make them finally do it. And some people just can't do it. Instead they'll torment themselves for the rest of their lives, for the sake of all those other people.

Rick Noss

Rick was born in 1960 and grew up with two younger brothers in north-central Iowa, near Sheffield, in Cerro Gordo County. The farm was about 450 acres when Rick was born, and it grew to about 800 acres. It was mainly a grain farm—corn, soybeans, and oats—and a hog operation. Rick lives in Omaha, Nebraska, where he works for a bank.

EVENTUALLY, I would like to live on about five acres outside of town, so I could have a couple of large dogs and maybe even a few farm animals. Farming doesn't interest me, but life on a farm does. I like the openness and solitude, but I would have to be in driving distance of an active gay lifestyle.

I wouldn't give up growing up on a farm for anything. Farmers are there to create. Their whole life is built on growing and maturing and harvesting. I value life a lot, and there are a lot of people who don't. Another thing is pride. Driving through farming neighborhoods, you can tell who takes pride in their farms and who doesn't. It doesn't take much to let the buildings get run down, or for weeds to grow up around the buildings, or for corn to grow up in the beans. My dad built his farm up on his own to where it is today, and his fields were always clean. Every summer, as a family, we walked all our beans and pulled out all the weeds and volunteer corn. I would feel not only that I was letting myself down, but my parents as well, if I did a bad job at my work or whatever I did. I'm closer to my dad now than I've ever been, and I've never admired a person more for the work they've done. A farmer has to do everything—be a veterinarian, a businessman, a laborer, a bookkeeper. Dad never went to college, just graduated from high school and started out on his own.

We raised about a thousand hogs a year, but Dad never really pushed us to become involved in the day-to-day farming operations. We'd help with special projects, like vaccinating pigs or sorting pigs to take them to market. If Dad asked us to do something, we'd do it, but he was very much of a perfectionist and preferred to do things on his own. I always felt kind of out of place, like I could never live up to the expectations he would set for me. But with each kid, Dad mellowed out a little bit, so each one down

the road got a little more involved. When he was younger he could handle it all himself, but as the farm grew and he needed more help he would
take more time to explain things clearly and show how it needed to be
done.

I liked working with the livestock, especially my own projects. My
brothers and I would raise our own calves or pigs, and I would get into
awful arguments with my dad over how he treated the pigs. Once one pig
bites another pig's tail and gets the taste of blood, it will eat and eat until
it kills the pig, or chews the tails off all of them. It can get to be an epi-
demic. Dad would just take a metal bar and knock the pig's teeth out so
it couldn't do that anymore. I would scream at him. I thought that was
the most cruel and awful thing. That was probably the one time I felt like
he thought I was a wuss.

I'm not a mechanical person, and I found the fieldwork really monot-
onous—going up and down the rows and never seeming to get to the end
of it. When I was cultivating I would get caught up in my own thoughts,
start to daydream, and wipe out rows of corn. We had an old Allis Chalmers
tractor that I hadn't driven all that often. When I was ten or eleven, I was
taking a load of bales over to my grandparents' place, and I forgot I had
to hit the clutch before the brake. I was pounding on the brake but the
tractor wasn't stopping, and I ran the tractor into a telephone pole. Dad
yelled at me, and I thought, oh my god, I've failed! He always gave me
the opportunity, but I never wanted to go out and do anything after that.
I never felt like he put me down, but I was always kind of in awe of what
he did, and I put a lot of pressure on myself.

Mom was a lot more jovial and outgoing than Dad, more the friend in
the family. She was the one who really got us interested in sports. Her whole
family was very athletic; two of my uncles played minor league professional
baseball. When Dad was out working on the farm, Mom would be hitting
us fly balls in the yard. Growing up in a small town, we had the opportunity to participate in about anything we wanted to. In high school, I
was in baseball, basketball, track, speech, band, choir, Future Farmers of
America. I had the most success early on in speech. I got the top ratings
in original oratory.

In FFA my freshman year, one of the competitions was to memorize
the FFA creed and present it. I didn't want to do it, but they talked me
into it because I was in speech. By the day I was to go to the contest, I had
managed to memorize it, but that was about it. I didn't know where I
wanted to put the most emphasis, where to pause. With my other speech
work I would rehearse and nit-pick and edit. I knew I wouldn't do the
best job I could, so I didn't want to do it. I told my mom to call my FFA

coach and tell him I was not going. She said, "If you want to do that to
your teacher and your team, then *you* have to do it." I called and used the
"I'm sick" excuse, and I was embarrassed for a week or two.[1]

By the beginning of my junior year in high school, I was six feet tall
and my success in athletics kind of took off. In basketball, I was the cap-
tain of our team my senior year. In track, I always ran the mile and had
just mediocre times, but in my senior year I developed some speed. I ran
hurdles and tied for the best time in the state in our class. When we had
districts at our school, I thought I was a shoo-in to make it to state, but I
hit the last hurdle and fell. I was devastated, but my track coach picked me
up, put his arm around me, and said, "You're still one of the best hurdlers
we've had. Now I need you to run in a relay for us." I thought, god, give
me a break, I'm grieving here! But I ran that relay and we placed in it.

Sheffield and Rockwell were archrivals in everything. Sheffield didn't have
a Catholic church, so I would go to catechism classes in Rockwell on Wed-
nesday nights with my friends from Sheffield. By sixth grade, all my friends
were dropping out, so I was the only Sheffield kid there, with fourteen or
fifteen Rockwell kids. I was starting to get picked on. Whenever we had
to memorize a prayer, the Rockwell kids would never have it memorized.
I would, but I would tell the teacher I didn't, and when I would read out
loud I would pretend like I didn't know a word, just so I wouldn't stick
out and give them anything else to pick on me about. It got pretty bad
for a while; I was so uptight, I was checked for stomach ulcers. One time,
on the way to catechism class, I jumped out of the car when we stopped
at a stop sign, and was going to walk the eight miles back home. Finally,
during the class, I raised my hand and asked the instructor if I could go
to the restroom. I left the church building, went to the local grain elevator, and called my grandpa to come get me. He took me home and I never
went back.

My mom was raised Methodist, but Dad wanted his kids to be Catholic.
He and I are both very stubborn, and we would butt heads on a lot of issues. My last year in high school, we were having one of our go-rounds. I
had decided I was not going to go to the Catholic church and Dad said I
was. One thing led to another, and I decided to leave home for a while,
so I stayed with a friend in town for a few days. Dad and I finally reached
a compromise where I would go to the Catholic church two times a month
and to the church of my choice two times a month. If it was a five-Sun-
day month, I'd go to the Catholic church the fifth one.

I checked out quite a few churches that I could get to—Baptist,
Lutheran, Methodist. I'm glad Dad and Mom gave me the opportunity

to explore those other churches, because if they hadn't I might have just chucked the Catholic church altogether. As time went on, I realized that even though I had some fundamental differences with the Catholic church, my major beliefs were still more Catholic. I haven't gone to services in quite a while, but I still consider myself a religious person. I still say prayers before I go to bed at night. I'm not sure I would classify myself as a strong believer in organized religion, but my belief is there, as far as a supreme being or whatever.

In Cub Scouts, all the other guys would be drooling and slobbering over the girls in *Playboy* and *Penthouse,* but it wasn't really doing the job for me. But it really turned me on when they'd have pictures of a man and woman having sex. I always thought it was just the act of sex, but now I think it was because there was a man in the picture. On one Webelos expedition we were playing "Truth or Dare," and one guy pulled down his pants and said, "Truth or dare." I said, "Dare," and he said, "Lick my penis." I said I wasn't going to do it, and they said I had to. They forced my head down, but they didn't make me do it. I remember thinking that night that I should've tried it. In fifth or sixth grade, I'd have friends stay overnight and we would sometimes wrestle around and touch each other, but we never really experimented with each other. When I was a freshman, I was in the same locker room as some of the seniors, and I was intrigued by the guys who had hairy chests, or more hair anywhere on their bodies.

I always had a date for the prom and things like that, and I enjoyed holding hands and kissing with a girl, but I never tried anything farther than that. I was very naive, as far as sex, and I sensed a differentness in myself. I masturbated a lot—often with *Penthouse* magazine, reading "The Forum"—and I would think about some of the guys in the locker room. I knew my friends masturbated, but I didn't know if they were thinking the same thoughts. It bothered me, feeling like I was different but not really knowing how or why.

I didn't date much in college. I felt that I was really ugly, and that no one would want to date me. In the dorm room next to me were two very attractive guys, John and Andy, who were supposedly gay. I knew the words, like gay and faggot, and I knew they liked other guys, but I didn't really grasp what that was about. They had a friend who was also supposedly gay but who was not attractive to me. I had a party in my room and they were all invited. I got really drunk, and this other guy supposedly took care of me and put me to bed. I took a lot of razzing from everyone about that. Later on, he and I had a drink together, and I'm sure he was hitting on me. It excited me but at the same time it repulsed me. I never spoke to him again.

After college, I started teaching school and lived with two other single male teachers. I saw the movie, *Making Love,* advertised and wanted to see it so bad, but I did not want them to know.[2] We only had one television, so I watched it at 3:30 in the morning. I was in the living room with the lights turned off, really quiet, leaned over, listening to the TV. I just sobbed at the end of it. That was my first inkling why I was different. After that I knew I was attracted to men, but I didn't know I could really do anything about it. Where would I look? I didn't know there were gay bars and gay athletics. And I'd never had sex with a woman, so I certainly wasn't going to try to have sex with a man. I just thought I hadn't found the right woman yet. But I would often think back to John and Andy and that other guy in college, and wish I had pursued something further, or at least found out what that gay thing was about.

My third year of teaching, I was the head volleyball coach and Dee was my assistant. We were going to a party one night, and she asked if I wanted to go dancing. I said I did, and she said, "I want you to know that where we're going to dance is kind of different." We went to The Max, in downtown Omaha, and I was just in awe. There were probably eight hundred people in there, men dancing with men, women with women, and women with men. After that, Dee and I would get home from volleyball trips at midnight, drive to Omaha to dance for an hour, go to breakfast with all our new "gay friends," and get home at 4 A.M. to be ready to teach at 7:30. We were running ourselves into the ground.

At The Max, the brother of one of my students asked me to dance. I said no. I found out later that another guy asked him if I was gay, and he said, "Well, I'm pretty sure he will be, but I don't know if he is now." The guy gave him his number to give to me, but I said I didn't want it. A couple of days later, I called him up and said, "I'm not going to take his number, but you can give him mine." We wound up going out for dinner. I took Dee with me, and he took his friend Andrea. I felt pretty comfortable with that, so then he and I went out on a date, and things just went from there. Suddenly, at twenty-five, I knew why I had felt different for the past ten or twelve years. I often wonder how much longer it would have taken if Dee had not asked me to go dancing at The Max.

I wish I had come out when I was younger. I have no doubt that if I had grown up in a city I would have come out in high school. It would have been tough for me to come out in my small-town high school because you can't hide anything. If there had been another gay person I was having a relationship with or just fooling around with, someone would have talked, and if it gets to one person in a class of thirty-two, it gets to everyone. I

In contrast to Christmas 1990, when his parents traveled to Omaha to meet his boyfriend, Christmas 1965 brought Ricky Noss a fancy Western gunfighter's outfit. Courtesy of Rick Noss.

knew practically everyone, my dad was president of the school board, my mom was involved in several organizations, and my parents were in three bowling groups, two card clubs, and booster club.

I've told my parents I was probably always gay, but I had no exposure to gay influences growing up in a conservative German Catholic farm family. There weren't even stereotypical gay people on TV that I can remember. It kind of surprises me that I didn't take advantage of the opportunities that were presented to me when I got to college. I guess I just held back because I wasn't sure what to expect, or what I wanted, or even what it was. It took me till I was twenty-five and it was right in front of me, where I just had to reach out and say, "Here I am—take me." I was readily accepted into the gay community here in Omaha.

When I came out, I decided I couldn't be gay and be a teacher. I was a very hands-on teacher and it made me very effective; kids wanted to perform well for me because I was their friend. I hugged my kids, I had slumber parties at my house for kids to come over, watch a sporting event on TV, order pizza, play cards. If word had gotten out that I was gay, no parent would have allowed their junior high boy to come over to my house. They would have thought there were ulterior motives. So I quit teaching.

I am extremely happy the way I am now, but if I had a choice I don't think I would choose to be gay. I've worked hard at becoming a good gay person. When I came out, I went through a period of putting my partying and social life ahead of my work life. I was just basically being a tramp—going to the bar every night, sleeping over at someone's house, and dragging my butt into work every morning. I was in a state of euphoria, and I wanted to experience it all. Thank god I'm through that! Maybe it's a stage that most every gay person goes through, or maybe it's just me, because I came out so late, but I wish I would have had those opportunities when I was in high school. I think it would have made it easier later on.

I've become what I think is a responsible gay person, and I like that. I'm a productive person; I've got a good career, insurance, and a savings plan for the future. I've got a great core group of friends—the friends I met the first few months I was out—but I've never had a real long relationship. I dated one guy for nine months, one guy for about two years. The person I'm with now, it's only been about four months, but I would really like to see it develop. If I had been heterosexual, I think I would have been at this point seven years ago. Being gay has kind of set me back, as far as my personal goals. But now that I'm here, I enjoy it and I'm actually kind of proud of it. I've come through. And now that I've gotten my own life in order, I can go beyond that and do things for other gay people, like volunteer work and political work.

In 1990, I was Mr. Gay Nebraska, and I started getting a little politically active, going to some fundraisers. But I still wasn't comfortable enough to say, "Hi, I'm Rick Noss, Mr. Gay Nebraska. What are you going to do on issues related to hate crimes?" I thought I could do it, but when I got into it I couldn't. We had a few really good role models for that in Omaha, but they're getting older now, and they're burnt out. We need people my age and younger to pick that up, and so far no one has stepped forward, so I want to try to do that. This weekend I'm volunteering my time at the AIDS Memorial Quilt, and I've got my application in to do public speaking for Nebraska AIDS Project. I would love to do that.

I'm only out to my mom, my dad, and one of my brothers. When my youngest brother came to visit me one weekend we went to a bar in Council Bluffs that's straight except from one to two in the morning, when it becomes gay. I introduced him to a bunch of my friends at the bar and

asked him how he liked them. He said he didn't think they liked him because they weren't talking to him. I said they liked him, they just didn't
know what they could say around him because they knew he didn't know
I was gay. He said he *knew* that's what it was, and we just laughed and
talked. I don't think I could have that kind of conversation with my middle brother, but I'm sure he's figured it out.

I'm sure my other relatives have figured it out too, but if they want to
know, they can ask me. If they do, I'll say "Yes, I am," and then we can
go from there. But it's not something I'll just come out and say if they
don't have the nerve to ask. Everyone knows at my job at the bank, and
I've had no problems. My friends at work and the people I know who are
straight ask me how my boyfriend is, and when he went into the hospital
the bank gave me time off. I think I'm doing a lot of good in that respect,
promoting gay awareness, and if I can do that with my friends, maybe
they'll tell their friends. That's what we need now.

When I came out, I thought there was no way I could ever tell my parents. I thought they would disown me, especially my father. They came to
visit me one Labor Day weekend, and I was planning to go to gay bowling.
When I said they couldn't go along, they were just crushed. I said, "I'm not
very good, and you know how I hate it when people watch me do something that I'm not very good at. You go shopping and I'll meet you later."
But I had made the mistake of telling them where the bowling alley was,
and at the end of the third game they came in. I said, "Oh my god! My parents are here," and it spread down twenty-four alleys. There's nothing more
hilarious than watching a hundred gay guys try to act straight. They tried
their darnedest for me, and my parents didn't say a word about it.

Dad and Mom were taking off the next morning, so I wrote them a
note. It was a chicken way out, but I did it. I told them to read it on their
way home, and that I was going to be gone all day. They said they started
to cry when they read it. The first thing they thought of was AIDS. The
second thing was that they would never have any grandchildren. They
wanted to come back and talk to me, but they knew I wasn't going to be
home, so they left a message on my machine. My dad called me at 6:30
the next morning to make sure he caught me, to tell me he loved me and
he didn't care. He called me and wrote me every day for a week, and my
mom called every day. There were great periods of adjustment—maybe
more for them than for me. First of all, they said they just didn't want me
to bring my boyfriend home. Two years ago, they came down to Omaha
to meet my boyfriend for Christmas. I guess that's what family means to
me—you overcome what you might not agree with or understand, but
they're still your family. I can't describe how much they mean to me be-

cause of that. I've always had a sense of belonging. I've always known, no matter how bad things are, I've got a home.

Notes

1. The FFA creed that Rick memorized was written by one E. M. Tiffany and adopted at the third national convention of the FFA. It is a gem of inspirational oratory from the early decades of this century:

> I believe in the future of farming, with a faith born not of words but of deeds—achievements won by the present and past generations of agriculturists; in the promise of better days through better ways, even as the better things we now enjoy have come to us from the struggles of former years.
>
> I believe that to live and work on a good farm, or to be engaged in other agricultural pursuit, is pleasant as well as challenging; for I know the joys and discomforts of agricultural life and hold an inborn fondness for those associations which, even in hours of discouragement, I cannot deny.
>
> I believe in leadership from ourselves and respect from others. I believe in my own ability to work efficiently and think clearly, with such knowledge and skill as I can secure, and in the ability of progressive agriculturists to serve our own and the public interest in producing and marketing the product of our toil.
>
> I believe in less dependence on begging and more power in bargaining; in the life abundant and enough honest wealth to make it so—for others as well as myself; in less need for charity and more of it when needed; in being happy myself and playing square with those whose happiness depends on me.
>
> I believe that rural America can and will hold true to the best traditions of our national life and that I can exert an influence in my home and community which will stand solid for my part in that inspiring task.

2. *Making Love* (1982) was a widely advertised movie in which a man reveals to his wife that he is gay.

Richard Hopkins

Richard was born in 1961 and grew up with three older brothers on the family farm in central Indiana. It was primarily a grain farm, about 450 acres, but they also raised horses and other animals—cattle, sheep, and chickens. Richard left the farm when he got married in 1979. He lives in Indianapolis with his best friend, Keith, and continues to parent his two children.

I GREW UP in a big, old, two-story farmhouse. Having the finest house on the road was not important to Mom and Dad. What was important was that you worked hard and everybody was taken care of and you ate and did what you wanted to do. Growing up that way made me realize how hard it is to get things and to maintain what you want. Nothing was given, everything was earned. We were very structured in the work we had to do. You may have done a lot of bitching about it at the time, but at least at the end of the day you felt good because you'd done it. Baling hay, you're sweating your balls off in the hayloft, one-hundred-plus degrees and chaff all over you. But when you're done, you go in and take that shower. There ain't nothing feels better than a shower at that point. And then you get something to eat and you relax and you know you worked—you can *feel* that you worked.

After I got married, I was going to college and working part-time and then going to the farm and working. I knew I didn't want to farm, but it wasn't the chore it was when I was growing up. I could see some value in it. I never got around to completing my college education, but I'm a successful businessman today. I do okay. Farming taught me how to work, to get by, to take care of myself. There's no question I know how to bust my ass if I need to. And it taught me to be responsible. When you say you're going to do something, you do it. It's not just lip service. And it has really made me appreciate the finer things in life. This is a wonderful house, and Keith and I have nice things, and they mean more to us because we worked hard for them. A lot of people think things are owed to them. Nothing's owed to you.

In high school, all my friends were driving Camaros and Monte Carlos, and I was driving a fricking baby blue '62 Ford Falcon, little junk car. It was about to drive me nuts. "Why can't they buy me a car? Everybody else is getting a car. It's so unfair!" I hated my parents at times, going through it. I never felt like I had any money. It took me until I had a family of my own and was trying to earn a living to realize—how the hell did they do it? Four kids and a farm that was relatively small—I know they didn't have any money. How they were able to do that, and do it well, really amazes me.

My oldest brother didn't like to do the tractor work, but he was really into the horses and tending the barns. My next-to-the-oldest brother, Ray, and I did the fieldwork. He was my favorite brother. I started riding tractor—plowing and disking and cultivating—when I was in the third grade. Nobody thought I could do it, but it was just something I wanted to do; you're always trying to make your dad proud of you. I enjoyed it at first, but it didn't take long for the fun to wear off and for me to think, "Gee, this is a bitch, doing this all day long." During planting season, I was riding the tractor in the fields, weather permitting, from 7:00 in the morning until 8:00, 9:00, 10:00 at night.

My dad always did the planting because he didn't think we could drive straight enough. He was a very difficult man, a hard man to please, but I was always trying to make him proud of me. When you're fourth in line, it sometimes doesn't seem like you're getting a lot of attention. I guess that's why I wanted to start farming as early as I did—to gain some attention. Dad showed no emotion except for when he was mad, and when he'd get mad he'd take his farm hat off and hit you with it. He'd never put a hand to you, but he had a temper. One time I saw him lose it and break a scoop shovel over a horse's head. We worked together all day long during planting season, and you always kind of hated to tell him if you broke something. Ray could do everything and just whiz right through it, but I had an innate ability to find every rock in a field and break a plow point or a disk blade or something.

Ray was quiet, cool, a good guy, and I always wanted to be like him, but he always wanted to be somewhere else. You could just tell farming was not what he wanted to do, and as soon as he was graduated he was married and gone. All my brothers, the minute they reached eighteen, they were gone. That kind of left the farming to me, because the brother between Ray and me would never drive a tractor, period. He had a fear of it or something, and Dad and Mom never made him do it. I resented the hell out of that, but it was *my* fault—I said I wanted to do it. But dang! Day in, day out, dealing with the breakdowns and this, that, and the other thing.

When we weren't in the fields, the horses kind of took up the rest of the time. We stood three or four stallions at stud service, so we had breeding mares coming in all the time, and we trained and boarded horses. I was big into horses, and I was good. I showed pintos and paints for national points, and I marvel at how my parents had the money for me to do that, because horses are an expensive hobby. You can make money showing, but not if you're a kid. I was out there for the fun of it, getting the points. Mom and Dad hired a trainer for me and he hauled me around to horse shows almost every weekend from April until Labor Day. We'd go to shows all over—Missouri, Tennessee, Illinois, Michigan, Ohio. We'd leave on Friday night and get back Sunday night. It was a lot of fun.

He was a real cowboy type, just a real good guy, and I was really tight with him—that first love type of thing. I was fourteen, fifteen, and he was nine years older. We engaged in quite a bit of sexual activity through two summers. We'd do the full gamut, but there wasn't the mature lovemaking that goes on when you get older—the kissing and the whole range of passion. It was more the act. I never had anal intercourse with him, but he did it to me. When I got my own driver's license, Mom and Dad dismissed him, but I don't think they ever had a clue I was doing anything like that. The whole time, I had my girlfriends and was doing everything to keep Mom and Dad happy.

There was always work to do, so we never took vacations, but we got to do all the activities we wanted to do in school. My oldest brother was very musical and he loved the horses. Ray was very athletic, a great basketball player and cross-country runner. He was kind of a wild one, really good at partying. My brother who's just older than I was a great football player, and any free time he had you could find him in town playing pool.

Basketball was my thing—I played all the way through school—and I loved music and was fairly good at the saxophone. In the seventh grade I got moved up into the high school jazz band because they needed a saxophone player. That put me in with an older group and they all liked me, so I was getting asked to do things with them. That's when a lot of deception crept in. I lied to my mom a lot to get to do all kinds of things I knew they wouldn't let me do. I wanted to go to a REO Speedwagon concert in Terre Haute when I was a seventh grader, and I knew they wouldn't let me go. So I concocted a really elaborate school trip, and she bought it and I went. I started drinking beer here and there. "No, I haven't been drinking." Driving tractor all day, I started smoking, and I'd lie about that, too.

Some friends had given me tickets to a Doobie Brothers concert on the night of my graduation day. After the graduation there was a reception at the farm, and all of Mom and Dad's friends were there, but who the heck cared? So about an hour and a half after that started, I said I had to take a buddy back to his house, and I never came back. I went to the concert, and then I had to explain that one. Mom and I were close, but I caused her quite a few problems from time to time.

Mom and Dad really tried to instill responsibility and religion. My dad smoked, but I never saw him touch alcohol—never in the house. Mother never smoked, no alcohol. We had a solid church upbringing, and Mom was the real drive behind church. She taught Sunday school, she taught vacation Bible school, she did the youth group. I was the first one out of my brothers to join church, and I went every Sunday. I played the piano in church, did the youth group thing on Sunday nights when none of my other brothers were going, did Bible school until I was too old for it and then helped out with it, went to church camp. In the back of my mind it was always to make Mom and Dad happy, especially Mom. I never wanted to upset them.

When I got married right after high school, it carried on. I became a deacon at the church, my wife and I took over a youth group on Sunday night, I was on the church board. When the divorce happened, all of a sudden I woke up thinking, "Where are all these people who are supposed to be there for you when things are going bad?" I walked away and didn't go back to church for a long time.

I learned sex from my brothers. We never talked openly about it, but each one of them had sex with me from when I was about ten to fourteen, fifteen. My two oldest brothers had a bedroom by themselves, and my brother just older than I shared one with me. With my oldest brothers it would usually happen when we were changing clothes after school. When they'd get horny they would just come in and pull it out and expect me to give them a blow job, forcing my head down on it. I was quite a lot younger and smaller, so there was nothing I could do. But I couldn't figure out why I was the one. Why were they grabbing *my* head and making me go down on this thing?

The majority of the sexual activity was with my brother just older than me. He'd come over to my bed. I cried real bad after the first time we had anal intercourse. The next time he wasn't as rough with me, but it still hurt. It happened for quite a while, until he got his first girlfriend. I don't want to make it sound like I was saintly or anything. After things got to the point they did with him, it was like, "Well, if you're going to do this, you go down on me. I'm not going to do this for nothing." So there was some sexual release for me as well. He went down on me a couple times, but I never had anal intercourse with him.

From first grade, I always had girlfriends. It was important to have girlfriends. But I knew there was something different, and it must be me. In high school, I would double-date with a good friend of mine, and after we took the girls home I'd give him a blow job, or he'd spend the night. Those times would start out, "Oh, suck me!" "Well, you suck me!"—that type of thing—and before you know it, "All right, whip it out!" Well, this guy had the balls to whip it out and I had the balls to do it. It's amazing what you can get that way. I had lots of friends through high school— guys I ran around with, double-dated with, went to parties with, played basketball with—and I had sex with all of them. But I lied all the way through it; I'm doing it, but I'm not gay. I'd wake up the next day and call my girlfriend and go on—find out where we were going that night, or she'd say, "The family dinner's this Sunday. What time you going to be here?" I did that all the way until I got divorced.

I watched my brothers grow up, graduate, and get married, so that's what I did. I got married right out of high school. Two to three years into my marriage, with two kids, I finally started saying, "I really *am* gay, I really am. What am I going to do about it?" I finally woke up and stopped some of the lying. I came home from being with a guy and I said to my wife, "I love you as a person and as the kids' mother, but this isn't working. I am just not happy here. I'm twenty-four years old, and I've got to figure out what's going to make me happy." My wife wasn't happy either, so we started mapping out what we could do about it.

I went back to my parents', but after about six months I realized you just can't go back. I was too old to be coming in at midnight with them still waiting up for me, or to be saying, "Mom, I'm not coming home tonight." That was a wild time. You're out all of a sudden, you're free to do what you want to do, and there's all this world out there you've never experienced. I'd had plenty of gay experiences, but I'd never been to gay bars, never experienced the nightlife, and I was trying to soak it up as quickly as possible. I got really out of control, but it didn't take long to pull myself back.

People get lost in the bar scene. I did at first. It was exotic, it was new, it was exciting. It didn't take long for that to wear off for me. But there are a lot of gay people out there who have no direction, no vision—the only thing that's important is being in the bars over the weekend, having something new to wear, and enough money to drink themselves silly. Keith and I are both very responsible and driven, and we want to work and be successful. I'm sure there are a lot of gay people out there who are the same way. But we have run into so many who are completely irresponsible, who think things are owed to them without having to work for them.

On the farm you are secluded; the people you interact with are pretty much your family. We were real private people, not telling everybody in the neighborhood all our problems. In fact, we worked real hard to keep our problems under wraps. I never saw my mom and dad openly do anything, and that's the way I've always viewed being gay—as a very private thing. I don't want to wear it on my sleeve. It's not open for discussion, and I don't ever intend it to be—with people I work with, the next-door neighbors, the family even. If you know me, you're either going to like me or you're not going to like me, but not because I'm wearing a banner up and down the street so everybody knows, or saying in your face, "I'm gay, like it or leave it."

I haven't been honest with my parents about being gay, but I've lived eight years with Keith and he's always welcome in their home, so I think they have a pretty good idea. I'm HIV-positive, and I've known that for about a year and a half, so I'm really to the point where I need to talk to Mom and Dad. We'll see, but I do think that's going to happen soon. It's time. But how can they not know I'm gay? Maybe they're just being pleasant all these years, not blurting it out, because we never talk about sex. As far as my brothers are concerned, I don't feel the need to tell them. I know they all know about it already, but I don't owe them an explanation. They probably feel responsible in some way. But I don't see the time I'm going to sit down with them and just lay my cards on the table.

Sex with a man, being gay, is what I'm comfortable doing. It's what I like to do and it's what I feel like I'm good at. When Keith and I make love, there is something that is right, completely right, and that never occurred with a woman. Yes, the act could be done with a woman, but the feeling, the passion, the pleasure is just right with a man. You've got to be born with something like that. Maybe my brothers saw something in me I didn't know about, something that was saying to them, "It's okay to do this to him—he wants to do this." I don't *blame* them for this. I don't blame anybody for this. But I can't help but wonder what they saw that allowed them to do that, why they thought it was okay, and if that's why I am the way I am—that I started enjoying it after a while, and continued with it.

I have trouble coming to grips with this because they all know they did it, and we've never talked about it, and they're all very standoffish with me. I think it makes them all uncomfortable. We interact, but there's no closeness. I really think I've made an effort throughout the years. I helped one brother build his house, and we've taken another brother's kids on vacation with us, and I've let my oldest brother spend the night with us numerous times when he needed to. They're the ones who really have a problem with it. I know I'm okay. I'm being honest, as far as my sexuality goes. The way they view me has made me a little stronger and helps me come to terms with it a little bit better.

My oldest brother is a mess, but the rest of us are all successful and responsible. Ray and I are not close now. It's not like we don't like each other. We just don't make time for one another. I don't get along with my brother just older than I, and I don't like my oldest brother at all. We've tried, but we haven't succeeded. He may be gay, too. Keith and I ran into him in a bar one night, so it was kind of tough to get out of that one. I was uncomfortable from the very get-go, and—in this big city—he was with a guy I'd dated before.

Who I am and why things have happened is something I'm trying to figure out right now. I've started seeing myself, and there are some parts I really don't like, and I've got to face them. Trying to make everybody proud of me, I spent a lot of time not recognizing who I was and lying about who I was. I tried for so long to do what I thought was the thing to do, to be the way I was supposed to be—and I tried all those things for all the wrong reasons. I had the two kids, which I don't regret at all—they're wonderful kids and bring me a lot of happiness. But it wasn't the reason to do it. I lied to myself. That's what I'm really struggling with right now. Throughout my life, there have been lies and then lies to cover lies, and lies and lies and lies.

Now I'm trying to figure out what role God has in my life. About a year ago, I started going with my parents to the church I grew up in, an Independent Christian church. I went real steady for about a year. I've yet to find me a church around here, but I really am trying to come to grips, because I do believe in God. I don't know what God thinks of me right now—that's something I need to work out.

Farming was in me, but I was never a Future Farmer of America. I think I saw a picture of my dad I didn't like—always having to work, never looking happy. But I felt sorry for my dad after we all moved away and he quit farming. He loved farming—I see that now—and after a man does that for years and just quits, I know it had to work on him. They leased the farm out, and he runs a farm machinery business so he still works like a dog. They still don't give a hoot about what the house looks like. It's not a run-down old shack, but they don't put money into the house or vehicles or anything.

My dad and mom, my uncle and his wife, my grandmother and grandfather—their commitment to one person has really been tremendous. Commitment to the right person is what I want, but when you have two men together it's too easy to just chuck it all and get out. Hell, divorce is too easy for married people these days, and with two men it's even easier. You have a fight, you move on to the next. There just doesn't seem to be a real effort to make it work. Keith and I are hitting our eighth anniversary. There have been troubles and struggles. I feel like I don't deserve him sometimes, because I've done some pretty nasty things. But the bottom line is we do love and care deeply about one another, and no matter how bad things get, that commitment remains the same. My son and daughter, twelve and nine, are here one day a week, every other weekend, and four weeks out of the year nonstop. We always do family vacations together. The kids love Keith—he is as much a father to them as I am. He is extremely successful—his drive is incredible—and his commitment to his job and to me and my family is very important to him. He will execute my will and the trust that's all set up for the kids.

I still love horses, and the farm is still a sanctuary to me. It's so open and free, being able to saddle a horse up and escape, get away, just get lost and ride. Sometimes you don't realize what you have until you don't have it anymore. I wish my kids could grow up in that environment, to learn how to care for things. They ride my horses, but it's not the same as being there day in, day out.

Just because I'm HIV-positive doesn't mean I'm not going to be here for a long time to come. It's taken me a while to realize that, but I haven't been sick, and all indicators are real good—going up, up, up. I'm healthy as a horse, I feel good, and I'm loved by a lot of people. There's absolutely no reason to think it's not going to continue for a long time. Down the road, I want to have five to ten acres, room for the horses and the animals, and then let Keith build a new house. I may be in the middle of beautiful Meridian-Kessler in Indianapolis right now, which is real nice, but there will be acreage in my future. I can guarantee it.

Lon Mickelsen

Lon was born in 1961 and grew up on a 780-acre crop farm in Mower County, southeastern Minnesota. He was the seventh of ten children, with three brothers and six sisters. Lon lives in Minneapolis and works in investment products marketing.

YOU HAD TO be the oldest boy in the house to become pals with Dad, the guy that he would discuss farm things with. When Ben, my next older brother, moved out of the house, I moved into his place, even at the dinner table. We'd all shift around the table. Now *I* was the oldest boy in the house, so all of a sudden I was pals with Dad. I didn't have to do anything to prove myself for that spot—it was by default. It felt good that Dad was treating me like he used to treat Ben, like more of an equal, like I would understand what he was talking about.

We farmed just shy of eight hundred acres, growing soybeans, corn and oats, and peas for Green Giant. My two older brothers were more involved in the farming work than I was. We had no livestock, so there weren't regular chores to do, but in the summer we had to do some of the cultivating and weeding. We were pretty involved in walking beans— walking up and down the rows of soybeans to pull weeds that were missed by the herbicides. Picking rock was a dirty, horrible job that seemed like an endurance test, but we were all expected to do it. The area had rich soil, but it was also pretty rocky, so about every two years we would pick up rocks off of all the fields. Year after year, the plows kept pulling up these ten, twenty, and thirty-pound rocks left by some prehistoric glacier.

My older sister liked mechanical things and wanted to be on a tractor as much as anybody, but in our family the guys helped dad in the field and the girls did the housework. Except for picking rock, which required a family effort, my sisters did not get involved much in farm chores. One of my sisters and I did a lot of gardening, partly because of our involvement in 4-H. With ten kids, the vegetable garden was a necessity, not a hobby. We were expected to maintain a good-sized garden, about a sixth of an acre. I was one of two males in my family who really liked to cook. Ours was a meat-and-potatoes family, and I liked to try things we didn't normally have,

251

like Oriental cooking, soufflés, and crêpes. For our family, those foods
were plenty exotic.

My parents were strict disciplinarians, which is a difficult thing to be
with ten kids. My mother was the one who really raised us. She only called
Dad in when she needed the heavy guns. Mom had a pretty gentle wooden
spoon, and we were not spanked much—although there were times I would
have preferred a swat rather than "a good, stiff talking-to," as my father
used to say. My mother, a devout Catholic, injected religion into the family whenever she could. When things were difficult, we would all get together and pray the rosary. From the time I was old enough to be carried
along to church until I left for college, the only time I ever missed a Sunday mass was when I was sick. And not just kind of sick; you had to be really sick.

There was an old German-Scandinavian work ethic, but there was a
play ethic too. We rarely worked on Sundays, and we did a lot of cookouts
and other fun things together on the weekends. My grandfather was an
avid golfer and bought his grandkids memberships at the local country
club, so we would golf with him and my dad. We had the misfortune of
living in one of the few counties in Minnesota that don't have any natural
lakes, so it was a big deal to go to a lake. A couple of Sundays each summer, we would pack up the boat and go fifty-some miles to water-ski and
splash around for the day. And in early August, after the cultivating was
done but before harvest, we would rent a cabin at a lake in northern Minnesota and go up for a week to water-ski, fish, canoe and just generally
play in the water.

I started band in fifth grade, played the French horn and then the trumpet. In eighth grade I got into singing and it became a large part of my
identity through high school and college. I was in just about every music
organization there was in high school, and I was also in a rock-and-roll
band that played in bars and clubs on the weekends. It was a Partridge
Family sort of thing—a family of five kids that went to the same school
we did. They brought in other people as they wanted to add instruments
to the band. I wasn't aware of it at the time, but two of the brothers in
that family were gay. I became very good friends with both of those guys—
there was sort of a relaxed understanding between us. I got to know them
at about the time they were coming to grips with their sexuality, probably ten years before I did.

Our farm had two large pastures, almost twenty acres, some of the best
grazing land in the county. There were creeks running through both pastures, and when I was little I would go there with friends just to explore—

Eating Apples, by Jeff Kopseng, based on a photo courtesy of Lon Mickelsen

in the creeks and the woods, along the railroad tracks, under the railroad bridges, up to the highway. You could get probably half or three-quarters of a mile from the house. I'd hike out there and sit, just to get away.

We lived very close to town, and there was a bunch of town kids that used to come down and play under one of the railroad bridges that crossed the creek. Playing "Truth or Dare" with a bunch of boys and girls, I was always more interested in seeing the boys naked. I went fishing a lot with one of the boys from town—probably the person I spent the most time with in my childhood. We spent three or four summers together, almost every day when I wasn't doing some kind of farmwork. In my youth, he was the only friend that I had any sexual encounters with. It started when we were fishing and decided to go skinny-dipping in a pool in the creek.

From there it was "you show me, I'll show you," and we felt each other's erections. That sort of thing went on for weeks one summer, probably in the fifth or sixth grade. But in high school, he and I were almost strangers; we could hardly look at each other and rarely talked. I think a lot of that was because we were embarrassed about those past summers, and didn't know how to deal with that as we got older and started to realize what it had been.

In my family, sexuality was governed largely by conservative Catholicism—that is, it was not discussed. When I was probably six years old and started asking enough questions about where the kittens came from, my mom had the talk with me about the birds and the bees. It was all presented in non-human terms. My mom and dad seemed to be reluctantly resigned to the idea that sex education should be taught in the schools, mostly because they didn't want to deal with it at home. Sexuality was held in an undercurrent. You didn't talk about it, and you certainly didn't openly demonstrate it in any way. When boyfriends and girlfriends came over to the house, they were expected to be prim and proper in front of the family. You were expected not to sit in the car with a boyfriend or girlfriend after you got home from a date. I suppose it was the convent sort of attitude—"Sex is evil, children"—not openly announced, but understood.

I dated all the way through high school, mostly to be one of the gang. I think I was aware that I had an attraction to boys, but I was trying to stay with the flow. My last steady girlfriend was in college. I went out with her for about two-and-a-half years, and broke up with her during my senior year. One night we were talking and finally I said, "Listen, I can't do this anymore." She said, "What do you mean, you can't do this?" And I thought, I don't know what I mean. Why do I want to break up with somebody I've been going with for two-and-a-half years, a person I actually love? The answer was obvious, but my mouth couldn't form the words: Because I'm not sexually attracted to her. I was dating her, but fantasizing about my male roommates.

A few months later, at home for spring break, I went for a walk down the railroad tracks one night and was sitting on the same railroad bridge that I'd played "Truth or Dare" under as a child. I was trying to figure out why I'd broken up with my girlfriend. After an hour or so, I finally came to the point of saying out loud, "I must be gay." I couldn't believe it, but I must be. As soon as I'd clicked that little switch, a hundred things rolled through my mind. I would have to somehow get used to it, though it seemed like it wouldn't work either way—I couldn't be straight, and I couldn't be gay. How could I ever tell my parents? They could never deal with it, because the Catholic church is against it. How could I ever meet somebody? Could I ever have a real relationship? I felt a strange, quiet panic; this was something I was going to have to carry all by myself. But I'd had enough of fighting it for fifteen or twenty years, and I was giving up. I decided to affirm it because I couldn't fight it anymore. If I could have fought it, I would have.

I'm still coming to grips with being gay. I've pretty much always seen myself as a homosexual trying to appease society by pretending I wasn't. I've never liked the word "gay." It doesn't bother me as much now, but I used to choke on that word. It seemed like a derogatory term, like black people calling each other niggers. I first went to my therapist to deal with a relationship, and in one of the first sessions he said, "We'll deal with this relationship first, and then we'll deal with your homophobia." I thought, who's he talking to? It was shocking to hear somebody say I was homophobic. To me that was something only a non-gay person could have. Then I realized you can accept who you are, but you can still be crippled by a fear of it.

Dealing with my homophobia has been an exercise in getting over avoiding being gay and making a conscious effort to tell people who I want to know about it. Part of that has to be to inform my family. But my parents are so reactionary, I don't know if or when I will ever tell them. It just might not be worth the hassle to me. But my first experience of telling a sibling was very positive. I told my sister who's a year older than me, as we went for a walk near my parents' house. It was very reassuring, but I knew it would be with her, and she had kind of suspected it anyway.

One of the first people I told was my old college roommate. He's one of the people I'd been most attracted to, and had he been gay I think we could have been very good partners. He's married to one of my old girlfriends, a sister of the two gay brothers in the band I was in. She and I were dating when we got to college, but I became very interested in him, and so did she. She got to know him from hanging around our dorm room, and they started dating. That was terribly traumatic for me. I was losing a girlfriend, who was a true friend and a social safety net to me, and at the same time I was losing the person who I was really sexually interested in—and I was losing them to each other. But the wounds healed fast. They've been wonderfully supportive, and they're still among my best friends.

I'm talking about it with people who have known for a year, asking them what their reaction was when I told them, talking to other people who are gay, finding out about their life experiences. The very first person I ever told was my last girlfriend in college, who for six years had been wondering why I really broke up with her. She's still a very good friend, and I made a special trip to the farm in central Minnesota where she lives with her husband and family, to talk to her. She was able to tell me about all the people who have been talking about me for the last few years. It's an eye-opening experience when you find that a lot more people are aware of it than you think or hope are.

It's been eight, nine, ten years, and I'm just now starting to put all the pieces together. Up until the last year or so I've chosen to conform and to give the appearance of conforming. My overriding passion has been to meet people's expectations, and I've always been able to do it, largely. That stems certainly from a childhood of doing what was expected of me by my parents. When I told my sister that I was gay, she said, "You've always stood out in my mind as the one person who wasn't in trouble with Mom and Dad for what you were doing on your dates." My sisters were always in trouble for sitting in the driveway necking in the car when they got back from their dates. "That's why you got off so easy," she said, "but now you're going to make up for it!"

I had three steady dating relationships in high school. I was physical with those girls, but not particularly sexual. I was one to emphasize getting to know someone emotionally and intellectually. In college, I was sexually active with one woman, but that was a very small part of the relationship. I've had very deep feelings for some of the women I've dated, and I could be physically aroused, but I was never fulfilled sexually. My masturbation fantasies were always about other males. When I was younger, my fantasies focused on the sexual experiences I'd had with my friend in fifth and sixth grades. As I got older, they were about guys I knew who I would like to have physical contact with, like college roommates. I don't remember fantasizing about someone I didn't already know pretty well. The sexual fantasy part of it came after the friendship was there. I've never been one to fantasize about celebrities or men in magazines.

I didn't have sexual contact with another male until I was a senior in college, so there was a long, dry spell. That first experience was with a college roommate. We had been friends for two years, but our encounter scared him so badly he barely wanted to talk to me after that. I haven't talked to him for years now, but what I've heard about his life is a sad story. He comes of an absurdly staunch Catholic upbringing, and has been trying to please his parents for years. He has actually moved back—a thirty-four-year-old guy who's living with his parents and constantly trying to make them happy. I wish he would throw all that off and get on with his life. I'm not Catholic now. I'm not even religious, and in many ways I feel like a more spiritual person now than I did when I was religious. But I never felt like I couldn't be Catholic because I was gay. I gave up religion before I came to grips with my sexuality.

A friend of mine who grew up on a farm near Omaha gave in to his homosexuality at about the same age I did. We were starting to deal with being gay at a time when many friends our age who grew up in urban areas were putting things together and getting on with their lives. It took longer to come to grips with being gay growing up on a farm, not so much because of the homophobia but because of the absence of homosexuality in that culture. It's not that homosexuality was frowned upon. It simply didn't exist. There were never any strong overtones about it being wrong, because it was never discussed. Of course, the adults were aware of it, but it was seen as more of a big-city thing that they didn't understand and didn't have to deal with, so they didn't. One of my uncles had a gay brother-in-law who moved back to Minnesota from New York when I was in high school. I never even knew he existed until then. My mom and dad would talk about him. "Oh, he's the guy that *thinks* he's a homo. Maybe a doctor could help him."

There was no role model anywhere in that community, so that I could say, "Here's a person who is like me, who's gay, who's an adult, who's not running away from it." I'm sure it's not that way in all farm communities, but I had to wait until I went elsewhere to find acceptance of it—to see it, even, and not be afraid of it—and to see people who were living as gay and not repressing it. I have friends who grew up in larger cities who talk about gay couples dating in high school. Seems like it must have been on another planet. Where I came from, anybody who was suspicious of themselves being gay in high school just didn't go out, period—or they asked a girl out just to stay with the flow. The two gay brothers who were in my band had prom dates, and I'm sure their mother was pleased that they were home nice and early.

Looking back at some of the people who still live in that community, I wonder if this person or that person is gay. My "Truth or Dare" friend from fifth and sixth grade dated my sister a few times. I'm pretty sure he's straight, but I don't know. He's one of the few people in my class who's not married. He stayed in town to take over his father's business. To this day, we're still embarrassed about the naked games we played as kids. When I go home at Christmas I see him at my parents' church and it's awkward. "Hi, how ya doin'?" "Good. How 'bout you?" "Great." "Bye."

A long-term relationship is something I aspire to, but right now I find it difficult to imagine myself with anybody on a long-term basis. And I like living alone so much. I think of a long-term committed relationship between two individuals as an ideal. And though it's hard to see myself in that kind of relationship, I've never been involved in a one-night stand either. I've only had sexual experiences with four or five guys, and I've always kind of held a low opinion of people who sleep around a lot. It seemed that they were chasing something that they weren't even coming close to finding—that their sleeping around was getting them farther away from what they were really looking for.

I came off of my first real gay relationship about four months ago. It wasn't a relationship I particularly wanted to be in, but it lasted almost two years anyway, so I think my lifestyle and remnants of my nun-induced morality lend themselves to a long-term relationship. But I haven't yet found anybody that would even be a possibility with. That's largely because I haven't been in the flow. I've been running from being gay, or trying to figure it out. I haven't been in situations where I could meet a lot of gay men I would find interesting or who would be a good match for me. There's a community of gay musicians and visual artists in Minneapolis. They're very campy, cliquish, they have limited interests, and when they have parties, straight people are not invited. I've never seen myself fitting into that, but as a singer and musician it's the only part of the gay community I've ever really known. I need to find out what else is out there, and that's very difficult to do until you've decided to be out with it. Over the next few months, as part of my therapy for myself, I intend to get out and about and see what's there. Minneapolis is a very connected city for the gay community, and I think I can find a lot of areas of common interest other than the arts.

When my mother did her living will, she named me and my oldest sister as the executors. I asked her why, out of ten kids, she chose us, and she said, "Because you're as logical as you are emotional." I'm not sure what that means, but I think I have an idea, and she's probably right. I've always thought my mother has had something of a soft spot for me because, more than the rest of her kids, I've been able to tell her exactly what I think without being too worried about it. She has looked for things from me as much as I have looked for things from her. It's been that way since I was probably ten years old. She and I have talked about moral and religious issues, which makes her uptight when she knows I don't see eye-to-eye with her on a lot of things. Many of my siblings don't either, but they're less inclined to talk to her about some of those things that she finds very threatening. I think she and I see the world similarly, but she's got a conservative, devout religious element that I don't have at all.

To my parents, a mixed marriage was a Catholic and a Lutheran. Diversity was okay as long as it wasn't threatening—somebody who was Danish instead of Norwegian or Swedish or German. Louie Anderson, the comedian, does a routine where he talks about driving down the street with his dad, and his dad says, "Well, look at that guy—what the hell? He's got a ponytail, for Christ's sake!" That's my dad, privately deriding people who don't conform to the local lifestyle. I never felt like I was friends with my father when I was younger, but I'm very good friends with him now. He's not aware of my sexuality, but when a kid gets to be thirty years old, and the only one of ten kids who's not married, I'm sure there are questions in his mind. But so far it has not gotten in the way of us being good friends.

Some of the most intelligent people I know are farmers in the community where I grew up. But to my dad, the reason for going to college was so you wouldn't wind up farming—as though farming were reserved for only the uneducated or unintelligent. It was always preached to us that we needed to aspire above farming, yet I think my dad really liked it, and still does. I wish he could see more clearly how much he really enjoys it, because you can see it in him. He retired last year, but he still helps his brother during planting and harvest. And I can see his face become more intense and involved when we talk about the crops, how big the harvest will be, or the latest farm machinery to hit the market. I think he discouraged us from farming because he felt that his economic fate was in somebody else's hands—that he wouldn't necessarily get ahead by working harder.

Looking back, the farm and my hometown seem like distant, impossible places—places where my life doesn't fit, and where "keeping it to yourself" is considered an admirable trait. But growing up on the farm didn't seem that limiting to me until I was no longer there. And though there were times when it was rough around the edges, my life on the farm gave me many of the things that I value most today: my appreciation of the importance of relying on others and allowing them to rely on me, of balancing work and play, of keeping a wide-eyed fascination in the world; my love of animals and nature, my work ethic, my desire to grow things. Every now and then, sitting in a twenty-story office building in downtown Minneapolis, I have the urge to hop in my car and drive until I see corn. Some of my urban friends feel panicky out there, but to me the big open spaces are very calming.

Steven Preston

Steven was born in 1962 and grew up with two brothers, one older and one younger, on his father's 300-acre dairy farm in south-central Wisconsin. They farmed another 200 acres owned by his grandparents. At the time of our interview, Steven was living on a small hobby farm in southern Wisconsin and working as a nurse.

I NEVER KNEW my mother. She left us when I was one and killed herself when I was nine. My brothers and I don't know anything about why she left, because my dad would never talk about it. She and my dad had separated, and one day she just left us with the babysitter and didn't come home. When my dad came to see us, Neil was running around in the snow barefoot and Kevin and I were so ill we had to be hospitalized. Kevin wasn't a year old, I was a little over a year, and Neil was two. My dad was so busy with fieldwork and the cattle that Grandma looked after us until we got to an age to help with milking.

My dad oversaw it, but my older brother Neil and I did most of the herd management. It was our job to select bulls for breeding, register the cattle, manage feeding, raise the young stock. Starting at 5 A.M., we would have maybe twenty calves to feed, repeated the cycle at night, then fed and bedded the cows. We raised all of our own crops. Haying was never-ending and basically took up our entire summer—at least ten thousand bales a year to get us through. Many summers, if it weren't for the neighbor kids we would never have had any contact with kids our own age, because we didn't leave the farm except to go to church. It was very isolating—Grandma and Grandpa and my dad.

Grandma's a stern old Norwegian who believed strongly in "spare the rod, spoil the child," so we did not miss an opportunity to be spanked. We always attended everything at the United Church of Christ, and it was very important that we were baptized and confirmed. If we whispered during the church service, my grandmother had this signal—a little nod of her head. She'd look at you just once, and if you didn't stop, you knew your ass would be cream when you got out of church.

Family functions were very important because we lived with Grandma and Grandpa, and everybody came there, but holidays were never relaxing or enjoyable. The week before was always hellish. We would clean the house three days before everybody came, and Grandma would be cooking and screaming at everybody, "Don't mess up the place!" Then they would come, and they would eat within an hour, we'd do presents or whatever, and they would be gone and it was clean-up time again. It was like feeding a threshing crew.

We would can corn from late June or early July, until we were done. It took weeks. Huge gunny sacks of sweet corn would be brought up from the fields and we would husk the ears. Every piece of leaf and silk had to be completely removed for Grandma, who would sit on a chair with a huge basin on a stool between her legs and cut corn for hours. I used to think, "That fuckin' corn doesn't taste *that* good," but it taught me that hard work and stamina is what it takes. Things don't get done by themselves.

I loved to visit our neighbors, an old couple with no children that lived around the hill from us. That's where I learned about chickens—what to feed them, what they need, and how to butcher them. I'd consort with all the women who had chickens, because I just had to know more about them. Poultry was one of my major interests, but my dad forbade it. I was not to ever get poultry. "You can't have those filthy things when you're on grade A." My dad's place was immaculate for grade A milk production. Everything was very clean, and the barn was whitewashed and limed within an inch of its life.

It took me years to get chickens, and when I did I got beaten for going against my dad's wishes. I was ten or eleven, and I drove the tractor over to the neighbors who had birds, a mile or two away, picked out what I wanted and paid for them, and brought them home. I thought I could hide them. My dad didn't want those goddamned things in his barn. They'd get in the hay and shit on everything. They were to be confined. Getting chickens was one way I could express that I didn't always have to be who he wanted me to be, I could be independent, and I didn't need his help with it.

The inside of the milk house had to be painted yearly to stay on grade A. When I was painting it one year, I slipped off the ladder and spilled paint on the bulk milk tank. I was afraid it might contaminate the milk, so I ran and told Dad and he told me to get some gasoline and clean it off before it dried. Well, I got to scrubbing, and when he came into the milk house I was getting light-headed because the fumes were getting strong. Then the gas water-heater came on and the whole place blew up. I had pretty bad burns on my arms, and ran out to the stock tank to put them in the cool water. I had to go to the doctor, and then the doctor didn't get there for another hour. My stepmother told me to be quiet. "It can't be *that* bad." Illness was not allowed—you had a job to do. You didn't go to the doctor unless you were almost dead.

My mother killed herself when she was twenty-eight. She took an overdose, I think. I've never gotten the full story. One night Dad was crying, and I'd never seen him cry. I thought he was made of stone—this big, strong, mean guy. We said, "What's wrong?" "Oh, your mother died." What are you supposed to think when you're nine years old and you don't know this person even existed? I went to bed wondering, what the fuck just happened? My dad was very somber that whole week after he had told us. I wanted to go to the wake so bad because I wanted to see her. Looking at her face, it was so bizarre—this woman I hadn't seen since I was an infant. By her head was a little flower arrangement my dad had purchased that said "Mother of . . ." and listed our names.

Never dare to think for yourself. Follow the herd. Don't be different, because people will talk about you. My dad would say, "What are people going to think if you do that?" I don't care what they think. We were told we had to at least try football one year. I quit after two weeks because the coach was such an ass. I got into canning that year in 4-H, and the other kids and their parents made fun of me. I was interested in sewing for a while, too, and I was the only boy in choir for two years. One day I went up to Grandma's to dig up some iris to plant, and when I got back with them my dad and the hired man and Neil and Kevin were sitting around the table, and Kevin announced, "I told them why you went to Grandma's"—like it was really femmy that I went there to get flowers. They all kind of snickered, but I didn't give a shit. I didn't ask for your approval when I started, and I certainly don't care for it now.

I knew I was gay from the time I was five. I was always attracted to boys and I always wanted to be more than friends with them. I wanted them to touch me, to be sexual. About the time my mother died, Neil and I looked up homosexuality in the encyclopedia. It said something about males who engage in sexual contact with one another more than six times. So we were sitting there counting on our fingers and decided we were.

Our father's brother lived with us until he went off to college. He was having sex with us when we were little kids, from when I was five or six. He was ten years older than me and would play little sex games when he would babysit. It wasn't painful or, in my mind, nasty, but I was real uptight and nervous about it when we were little because I didn't understand it. Nobody ever talked to me about my genitals, and then all of a sudden somebody's rubbing them. It would develop a little sore, it was painful, and who could you tell? But as I matured, it felt good. We did everything—oral, anal, fondling, masturbating. Even when he was married, he'd call us up and say, "Can you guys come out and help me with a load of rocks?" We'd go up to his place, his wife would be gone, and he'd be in the living room in his underwear wanting us to fuck him.

My brothers and I had sex together until we became adults. It was very natural for us to be sexual—it was part of our rearing and it was acceptable to us. After all, our uncle did it with us. I became sexually aggressive with my cousins and with neighbor kids. We'd be taking a pee and then start playing with each other's penises. It was mostly fondling each other, masturbating, some anal sex. It just happened, it was never planned. We usually did it in the cow passes under the roads, or in the woods, or up in the hay barn. I had a cousin who liked to get fucked, and we had sex a lot. I'd go down to get the cows in the morning, and his bedroom was on the first floor. He'd roll over when I came in and I'd screw him, then go chase the cows home.

One day Dad was milking and I was washing cows for him. The man who did milk testing was there and was talking about how he was just disgusted by one of his neighbor's children who had had sex with another boy. He said to my dad, "What would you do with that kind of shit in your house?" My dad just shook his head. "Oh, that's just sick," was written all over his face. I thought, if you don't try it, you'll never know, Daddy.

I dated three or four girls throughout high school, one very steadily. I enjoyed the emotional part of our relationship a lot more than I enjoyed the sexual. The genitals of women, and their breasts, were just repulsive to me, but I kept at it and kept trying. Neil and I talked with each other about men we were attracted to, but we both denied it a lot and fought it and tried to go straight. When Neil got a woman pregnant and married her right out of high school, he made it real clear to me. "I'm not gay anymore, and we're not going to be sexual anymore because I'm straight now, and I'm married."

I was very out my senior year of high school. I decided that if I was going to be my own person, I had to be honest with myself. And I think maybe I was making it known to get other people's reactions. I took a lot of shit from the other boys about it, and would get into knock-down, drag-out fist fights in the middle of the classroom with those little assholes. They'd call me a name, I'd smack them in the face, and all hell would break loose, but I didn't care. It only made me stronger. It made me think, "I am so glad I do not have to stay in this one-horse town for the rest of my life. I get to leave here, and I have their permission because they don't want me here." I didn't have to worry about what anybody thought. It

was safe past the town limits—"on the other side," as I always called it—
where people didn't know me and I could be who I was.

At seventeen, I was going to the bars in Madison, and I had quite a circle of gay friends. My stepmother was supportive about my coming out,
which encouraged me to find out who I was. Without her, there would've
been a lot more fumbling and confusion. But then she turned around and
told everybody in town I was going to the gay bars, and would ridicule
me behind my back. If you can't say it to my face, say it to my back, bitch.

The godawfulest day of my life was when I had just turned sixteen and
went to the driver's license place with my dad. Driving there, he said, "This
is going to be your last fuckin' chance to get this goddamned license this
summer, so you'd better not fuck up on the test." When I showed him
that I got my license, he said, "Oh, thank God!" and onward home we
went. He was so derogatory. I look the most like my mother, and when I
would cry he would say, "You look just like your goddamned mother." I
thought, "Good. At least I don't look like you, you asshole."

My dad would fly off the handle and beat me, punch me—I would be
so bruised up. I remember wanting him dead—wanting him to suffer a
bad, painful death. I went with him one day to pick up a bull. He was
being a real smart-ass, and got in the cattle trailer and whacked the bull
on the nose with a crowbar. The bull went ape and nailed him, just smashed
the shit out of him, and I couldn't do anything. This two-thousand-pound
bull was goring my dad, and all these memories came back of wanting him
dead. He was very badly hurt, and on the way home he said, "What were
you going to do? Stand there and let the son of a bitch kill me?" And I
thought, "You perfect fucking asshole, yes, I should've." I have never been
afraid to swear. That was part of my survival, growing up. I couldn't hit
him back; all I had was my sassy little mouth.

One of my summer jobs was to cut hay. It was a big, hot bitch of a day,
and I got there at eight in the morning and didn't quit until 3:30 when I
finally cut the last windrow. It was a forty-acre piece that would never end—
full of dead furrows and rocks that broke teeth out of the haybine. I was
hot and thirsty and tired, but I was proud that I had gotten it done and I
thought Dad would be happy. When I got to the gate, he was coming up
the hill. Looking around at the field, he said, "How in the hell am I supposed to bale this, the way you've cut it?" We got into a huge argument
and he jumped up on the tractor and started hitting me. It was never civil
or calm, it was always explosive. Everything escalated into, "My God, how
could you do something so fucking dumb?" I left, moved out that day. I
was seventeen years old, suicidal, and to get out of there was saving my

life. I wanted to be independent of him, to never have to rely on him for anything. And I never wanted to look at a farm again.

I moved to Madison when I was eighteen. I was young and kind of cute and men were attracted to me. I was using drugs and drinking a lot and I slept with a lot of men and had a wonderful time. It's lucky I didn't get AIDS or god only knows what. For the first time I felt like a feeling person. I was free from my dad, experimenting with sexuality, and able to try anything. It got old real quick. Within the first year, I thought, I want to be involved with somebody, but all these people are flakes and they're out for one thing and one thing only.

Was I going to follow my sexual choice or do what society wanted— get married and have a family? At that point I was suicidal, because I was so torn. If I'm straight, I'm not going to be happy. If I'm gay, I'm not going to be happy. I didn't belong to either side. I was very confused and I didn't have anyone to talk to. I ended up living with a woman for nine months and getting her pregnant. She decided to have an abortion, and I was very glad at the time because I was nineteen and I was a mess.

My first long-term relationship was with Michael, a school-teacher. It lasted seven years. He drank too much, but that was a very small part of the problem. We didn't have a thing in common. He didn't want to farm, he wanted nothing to do with livestock. I would talk about wanting to get a place in the country, and that was so unappealing to him. He would've rather had me cut his foot off.

Hank and I have seven acres, mostly pasture for the heifers. Three acres are rented, four we own. We raise dairy heifers, breed them at fifteen months, and sell them as two-year-old fresh heifers. We like to have a milk cow to make our own cheese and butter. We produce our own eggs and chicken for eating, and raise our own pork. When we have a fresh cow, we buy some pigs and feed them out on the milk by-products until they're about two hundred pounds, then have them butchered.

We raise our own corn and most of our own vegetables, and I've planted thousands of annuals throughout the yard and garden. Every year, we have a large vegetable garden and are able to give a lot of it away. We have between three and five hundred hills of potatoes every year. To share the garden with others gives me so much pleasure. God lent me this ground to grow something on, and I think God would be so happy that it's either beautifying or providing food for someone.

I loved going to poultry shows when I was a kid, and I still do. I think I drive Hank crazy, because we've got to go to every show and they're all basically the same. Runner ducks are my specialty, and I've won trophies and ribbons with them. We're also raising white leghorn banties, which I really like—they're cute little chickens. Blue andalusians are another favorite; very few people have them. We've raised them for three years, keeping our lines going. We'll start out with about twenty-five baby chicks in the spring and the number increases. "Oh, we can get twenty-five more." By the end of last summer we had 250 chickens.

I've always liked to milk cows. Maybe it's the closeness of the animal and seeing the results of massaging the udder when she lets her milk down. If you like cows, you get to know individual animals—what their moods are, when their heat is strong, when they're sick. I've been an advocate of the cow's gentle nature since I was quite young. I really preferred being with the animals to fieldwork, and I loved showing the cattle—trimming their feet, cleaning them, and getting them all sparkly white. I had a pet cow named Lily, the first heifer I'd raised and shown in the 4-H fair, and she was just a big docile old lunk. She didn't milk worth a shit, and she was basically worthless, but she was my pet. Lily was so tame you could sit on her or curl up next to her when she was laying down. I drove my dad crazy with my carrying on if he even mentioned selling her, so old Lily hung on more years than she should have.

Hank and I always have a calf or two around. We like to watch them grow and mature and become milk cows. We recently sold a two-year-old heifer, quite a beauty. Hank felt bad that we had to sell her, but I needed the money for school. She's got a good home, and that's more important to us than holding onto her. I keep telling Hank we should buy a Jersey herd, about thirty cows to milk, and run a small operation to raise enough crops to feed them—under two hundred acres. That wouldn't support us, but it would be so wonderful to be your own boss, just to have the sounds of your own voice and the cattle bellering, and the quiet.

I want to be romantic, not to be taken for granted, to be kissed a lot, to be told I'm loved. I want the country life, and he must like chickens and cattle, and baking and eating, and drinking champagne and wine. He must know how to enjoy life and not be afraid to get some shit on his shoes and some dirt under his fingernails. I want somebody who is going to be honest and monogamous and very sexual. My early experiences formed a big part of what I like now sexually, and it really stripped away my inhibitions. I enjoy sex immensely and I feel very comfortable expressing myself. Sex is one of the better parts of life, I think.

I'm very open with my family and have made it clear what my relationship with Hank is. Take me or leave me. I've been through enough with them that I don't have time for that shit. My dad has said, "What are you going to do when you get old? You're going to be alone. You won't have any kids." He's got three kids and we all resent him. Ain't it great to have kids?

My brother Neil is also gay, and he is the only family I feel like I could count on if I really needed some emotional support. Kevin's so different from me and Neil—he's like my dad. He doesn't talk about anything but what's on the surface—hunting, crops, what cow is testing highest this year, the new bull that's out from this or that company. A typical conversation with Kevin: "How are you and your wife doing?" "We separated." "Oh, what caused that?" "Well, I was hunting all the time, and she didn't like that I was gone." End of conversation.

My dad looked down on dairy farmers who were grade B, and it was like a big joke to him if a farmer had trouble. "Did you see so-and-so tipped a wagon over? What a stupid damned thing to do." I was raised to be real negative and critical of what other people did, and to judge them if they weren't successful. There was always competition—your animals have to be better than the neighbor's, and you have to have all purebreds. Throw out the old. Newer means better and more important and richer. "I've got new self-unloading wagons to fill the silo with. Zoellers are using their old machinery, and they're beating it into the ground. They must not have the money."

You're on your own in this world. My dad really made that clear. If I was going to survive, it was up to me. Dad didn't care about us in the way a father should. He was more worried about what Joe Blow over the hill had, and what they were doing, and what sports their kids were in, and why weren't *we* doing as well? Shit, we were good students and we helped him. I feel like I have to work every day not to be like my dad. When I'm upset, I tend to go immediately for the negative. Now I think, slow down and start thinking rationally. I'm a sensible, logical person who can figure this out without losing my cool. I was taught to react now, react quick, and then it's over with. And after he'd beat me bloody, he'd smile and say, "What's for supper?" "Hey, what do you want for supper, Dad?"—as I'm wiping my eyes and my wounds and thinking, "Get me the hell out of here." I always wanted his approval but always hated him because of it.

How is it that some people grow up with all this baggage and actually are productive adults, and others just never can cope? They're in the bottle or trashed on something all the time. Somehow you either cope or you give up. I guess if you're a fighter or a survivor, you manage—because you want better, you want to improve your life, you want to be happy. I really feel good about my life and where it's at right now. Some of the anger will never go away, but I'm not looking for a quick fix.

I believe God created me, so therefore he must love me. If I am a sinner, then he will forgive me. I believe in an afterlife, and that I will go to heaven. What do you want from your life, what will make you happy? Can you find your happiness within without destroying yourself getting there? A lot of people are destroyed. My mother is an example of that. Will it make you happy to walk through the woods and hear the birds sing? That's as close to God as I will ever be.

Connie Sanders

Connie was born in 1962 and grew up with three older brothers and two younger sisters on a farm in Franklin County, southern Illinois. They farmed about 120 acres, on which they grew corn, wheat, soybeans, and hay, and raised beef cattle, hogs, and chickens. Connie's father worked full-time as a coal miner. Connie lives in Chicago, where he teaches in a college.

MY MOTHER CALLED last night and was telling me about all these people she knew who were sick or dying. I told her I had just come from visiting a very sick friend at the hospital. She asked what was wrong, and I said, "He has pneumonia, and I think he has AIDS—actually, I know he has AIDS, and he knows it too." And my mother said, "Oh, that's really sad." Her tone made me think that she meant it was sad that people do that to themselves. She said, "How do you know him?" and I said, "He's a friend. I'm better friends with his friend Gary." I didn't allow myself to go ahead and say, "Actually, Gary and Kurt are lovers, and I've been friends with Gary for years, and they've been such a support for each other, and Gary's being so strong and so nurturing right now, and I don't know what Kurt would do without Gary being there." I wanted to say all those things, but I didn't.

Sometimes I think it makes sense to come out to my parents, and then I go home to visit and I'm back in a world that's so completely different from the world I know now. Where I grew up, everybody was pretty much the same—white, working-class, rural, Protestant. People trusted each other, neighbors kept an eye out for each other, and the church was like an extended family, very communal and secure. But it wasn't a place where diversity was valued. It was like homosexuality didn't exist, except in a sermon or in a Bible verse condemning it. There was no one to talk to about things like that, at least no one I knew of.

I rode horseback every chance I got from the time I was nine years old until I was about fourteen. Sometimes I rode with friends, sometimes with Dad, but most of the time by myself. I craved the time alone in the wide-open countryside, the physical contact with my horse, the sense of independence. And I spent a lot of time in my bedroom, reading and writing in a journal, with a sense of being alone. I think that kind of experience contributed to my being a spiritual person. I've had to go inside myself so much to get a sense of who I am and how I fit into the world, what's important and what's not.

Sometimes I feel that I was this person sort of planted on the farm. I always felt sort of outside of them all. Now that I'm in an urban environment I feel so comfortable, it's almost like coming home. But I have a good time when I visit my parents now, when it's just my parents and me. I dreaded it for a long time because I'd have to edit out quite a bit of my life to be with them. One of these days I'm going to stop limiting myself, and I'm going to talk to them about it.

I wasn't as involved in the farmwork as my older brothers. I helped deliver baby lambs and calves, and my everyday chores were gathering eggs, carrying hay, and watering the cattle—sometimes by using an axe to break the ice on the pond. I liked doing things that let me get out on the tractor by myself and just go from one end of the field to the other. I would daydream or sing—songs from church camp, songs from musicals, or songs we had sung in choir at school.

I hated picking corn. We had a corn-picker that was pulled behind the tractor, with the wagon hooked on behind it. It was a jalopy of a thing, and a hassle. I'd have to ride in the wagon, and when the corn piled up too high I'd knock it down and even it out. Before we got the corn-picker we picked corn by hand, which took forever. When I was five years old, I missed being in the big Halloween parade in town because we were out picking corn. It got late, and my dad had to get the job done. Mom said I wouldn't be able to go because she thought I was coming down with a cold—but I was out there on that corn wagon, for god's sake!

The next year, in first grade, I was on a float in the Halloween parade. It was supposed to be about Illinois history; there was a farmer, a minister, and an Indian. Agriculture, faith and heritage. I was the minister. I represented faith. I had a big Bible and my little black suit, and I waved at people. I really liked that, because I was a very religious kid and I enjoyed being the star. My parents were involved in the United Methodist church, and my mother especially was very religious. I was sort of the favored child with my mother, and I was the only one of the kids who ever took religion as seriously as she did.

Dad would come up behind Mother at the kitchen stove and start rubbing her neck, and she'd start giggling. They were very lovely-dovey with each other. Dad would sometimes tease Mom by putting her over his knee and spanking her while she giggled and pretended to try to stop him. They obviously wanted us to see a healthy, playful attitude about sexuality in marriage, but they were embarrassed to talk about it, especially Dad. One time, when we were breeding rabbits, I asked him about how rabbits had babies. All he would say was, "Well, they do it just like any other animal does. The buck fucks the doe, and she has babies."

My dad was very hard-working, he knew what his priorities were, and taking care of the family came first. He was a fairly typical farmer, blue-collar kind of father and could have a coarse sense of humor. I, being a self-righteous little kid, sometimes got offended by things he said. I liked to watch shows like *The Waltons*, but Dad was more into cowboy shows.[1] And there was nothing worse for him than having to watch TV musicals like *Oklahoma!* or *The Sound of Music*, which I loved. Dad and I were so completely different in so many ways, we just didn't connect. With my brothers, at least he had to do things like giving them condoms to keep them out of trouble with girls. I guess he thought I was such a goody-two-shoes, he didn't need to bring that up with me.

Fall was my favorite time of year, but I always knew there would be a re-vival meeting at the church. From my infancy until I was about fourteen, I went to revival meetings every fall, where I'd hear a lot of preaching and fist-pounding about hellfire and brimstone. In high school, I started going to a holiness camp where they were into something called sanctification, which they interpreted as instantaneous perfection and holiness. I yearned for perfection, strived to attain the love of God, and had constant guilt. When I noticed my attraction to another guy at school, I would pray, "Thank you, God, for beautiful people. Help me not to be lustful." I had gotten this prayer idea from an advice column in a Christian youth mag-azine.

I was usually a gregarious kid, very good in school, and active in band, speech team, church youth group, and other things. During my junior year, however, I started dropping out of activities and didn't talk to my friends as much. My grades went from A's to C's and D's. I was depressed and started feeling guilty about things like being in the marching band, because of the baton twirlers' sexy outfits, or because we played "The Strip-per" at some of the basketball games. When my parents talked about buy-ing some new furniture, I told them they didn't need it, that they should save their money and be good stewards.

My church often had altar calls during the invitational hymn at the end of the service. The minister would ask those moved by the sermon to come to the front of the church to kneel and pray, to get right with God. It was not something most people did every week. Maybe they did it once and considered themselves "saved." I started doing it a lot. The fall of my junior year, I'd spend whole days thinking about what I could possibly have been doing that was sinful in the past half hour, and asking God to forgive me. My parents saw how depressed and fanatical I was becoming, and Mom got upset and started crying a few times. She took me to the family doctor to get a prescription for an antidepressant, which didn't seem to help much.

One Sunday morning when I had been praying and crying by my bed, my dad told me, "Look, your mom's going to church and we're going to have a talk." Dad and I went out to the backyard and sat under a tree. He began by saying, "You're hurting your mother, and I want it to stop. You're a good-looking young man, it's the fall of the year, you've got everything going for you—you're smart and you're popular. You have to pull yourself up by the bootstraps and get over this." Then we actually started talking about things, and he asked me a lot of questions. "Do you have homosexual desires?" He didn't ask it in a judgmental way, but I lied and said no. He asked me about erections and masturbation, and I told him I believed I had arrived at a spiritual plane above all that. I think that was one of his first clues that I was really fucked up.

As I got worse, I spent hours on my knees by my bed, praying and crying. I could hardly eat, and started choking on my food. I'm a diabetic, so my parents decided they had to do something. They called another farm family, because one of their sons had had a breakdown, got the name of his psychiatrist in St. Louis, and took me there to get treatment.

The hospital was a liberating experience for me. Here were all these people who were urban, educated in a different way, who didn't measure everything by the church and by what the neighbors thought. They challenged my beliefs in ways that sometimes seemed harsh and cynical to me then, but they helped me begin to look at belief more critically. Though it was painful and terribly frightening, it helped to free me. After a few weeks I was released, and after a few more weeks I got off the medication. I had never before realized that I could be just a normal kid. Finally I was able to believe that God loved me as much as anyone, and I could stop spending so much time worrying about it.

When I was sixteen, after I got out of the hospital, I started dating girls. My parents always liked the girls I dated; they were all pretty safe choices. I became very close with a girl who was active in the church youth group. We both ended up going to the same Free Methodist college, where students had to sign a statement promising not to have sex or to drink or smoke on campus. My junior year in college, I dated a girl my parents liked very much. Karen was a Baptist girl who used a lot of makeup and was pretty in a sort of artificial way. She worked with handicapped kids and was a very sweet, giving person—almost neurotically giving. When Karen met my family, she really won them over, so much so that everybody was upset with me when I broke up with her. I later started dating a girl who was not very physically attractive in the traditional sense. Diane was very intelligent, a math major. We watched *Masterpiece Theatre* together and talked about philosophy.

After my parents met Diane, they sat me down and told me how girls like Karen only come along once in a lifetime. My mother did this whole psychoanalytical thing about how I always rejected the things I wanted. She recalled how she had tried to buy me some cowboy boots when I was five years old, and I cried and cried in the store because I didn't want them, I didn't like them, and then when she brought me home, I wouldn't take them off—I wore them and wore them. Now I was rejecting Karen, this girl they loved and thought I was in love with. Why was I doing this to myself? Why couldn't I just give myself what I wanted? When I tried to explain what Diane and I had together, my dad said, "Don't give me all this about intellectual and spiritual relationships. Physical attraction is very important." I'll be sure to remind him of that when I explain my sexuality to him.

As a young child I saw *Cinderella,* with Lesley Ann Warren. I was just enchanted—with her, but also with the prince. I was very concerned about whether I would grow up to be handsome like the prince, perhaps because I was very drawn to him—wanting to be like him and wanting to have him. I had crushes on men who were authority figures—my minister, several teachers. When I got into high school, I started having crushes on other boys my age.

In a religious magazine for kids called *Campus Life,* a guy wrote a column about dating and sex, and every once in a while he would respond to a letter about gays. He would give advice like, "It's a wrong way to live your life, but God loves people that feel this way." I was fourteen or fifteen, and that's when I started realizing, "Yeah, this is more than just a passing fancy. This is really the way I am." That's when I started acknowledging in my prayers that I desired other boys, and asking God to help me not to lust after them.

On a school trip to St. Louis we went to a shopping mall, and I wound up in the gay novels section of a bookstore. I was fascinated, but it bothered me because I thought people shouldn't really be reading about homosexuality, except as a problem to be solved. One book, with a picture of two young men on the cover, was described as "one of the best homosexual love stories ever written." I could hardly tear myself away from it, but I couldn't bring myself to buy it.

"Sometimes I feel that I was this person sort of planted on the farm. I always felt sort of outside of them all—the farm kids and even the other kids at school." Connie Sanders on his home farm as a preschooler. Courtesy of Connie Sanders.

My masturbation fantasies were always about a man and a woman. That was how I got around feeling guilty. Once when I was in college, I worked up the nerve to buy a *Playgirl*. I had two orgasms in the car in the parking lot and another one while I was driving. Throughout college, I remained celibate, telling myself that although I had these feelings, I could never act on them.

After graduating from college, I went to Urbana to work in the library at the University of Illinois. It was a few months before I realized there was a gay community there. I resisted exploring it for a long time, but my life seemed really empty and depressing, so one night I went to a discussion at the student union about safe sex. I thought I could hide in the crowd, but there were five people there that I knew from campus, including my boss and a couple of co-workers. I was amazed, and decided that since people had seen me anyway, I might as well go to the gay bar.

Connie Sanders on a visit to the farm. Courtesy of Connie Sanders.

In the bar, I was so scared that I couldn't look anyone in the eye. I struck up a conversation with the first person I made eye contact with and we left together almost immediately. He was from out of town, about ten years older, and very melancholy. I had no interest in him, except that I had to try it, to get it out of my system. I was twenty-three when I had my first sexual experience with a man. It was just an experiment—I told him I didn't want to be gay, which is what I believed. After him, I met another guy I had nothing in common with. He was an alcoholic and a mess emotionally, and we had a very short and awful affair.

The first time I met someone I really cared about, he was a law student at the University of Illinois who approached me in the bar. He looked like the boy-next-door and we had a light summer romance—we actually had fun together. When he broke up with me I began to understand why people use the term "broken heart." That's when I realized I was no longer just experimenting.

What first allowed me to feel okay about being gay was the realization that there were gay people who were married—committed to one another and monogamous. So I decided the only way I wanted to be sexual was to be in a committed relationship. If I had sex with someone, we were automatically going to be lovers and it was going to last forever. It didn't take long to realize that that wasn't realistic.

Then I started just dating around and picking people up—being safe, but realizing that sometimes sex was just fun. But after living in Chicago a couple of years, I decided to give up casual sex for Lent. I tried to get through forty days and forty nights without being with anybody unless I thought it would be something significant. I sort of broke my promise once when I couldn't resist going to an underwear party, but that was the only thing the whole time.

On Easter morning, I decided to go to church. I hadn't been for a long time. At the coffee hour after church, I met Matt. He gave me a ride home and called me two days later. He said he'd get me up to go running if I would get him up to go to church the next week. We had a date that weekend and ended up having pretty wild sex.

Matt and I have made a beginning commitment to be monogamous and just see where it goes. We both want it to be a long-term thing, but we're trying not to write a script. We decided to meet each other's families before we moved in together, and it turned out to be a very positive experience. Dad took us horseback riding and we all had a good time and my parents liked Matt a lot. They've always liked the guys I've dated, but they haven't really known who these guys have been to me.

Terry was a rough-and-tumble girl, a year or two older than me, who grew up next-door. When we were out horseback riding or camping, she'd say things like "Goddamn it!" and then she'd apologize because she knew it offended me. Terry has been living with a woman now for about thirteen years. She had a daughter when she was about fifteen. One time when I was home from college, Terry and her lover came to the Christmas program at church to see her daughter. Her lover kind of fit the stereotype of a masculine lesbian. My mother and I got into a conversation about them at home, and my mother said, "I don't want to talk about this. You know about Terry and that woman, but we don't talk about it."

About a year ago, when I was home, Mom told me that Dad had been horseback riding with Terry and Joanne. I said, "Wait a minute! You mean

Terry from next-door and Joanne, the woman she's been living with for years?" Mom said, "Yes, they had a great time," and she just went on with the story. I know my parents know they're lesbians. In the country, I guess, it's the kind of thing that's okay if you don't talk about it—if you don't "rub it in people's faces." My parents' attitude is that God intends sex to be something within a marriage and between a man and a woman. But I've heard Mom say that she thinks people should have the right to live their lives the way they want to, even if she doesn't approve of their choices.

My mother's experience is so drastically different from mine, on their little farm out in the middle of nowhere, where the center of her life is the little Methodist church up the road. I haven't talked with her about being gay because I feel guilty about hurting her. I've always been the good kid. My older brothers got in trouble, my little sisters got in trouble, but I never got in trouble. If there's something painful in my life, or something that would make my mother unhappy, I don't tell her. We're not a communicative family about a lot of things. Everything is indirect, and we don't talk about things that make us uncomfortable.

I was in a show with a community theater in Urbana, and Mom said she wanted to come see it. I said, "Well, Mom, I don't know," and she said, "Oh, Connie, you know how much I love to come see your shows. What's the show?" I told her it was *La Cage aux Folles* and she said, "Oh, I've heard of that. Didn't that win a Tony award? I'd like to see it." When I said I thought she should know what it was about, she said, "Isn't it about a bunch of men who dress up like women and perform?" She probably got it from a talk show. She loves *Oprah Winfrey* and all those shows. I said, "Well, Mom, there's one more thing I should tell you. The two main characters in the show are a homosexual couple, and they're portrayed in a positive light." She said she wanted to see it.

She came for the last performance, and during the whole show I kept thinking, "My mother's here! What am I going to do?" The show has a lot of sexual innuendo, and we really milked that for all it was worth. I came out in crinolines and fishnet stockings, doing the can-can, and in a bird suit with nothing but a skimpy leotard and high heels and feathers. I came out in big blue pajamas and a boa, tap dancing in fishnet stockings and high heels. I also had a brief scene as a male waiter and danced in "The Masculinity Dance"—so I got to be a man too, which was sort of comforting.

A man who weighed about three hundred pounds had come to see sixteen performances of the show in various states of drag. Sometimes he'd come in full drag and sometimes he'd come in a three-piece suit. The last night he came in a suit with a tiara, and we presented one of the boas to him at the end of the show. I wondered what Mom thought about that.

After the show, I was in the back with one of the few straight guys in the chorus, and I started to cry. He said, "What's wrong, Connie?" and I said, "I think I just came out to my mother, and I don't want to go out and talk to her." He said, "Come on, let's go meet Mom." She was dabbing her eyes, and I thought, "Oh no, she's upset." But my mother's a sucker for a happy ending, and this show had one—the two lead men dancing off into the moonlight, celebrating their love for each other. She said, "Oh, I just had the *best* time. That was so good! You know, I couldn't figure out whether that was a man or a woman. Almost to the end of the show, I just wasn't sure. And it took me forever to figure out which one was you."

We had to strike the set that night, so she sat and looked through photographs and watched people. There was no way to get away from the campy comments and affectations. She just sat there soaking it all in. Every once in a while, she'd look at someone kind of funny, but she was really a good sport. I worried a little bit about coming off to her as a big drag queen, but I think she knows I just love to be a ham and to be on stage.

I've known people who were just sure their parents knew they were gay—they could even sort of joke with them about it. But when they directly confronted them with it, it became messy, because then their parents had to really deal with it. They couldn't use denial anymore. My parents are probably doing major denial. With all the stuff my mother would have to deal with (did she cause it? am I going to hell?) it would be important for her to have some kind of support. I just don't know if there are enough people there who would give her the support she needs and tell her the kinds of things she needs to hear, or if she'd be surrounded by people who were just as uninformed as she is, or more so.

My dad I'm not quite as concerned about. He sort of reacts to things according to how it affects my mom. His attitude tends to be "I hate to see your mother hurting like this." My prediction is that he'll be upset because my mother is, or he'll hide his upset feelings. I can see my mother working through it, dealing with the emotional things and loving me anyway. I think my dad is a lot less flexible, less verbal, and less able to grow. I can see him saying, "It's sick and it's wrong." But my parents have both surprised me many times by coming through with amazing intelligence. My mother watches a lot of television, and I think she sees more and more images of people who aren't sick or unhappy because they're gay. And in many ways, my dad is a very practical, sensible man. So who knows?

All through my life, I've been influenced by the church. An assumption of evil and rejection from God taints my perception of almost everything, and it comes out in very subtle ways. That voice in me—a former therapist called it "The Preacher"—had to do with my breakdown, it had to do with my difficulty accepting myself as gay, and even now it interferes with relationships. One of the first books I read when I was struggling to come out was *Embracing the Exile,* by a Christian psychotherapist. It was all about the spiritual journey of recognizing and embracing yourself as you are, as a gay person loved by God.[2]

My favorite show when I was growing up was *The Waltons.* The show's values comforted me, and I identified with John-Boy, the sensitive son who wanted to be a writer. He belonged there on the mountain with his family, yet he sensed that he was different and that he was often misunderstood. At times I would lay in my bedroom feeling like I was missing everything. There were boys I wanted so badly to be close to, and those were exactly the ones I avoided. I was frightened by boys who were very uninhibited and masculine and joked around about sex. I realize now that I was drawn to them, and I was afraid of giving that away, afraid I was too transparent to them. So I spent a lot of energy acting uninterested, or being shy, or thinking they shouldn't curse the way they did.

Sometimes I still feel like a misfit, even with gay people. My values are much more liberal than the values I was brought up with, but in an urban gay environment my values make me look sort of moralistic. There's something about camp humor, for example, that I've never been comfortable with. It seems like it's easier for urban people to have a harsh, cynical sense of humor about everything. Maybe it's a guy thing—wanting to make everything into a joke—and maybe it's an urban gay subculture thing too, but sometimes I want to say, "Just drop all this shit and be real. Stop thinking you're always on stage and talk to people like human beings." Matt says I need to loosen up, but it's hard for me to just let loose and think anything's okay. I still see certain behaviors as healthier than others. Matt is a lot more comfortable taking people at face value, without judgment. So he helps me loosen up a little, and I help him think about things in ways he wouldn't have before.

NOTES

1. *The Waltons* (1972–81) was a long-running television drama series that portrayed the life of a large family in rural Virginia during the 1930s and 1940s. The stories were seen through the eyes of John-Boy, the gentle and emotional eldest son and hopeful writer. Though the series was not a big hit in large cities, it was one of the most-viewed television programs in middle and rural America.

2. *Embracing the Exile: Healing Journeys of Gay Christians* (1982) by John E. Fortunato. New York: Seabury Press.

Randy Fleer

Born in 1963, Randy grew up with two older brothers on a mixed livestock and crop farm near Wayne, in Wayne County, northeastern Nebraska. He lives in the Chicago area. In this brief narrative, Randy recalls coming out—to himself, to his parents, and to a small circle of gay men in his hometown.

AS A YOUNG child, I had vivid fantasies about rough-housing with my uncles, riding on their backs and shoulders. In adolescence, I really didn't have any thoughts about girls or boys my own age. I was interested in men. My sophomore year of high school, about the time of Anita Bryant's big campaign, I started hearing the word "gay."[1] One night there was a TV show with a character telling his best friend he was gay, and I asked my mom what that meant. In her, "Okay, we're talking about sex now" half-whisper she said, "That's a man who loves other men instead of women." The light bulb went on.

The summer before my junior year in high school, my parents and I went to Omaha to see a family show. During intermission, I was in the rest room relieving myself and noticed that the guy next to me was watching me. I started watching him and we ended up going into a stall and touching each other. That was my first experience and I was very excited by it.

One night, about six months later, I called Larry—a gay man in Wayne that everybody knew about. I said, "I think I'm gay, and I don't want to be like that. I was wondering if I could talk to you about it." I went to his apartment and we talked. He told me, "You are gay and there's nothing you can do about it. You're not bad, and you're going to have a fine life just as you are. You don't have to fit the mold." I listened to him, but deep down I didn't believe him. When I said, "It's not right, I'm not normal," he said, "What is normal?" But I wanted to fit in. I wanted to be like everyone else, find that woman and get her pregnant and all that stuff.

I won a trip to Germany the summer before my senior year in high school. Up to that point, all I knew was Nebraska. Suddenly, I saw New York City, flew to Germany, spent a week at a youth hostel in Berlin and three weeks with a family in Nuremberg. While I was in Berlin, I wandered around the subway and picked up or was picked up by men on a few occasions. How does that song go? "How you gonna keep 'em down on the farm once they've seen Paree?"

I came out to my parents on April 2, 1980, near the end of my senior year of high school. I remember the date because I had been working up to it for a long time, and I was ready to tell them on April first, but decided April Fools' Day was probably not a good idea. I was taking a bath in the evening, thinking of what I was going to say, and by the time I was ready my father had already gone to bed. Mom said that I could tell her and she could tell him, but I said it was something very important that I had to tell both of them.

Dad hadn't fallen asleep yet, and I went through the usual half-hour build-up. "I've got something to tell you. . . . It's important for you to know this. . . . I don't want you to think any different about me. . . . Bla-bla-bla-bla-bla." Finally I said, "I'm gay," and my dad said, "What did he say?" My mom said, "He said he's homosexual, dear." I told them I didn't feel good about it and was trying to see if I could fix it myself. It would be two more years before I felt being gay was okay.

The summer before I started college, Larry was having a get-together with several other gay men he knew around town. Mom answered the phone when he called to invite me, and when I was getting ready to go into town that night, she stopped me and said she wanted to know who I was going to see and what I was going to be doing. I wouldn't tell her and said that she shouldn't worry.

That night at Larry's, I thought, "Wow! Four men in a room, and they're all gay!" In Wayne, where everybody knows what you do, Larry's place was a comfortable island where we could get together and talk. In a way, it's too bad that we could only feel safe talking there, but it was kind of exciting to get together with the girls and gossip. It was almost an underground thing, hearing them talk about some cute boy in town, or "Watch out for so-and-so—I think he's got an idea about you." I haven't seen anything like it since leaving Wayne. In Lincoln there were so many more gay people around, and bars for them to go to. And in Chicago there are ghettos with blocks of businesses that cater to gays.

A guy that I became friends with in college grew up doing some hustling in Omaha on the Milk Run, the area of town where men drove their cars around. When I first met him, I was envious of all that. Now I'm glad I came of age and came out the way I did. And despite the isolation, I'm glad I grew up where I did. I had to learn so much on my own, and some of that was not so good, but in a large city you can get so immersed in gay culture that you forget to grow up in other areas. I know a lot of gay people who almost cannot function in the heterosexual world.

There are some gay people I would like to be associated with and some I wouldn't. I think everyone should try to make the world a better place, live and let live, take care of and pick up after themselves, not be a burden on others. I see so many young gay men with no direction in life, who just go from one bar to another. They need some maturity, to start being responsible for themselves. It's scary that there's a whole generation of people like that. What's their situation going to be in ten or fifteen years?

NOTE

1. In 1977, Anita Bryant, evangelical singer and former Miss America, led a highly emotional and widely publicized campaign to repeal a gay rights ordinance in Dade County, Florida.

Ken Yliniemi

Ken was born in 1964 and grew up with two older sisters and two younger sisters on a small dairy farm in northwestern Minnesota, seven miles from Ponsford, in Becker County. He lives in the Minneapolis area and works in horticulture and plant biology.

THROUGHOUT growing up, one of my goals was to please my parents, and by working hard on the farm I pleased them exceedingly. I was not a rebellious child and I tried to maintain the best relationship possible with them by doing all the right things. I thought it was just the greatest thing when the neighbors, who had a son about my age, would tell my mom they wished their son could be just like Kenny. I thought, "Wow! I must really be doing everything right."

From the beginning, I went out to the barn with my dad and was extremely involved in the work on the farm. As a little kid I started out feeding milk to the young calves and as I got older I learned how to drive tractors. But in the back of my mind, I didn't know if I'd be good at farming. I could handle the animal husbandry and field crops part of it, but I wasn't very good at all the mechanical work. I was just amazed at how my dad did it, but I never really learned it from him. If he was working on something and needed help, he would ask me to help him, but I never had an interest in it and he never pushed me.

My dad became extremely allergic to cattle and hay dust. On top of that, we had a bad drought in '76, and hay prices were very high. He decided he wasn't going to feed the cattle through the winter, and sold them all. Six months later, in the spring, my mother decided she wanted to start farming and asked me to help her. I was all for it, because I actually missed the cows. From that point on, my mother and I did most of the work. We were responsible for milking the cows twice a day, feeding them, and cleaning the barn. My dad had found a job in Detroit Lakes, about thirty-five miles away. He did a lot of the fieldwork, but that became a big part of my responsibility too. Putting up the hay was a never-ending summer chore.

Before I started college, I considered farming. But that was in the early '80s, and the farm economy was just horrible. Farms were going under

284

"As I got older I learned how to drive tractors . . . but I wasn't very good at all the mechnical work. I was just amazed at how my dad did it, but I never really learned it from him." Kenny Yliniemi looks on while his father works on mowing machinery in a hay field, about 1970. Courtesy of Ken Yliniemi.

left and right, and prices were very poor. In order to take over my parents' farm, I would have had to borrow a great deal of money. When I went away to college, my mother sold all the cows. I've often wondered if I did the right thing. If I had stayed at home and not gone to college, I'm sure I'd be farming today. But my parents always told me I needed to do what I really wanted to do. They would have been very pleased if I had taken over the farm, but I knew farming was not what I wanted to do for the rest of my life.

There was a division of labor in our household: the girls were in the house and I was in the barn. I would usually get up around 5:00 or 5:30, do milking for an hour, grab a bite to eat, take a shower, and catch the school bus around 7:15. When I got home I did milking, and after supper I had homework. So it really got to be a long day. I was never encouraged to do any of the household activities, but I liked doing those things. I would bake on occasion, and my mother was very much into canning and freezing and often needed help with that. We would can chicken, peaches, pears, and canning tomatoes was a big one in the fall. Vegetables would always be frozen. I really liked helping to pick them, clean them, cut them up, and blanch and freeze them. When I was married, I did a lot of canning and freezing. I would call up my mother and ask her, "How do I do this? What's the recipe you use for this?" I'm sure she kind of wondered about me sometimes, but she was always very encouraging and willing to share her recipes and ideas with me.

In high school, I really wanted to do acting, but I couldn't because of the farm. Most of the play practices took place in the evening, and there was no way I could do that because we lived twenty-one miles from Park Rapids. So I got involved in technical theater and did that all through high school. Light design was my specialty. I worked on it right after school, so the late bus would get me home in time for milking. I would have just loved to do the summer musical, but we were busy with making hay and other summertime farmwork. I envied the freedom enjoyed by the kids who lived in town.

Our community 4-H club was started my senior year of high school, and I got involved in it right away, but I wasn't interested in doing any of the farm activities. I wanted to get into drama and speech. They had what was called "Share the Fun." Each club in the county put on a skit and competed with each other, and one skit from the county went on to perform at the state fair. That first year, I designed the whole act and got costumes for everyone, and we made it all the way to state.

We had a Finnish sauna in the basement, and one time when I was in junior high my cousins came over to take a sauna. Two or three of them went in together. My bedroom was in the basement, so I went down and laid on the floor under my bed and tried to peer into the sauna through the cracks in the wall and watch those guys who were several years older than I was. Then they came out of the sauna and started walking around without any clothes on. They thought they had the whole basement to themselves. Oh god! There I was, a gay adolescent with those naked guys in front of me, and I couldn't even look at them because I was so afraid they were going to find me and beat me up. When they went back in the sauna, I was so disappointed I had missed most of it.

On the school bus, all the older guys would ride in back, and I would listen to their rough and gruff conversations about women. I was intensely turned on by those guys. During junior high, my hormones were just racing, but it wasn't something I thought about at all. It wasn't until I got into high school that I realized I was different from most people. It became very evident to me that I didn't have the same interests the other guys did, and an awful lot of my friends were girls. I just didn't relate well to guys my own age.

Whenever my parents went to town—and then when I got old enough to drive—I would go to the drugstore and buy *Playgirl*. I'd buy a *Playboy* with it, to make it look like I was buying one for me and one for my girlfriend. Detroit Lakes was usually where I went, because I didn't go to school there and didn't know anybody in the store. When I first got my driver's license, I wouldn't even make it all the way home before I ripped open the *Playgirl* on the side of the road. I didn't keep too many magazines around at home because of the chances of someone finding them. After I had used one for a couple months, I would burn it. I would hide the magazines at the bottom of the garbage, so if something happened to me and I suddenly died, they wouldn't find them. They'd just take out the garbage and they wouldn't know any different.

Saturday night was sauna night, and as an adolescent I went by myself. I'd always take a magazine into the sauna with me because it was a perfect place to jack off. One time I forgot my magazine on a bench in the dressing area. It wasn't until late that evening, after everyone had gone through sauna, that I realized I'd left my jack-off magazine down there. And it wasn't just a *Playgirl*, it was an obviously gay magazine. I was mortified that someone had found it. When I went down and looked, I found that it had slipped behind the bench. If anyone saw it, no one ever mentioned a thing to me.

Paul was about my age and lived on another farm in the area. I would sit next to him on the school bus, and then we started doing things together, like going for snowmobile and horseback rides. One beautiful summer afternoon, when I was fourteen or fifteen, I was painting my parents' house and Paul came over. He asked if everyone was gone, and I said they were. Then he said, "Let's go inside." We went down to my bedroom in the basement and jacked each other off. Paul knew exactly what to do—led me through the whole thing—and I really liked it. I was just shocked, couldn't believe it. I'd never had anyone touch me there before, and I was so turned on. I was thinking, "I shouldn't be doing this, but, oh, it does feel really good! Oh, well, I'm not doing anything. I'm letting him do it all. I'm not encouraging this at all." But when he went home, I was so guilt-ridden I was ready to tell my parents and my pastor everything that had happened. But I was so terrified, I couldn't even bring myself to do that.

I vowed I would never let it happen again, but Paul came over a couple of days later and the same thing happened. This continued all through
high school. He would come over, or he'd invite me to go do something.
He was always the one who instigated it. I thought if I didn't instigate it,
it was okay—I wasn't really like that. But if a week had gone by and I
hadn't heard from Paul, and I was really horny, I'd get on the phone. "Do
you want to go do something? Let's go horseback riding." If he wasn't
home, I'd want to know when he was coming back. We arranged that if I
was home alone, I would call him. And whenever he went by my place, he
would look at what cars were in the yard to see if maybe I was home alone.
Then he'd call, and if I was alone he would come over and we could do it
wherever we wanted in the house.

Paul knew where my crotch was all the time—he knew how to get me
hard right away, and then give me a good blow job or jack me off. It was
strictly sexual gratification on both of our parts. We never kissed. I hated
his guts a lot of the time, because I was really guilted out by the whole
thing. But if I hadn't seen him for a couple weeks I'd want to call him up
and have him come over. We did it just about any place we could. We'd go
out in the middle of the woods on horseback or on the motorcycle. We'd
go swimming at Big Basswood Lake, down the road about a mile, late at
night when no one could see us. We'd soap each other up and have a really good time. In the wintertime, we'd do things in the barn loft because
it was fairly warm, and if we knew no one was in the barn, we'd do it there
too. One time my parents and sisters were gone for three or four days to
visit relatives in North Dakota. I stayed on the farm to milk the cows and
take care of everything. Paul helped me with some of the chores, and for
three or four nights we slept together in my bed. We'd wake up in the middle of the night and get each other off. I felt guilty as usual, but I thought,
"I'll grow up and get married, and it'll be okay."

My parents never once sat down and told me the facts of life. But if a
girl in the neighborhood would get pregnant, my parents made sure they
pointed it out with comments like, "I just can't believe it. I don't know
what she was doing. Why couldn't she wait till she was married?" We never
had any real sex education at school. I would read anything I could find
about sex. I would pore through home medical books, and whenever I'd
find a new term I'd look it up. I wasn't looking for things about homosexuality, because I was trying to deny that. Even though one side of me
was having fun fooling around with Paul, the other side of me was really
wanting to find out how things worked heterosexually. On the farm you
see how nature does it, but you don't really know. As a little kid I asked
my dad how a cow gets pregnant, and he said, "Well, the bull gets up there

and sticks his peter in there." When I said, "No he *doesn't*, Dad," he got mad and said, "Well, don't believe me then."

My parents had me baptized and confirmed in the Apostolic Lutheran church, which is very conservative and primarily Finnish. I did everything in church I could do. I didn't miss Sunday school and I made sure I had my lessons done. I went to Bible school, and when I got old enough I taught Bible school. All through my teenage years I was very much involved in the young people's group at the Ponsford Community Church, where they preached born-again Christianity very strongly. I had a wonderful time at their summer camp—Camp JIM, which stands for Jesus Is Mine. A lot of people sent their kids to Camp JIM to become born again. I had so much conflict as a teenager, because Paul would come over, and then I'd go to church. The pastor emphasized making sure you came to communion with a clean heart, so I'd make sure I had confessed and asked forgiveness in a personal prayer. But that always reminded me I was a sinner.

Most kids, when they go away to college, go out and party and get drunk. Instead, I got so intensely involved in religious-oriented campus organizations I would sluff off schoolwork because I had Bible study that night. I fell in love with a guy who introduced me to some of those groups, but both of us were so involved in our religious activities there was no way anything could ever happen. I remember once giving him the biggest hug and not wanting to let go, and he wouldn't let go either. That was the closest I'd ever been with a man emotionally, but I wouldn't acknowledge anything about being gay connected with those feelings. After he graduated, I went up to visit him at his parents' farm, and he said, "I think I'm going to get married." I said, "You are? To who?" "I don't know yet, but I'm going to get married," and within about three months, he was married. I was crushed.

Eventually I got away from the religious groups, started dating, fell in love with this wonderful woman, and we got married when I was twenty-three. I was married for four years. My wife was the turning point in my coming out, because she had been raised very differently than I had, in a very liberal family in the city. She didn't take any shit from anyone, and she taught me a lot about being who you are, expressing yourself, talking back to your parents. People have said that I was such a conservative thing, and that she's the one who really brought me out and made me gay. She didn't make me gay, but she helped me feel comfortable in being who I am. The summer of 1991 was when I really came out to everyone. I came out to myself about a year earlier and had gone to a support group at the

Men's Center in the Twin Cities. It was safe to go there while I was married because it was not a gay organization.

I was sleeping with men while I was married, and when I got divorced I told my wife I would never expect anyone to be faithful to me. I would just expect that somewhere down the line they would probably cheat on me. That sounds really sad, but some part of me really does believe it. I've been seeing a lot of men and getting involved in relationships with them, and I feel like I'm walking on very unstable ground. I thought one guy I was involved with was really honest and up-front, and I found out he was cheating on me. It just ripped me apart. How do I adjust? Do I not expect honesty from now on? Do I not expect people to be faithful to me? Did I set myself up for that because I expected it to begin with?

Honesty within a relationship is very important. You talk about how you feel, what you want. Everyone changes, but that's okay as long as you're honest. I want more than anything else in a relationship for both of us to be happy. That means if one of us decides it's not for him, that's really the end of it. You want it to work and you hope it will work, and everything tells you it should, but is that reality? I think honesty and happiness are more important than long-term commitment. I don't believe relationships should be like typical heterosexual marriages where the couple stays together just because they're married. You should be together because you really love each other and you really want to be together, not just out of habit, because that's all you know and you're scared.

I'm trying to come to terms with the guilt the church put on me for being gay. I felt guilty about doing something that was wrong, and would go over and over passages in the Bible that were supposedly referring to homosexuals. I never really understood it, but I had to believe it, and I had so much conflict. My mother would watch *The 700 Club*, and a lot of their programs really denounced gays. I would watch it and think, "Thank goodness I'm not really gay—it's just a passing thing." Every once in a while there would be something on the news about a gay pride parade, and I'd think about "those faggots that live in the cities—I'm not like them at all. I'm not one of those." I tried very hard to be straight—got married and did that whole route—and it didn't work. Finally, I was able to come to terms with the fact that this is who I am and it is okay, it's fine. I was created with just as much purpose in life as any heterosexual. I wish there was some way I could convince my parents and my sisters of that. God made me exactly who I am, and God wouldn't make me like this just to be cruel, or to live the life religion teaches: If you're gay, well, it's okay, but just don't practice at all.

Paul, my high school friend, identifies himself as gay, but he will never admit it to anyone else. I think everyone in the community knows, but no one talks about it. Paul's life is the flip side of mine. I strove to please my parents, to work hard and to excel, and he did just the opposite. When I went away to college, Paul was still on the farm, and sometimes when I'd come home on weekends we would get together. When I started seriously dating women, I really didn't want to see him at all, so it ended. Occasionally, Paul would call me when I was married, and I would tell my wife it was just a guy from back home. He called this summer, when I was home for my high school reunion. He had heard I was divorced, he was drunk, and he wanted me to come over to his place really bad. I told him I had a boyfriend, and even if I didn't I wouldn't want to come over to his place because it was nothing more than just sex.

Clark Williams

Born in 1965, Clark grew up with four brothers and sisters on a small honey and produce farm near Eau Claire, in Eau Claire County, northwestern Wisconsin. Clark's introduction to his sexuality at rural, highway rest stops is the focus of this brief narrative.

MY PARENTS WERE pretty open about sex. It was never something to be ashamed of or to hide from. We all had "the talk," and if we needed birth control, that was fine, we could have it. But homosexuality was never discussed. As much as my parents allowed us to explore who we were, being gay was not an option.

When I was nineteen, I was walking in downtown Eau Claire one night and a guy pulled over and said he wanted to give me a blow job. So I had my first sexual relations with a man, in his car. I told myself I would never do it again, but a couple weeks later I found myself walking down the same street, looking for the same man. I didn't find him, but I found someone else, and that started the whole thing. Suddenly I realized there were men everywhere who were looking at me and who would have sex with me.

After I got my first blow job, I went gangbusters. The rest areas that dot the rural highways were very active if you knew where to go. There was a lot of great sex going on out there, some of it young—sixteen- and seventeen-year-old boys. But most of the guys that I'd have sex with were married. Sometimes they'd take their rings off, sometimes they wouldn't. One time I had sex with the father of a kid I knew at school. Sometimes people my own age would come by, but for a long time my only experience was with older men. I didn't have to do anything but lean back.

There was a very active rest area about two miles down the road from the farm. It was dangerous, not knowing if the state patrol would drive up or if my dad was going to pull over to take a piss. But I really got into that game one summer. There was always a wide variety and I was good-looking, so I never had any problems. I could do that and still date women. I never really bothered myself wondering whether or not I was gay. It was just something I was doing at the time, and I did it until I was about twenty-three.

I wish I hadn't had to go through all that. I wish I could have fallen in love with a boy at sixteen and had all the experiences that two sixteen-year-olds should have with each other. My first role models were the older men I was having anonymous sex with. I'm glad I was able to break away from that, because I know a lot of people don't, and they go on and perpetuate it. I've always wanted to know about those men—what they thought, why they were like that, how they could do that and stay married for so many years. They're still doing it, with someone younger than me who's taken my place. They taught me about sex, but not once did one of them say that what we were doing was okay. It was always over quickly. They were always wary: "No, don't give me your phone number. Let's meet tomorrow night at 9:00." I wonder what I would have done if one of them had said, "You really should find someone your own age, and I think I can help you do it."

Joe Shulka

Joe was born in 1966 and grew up on a 500-acre dairy farm near Prairie du Chien, in Crawford County, southwestern Wisconsin. He grew up with four sisters, one older and three younger. Joe lives with his partner, Dallas Drake, in Minneapolis.

MY BEST FRIEND Mike, who lives here in the Twin Cities, I've known since kindergarten. There were six of us who hung together from almost the very beginning, and five of us are gay. There were also peripheral friends who liked to hang with us because we had a lot of fun together, and all of them are gay. They were all town kids, so after school they would do things together and I would want to be there, but before I got my driver's license I had to go home on the school bus. And summers, they were lounging around the house watching cable while I was throwing bales and milking cows. But we were inseparable for most of high school, and four of us went to the same college. I had friends in college who didn't know any straight men from Prairie du Chien. They wondered if it was something in the water. Out of a class of 138, we've identified thirteen men and eight women. When my mother clutches her bosom as if to say she's the only mother who gave birth to a gay son, I say, "Mom, would you like the names of the other mothers? They all live here. Maybe you could get together and have a kaffeeklatsch or something."

If there is a checklist to see if your kid is queer, I must have hit every one of them—all sorts of big warning signs. I was always interested in a lot of the traditional queen things—clothes, cooking, academics, music, theater. No high heels, nothing like that, but my god, my parents *must* have seen it coming. A farm boy listening to show tunes? From sixth grade, I was in various choirs—large choir, madrigal groups, solo ensemble. My four friends who happened to be queer were also in the choir group—five men with forty-five women.

I was involved in high school play productions. I had no idea then, but I'm sure the guy who directed our plays was gay. As a round teenage kid who had no clue what was going on, I was totally infatuated with him. He was six-foot-two, blond hair, green or blue eyes. One of my best images is of him showing up for play practice one night, sweaty, in a pair of lycra running shorts and a tank shirt. He got a lot of flak because he taught English and directed plays in a jock school. I would love to meet him again, to have lunch with him and chat, because I'm sure he must have seen it in all of us; he must have known we were little fledglings just waiting for it.

My parents very much frowned upon my activities because they took me away from farmwork. They didn't attend my concerts or plays, and that hurt. We've tried to work through those things, and I understand where they were and what was going on. My parents had a hard time dealing with me because I was so different from the young man they had hoped I would be. God, it's amazing what you think when you get to be an adult. I sound like I've gone through the Twelve Steps, and I'm now at peace with my Higher Power. Memories of me just *screaming* at my mother come to my mind, and now I say, "We had different sensitivities and sensibilities."

Right after my parents' wedding, it was one child after another—five kids in six years. From a distance, we must have looked like the most perfect little traditional farm family. Mom dressed us all the same—the vogue thing to do in the seventies. She'd buy cloth by the bolt and all of us kids would have matching striped shirts and plaid pants. My maternal grandparents lived on the same farm, so we were almost like the Waltons, which we've always joked about—and even the Waltons had their deep, dark little secrets.

My sisters and I had rotating shifts to do weekend chores. We did the milking, cared for the cattle, and cleaned out the barns. There was always a lot to do on a day-to-day basis, and summers there was the planting of oats and corn, and baling hay. My grandfather was our hired hand, so he and Dad took care of most of it. I would help, but I think Dad saw my resistance and just kind of gave up after a while.

Dad bought the farm from his father, and as soon as he had a son he figured it was going to continue on for generations. There was a lot of disappointment and strife when I went off to college. My mother would ask me, "So, when are you going to stop this college stuff and come home and work at the farm?" The farm was seen as the place where *real* work was done; when you work, you get your hands dirty and you sweat. Mom has only a high school education, and Dad doesn't even have that. He dropped out of school during the Depression to work the farm and support the family. I'm the first generation ever to graduate from college, and my parents wouldn't even attend my graduation.

My father just turned seventy, my mother is forty-six. Dad grew up in the Great Depression, Mom came of age during Vietnam, so it was like Woodstock and the Waltons. I have always been much closer to my mother;

"I laugh hardest when I'm with my sisters. Within ten minutes we're just screaming, tears rolling down, almost wetting ourselves." Joe Shulka, age 5, with sisters, *center*, Krista, and Vicky. Courtesy of Joe Shulka.

we have the same perspective on a lot of things, the same sense of humor. My father and I are as different as night and day, and have been kind of distant, but we're getting closer now. There was so much work to be done that we didn't see each other a whole lot. When I'd get home from school, he was out working in the barn. We didn't have a whole lot of conversation. Summers there was some, but then Dad would start talking about the Depression and the eyes would start rolling.

At six, I was totally infatuated with other boys my age. I have a cousin, two years older, who grew up to be an absolutely stunning man. All the really good looking genes of the family just funneled their way toward him—all the tall, broad-shouldered, narrow-waisted, chiseled features. Baling hay with him was always a joy! When I was ten, eleven, twelve, I palled around with my cousin Allen. He lived on a farm adjacent to ours. I hung with him a lot and almost idolized him, because he was thin and wiry and a lot of the things I wanted to be. I was making a real conscious effort to be more like a boy, more like I thought my father wanted me to be. I never hunted or fished until I started palling with Allen. He was a very good hunter, but I would walk around in the woods with him and purposely step on sticks to frighten squirrels, and he would get very irritated. I had then the attitude I have now: Why should you go out and kill some little forest creature when you can run down to the Piggly Wiggly and get something larger and better-tasting that doesn't have fur on it?

I was an obese child, so physical education was the worst possible thing, just awful. Basketball was my least favorite, because we always played shirts and skins. Allen taught me how to play basketball, and I really made an effort—played every chance I got for almost a year—but I still sucked so bad. I've been called faggot by other boys since I was probably seven. Even my sisters would call me faggot or queer when they were pissed at me. I don't even want to think about what kind of messed-up straight boy I would be if I had been jeered and mocked and taunted as a kid for being a faggot and a queer, and I *wasn't*.

I entered puberty late, when I was maybe a junior in high school. There's something about the hormones that pump through you when you're seventeen years old that just galvanize locker-room images. There was a classmate of mine in high school, Greg, whose father owned a tractor dealership, so my dad did business with his dad. I don't know how Greg's dad gave birth to seven sons who were just—oh my god!—every single one of them was better than the last. All of them played football, all of them played basketball, they were big, they were beefy, they were brawny. It was like they all entered puberty at seven and started shaving by the fifth grade. To this day I remember Greg's broad and hairy chest, and his very tight blue jeans. My friend Mike, who's a quintessential size queen, happened to see Greg naked once. I guess he was quite amply endowed.

I didn't date at all in high school. Isolated on the farm with just the family, miles away from town, it was easy not to have to deal with a lot of that. I think my mother would have liked to see me date, because I know she had inklings. When I was twenty, she and I were having one of those bizarre conversations where you think you're talking about the same thing, but you're really talking about different things, but you're answering questions based on what you *think* you're talking about. My mother turned to me and said, "Well, *have* you?" And I assumed she meant "Have you had sex?", and I was still a virgin, so I said, "Well, no—no, I haven't." Then she realized what the question I was answering was, and she said, "That's *not* what I asked. But what do you mean you've never had sex? It's fun! Live a little!" That's not what she told her daughters.

I came to terms with being gay long before I had sex. I think that's the way I needed to do it. Again, I found a clique of friends in college who all turned out to be gay. There was one October where thirty men came out to me. It was ridiculous! I was in a male choir in college, and the men who slept with women were definitely the minority. We did a tour of women's colleges in the Midwest, and those poor girls didn't get anything. We would sing and go back to our own rooms, all paired off. I've known a few women who *thought* they were dating me, but I've never dated women, and I didn't date men until my third year in college. I thought dating was supposed to be fun, like on *The Brady Bunch*. Greg and Marcia looked like they were having a blast. Dating is a horrible, awful, vicious thing! I once defined "a date" as the two to three hours of shared activity men display in public preceding sex.

When I was twenty-one, my first lover and I went out for about a year. It would prove to be the first of several relationships that were really bad choices for me. When we started having problems, Rob started to show signs he was not going to make it easy on me when we broke up. I had pretty much decided to tell my parents I was gay, and was trying to schedule time to go home to talk with them about it. Rob beat me to the punch by just a few weeks. Out of the blue, he wrote a letter to my parents and told them in no uncertain terms *what* their son was and who *he* was. It was addressed to my father, but thank god my mother opened it. My grandmother happened to be in the house when my mother read the letter and burst into tears. They kept it from my dad for a year or two, thinking he didn't need to know and that it would be too hard for him. It was real difficult for about six months, and there were two or three months where we didn't speak at all. They just shut me out. We said some awful things to each other. My sisters were working on my behalf to try to open things up.

It took a year or two before my mother was able to say the word "gay." She would always refer to it as "his lifestyle," and when she said it she would drop her voice. She's getting better about it, and so is Dad. He and I have not had "the talk," even though he's met Dallas. It's just one of those things I don't think my dad and I will talk about a whole lot. My parents haven't had much exposure to people who are different, but they happen to have given birth to five very enlightened, feminist kids. And having a gay son and a lesbian daughter has kind of pushed them, kicking and screaming, into realizing there's a lot of differences in the world.

Grandma took my being gay pretty tough, because she and my grandfather had only one child, my mother, and I'm the only grandson. So there's a limb on the family tree that's pretty much snubbed. My dad looks at it like that, too; the family name ends with him. They may still hold near and dear to their hearts that if the right woman comes along I'll be swayed, but I'm sorry, it's just not going to happen. I'm a Kinsey six.[1]

I am so envious of men who came out in high school. But if I had clearly known I was gay at thirteen, I don't know what I would have done. There was no one to turn to and the resources were just not there. God, I wish there *had* been something to hide underneath my mattress! It would have been so nice to have known at that time, because I wasn't putting a name to how I was feeling. I wish I had known there were so many of us—that I was not alone. My friends and I were all going through this big battle that a lot of us didn't even know we were fighting, and that we would have no clue about for years. We tried to peg feeling different on other things. It's such a heterosexist world at that age, and sex was one subject we never talked about when we were in high school. None of us experimented with each other in high school, either. College was a different matter.

I learned about sex from the *World Book Encyclopedia* in the sixth grade. Since AIDS, I think the sexuality stuff is starting to infiltrate school systems in smaller cities. I know it is in my hometown. Whether or not it's happening in a positive way, I don't know. I feel so much for kids in small towns who haven't got an outlet. It would be so much easier to come out if you felt like you had a safe place to come out to. My partner Dallas and I have done some public speaking in small towns in Minnesota. We have little cards for the Gay and Lesbian Helpline here in the Twin Cities, and we go into libraries, find the books and files that have even the vaguest of references to homosexuality, and slide these cards in them. Some kid is going to search out that book, find the card, call the 1-800 number, and talk with a friendly person who might actually say some positive, affirming gay thing to them.

Nobody told us that some of the authors we read in high school were gay, that some of the music we heard was written by gay men. I feel like I was cheated out of a whole culture. At college I was able to get a better connection with it, and when I moved to Washington, D.C., I really saw there was a culture, it wasn't just a bunch of men having sex. We had art, we had history, we had music. It seemed like I found a home. There's so much about gay culture I like. It's fun, it's creative. It's also catty and vicious, but it's just so colorful. I wish you could inspire young kids who are coming out to look at what's available to them. They don't have to do mainstream America. I know gay men who would love to be straight. My god! White, middle-class, Protestant, college-educated. If it weren't for being gay, I would be part of the horrible majority. I don't see Range Rovers and car-seats in my future. I see gala balls and Halloween masquer-ades and horrible drag shows and pride festivals, tit-piercing and tattoos and big, burly lesbians in leather jackets. And then there's that whole other side of it, where they take off the leather jackets and teach Sunday school.

I live in one of the gay neighborhoods of the Twin Cities, and a cou-ple years ago I was beaten up two blocks from my house. A friend and I were walking across the street and a car ran a stop sign and tried to hit us. Then he got out and beat the shit out of me. There was nothing overt about us. Neither of us were wearing any gay insignia; we weren't even talking at the time. But people see us and jump to that conclusion, and there's a segment of the population that will act viciously on those as-sumptions. I learned a lot from the experience and became very vocal about my bashing; I did a lot of public speaking and interviews. Now Dallas and I make it a point to make public displays of affection. You try to explain it to people who are not gay by telling them to imagine going out with their date and not being able to kiss them or hold their hand or put their arm around them.

I grew up eight miles from town, and I always thought it was a great dis-tance, mostly because my father drove only about thirty miles an hour. "Set the cruise control for thirty? Come on, Dad, cars can go faster than tractors!" The isolation was compounded by the whole sexuality issue and by my strengths being in academics. That sense of isolation pushes you to-gether. It's infuriating to have seven people in a house with four bedrooms and one bathroom, but you overhear each other's conversations, you talk to each other, you bump into each other constantly, you really get to know each other.

Despite living in different cities and states, we're a pretty close-knit family and they're very important to me. I call my mother two or three times a month and we'll chat. When I was having such a problem with my folks about my sexuality, I was furiously angry, but there was no way I could cut them out. They're too important. I need their support so much, to hear good things from them, to hear about what's going on back home.

I laugh the hardest when I'm with my sisters. Within ten minutes we're just screaming, tears rolling down, almost wetting ourselves. My dad just looks at us like "What is *with* those kids?" Lisa is a lesbian, very open, very vocal. She's thirteen months younger than I, but it's like we were switched at birth. She was such the tomboy, and I was such the wuss. I would be given toy trucks and rifles, and Lisa would play with them. I would play with dolls and she would have war games and blow up my GI Joes. To have it be a surprise for either one of my parents—come on! Were you guys paying attention for fifteen or twenty years?

Lisa is the sister I'm most like, for a variety of reasons, our inverted sexualities being one of them. We feel like the odd people out, the other part of the family tree, and that kind of pulls us together. I love her dearly, and she's the one I wish I was closest to, but we have different ways of getting things done, different views of the world and politics. In particular, she is becoming a real man-hating dyke, a separatist. Every year her hair gets shorter.

Lisa has been in a relationship now for almost five years. Her girlfriend, Pam, is such an integral part of the family. She has been at every Christmas, every Thanksgiving, everything, first as my sister's roommate, then as her partner and lover. So when my parents choked on my sexuality, I said, "Wait a minute! What do you mean I can't bring anybody home? You have a lesbian daughter who's been bringing her girlfriend home for years, and you know it." But I don't think my parents could conceive of a sexual relationship between two women, whereas—very graphically and luridly—my mother could picture her baby boy being sodomized. My mother is convinced that all gay men do is have sex, and Lisa perpetuates it when she says, "All you do is fuck." Lisa says when she goes to Gay Pride she sees the lesbian couples with their babies, and a lot of single men being bawdy and ostentatious. She doesn't realize that kind of overt sexuality and camp is very much a part of our culture.

It's not just lesbians who are out there having long-term committed relationships. I think a lot of gay men are looking for one person to share their life with. A lot of us want and hope for that. Whether or not we have the skills to get it is a whole different thing. I learned a lot about relationships by not falling into one, by making it a point to be single for almost two years. Dallas and I have been together a little over a year, and he is the only partner I've ever wanted to bring home. I say partner because the rest of them have all been boyfriends, and I see Dallas in a whole different light.

I never would have thought I would be able to bring Dallas home, but about two months ago we were going to be driving to Chicago and he asked me if I wanted to stop at my parents' place. I suggested it to my mother, just off-the-cuff. "But I'm not coming home with any pretenses," I said. "Dallas is coming as my boyfriend. And *no*, we're *not* going to have sex on the kitchen table." Mom was really taken aback, but I had given her time to ask Dad and Grandma if they would be comfortable with it. They had a lot of preconceived notions, having never met any of my boyfriends. I'd had a couple of really awful relationships, Rob being the first one. Then I had a lover when I lived in D.C. who turned out to be a psychotic killer. Mom knew about that one, too, so she was probably wondering what kind of Jeffrey Dahmer look-alike I was going to be bringing home, or what kind of flaming, ostentatious queen wearing a tutu.

I told Dallas, "You're not only going to be meeting my parents, you're going to be meeting my entire family. They've all found an excuse to come home this weekend." When Dallas and I pulled up and he was just a real average-looking, nice, cordial kind of guy, I think it blew them all to hell. The stress level was high, but they were all really nice, very civil, and a lot of fun. Dad talked to Dallas more than he talked to me. My grandma was a little jittery, up-front and personal, and her smile was stretched very thin, but she was very cordial. Everybody was being civil about as long as they could. When we pulled out I said to Dallas, "I think if we had stayed another hour, my grandmother would have had a stroke."

When I was maybe ten, Dad fell down beside a cow and was repeatedly kicked. His leg was broken in many places and his ribs were cracked. It happened in April, just as planting season was starting, and he was in a wheelchair and crutches for a long time; the cast came off in November. Dad came from a large family, so we had lots of help that entire season. There were crews to do the planting, the cultivating, the haying, and to help with the milking. I had cousins I hadn't even known about. I don't know of any other occupation where something like that would happen. It's not just an occupation, it's a whole culture.

In the last six months, my father has decided to sell the farm. I'll be glad to see Dad not working so much, but it's going to be hard to sell the farm, because it really is a part of every one of us kids, and very much a part of my father. With Dad planning to sell the farm, there's a lot of people who are looking on it as a real loss, because he's been at it for fifty years in the same place, and the farm has really changed under him. I feel some guilt, but I think Dad and Mom have come to terms with the fact that I've chosen a life of my own. I know there's been a real longing for me to be there so that it would continue, but Dad has said he doesn't want his kids to do it, because you have to work too hard for too little money and recognition. He wants his kids to have a better life, and he sees it off the farm.

I never thought much of the farm growing up; it was just where I always was. Then there was a time when I thought the farm was a really bad place to grow up, because I felt I missed out on a lot of things. Now I realize how important it was, and I know that huge tract of land so intimately. I can traipse around in the woods and know my way in and out. We used to joke that we lived on Walton's Mountain, because our farm is perched on top of a very steep hill. It's a very bluffy area, but it wasn't until I went away that I realized how beautiful the area really is. When I look down those precipices, those virtual cliffs we pushed ourselves off of on toboggans, sleds, and inner tubes, I'm amazed that we weren't killed!

Postscript: In 1994, I set up the "Shulka Scholarship for Social Equity" at my high school in Prairie du Chien, Wisconsin. Applicants were to write essays on topics such as government, gay history, AIDS, racism, and leadership. The school was eager to offer a scholarship from an alumnus, but when the school board found out I was gay they attempted to bar my scholarship. Although it ended up being allowed, the climate that was created resulted in no applications. In its place, I purchased two dozen books on gay, lesbian, bisexual, and transgender themes for the high school library. I hope that these books will help educate students so that they will be eager to apply for my scholarship in coming years. I am working with several other gay alumni to set up additional gay-positive scholarships at Prairie High and in surrounding small towns.

NOTE

1. In describing himself as "a Kinsey six," Joe is referring to a scale developed by sex researcher Alfred C. Kinsey, who viewed homosexuality and heterosexuality as parts of a continuum. An individual's position on the seven-point Kinsey scale was based on both psychological reactions and overt experience. The scale ranged from zero (those whose histories were exclusively heterosexual) to six (those whose histories were exclusively homosexual).

Todd Ruhter

Todd was born in Hastings, Nebraska, in 1967, and grew up with a younger brother on a farm/ranch near Prosser, in Adams County, south-central Nebraska. His father and two uncles farmed about 2,000 acres of row crops—corn, soybeans, wheat, and milo. In addition, his father ran and calved out about 500 head of cattle. At the time of our interview, Todd lived in Omaha.

BEING GAY HAS never really bothered me—there it was and that was it. I'd always been different in every other way from everybody I grew up with. What the hell was one more thing? And nobody else around me had ever been perfect. I still couch it in terms of, "Okay, I'm not perfect, but nobody else is." Friends will say they wish they were straight, but it's kind of silly to wish for something you're not. And being gay is my only claim to minority understanding. Otherwise, I'm a complete majority person: white, male, Republican. If I wasn't gay, would I know that there's a whole other world out there besides Prosser, Nebraska? I really would have missed something if I didn't know anything besides my family, my farm, my church, my small town. So, in that sense, maybe being gay is the best thing for me.

Where I came from, social life consisted of dating the girl you were supposed to marry, going to a movie, and sitting in a hometown bar talking about the same things every day. When I was twenty-two and first came out, the gay scene in Lincoln seemed ultra-exotic and fascinating. There were new people to meet, new ways to talk and think and dress, new music. I had no clue how to operate socially, but it was fun to learn, to figure out how to fit in. Here in Omaha I know I've been laughed at and looked at as stupid because I come from the country, so a lot of times I don't tell people. You just kind of dust over your tracks. You try not to talk like you're from the farm, you don't act like you care about the weather. It's almost like being gay twice; you hide two things instead of one.

Some people assume that if you're gay you're going to move to the biggest city and wear the flamiest clothes and learn how to walk the swish. I would rather be able to go back to live in my hometown—maybe not find the perfect mate, but be happy with what I'm doing. I've never met anybody else who loved where they came from as much as or more than they loved being gay. Where I came from is as important as what I am. In fact, it's hard for me to separate the place from the person. I listen to country music and I go out of town to do rodeo on as many weekends as I can. I have the big belt buckle I won in college and I have the big black hats in the closet, which I like to wear. If I go home for a weekend, I start talking like a redneck. When I get boisterous, I'm very physical. My family was not above rassling, and it wasn't unheard-of to hit somebody if you argued.

My brother Tony and I started driving the pickup on the farm at age six, as soon as we could reach the pedals. We also learned how to drive a tractor right away; we started out doing the things that didn't require a whole lot of brains. Disking a field a quarter-section in size didn't require driving straight. You could just drive and tear up dirt. When you got into junior high, you were old enough to cultivate corn. Hopefully, along the way, you'd learn to do all this right and you'd pick up all the mechanical skills. I never did. I was always saying, "Dad, I don't know what's wrong, but it's not working." I felt I had to prove I could do things, but I wasn't getting it and Tony was. Until Tony came along, my dad would tolerate teaching me things. But it was obvious that Tony was what my father wanted—the next generation of farmer. There was something that was drawing them together—or at least not pushing them apart—that wasn't there with Dad and me. It drove me crazy! From then on, my father and I grew further and further apart.

Riding along with my dad, meeting people, I picked up the ability to do people and to bullshit. He knows everybody for a hundred miles around and can buy and sell livestock at the best price. I can still meet someone and, just like he does, pick up and go with it right away—have a best friend within five minutes and forget their name within ten. But as much as my dad can read other people and figure them out, I don't think he's ever been able to figure me out, and I've never been able to figure him out. It's probably been like that from the minute I hit the ground. It always seems like he's so far across the room from me, and there's a big, invisible wall between us.

In the early eighties, things started to get really tight financially. If we didn't get rid of the farm, we were going to lose it. So we consolidated—kept the cattle and got rid of the farm. We bucked up and went on, but it was really tough, because my family was pretty well-known. It was a small town and they were all related or knew each other somehow. All of a sudden, our finances went public. My family was devastated by that. We were a very uptight, anal-retentive German farm family that wanted things done so it looked nice, no matter what. My family auctioneers on the side. Here we had been selling people out, and now *we* were getting sold out.

My father would stop at the local bar and stay until it closed, and Mom would sit up and wait for him. She would be so angry with him, and she'd be angry with herself for being so upset. You knew when she put a Hank Williams record on that she was waiting for him to come home. Lying in bed, seven years old, listening to Hank Williams, I knew there was trouble, that it was going to be cold, cold, cold the next day, and it was going to be my job to put her in a good mood. I spent a lot of time with her and got to hear a lot of her gripes. That probably explains some of the distance between me and my father.

I got glasses at an early age. A quiet, skinny, sandy-blond kid, I was never terribly social, and I talked to myself a lot. I started to read a year and a half before I was in kindergarten, so you could usually find me in the quietest place in the house with a book. People lived so far away that I didn't know the kids I went to school with. I excelled in school, but I kind of kept myself separate, and would just go home at night and do my little things. The farm was a half mile from the Platte River, in a beautiful valley with rich pasture and great big cottonwood trees. I had collections of rocks and leaves, and I could tell you what every kind of plant was.

My uncles and grandparents could discipline us just like my mother and father could. Everybody and everything was community property. And everybody in town knew me as one of Stan Ruhter's boys. I would stay at my grandparents' in Prosser for days on end, almost every weekend. They had a big house with empty rooms where my dad and my three uncles had lived, so I had my own room there. Like my father, my grandfather was gone a lot, buying sheep in South Dakota and Wyoming. I was my grandmother's replacement for my grandfather and her sons like I was my mother's replacement for my father. I was the first grandchild, and males were always the center of attention, so I had the run of the place for a long time.

Grandma taught me things most guys never learned because they were too busy doing whatever with their fathers. She would buy books for me and take me to the library. She taught me how to take care of plants, how to know what's what, how to garden. Her mail-order catalog from Gurney's of Yankton, South Dakota, the biggest seed farm in the Midwest, came every January when it was really cold and nasty, and I was just enthralled with it. My grandmother would come down and check out my garden and give me advice. My parents' thing was that they were going to be the perfect role-model family. So, when I was doing weird things like planting a humongous garden at age ten, they had to find some way to explain why I was at home doing the gardening and not out farming like my brother, who was only seven. So it had to be the *best* garden there ever was.

If you were a guy, you were born to farm. You were born to be a total, typical, straight male—to play sports, to hunt, to do everything a guy was supposed to do. I knew from the beginning that I didn't fit into that. Everybody else knew it too, so they pushed me for a long time, until I was in junior high and they realized it wasn't going to work. The whole time, my father and I battled each other. It was a long, drawn-out warfare. If he said up, I'd say down. If he said black, I'd say white. Neither of us would ever admit that the other one could be right. I was frustrated that I couldn't be right on his terms. I wanted to be, but I just couldn't think like him.

I'm turning out to be just like my father was—in my temper, my ability to filter facts so I don't give out too much information about myself, my inability to communicate how I feel. I've become this big stoic man around the house who just works a lot and doesn't come home, who pays the bills and ignores everything else. My family's not an emotional family, not physically expressive at all. We can't get past a handshake. Like the Germans who never smile in their pictures, we just kind of sit around with grim faces. A horrible way to live, but I still lapse into it if I don't think about it.

Since my father stopped drinking in 1985, '86, he and I are starting to get along a little better. He just turned fifty and he's starting to realize he can't be on top of everything forever. Now we talk, and he listens to what I say and agrees with me occasionally. He calls to ask for advice, and we talk about cattle prices, the weather, who's got a new pickup. I ask him for advice, which is a change for me, and he tells me—or says he doesn't know, which is new for him. He's mellowed, and I don't feel like I'm in competition or trying to prove anything to him anymore, so I can learn things a lot easier. For years I couldn't figure out how to do things, because he told me I had to.

I don't feel the need to talk to my mother as much as I used to. I try to keep it down to once a month. She probably thinks things are getting more distant, but I think things are just moderating after all these years. I used to talk to her a lot more simply because I felt I had to, to make her feel good about herself when she felt lonely and double-burdened. My mother is the ultimate farm wife. She can pull a calf, muck through mud, load fifty head of cattle on a truck, stand in five-degree weather for hours. Since conception, she taught me how to ride a horse. She would take me to horse shows and leave me in the playpen on the shady side of the horse trailer while she rode. She can cowboy with the best of them, she's tougher than nails, and she still manages to dress up and go out. If I had to have a wife, that would be the kind I'd want.

I'm not out with my family. There's really no point, and financially it would be stupid. All the money I make, beyond what it takes for me to live, I send home to put into cattle and investments there. The money goes into one account and pays for everything, so I have a share in the deal, but no legal recourse. I'm in the will, but I'm not legally in the partnership. So I sure don't want to do anything that would jeopardize what I've spent seven years working for. I don't know if my parents would do anything, but I would be scared to find out. And I'm not really big on telling them too much about what's going on in my life in the first place. My mother knows something is up, and I think she always has, but she has never asked. They're very appearance-oriented, and as long as they don't actually know it, it's not real.

If you want to educate somebody, tell them you're gay. But there's a time to tell people, when they're able to learn. My parents aren't ready to know this yet. They're just figuring out where *they* are at age fifty and forty-eight. I wouldn't want to infringe on that to save my life. Whenever they're ready to hear, which may never happen, they can hear. I don't have any problem with telling them. I haven't done anything else they've expected me to do. But even if I thought they might be ready, I'm not sure I trust my judgment enough, considering what they have of mine financially, and how they could really hurt me. They are the keystone of my physical safety and my ability to interact in the community where I grew up.

There will come a time, when my father is done working, that I'll have the option to go home. I'll have half of what he has, if I don't screw it up. I wonder what he would do if he knew. The whole thing with my family has always been, if it's wrong, don't tell anybody, and make sure it's not wrong in the first place. To make sure I never told anybody at home would be the ultimate damage control for them, because for anybody there to find out would theoretically destroy the business for them and destroy the way they're treated in town. I understand and respect that, and I don't want to push them too hard, but I also want them to make sure that if they can't deal with it, they don't force me to tell them. So we kind of have a little standoff.

Tony and I beat the bejeebers out of each other for the first fifteen years, but we've gotten to be pretty close. He'll come down and see me, or I'll go see him, or we'll go to Denver or Lincoln together. Sometimes we rodeo together. It's frustrating, because rodeo is a straight world, but it's fun. I've gotten involved with gay rodeo; there's one in Kansas, and they're starting one here in Omaha. When I first heard about it, I thought,

Yes, all right! I'd love to meet somebody in a gay rodeo. Then I realized that a lot of people were doing it as just a humorous sideline. I'm learning to get into that, but it makes my teeth itch a little bit. If rodeo's not done traditionally, the way I'm used to it, I shy away from it. Where I grew up, rodeo was serious stuff—fun, but not campy fun. Everybody who was worth anything rodeoed. If you were a cowboy, you were cool. We always said, "Cowboy is as cowboy does." It isn't necessarily a big hat and big boots. It's what you do and how you think. I have a little fetish for straight cowboys.

It was preordained that I wasn't going to farm. My family knew as well as I did that it wasn't working for me, and I don't think they relished the idea of having to work with me, so they just kind of hustled me out. Since then, I've learned how to judge livestock and how to ride and rope better. I started riding big feedlots to check the cattle, rope the sick ones, haul them out, doctor them. It was hard work but great money. I've worked on ranches in the sandhills in western Nebraska two summers—fixed machinery, changed tires, moved livestock, fixed fence, tore pickups apart and rebuilt them. Things I supposedly didn't know how to do, I was able to do spontaneously and very well. I've realized the reason I didn't like to do it, or wasn't good at it, was because I didn't want to.

I'm moving back home in about a month. My father is going in for surgery, and he'll be incapacitated for three months. He's got cattle to take care of, so I'm going to be the rancher I never was. We live on Big Island, about eleven miles long, three miles wide; the Platte River goes around it. It's very swampy, so most of the work on the ranch has to be done on horses. My mother and I are going to calve out five hundred head of cattle by ourselves this winter. I've learned how to do all the basics of it, but I've never proved it on my home turf. I haven't done that kind of physical work for years, so it'll be tough. It's going to be cold, and I'm sure there are going to be times when I'll wish I hadn't done it, but I think overall it's going to be fun. I've wanted to go back anyway, to prove to myself I could do it, so I'm going to do it until May, come hell or high water. If it works out, I'll stay longer.

When I've gone back home I've sometimes thought it must be obvious to a lot of people that I'm gay. It really wasn't, though, because they couldn't conceive of it; it just wasn't an option. But now that gay people are moving back to Hastings and Grand Island and coming out, and people are starting to learn and understand more, it may be harder for me to keep my cover. But no matter what, I'm one of theirs. Even though people there are very cliquish and they know what you do and talk about you,

you really can do what you want as long as you're their own. They'd tolerate just about anything as long as you paid your social dues and didn't push it. If I were HIV-positive and got sick, I'd go home. No matter how much they would hate the idea, they'd take care of me back there, because I'm one of theirs.

Most of the gay people I've met who come from farms have ditched everything they came from. They believe they had to leave the farm if they wanted to be gay. They have never seen it as, "I'm gay, I'm from a farm, I'm proud of it and it's still a part of my life, and I will go back there." They think farm life is horribly boring, it's so repressive, country music is so stupid, they all dress so dumb, they all have such bad hobbies, they're all so fat and dumpy. But it wasn't that bad. It wasn't any worse than life here in Omaha, or in any city. I wonder why we're brave enough to face some of the things we put ourselves through here every day, but we can't face the idea of living at home.

So many times I've felt like I'm out here on my own, a whole different breed from the people I see in the gay communities of Omaha and Lincoln. I'm always searching for the person who's going to match me, for someone who comes from my background, is not embarrassed or intimidated by it, and is willing to make sacrifices to go back to it. I would love to have somebody significant in my life who can tolerate it, because we won't be able to be as close there as here. Nobody's dumb enough to be openly gay there, and it would be pushing it to live together, not because people would scorn you but because they could physically hurt you. Living together might be okay in Hastings or Grand Island, as long as you didn't hang out too much with the neighbors.

I'm anxious to see what kind of people I meet when I go back, because now I know what I'm looking for, and I know how to spot someone else who's gay. There used to be a gay bar in Grand Island, so it'll be interesting to see where people are meeting, what bathrooms are cruisey. It'll be interesting to see if there are people back there who made the choice to give up the career life or the social life to live where they wanted.

Afterword

IN THE COURSE of working on the Gay Farm Boys Project, I happened upon a book titled *Farm Boy,* by Archie Lieberman.[1] A photographer for *Look* magazine, Lieberman became acquainted with a farm family in northwestern Illinois in the mid-1950s and gained their cooperation in creating a wonderful photographic record of farm family life from that time through the 1960s. The book's primary focus is the family's only son: his childhood and adolescence, coming of age, marriage, fatherhood, and inheritance of the family farm.

Lieberman's work celebrates the life of a boy who grew up to fit the mold of farm culture, to follow a conventional life path, to complete the generational cycle of family farm continuity. He managed "to be the square peg in the square hole," as James Heckman put it in our interview. I have seen the Gay Farm Boys Project as something of a tribute to the lives of boys who come to discover that, however much they may have a sense of belonging on the farm, something fundamental in their natures makes misfits of them in farm culture. A few of the men whose life stories are presented here have remained in rural communities or have gone back to them, but most of these men have responded to their feelings of being misfits by removing themselves from the farm to the city or suburbs.

In light of this rural-to-urban migration, these men's stories describe how their midwestern farming heritage has influenced their choices and identities as gay men, how they see themselves in relation to gay men from urban or suburban backgrounds, and how they fit into their local gay communities. For many of them, the dislocation of living in an urban culture after growing up rural was in some ways similar to that of being gay but living in a heterosexist culture; in both regards, they felt like outsiders. "Here in the city I'm kind of out of my element," said Wayne Belden, who had lived in Chicago for about twenty years. "I just have to get on as best I can, gaining some things and losing some."

What had these gay men lost and gained in leaving the farm communities of their childhoods and leading more urban lives? Certainly they had lost the ability to pursue farming on a day-to-day basis as either a livelihood or a way of life. To varying degrees, they had lost intimate connections that had developed during their childhoods—to their homelands, their home farms, their families and home communities. For some men,

Boy in Calf Pen, by Jeff Kopseng, based on a photo courtesy of Todd Moe

losing these relationships with places and persons had sparked significant crises of identity.

But their losses seemed to have been tempered by important gains. Putting some distance between themselves and the farm had made it possible for many of these men to come out more readily to themselves and to their parents and other family members. And as they had distanced themselves from the rural communities of their childhoods, many of them had gained a broader perspective on their lives. Greater exposure and access to resources and role models had helped them explore and discover what it can mean to be a man beyond the confines of the traditional gender roles with which they grew up. Most of these men had achieved a reasonably comfortable acceptance of their own ways of identifying and living as gay men. Exposure to the urban diversity of gay men's lives had led some of them to become more comfortable with ways of being gay that differed from their own.

In the city, these men were more able to connect with others like themselves, to cultivate friendships as well as intimate and committed relationships. They were more able to develop community connections across the boundaries of sexual orientation, interweaving their lives as openly gay men with those of gay and non-gay friends, neighbors, acquaintances, and coworkers. Many of these men had benefitted from the greater range of opportunity afforded by city life in education, employment, entertainment, spirituality, and volunteer involvement. Becoming politically involved in issues related to sexual orientation had led some of these men to move beyond the "that's just the way things are" fatalism that is often characteristic of farm culture.

What had farming communities lost and urban communities gained as many of these gay farm boys had become city men? This question acquired a particular significance for me on a recent day in early spring. Taking a break from writing, I had gone for a walk with my mate Bronze in a nearby park that is home to scores of Canada geese in the heart of Milwaukee. On the occasion of a visit to my home farm, Bronze had suggested that we take a bushel of corn back to Milwaukee to feed the geese that raise their broods in the park. As we threw handfuls of this corn to the hungry flock, it occurred to me that Bronze had found an urban outlet for the animal husbandry impulses rooted in his own farm upbringing. In addition to feeding the waterfowl, Bronze makes occasional efforts to clean up the forlorn park by collecting litter and salvaging trash cans and picnic tables that have been pushed into the pond by neighborhood vandals.

Had they felt there was a place for them in farming, some of these men would have no doubt brought to their farmwork a meticulous aptitude and commitment to animal husbandry and the "housekeeping" involved in caring for livestock. Though it is unlikely that most of them would have engaged in fieldwork with as much enthusiasm, they would have no doubt been similarly painstaking in their care of machinery, fields, and crops. Having grown up in families in which it was common for the household economy to depend on the labor of children as well as adults, it is likely that their approaches to farming would have been informed by a hardworking, persistent passion to be productive and nurturing. In their urban communities, many of these men had found outlets for these impulses in their employment as well as in family, community, church, and volunteer commitments.

In losing many of their gay sons to the cities, farming communities had lost solid citizens. In gaining these transplanted citizens, the cities had acquired some exemplary homemakers and gardeners. Many of these men tended to be homebodies, oriented more to domestic life than to social life. In their perspectives on matters of politics, gender, and sex, they leaned toward the conventional and conservative. Their views on the relation of gay people to the mainstream community were consistent with the rural preference for blending in rather than setting oneself apart. Often feeling like outsiders in their urban gay communities, they tended to see their own views as representing a sensible and pragmatic counterpoint to the more extreme positions of their city-bred peers.

In ways that reflected their diverse personalities, nearly all of these men seemed to believe that changing anti-gay attitudes depended on gay people being good citizens—responsible, self-reliant, productive, "regular" people. "It makes me very sad that a lot of people think we're all a bunch of perverts running around," Everett Cooper commented in our interview. "And not only do they think that, but they *choose* to think that— they choose not to know the other side of it. I would like somehow to become politically forceful in changing that perception." Many of these men seemed to believe that the only way to effect this kind of progress was for gay people to go as far as they could to make their sexual orientation known to all with whom their lives intersected. However, several men saw this kind of openness as counterproductive, and inconsistent with being "regular" people.

If the prospect of staying in their rural communities had not appeared to be so incompatible with leading honest, unconstricted lives, more of these men might have made their homes in farm communities—some of them as farmers, perhaps. If they had been able to live in these places as openly gay men, they might have helped to diminish the silence, ignorance, and prejudice that surrounds homosexuality by demonstrating to their rural communities the possibilities of living fulfilling, meaningful, "wholesome" lives outside of the mainstream mold. From their homes in the often more diverse and supportive environment of the city, many of these men hoped that their efforts for social change would eventually reach the minds and hearts of those back on the farm as well.

Since the late 1980s, AIDS has prompted an unprecedented reversal in the rural-to-urban migration of gay men, as many HIV-infected men have moved back to their parents' rural and small-town homes. "If I were HIV-positive and got sick, I'd go home," Todd Ruhter remarked in our interview. "No matter how much they would hate the idea, they'd take care of me back there, because I'm one of theirs." Unlike any other force, AIDS has pushed rural midwestern communities to acknowledge that gay men's lives are connected intimately to their own.

Many of the HIV-infected men who have returned to their home communities have found that attitudes toward homosexuality remain grounded in ignorance and prejudice. In many cases, AIDS and homosexuality have simply been lumped together in the same swaddling of silence. Perhaps the devastation of HIV will provide an opening to greater understanding and acceptance of the diversity of affectional and sexual identity. However, if the disease elicits little more than a resigned and pitying "taking care of our own" response, intolerant attitudes and beliefs will be left essentially unchanged and the tragedy of AIDS will be amplified. Will families and communities move toward truly embracing their gay sons and brothers and neighbors, more as "one of *us*" than as "one of *ours*?" Or will their response be little more than the embrace of smug samaritans extending love and support to those wayward souls who have come home to die?

Among the many things that have influenced my approach to this project has been my acquaintance with the life and writings of Willa Cather. A lesbian who grew up in rural and small-town Nebraska in the 1880s, Cather was a quintessential misfit who felt that she couldn't live in her home state as an adult. But from the comfortable distance of the urban Northeast, she was able to write many novels and short stories based on her Nebraska childhood. Cather made frequent visits to her home-state throughout her life. In her late forties, she reflected on her life in New York City, on her Nebraska visits of earlier years, and on what compelled her to write her first Nebraska novel, *O Pioneers!*[2]

> There I was on the Atlantic coast among dear and helpful friends and surrounded by the great masters and teachers with all their tradition of learning and culture, and yet I was always being pulled back into Nebraska. Whenever I crossed the Missouri River coming into Nebraska the very smell of the soil tore me to pieces. I could not decide which was the real and which the fake "me." I almost decided to settle down on a quarter section of land and let my writing go. . . . I knew every farm, every tree, every field in the region around my home, and they all called out to me. . . . I had searched for books telling about the beauty of the country I loved, its romance, and heroism and strength and courage of its people that had been plowed into the very furrows of its soil, and I did not find them. And so I wrote *O Pioneers!*[3]

Before Cather got around to writing this novel, which celebrates the European settlement of Nebraska, she had written short stories related to pioneer life in Nebraska. According to one Cather biographer, her response to her homelands in these works was one of "almost unmitigated hate and fear. . . . In her early stories she rendered what was hard and bleak and cruel in the state's way of life—the collapse, for instance, of minds and bodies in the struggle with the land, the pressure of convention in the village, the imperviousness to art. . . ." Her reaction was said to be in "opposition to forces that seemed to her monstrously strong and a threat to her differentness, to the core of what she felt herself to be. To look at Nebraska otherwise, to contemplate it with some objectivity and appreciation, Willa Cather needed to go away for a long time and to achieve success."[4]

As freedom and distance changed Cather's perspective, those same conditions have been important for most of the men whose stories are presented here. This is not to say that all of these men were inclined, as Cather apparently was, to look back on their childhoods objectively and with appreciation. Their recollections and assessments range from the sentimental to the severe. But like Cather, many of these men brought to their life stories the unique perspective of individuals who had gone from being misfits in their rural communities to being misfits in the more urban communities they had come to call home.

"In certain ways," Richard Kilmer observed in our interview, "growing up on a farm and moving to the city was like being from a different country and moving to the United States." Perhaps this conjunction of rural and urban experience, somewhat like the experience of being an international immigrant, had made it possible for many of these men to achieve richer perspectives on life than would have been afforded by either rural or urban life alone. So it seems to me. Whether I have found myself reacting to their stories by nodding my head or by shaking it, whether their words have roused me to laughter or to despair, my own life has been enriched by collaborating with these farm boys in telling about their lives.

NOTES

1. Archie Lieberman. 1974. *Farm Boy.* New York: Abrams.
2. Willa Sibert Cather. 1913. *O Pioneers!* Boston: Houghton Mifflin.
3. L. Brent Bohlke, ed. 1986. *Willa Cather in Person.* Lincoln: University of Nebraska Press, p. 37.
4. Edward K. Brown and Leon Edel. 1953. *Willa Cather: A Critical Biography.* New York: Alfred A. Knopf, p. viii.

Postscript

"What storytellers, and what stories!" a man in Nebraska wrote to me after reading *Farm Boys*. Although he had grown up in a small town on the North Carolina coast, he wrote, "the emotional experiences these guys describe sound very familiar. Their crushes and loneliness and hobbies I can easily relate to. It's fascinating to me that while some of them enjoyed working outdoors and others were more drawn to housework, except for one or two they all hated basketball! Me too!!"

As I awaited publication of *Farm Boys,* I was a little concerned that some readers might object to my generalizations about "the gay farm boy." What if there had been great bias in the composition of my group of interview subjects, leading me to create a portrait that was lopsided or incomplete? Although I did not intend this work to be definitive, I did not want it to misrepresent.

It has been a pleasure to find that every response I have had from "gay farm boys" affirms the general portrait. "That's *my* life you're talking about!" is something I have heard from many readers. "It's strange," a man in a small town in western Pennsylvania said, "but even now, so many years away from my farm days, it is still reassuring to know that that bewildered, scared, goofy, gawky kid was not so strange after all."

A man in Seattle who grew up on an Iowa farm in the 1930s and 1940s wrote:

> I identified with nearly every case history you presented, in one aspect or another. The book recalled my own feelings of confusion, and the utter lack of anything gay to which one could relate. Most of my friends grew up in some kind of urban situation where they eventually made contact with other gays. They find it difficult to understand that I had no idea of what being gay meant until I went into the Army in my mid-twenties. I know that young gays just coming out today have problems they have to face, but they have no idea of the kind of isolation that I felt.

After immersing himself in *Farm Boys* over a long weekend, a man who grew up on a farm in Indiana wrote:

> On almost every page I found myself thinking, "That was me!" How I wish I could have found a book like this years ago. I am a Roman Catholic priest, the pastor of a very large parish. For twenty years, I was the Catholic chaplain at [a midwestern university]. I had many occasions to

317

counsel young men in the course of my work. As you can guess, I was not open about my own orientation, but I'm sure there was little doubt in the minds of most. I pray that I was able to be of help to some. In fact, it was partly through talking to the students that I came to be accepting of myself. I am still not open with most people, but I think I have arrived at a healthy understanding of myself and am very comfortable with my orientation. It has not been an easy journey.

A Nebraska farm boy now in Seattle wrote:

My memories are not as bad as those of the man who was bound and flogged by his father, nor are they as good as those of some of the farm boys who had many playmates and a life full of FFA and 4-H activities. I did notice that almost universally the farm boys saw their religious experiences as being harmful to them. With that I can certainly identify. I would be hard pressed to think of one positive memory from my Catholic and Catholic school background. After graduating from college in Omaha, I lived in Germany for six years and didn't even return to the States for a visit during all that time. I came out there. In a very real sense, I *went* to Europe to get away from Nebraska, from the narrow social control of the people whom I knew.

"Really, these stories are all of our stories," said a gay man who grew up Jewish in Chicago. A man in Minneapolis said that many of the experiences of gay farm boys resonated with his ethnic urban upbringing. It has become evident to me that, except for the often greater social isolation of farm life, city boys growing up gay in tightly knit ethnic communities have much in common with these farm boys. As a man in Chicago wrote:

I'm sure it wasn't any easier for my boyhood friends and me to come to terms with our homosexuality on the conservative northwest side of Chicago. Our city was settled by the Yankee and German stock you mentioned, but we had the added trauma of our ethnicity (Italian, Irish, Polish) and the wonderfully progressive Catholic church to contend with as well.

I do agree that openness leads to the smashing of stereotypes. I continue to reside on the northwest side of the city. Like the farm boys who feel disconnected from urban life, I feel a certain discomfort in Boys' Town [a gay neighborhood in Chicago]. A nice place to visit, but I wouldn't want to live there, much to the chagrin of some of my dearest friends. As a teacher at an all-male secondary school, I find it heartening that my students feel comfortable "coming out" to me. I could never imagine, in our generation, displaying that kind of self-confidence and courage.

Besides enhancing self-understanding for many men, *Farm Boys* has opened a window on men's lives that has been illuminating for others. A woman in Milwaukee commented that *Farm Boys* helped her to better understand how her husband's farm background had likely delayed his sexual development; their sexual relationship was his first, at age twenty-eight. Another woman wrote to me after attending my *Farm Boys* slide show in Cedar Rapids, Iowa.

> My late husband and I were married in 1970 because it seemed to be the thing that society expected of us. Neither of us were really aware of our sexual orientation at that time. As time went on, I began to acknowledge my attraction to women. My husband had a difficult time with this, and also with acknowledging who *he* was sexually. He was an extremely unhappy man, full of rage, and terribly addicted to religion. The stories you shared have helped me to understand my husband more and have brought healing to me.

A man who spoke with me after the slide show in Bloomington, Indiana, told me that he was gay, married and in the process of coming out. I was to do the presentation in Indianapolis the next evening, and he said that he was going to ask his wife to attend with him. They were both there that night, in the front row, two of about forty in attendance. He had brought a notebook for taking notes. She thanked me afterward and said that the presentation was very important for her.

"I have just finished laughing and crying myself through your book," declared a man who grew up on a farm in Mississippi and now lives in a small town in that state. The emotional effects of the stories in *Farm Boys* are as diverse as readers' lives. "If there is one emotional reaction I'm experiencing, it's a renewed anger at Christianity," wrote a man in California, "when I read again and again the feelings of isolation, pain, fear, even terror, and the accompanying denial these brought about."

A man in New York City said that, growing up, he had been eager to leave Iowa, which he did thirty years ago. Now he felt torn between the two places.

> I have just read *Farm Boys* and found it a great joy, even though at times tears were flowing when reading of the lives of these wonderful men with whom I could relate totally. Although I didn't grow up on a farm, I did live in several small towns throughout Iowa, some no larger than a hundred people. The schools were made up of about ninety percent farm kids. I always marvelled at how hard they worked on a daily basis, work I also did on occasion when trying to make extra money. How I love those simple yet wise people who grow and cultivate our food on land that is as true and constant as they are.

Farm Boys has stirred some men in especially distressing ways. This was apparent following several slide shows when men with rather stricken expressions came over to shake my hand and say, "Thank you," unable to say much more. And there was this earnest letter from a man in Iowa who asked me to help him connect with other men in his area, and to forward his letters to two of the men in *Farm Boys*.

> I have read your book twice in the last three weeks. It has occupied my
> thoughts continually and caused me sleepless hours at night. To realize
> there are guys out there that I so identify with. I have lived a straight life,
> always being so good. I have been married thirty years, have children and
> grandchildren, and am a good provider. But I remain alone and apart. I
> have *never* had a friend. Absolutely no one knows me. Because I live
> one life on the outside and another on the inside, the mental turmoil,
> depression, and loneliness are constant. That's what so terrible. To keep
> living like this. Maybe your book will give me the impetus to do some-
> thing about it. Or maybe I am too old to hope. I can't change my
> situation and abandon my life as it is.

Because these stories are able to illumine, to affirm, and to stir, many people have found ways to put the book to use. A minister's wife in Indiana suggested that it would be important to get *Farm Boys* into both small-town public libraries and seminary libraries. A man in upstate New York, whose sister gave him the book as a Christmas gift, wrote, "I have never in my life so far received such a special, thoughtful gift from one of my family members. I will treasure it as long as I am on this earth. If I had had a book like this sixteen years ago, I could have saved a truckload of angst and hours of time in a therapist's office."

A woman in Wisconsin gave *Farm Boys* to her thirty-eight-year-old brother-in-law. "He struggled a lot before he figured out that he was gay," she said. "He has shared this with some of our family, but not all. He has gotten some great support and some really awful reactions." She also gave a copy of the book to the twenty-year-old brother of a woman friend. "He just came out to her last night and is struggling with how to confirm his mother's suspicions. He is very creative, lots of fun, and a wonderful uncle."

A college English professor in Missouri wrote to me about a male student in one of his classes who had written a poem about his twenty-two-year-old friend, Jeremiah, struggling with his sexuality in rural Missouri. "He must be retaught his loveliness," the poem concluded. The professor gave the student his copy of *Farm Boys,* to give to Jeremiah. "I'm talking about utility here," the professor said, "and what more useful thing can a book do than save a man from suicide?" Through this book, he said,

"Jeremiah might rediscover his loveliness. He might discover self-worth, affirmation, useful labor, and hope. He might be encouraged to go on."

It was this kind of impulse to *Farm Boys* evangelism that provoked Stan, who grew up on a western ranch, to spread the word about the book. From the midwestern college town he has long called home, Stan distributed *Farm Boys* bookmarks, and newspaper articles about the book, to scores of people on his university campus, around the city, and beyond. "I am telling the professors in our department that if a male student comes out to them and is having a hard time dealing with his sexuality, point him to the book, especially if the student is from a farm," Stan said. "I am only doing this because I really believe in the book, and that it will help rural youth."

Many men who have encountered *Farm Boys* have been stirred by a desire to tell their own stories. Several have sent autobiographical manuscripts for me to read. Others have asked me to keep them in mind as interview subjects if I should do another book. In a note expressing his interest in being interviewed, a man in Wisconsin confided, "I got my sex education at the early age of eleven or twelve from the sixteen-year-old hired hand, in the convenience of a bunk house on the farm. I'm gay and still in the closet in this small river town. But I do enjoy male sex, if the opportunities present themselves. I told my minister friend that I could write a book about my experiences. He said, 'Yes, but you'd have to leave town.'"

The desire to make rural connections—with the land or with gay men from farm backgrounds—has been evident in some letters. One man wrote to me after attending the *Farm Boys* slide show in Chicago:

Hearing the stories you tell validates my experience of isolation and shame as a gay farm boy from New York. I can now look at my own past compassionately and know I'm no longer alone.

I'm now as certain as I can be that I'm moving back east next spring to live in the country. I came to college in Chicago and haven't left yet. I haven't liked being here for a few years; the city is noisy, crowded, ugly, and stressful. But I haven't been ready to leave until now. What makes me ready is my plan to seek out and rely on the support of my twelve-step recovery programs, whatever welcoming and affirming church I find, and the community of other gays and lesbians. By "community" I mean honest and intimate friendships; I've always been ill at ease with the conspicuous forms of "gay life"—bars, clubs, gyms, cruising, promiscuity.

I plan to live near a small city that has a reputation for being gay-friendly, and where people are out. I'll be visiting Ithaca, New York, Burlington, Vermont, and Amherst, Massachusetts, to see what they're like. The bottom line is that when I move to the country my support will continue to be God, in the forms I have mentioned.

"Reading stories of other farm boys has reminded me of the importance of my own childhood on the farm," said a man in Washington, D.C., who grew up in Nebraska. "I only wish I had men in my circle who were also from farms. Maybe I'd finally fall in love!"

A shared musical passion prompted a man in Chicago to ask if I would help him make a pen-pal connection with one of the men in *Farm Boys*. "It would be a great pleasure to correspond with Dave Foster, who seems to be fond of Opera but has no friends with the same inclination. I have attended more than four hundred opera performances and have heard all the great singers of the past sixty-five years. My favorite opera is Verdi's *La Forza del Destino,* which I have seen eight times, including a performance at La Scala in Milan fifteen years ago."

A photographer in San Francisco sent me samples of his work celebrating men's bodies and enclosed a brief note: "Enjoyed your book tremendously. How do I get to know a farm man? If you are ever in San Francisco, I would love to photograph you."

After reading *Farm Boys,* the owner of a gay resort in Iowa got the idea to host a "Farmers & Cowboys Round-Up" during the Iowa State Fair. "In the evening we will gather around a campfire on the banks of the river to reminisce and tell our stories," the brochure said. "We are providing a place and a time for farm boys to make a real connection with each other and to celebrate our gay heritage."

After my *Farm Boys* slide show in Cincinnati, one of the men there offered to give his old Future Farmers of America jacket—dark blue corduroy with gold decoration. During my talk I had mentioned that I had never had a FFA jacket, and that its colorful embroidery had a certain charm. I had also commented that the FFA emblem had inspired the "Fabulous Farm Boys" design on book-promoting apparel.

This generous farm boy's old FFA jacket arrived in my mailbox a few days after I returned home, and I have made it a part of book-related events since then. His letter said that he had been a state 4-H president and a FFA regional vice-president. "One of my first loves was my state 4-H vice-president. Truly a story of fabulous farm boys," he said. "As young men whose whole lives were centered around agricultural activity, being gay was not easy. I hope that this jacket serves some meaningful purpose in your efforts to broaden the world's perspective of who and where we are."